DISCARD

LB
1028.3 Hopkins
.H66   Educational research

Educational Research:
A Structure for Inquiry

Educational Research: A Structure for Inquiry

Charles D. Hopkins

Indiana State University

CHARLES E. MERRILL PUBLISHING COMPANY
A Bell & Howell Company
Columbus, Ohio

Published by
Charles E. Merrill Publishing Company
A Bell & Howell Company
Columbus, Ohio 43216

This book was set in Baskerville.
The Production Editor was Linda Lowell.
The cover was designed by Will Chenoweth.

Copyright © 1976 by Bell & Howell Company. All rights reserved. No part of this book may be reproduced in any form, electronic or mechanical, including photocopy, recording, or any information storage and retrieval system without permission in writing from the publisher.

ISBN: 0-675-08624-8

Library of Congress Catalog Card Number: 75-36961

1 2 3 4 5 6 7 8 / 83 82 81 80 79 78 77 76

Printed in the United States of America

Preface

Educational Research: A Structure for Inquiry is a textbook for the first course in research. The four major divisions organize a comprehensive study of how to answer basic questions about the educational process:

    Part   I: Orientation to Research as Inquiry
    Part II: The Problem: A Question and Its Answer
    Part III: Inquiry Methodologies
    Part IV: Aids to Inquiry

The *purpose* of this book is to help a person who is to be actively engaged in research to become a good researcher. It is intended to develop within the individual a feel for researching, as well as to provide specific direction for proceeding. My piano playing leaves much to be desired. Although I can read, play, and give each note the correct amount of time, the product is less than acceptable as music. I have not developed the art of "putting it all together." This book is intended to help those persons engaged in educational research to learn some specific ways of functioning in research, but more importantly to "put it all together."

The *reason* for writing this book is that most textbooks designed to introduce students to research fail to develop the *art* of researching. It may be that a book cannot do that by itself, but I believe that the art can be furthered by a new approach. Some authors have attempted to do this with a do-it-yourself kit, but most have not been able to do what is attempted here. I hope the contribution of the book lies in its ability to guide students to develop within themselves a way of answering questions about educational concerns and reporting them to the profession.

The *theme* of the book is *research as inquiry*. The process of research is viewed through a scientific approach to problem solving that leaves room for combining the components of problem solving into an integrated research strategy. Mark Twain is reported to have reflected about his wife's swearing, "She knows all of the words but she can't quite get the tune." I hope that this book helps the student get the tune through the structure, even though it does not cover every detail that the researcher will need in every situation while conducting research.

Clear distinctions are made among research and other closing related areas of inquiry, and the focus of the book is restricted to inquiry procedures which culminate in new knowledge about educational concerns. As a book on research it develops an understanding of the research process to allow the student to develop a plan—the proposal—to answer educational questions and to carry out the methodology to a set of valid conclusions. In addition the understanding of the research process allows the student to judge the procedures used in research studies that are reported in professional literature. The basic premise is that the understanding of a process serves the student by preparing him or her to (1) become a critical consumer of research by others, and (2) conduct his or her own research studies.

While my intent has been to put together a sequence of materials which is practical, this book is not a "do-it-yourself kit." It is beyond the scope of any book on research to cover all specific points for all possible research studies. What is possible in an introductory book is to build a structure that allows one to fit the intricacies and peculiarities of a specific study to the basic framework common to all research techniques. Although the subject matter of this textbook is based in educational inquiry, the structure is much the same for other areas, and it can serve as a basic text for other courses, where appropriate, and as a widely applicable resource book for research in general.

The titles of the four parts of the book point up the intent to keep inquiry as the strand that ties together the discussion of the research process. My experiences with those persons who are engaged in the study of research for the first time have indicated a general lack of understanding of what research is and what its role is in education. In the past the lumping of too many different things under the umbrella of research has fostered the confusion about what can be considered researchable and what should be attacked by other inquiry strategies. The first part of the book is intended to give needed information about what research is. The justification for a rather lengthy section is that, without the needed orientation, there seems to be no reason to discuss procedures with nothing to relate them to. A lack of direction for the person new to research seems to be a major deficiency of most books written for this course.

I have chosen to omit any separate section on statistics. Certain coverage is given to selected topics that seem to be an integral part of the material, but, in general, I have held to my deep conviction that one course cannot attend adequately to both research and statistics. The decision to omit the statistics section was made on the basis that any coverage would be inadequate and that the student would benefit

Preface

from the study of research from a research textbook and the study of statistics from a statistics book. Knowledge for most statistical topics which are appropriate for the beginning researcher can be obtained satisfactorily from self-study texts. As a subject, statistics is especially amenable to programming, and self study also releases class time to a more in-depth study of educational research.

In an effort to make the book practical, some very specific direction is given to the student, but wherever possible the thrust of the book is on the structure of research. Throughout the book the student is guided to other materials that expand on the most important concepts and procedures. Difficult topics have not been avoided, and, where differences of opinion exist in the field, I have no doubt let my biases show. But I have attempted to offer the student some alternatives whenever possible, and have included a rationale for my own personal biases.

Acknowledgement for all of the assistance in putting together a manuscript for a book such as this one becomes an impossible task. I can claim few of the ideas or procedures used in this book as solely my own. To name one source would require an endless list of the many students, colleagues, teachers, and others who have contributed to what I know about research and who have caused me to think about it in so many different ways. If there is a contribution to better understanding of research through the concept of inquiry structure, all of them must share my satisfaction.

For the mechanics of getting the words into book form, I would like to express my indebtedness to Rebecca Rutherfoord, who took the first handwritten pages and put the words into type script, and Jane Angell who took that first copy and helped in so many ways to improve the manuscript. To my readers—John Follman, Larry Braskamp, and Leo Harvill—I express sincere thanks for the many suggestions for improvement and coverage. The responsibility for the final manuscript is mine, and any errors in choice of content or omissions remain my burden.

Contents

PART I   **ORIENTATION TO RESEARCH AS INQUIRY**   1

    1   **Inquiry**   3

        Deduction; Induction; Problem solving; The scientific method; A scientific method; What research is not; What research is; Research characteristics; Summary

    2   **Educational Research as a Science**   15

        An early use of educational research; Education as a science; Applying the scientific method to educational problems; Evaluative procedures; Developmental procedures; Research procedures; Does research make a difference?; Summary

    3   **Structuring Research Activities**   23

        Planning stage; Investigation stage; Generalization stage; A structure for the plan; Summary

    Bibliography   31

PART II   THE PROBLEM: A QUESTION AND ITS ANSWER   33

4   Problems and Hypotheses   35

Sources of educational problems; Problems generated from practice; Problems generated from theory; Selection of a problem; Problem clarification; The hypothesis; Proof within research; The unhypothesis; Theory development; From a problem to hypothesis; Summary

5   Planning the Study   53

Selecting sources of information; Selection of subjects; Sampling techniques; Framework for a study; Data collection; Organization of data; Treatment of data; Summary

6   Observation   77

Psychological factors of observation; Observation and hypotheses; Objectivity in observation; Techniques of direct observation; Supplementing direct observation; Observation in educational research; Sampling observation; Summary

7   Measurement   93

Measurement: a definition; Four levels of measurement; Measurement in educational research; Characteristics of measuring instruments; What test to use; Developing a test; What kind of data?; Summary

Bibliography   113

PART III   INQUIRY METHODOLOGIES   115

8   Studies Based in Historical Inquiry   117

Nature of historical research; Steps in historical research; Historical Writing; Tools for historical research; Summary

9   Descriptive Studies for Inquiry   135

The status study; Nature of descriptive research; Steps in descriptive research; Sources of data; Types of data; Tools of descriptive research; Summary

10	**Use of the Experiment in Inquiry**	173
	Nature of experimental research; Steps in experimental research; Experimental design; Sources and types of data; Tools of experimental research; Summary	
11	**Drawing Conclusions**	203
	Bases for research conclusions; Generalization; Implications and recommendations	
	Bibliography	212
PART IV	**AIDS TO INQUIRY**	215
12	**The Library**	217
	Indexing the library; Abstracts; Reviews of literature; Encyclopedias; Guides; References to references; Dictionaries; Organizing the information; Summary	
	Bibliography	231
13	**The Research Proposal**	233
	The proposal title; Background of the problem; Presentation of the problem; Methodology; Bibliography; Preparing materials; Summary	
	Bibliography	242
14	**Writing the Research Report**	243
	Form and style; Planning; Investigation; Generalization; Reference materials; Abstract; Writing journal articles; Writing style	
	Bibliography	252
APPENDIX		253
GLOSSARY		271
INDEX		279

PART I

Orientation to Research as Inquiry

Since this is a book designed for an introductory course in educational research, the notion of research will vary among individuals engaged in this study for the first time. Part I is included to first acquaint the reader with the relationship of inquiry to research, and then to specifically relate systematic investigation to educational research.

Inquiry is not new to any reader of this book since it is a part of human life from birth. What may be new, however, is the idea of a structure for inquiry through procedures that have little likeness to trial and error or other informal approaches that give answers to questions that arise in our day-to-day activities.

Part I is intended to set some ground rules and give common meaning to what research is and what research is *not*. A very broad structure for research in all areas is presented as a base for developing the following sections, those dealing specifically with the various parts of educational research.

1

Inquiry

> *Like most men I hold certain cherished beliefs which I think valid because they follow logically from known and obvious facts.*
> — Carl L. Becker

Humans are questioning beings. *Inquiry*—more than any other characteristic—has caused the elevation of humans to a special place in the world. Ignoring the disputes of creation and evolution, our uniqueness is, to a large extent, based on our ability to ask questions. Unlike other animal life humans are able to question, seek answers, and record the outcomes for future generations. Each generation is able to build on previously gained knowledge without starting anew with each succeeding generation, as other animals are required to do.

The questions of the earliest people were based in the mysteries of the physical world and dealt with the phenomena of physical nature. Evidence of these questions is found in ancient myths, where questions about nature were answered by mythological explanations in stories passed from generation to generation. The answers found as primitive man's stories are evidence of the unwritten, but implied, questions that formed the bases for those stories. A study of various definitions of *myth* finds agreement that myths are stories used to explain and answer questions about deity and the origin of the universe. Myths attempt to give the reasons for the mysteries of natural phenomena by personifying forces of nature.

Each primitive culture has evolved its own set of stories. Investigations of the patterns in myths, folk tales, and legends make interesting studies in literature. Every developing culture has an accumulation of myths, which collectively represent the answers to that culture's early questions. Since early humans were directly affected by nature and its physical aspects, it is easy to see why the first questions were centered around that which was the closest to humans. Norse, Greek, and American Indian myths, for example, each take different characteristics and vary in their levels of sophistication, but common to them all is the theme of *explanation* that is testimony to early people's development of the question. The Greek story of *Phaethon,* the Norse tale of *Balder and the Mistletoe,* and the American Indian tales of *Determination of Night and Day* and *Determination of the Seasons* are examples of how different cultures explained the phenomena associated with nature through "weather myths."[1] The type of weather is also reflected in the stories. Ideas of deity and the concepts of gods were in large part a result of the climate in which the culture developed. Review of Norse myths finds that the cold climate affected the stories and the types of gods worshipped.

The development level of the questions can also be determined from the answers. The myths reflect questions about nature. Legends and hero stories that appeared later reflect the questions about more sophisticated aspects of human relations and expose the development of the human mind to today's world. Greek myths contrast with most other cultures' stories in that they deal more with the cosmic forces of nature, human traits, and human emotions. The development of a deeper philosophy is exhibited by the Greeks. Present day inquiry continues the move to ask more and more complex questions.

A study of the evolution of music reveals that songs, too, can be thought of as answers to questions in the minds of people. Studies of literature and music from all eras can be viewed as attempted answers to the questions that were on people's minds in each of those times.

Throughout the centuries information was gathered by inquiry through observation and personal experience, and this knowledge came to be used to establish what common sense revealed as cause-and-effect relationships. When the questions were answered knowledge was created, and as people gained knowledge of the world they became aware of the orderliness within the universe and learned to make some predictions with reasonable degrees of accuracy. As the questions became more sophisticated, less accuracy was found in predictions based on common-sense answers. The following quotation points up a major deficiency associated with common-sense answers, and provides an added warning about gathering knowledge in bits and pieces with no unifying feature in the process.

> I am presupposing therefore that no one learns anything unless he puts a question to experience and that knowledge is a series of questions and answers.
> . . . We do not add one by one new atomic truths to our accumulated store of truths. There is always the possibility that the whole edifice which we have erected on the foundation of the past may topple like a heap of jack straws at any moment. Hasty generalizations, neglect of negative instances, fallacies in inference, wrong identifications, all are symptoms of the weakness of our knowledge. And I confess to being incapable of explaining this if knowledge is a complex of elementary sense-data.[2]

A major defect in attacking questions through common sense alone is that human beings are involved in the process. The observer may consciously or unconsciously select evidence to support what he or she already believes, may generalize from insufficient data, or may, knowingly or unknowingly, ignore important contributing factors. Personal feelings, opinions, biases, and prejudices can strongly influence what the observer observes and the conclusions that he makes. To overcome the mentioned shortcomings man developed more sophisticated procedures of inquiry by structuring his thoughts systematically while searching for explanations.

---

1. Stith Thompson, *Tales of the American Indian* (Cambridge: Harvard University Press, 1929).
2. George Boas, *The Inquiring Mind* (LaSalle, Ill.: Open Court Publishing, 1959), pp. 4-5.

DEDUCTION

The first systematic approach to inquiry utilizes the *syllogism* as a model of thinking. The syllogism is a form of deductive reasoning which moves from a generalization to a specific case. The syllogism is limited by dependence on the generalization that is used as a premise. If the basic generalization (called a *major premise*) is false, then the conclusion will be false.

> Major premise: All animals with black fur are cats.
> Minor premise: This animal has black fur.
> Conclusion: This animal is a cat.

The model is consistent within itself but the fact that the major premise is not true could result in an error in the conclusion if the animal were a dog or some other animal with black fur. Since the syllogism could not establish truth for early humans it served little to add to what was known.

INDUCTION

Much later in time the technique of arriving at generalizations by gathering data from many specific observations was attempted. Although early people gathered information through a form of the inductive process, *formal* inductive reasoning came much later in time.

Inductive reasoning moves from many specifics to generalization. It is limited by the fact that an observer can rarely observe every case. The selection of what *is* observed may be biased, knowingly or unknowingly, so that the generalization developed has little, if any, credibility.

A technique that combined the inductive and deductive methods was produced later, and was utilized in formal studies of observed variations in the events of nature when the need was to make inferences about causes underlying the variation. A combination of the inductive and deductive processes that uses the inductive method to generate a hypothesis and the deductive method to test that hypothesis is a technique utilized to answer many present day questions. Refinement of inquiry techniques has brought us to the present conditions for investigating important questions in the minds of people and solving important problems. We are in the midst of an evolution to sophisticate techniques of investigation. Today the knowledge that is created through research procedures is organized into a dynamic functional body of knowledge covering operation of general laws, rather than being limited to a status state where banks of knowledge hold facts in isolation as bits and pieces with nothing to tie them together. Future improvement of procedures will undoubtedly move us far beyond our present state of affairs. The purpose of this book is to move a little further along in the evolution of the inquiry process.

PROBLEM SOLVING

The gradual replacement of the major premise used in the deductive method by a research hypothesis provided an opportunity to structure inquiry into a technique commonly referred to as *problem solving*. As early as 1910, John Dewey in *How We Think* presented five stages for the act of problem solving in his analysis of reflective thinking. He said:

> Upon examination, each instance (of reflective thinking) reveals, more or less clearly, five logically distinct steps: (i) a felt difficulty; (ii) its location and definition; (iii)

suggestion of possible solution; (iv) development by reasoning of the bearings of the suggestion; (v) further observation and experiment leading to its acceptance or rejection; that is, the conclusion of belief or disbelief.[3]

In 1959 the philosopher George Boas gave this view of the human mind as a problem solver:

> It has been traditional in philosophy to consider the human mind as a sort of mirror reflecting a world which is alien to its nature.
> . . . Whatever it is, it [the world] is always objects seen, observed, contemplated, enjoyed, apprehended, intuited, as if knowledge were a simple dyadic relation between two terms, the knower and the known. At times, as in the so-called empirical tradition, the known is the starting point of knowledge; at times as in Platonism and mysticism, it is the terminus. The purpose of these lectures is to suggest, if not to prove, that it is more fruitful to consider the human mind as a questioner, a doubter, as solver of problems, and that *knowledge is always the answer to some problem.*[4] (Italics added.)

All of our present knowledge is an outcome of literally billions of questions that needed answers, and problems that needed to be solved. Many times—probably most of the time—the search for an answer generated more questions. This phenomenon required that some kind of structure be used to direct people as they went about the business of finding answers to questions. The need for structure has given rise to a scientific approach to solving problems. The scientific approach, which is intended to be more efficient than trial and error, is designated as a model to structure the attack on new questions and old questions which have not yet been answered satisfactorily. The combination of the inductive and deductive processes has produced a modern scientific approach to problem solving that is known as the *scientific method*. An integral part of the scientific method is the *hypothesis*. The hypothesis is an outcome of thought processes about the problem being considered—presented as a generalization. The input for the hypothesis is all of the information that is logically connected to the problem. The level of credibility of the hypothesis will depend on the input available to the person stating the hypothesis. Hypotheses range from near-blind guesses to quite well-developed statements that approach the level of a theory.

Dewey said, "There is a distinction between hypotheses generated in that seclusion from observable fact which renders them fantasies, and hypotheses that are projections of the possibilities of facts already in existence and capable of report."[5] A hypothesis is generated from gathered information and is developed to provide a guess that can be tested deductively. The reader should keep in mind that the hypothesis in problem solving can best be viewed as the proposed answer to the question that has been asked by the inquirer.

Some hypotheses can be tested directly. The direct test of the hypothesis will be found in questions based in the physical sciences where matters are most subject to full intellectual control. For example: If the commuter bus that is scheduled to ar-

---

3. John Dewey, *How We Think* (Boston: D. C. Heath & Co., 1910), p. 72.
4. Boas, *The Inquiring Mind*, p. 1.
5. John Dewey, *The Quest for Certainty* (New York: Minton, Balch, and Co., 1929), p. 78.

Inquiry

rive at 7:45 A.M. does not come by at the expected time, several hypotheses could be offered as the reason why it missed the time as scheduled. The implied question being: Why did the commuter bus fail to arrive at 7:45 A.M.? Possible hypotheses (proposed answers):

1. The scheduled time has been changed.
2. The bus has been delayed but will be by later.
3. The bus has had mechanical trouble and will not be by at all.
4. The bus drivers are on strike.

Each of these proposed answers that are viewed as hypotheses can be considered as a reply to the question implied by the problem question: Why did the commuter bus fail to arrive at 7:45 A.M.?

Each of the above hypotheses (and others that can be proposed) could be tested *directly* by information that would be generally available. Another problem example that could be tested directly is the common problem of turning a light switch and not having the bulb light up as expected. What question is implied? What proposed answers (hypotheses) are suggested by the light-bulb problem question? Can the hypotheses be tested directly?

Hypotheses that can be tested directly are those that can be investigated by the use of public facts—that information open to interpretation without deduction and on which general agreement can be obtained through many independent observations. If the following question is asked, the answers from many independent observations will undoubtedly have a very high degree of agreement.

Is diamond a harder substance than glass?

Most questions based in the natural sciences are testable by *direct* methods. The fact that natural sciences deal to a large degree with public facts is not to be interpreted as meaning that all of those questions are easily answered. However knowledge based on public facts is, in general, accepted as the most reliable knowledge and, in turn, the most trustworthy.

Questions generated in the social and behavioral sciences are primarily answered by facts not equally available to all observers. Personal data about attitudes, fears, emotions, achievement, aptitudes, and other equally important traits are located deep within the individual. They cannot be observed directly. One observer's interpretation may not be agreed with by other observers, and the information derived is more open to revision as a result of more probing by investigation.

Problem solving is to be considered as a way of structuring an attack on a question that utilizes the *inductive* approach to generate a hypothesis. The *deductive* approach is then used to test the hypothesis by providing support for or evidence against the hypothesis. The hypothesis is the integral part of the problem-solving process that bridges the gap between a generalization obtained inductively and the deductive approach of testing that generalization. A widely used model for organizing procedures for problem solving—the scientific method—is described in the next section.

THE SCIENTIFIC METHOD

There is no dearth of material about the *scientific method*. Wide reading about this subject reveals one point very clearly—there is no such thing as *the* scientific method.

This becomes evident as different writers explain what they mean by the term *scientific method*. Usually the writer discusses it by describing the steps in the process that organize progression from problem development to problem solution. The steps may vary in number from three to as many as ten or more, depending on how the writer views the process.

Another point that becomes clear in the mentioned reading is that all of these writers are discussing the same thing—a *structured approach* to solving problems. Only in this synthesis does the scientific method exist. It must be that general model which is used in different ways as a structure of inquiry for solving different types of scientific problems. Dewey's five stages for the act of problem solving in his analysis of reflective thinking have been widely used as a basis for steps in the scientific method.[6] By 1933 the five aspects of reflective thought that were mentioned earlier had developed into: (1) suggestion; (2) intellectualization; (3) the guiding idea, hypothesis; (4) reasoning (in the narrower sense); and (5) testing the hypothesis by action.[7]

The primary goal of science is to understand—to understand all of the problems that perplex humans. The scientific method may be reduced to a set of rules, accepted by scholars, that is used to explain phenomena through systematic pursuit of knowledge. It provides a vehicle to extend and test what common sense gives as explanations to problems.

A SCIENTIFIC METHOD

Moving from the general model to a specific example, a scientific approach to solving problems could be structured in seven steps:

1. A felt difficulty
2. Problem identification
3. Information
4. Hypothesis
5. Experimentation and/or observation
6. Conclusions
7. Replication

Let us now turn our attention to each of these parts in isolation.

A felt difficulty. The process is set in motion by a doubt, barrier, obstacle, or an experience that causes bewilderment. The way to an end or goal may be blocked. An unexpected or unexplained event may result in a perplexity.

Problem identification. This phase brings the difficulty under study so that the problem is clearly recognized. It is limited so that the expanse of the study is brought into focus for the investigator and others interested in the same area. The problem is usually phrased in the form of a question. The answer to that question becomes the product of the study.

Information. The first search for the answer should be made within present knowledge. If the answer is found to the satisfaction of the investigator, of course, this is the terminal phase of the process. If the answer is not found in present knowledge, closely related information gives a background for further study, and for hypothesis development.

---

6. Dewey, *How We Think*, p. 72.
7. Dewey, *How We Think* (Boston: D. C. Heath, 1933), pp. 107-15.

Hypothesis. If the answer is not found in present knowledge the most logically developed proposed answer is stated as a hypothesis. The hypothesis is stated in a declarative sentence and serves as an explanation to be tested by vigorous investigation. The hypothesis is formed inductively as a generalization. It serves as a major premise to be deductively tested by empirical means.

Experimentation and/or observation. A well developed design is produced to collect, organize, and analyze data pertinent to the question under study. The results will be organized as information to reach a decision about the tenability of the research hypothesis.

Conclusions. The results are used as bases for the conclusions of the study. The researcher interprets the meaning of the results as it relates to the problem under study. This phase will (1) verify and support the hypothesis and in turn any theory that it is linked to, (2) cause the researcher to reject the hypothesis as untenable, or (3) bring about a modification of the hypothesis to be tested with new data.

Replication. The hypothesis should be retested using new data gathered from the same design. Retesting a hypothesis under different conditions of time, location, and/or other factors will strengthen the value of the original results if the same outcome is observed. If a different outcome is found it may indicate (1) a previous wrong decision, (2) the hypothesis does not hold under different conditions, or (3) the hypothesis is now invalid. The pooling of the results of many studies will provide data that are more trustworthy. If the same study is conducted fifty different times with different subjects and the same outcome is found for forty-seven of those times, it is likely that the supported outcome would be difficult to debate. The tendency to let one study stand alone as testimony causes this phase to be often overlooked.

A scientific method depends on a problem to make it work. Without the problem there is no scientific method. The use of the hypothesis allows the researcher to develop a clear idea of a possible answer to his or her questions, and permits him to place part of the problem-solving activities outside of himself. This is the power of the scientific method and why it is so widely used in inquiry today to answer questions and to add information to the body of knowledge.

This well developed approach to solving problems brings us to the term *research*. Let us now turn our attention to the topic of research, viewing it as a way to structure the production of answers to important problem questions and, thus, as a generator of knowledge.

WHAT RESEARCH IS NOT

Research is *not* going to the library or other source of present knowledge to find the answer to a question that either a teacher has asked or is in the mind of an individual. This does not preclude historical research as a producer and synthesizer of knowledge. Use of present knowledge and knowledge of the past to answer *new* questions is indeed to be considered as scientific research, assuming acceptable procedures are used.

To read widely about a subject and write a review of the writing *or* the finding of an already known answer will not be considered as research here, although the teaching-learning process may find this to be effective pedagogical procedure. Best says:

> Teachers frequently assign a so-called "research project" that involves writing a paper dealing with the life of a prominent person. The students are expected to read a number

of encyclopedias, books, or periodical references and synthesize the information in a written report. This is not research, for the data are not new. Merely reorganizing or restating what is already known and what has already been written is not research, valuable as it might be as a learning experience. It adds nothing to what is known.[8]

Helmstadter says that "once a problem has been solved and recorded, the transmission of the information to others is a matter of communication and teaching, not research."[9]

Research is neither an evaluation process nor a development process, though these two strategies are closely related to research. Confusion in dialogue often arises because of a tendency to lump many techniques that structure inquiry under one large research umbrella. A major step toward ordering this confused state is found in the article "Toward a Taxonomy of Empirically-based Problem-Solving Strategies" that evolved from a series of symposia of professors of educational research held in the fall of 1972.[10] The taxonomy has been developed "to sort out the confusions about complex relationships among the empirically-based processes of evaluation, development, and research by suggesting a taxonomy of empirical methods."[11] The taxonomy associates the "need to choose" with evaluative procedures that have the major purpose of providing "information which rationally weights each of the alternatives in a specific decision situation."[12] It in turn associates the "need to do" with development procedures that have the major purpose of producing "the tools and procedures needed in operations."[13] Other problem-solving methods could be built into the taxonomy and probably will be as modifications of the taxonomy are developed. Where does the research process fit in the scheme of problem solving? This matter is attended to in the next section.

WHAT RESEARCH IS

The taxonomy associates the "need to know" with inquiry procedures (research) that have as their major purpose *the creation of generally applicable knowledge*. There is agreement in contemporary definitions of research that research procedures are problem-solving methodologies designed to add to present knowledge. McGrath says:

> Research is a process (tool) which has utility only to the extent that the class of inquiry employed as the research activity vehicle is capable of adding knowledge, of stimulating progress and of helping society and man relate more efficiently and effectively to the problems that society and man perpetuate and create.[14]

---

8. John W. Best, *Research in Education* (Englewood Cliffs, N. J.: Prentice-Hall, 1970), p. 9.

9. G. C. Helmstadter, *Research Concepts in Human Behavior* (New York: Appleton-Century-Crofts, 1970), p. 4.

10. William J. Gephart et al., "Toward a Taxonomy of Empirically-based Problem-Solving Strategies," *Similarities and Differences in the Research and Evaluation Processes* (Bloomington, In.: Phi Delta Kappa, 1973), pp. 39-43. *The content of this article evolved out of the three 1972 sessions of the National Symposium for Professors of Educational Research. Credit for these ideas must be shared with Robert B. Ingle, University of Wisconsin, Milwaukee; Gary Saretsky, Phi Delta Kappa; and the many participants of NSPER 1972.

11. Ibid., p. 39.

12. Ibid.

13. Ibid.

14. J. H. McGrath, *Research Methods and Designs for Education* (Scranton, Pa.: International Textbook Company, 1970), p. 20.

Inquiry

Helmstadter notes:

> In summary then, an operationally useful (though not rationally perfect) definition of research can be given: Research is the activity of solving problems which leads to new knowledge using methods of inquiry which are currently accepted as adequate by scholars in the field.[15]

Kerlinger reluctantly "attempts" a definition:

> Scientific research is systematic, controlled, empirical, and critical investigation of hypothetical propositions about the presumed relations among natural phenomena.[16]

The following synthesis of current views of research provides the definition of *research* used in this book:

> *Research is structured inquiry that (1) utilizes acceptable scientific methodology to solve problems, and (2) creates new generally applicable knowledge.*

The taxonomy in figure 1.1 is designed to show the relationships among problem-solving strategies and, at the same time, to point up the differences.[17] Readers will find it helpful to study carefully levels I and II to check their orientation to the research process and to reflect on how research activities of business, industry, government, physical sciences, biological sciences, social sciences, behavioral sciences, and education differ from those procedures associated with the development and evaluation processes for those widely varying fields. The first level is the foundation used by all three strategies based on a philosophy of science — the scientific method. The second level is designed to organize problem-solving activities, rooted in the scientific method, into more specific problem areas and associated strategies.

All fields utilize many strategies for problem solving. Some of these procedures are associated with evaluation and, at level II, channel into the branch to the left. Others are procedures of development and, at level II, channel into the branch to the right. Still others are procedures of research and, at level II, channel into the center branch.

The use of research and development centers and divisions in the above mentioned fields points out the separation of procedures for problem solving. In industry, for example, the difference between research activities and development activities is clearly defined although the two work hand-in-hand to accomplish a goal for the sponsoring company. The same is true of evaluative procedures in industry: a clear-cut division in terms of activities and roles. Geographically the divisions may be housed together but distinct differences exist within the organizational structure. A listing of research characteristics in the next section will help in identification of research procedures.

---

15. Helmstadter, *Research Concepts,* p. 5.

16. Fred N. Kerlinger, *Foundations of Behavioral Research,* 2nd ed. (New York: Holt, Rinehart and Winston 1973), p. 11.

17. Gephart et al., *Similarities and Differences,* p. 40.

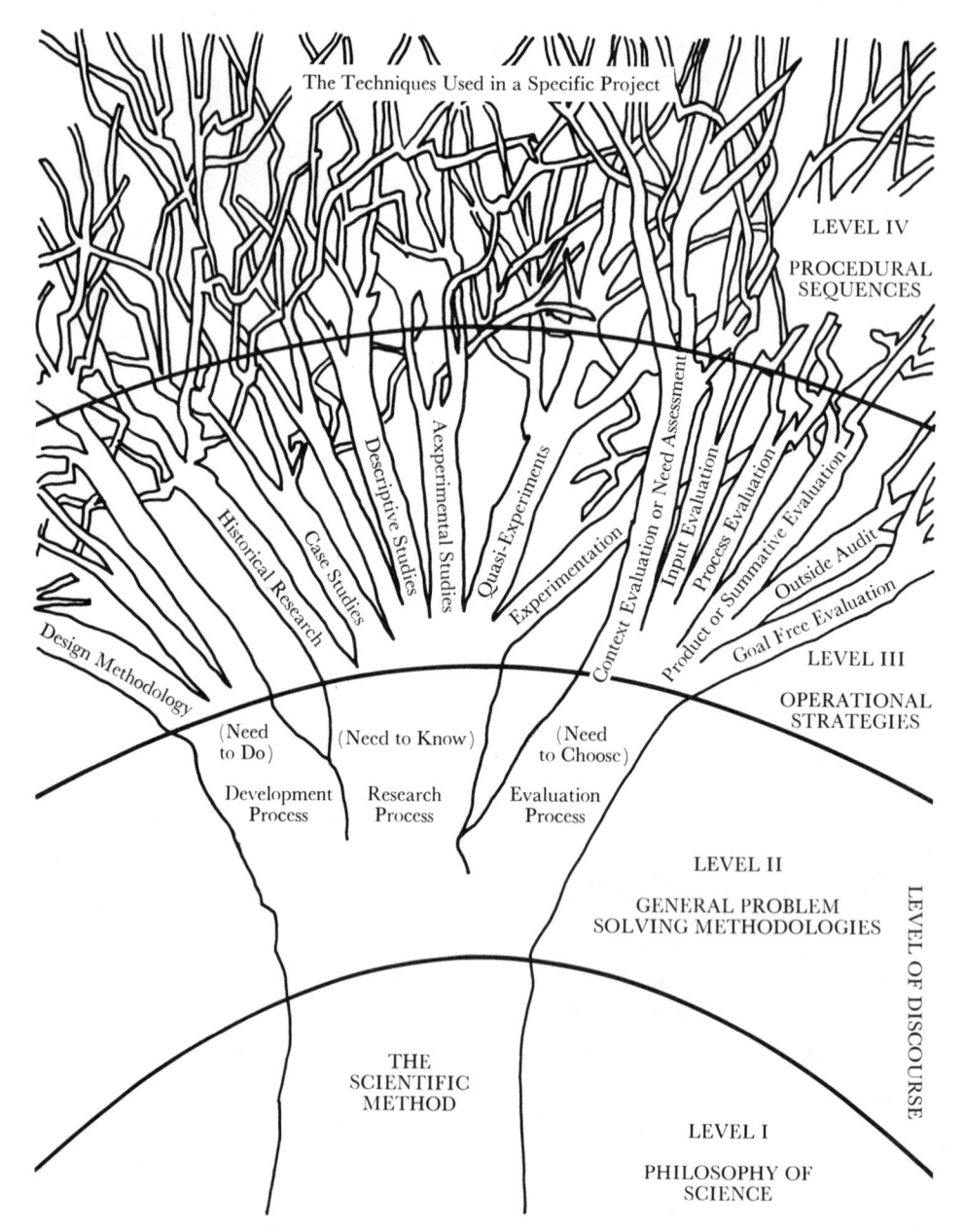

FIGURE 1.1 Taxonomy of Problem-Solving Strategies*

RESEARCH CHARACTERISTICS

The special use of the scientific method in the research strategy structures the procedures into a systematic logical sequence. The methodology of research can be overviewed by the following list of research characteristics.

---

*SOURCE: William J. Gephart et al., *Similarities and Differences in the Research and Evaluation Processes* (Bloomington, In.: Phi Delta Kappa, 1973), p. 40. Reprinted by permission of Phi Delta Kappa.

1. Research activity points to the solution of problems. Research is an outgrowth of the age-old desire of humans to explain the universe as completely as possible, through inquiry.
2. Research is conducted only after all other sources of answers have been exhaustively examined. There is no need to engage in research if the proposed question has been answered to the satisfaction of the asker, and is currently available in present knowledge.
3. The research process is directed to problems based on a "need to know." The research role does *not* include problems based in formative or summative evaluation or problems based in development of tools, programs and procedures.
4. Research processes study presumed relations among natural phenomena. Studies are designed to either (1) establish relationships and/or (2) study observed relationships for the cause-effect direction between or among variables.[18]
5. Research is used to test hypotheses — the more important of which are tied to a general theory. The hypothesis is used to bridge the gap between the generalizations proposed by inductive investigation and the testing of the generalization by the deductive process.
6. Research findings add to knowledge by providing new knowledge. Communicating already existing knowledge is not to be considered as a research activity.
7. Research is an orderly investigation that provides outcomes that withstand criticism of persons in the field. Findings should be free of legitimate attack by knowledgeable colleagues. The procedures are reported in detail so that the findings are subject to the reactions as a check against the investigator consciously or unconsciously committing human errors. All parts of the research activities connected to the inquiry are open to scrutiny by experts.
8. Research can be thought of as a chain of reasoning starting at problem formulation through investigation to findings. The total process from problem isolation to the addition of new knowledge is a logically structured inquiry into some well-defined problem.

SUMMARY

A brief review of the inquiry methods of humans has been given as background to present methods of attacking problems through a structure of inquiry. Through history, the development of problem-solving techniques culminated with the hypothesis serving as a bridge between the inductive method, which provides generalizations, and the deductive method, which moves from a generalization to specifics.

The scientific method has also been discussed as a problem-solving technique. The process was broken down into seven steps to direct a study of the parts and their relationships. The process is organized around (1) a felt difficulty, (2) problem

---

18. A variable is a characteristic, trait, or property to which numbers, classes, or values may be assigned for members of a group to indicate differences between subjects. Examples of variables: height; eye color; hostility; creativity; number of cars owned; and annual income.

identification, (3) information, (4) hypothesis, (5) experimentation and/or observation, (6) conclusions, and (7) retesting of the hypothesis by replication.

Further, what research is *not* has been discussed, to develop a focus onto what research *is* — a strategy to use when the problem is based in a need to know. The following definition is synthesized from contemporary writings about the research process:

> *Research* is structured inquiry that:
> 1. utilizes acceptable scientific methodology to solve problems;
> 2. creates new generally applicable knowledge.

Research characteristics have also been listed to extend and clarify the definition of research that is used in this book. Further clarification of the role of research was also attempted through a taxonomy designed to categorize and classify the problem-solving strategies of evaluation, development, and research.

The focus of the rest of the book will be on investigations that structure inquiry using research techniques. No judgment about the relative value of the different strategies has been made or intended, as each must be viewed as important in its own right. The capability of each particular strategy to solve problems of a specific type equates their relative value.

Three major research methodologies are given attention in major chapters. The first covers questions based in the past and is given the name *Historical Research*. The second covers questions based in the ongoing events of the present and is given the name *Descriptive Research*. Finally the third covers questions based on a need to manipulate certain conditions in a laboratory-like situation, to study the effects of the different conditions, and is called *Experimental Research*.

2

Educational Research as a Science

> *There is nothing more powerful than unfettered scientific thought.*
> —Vladimir Vernadsky

Many of the problems that arise are problems to be solved by evaluation or development procedures and, of course, cannot be considered as answerable through research strategies. The role of research is to attack those questions that are generated by a need to know. Answers to these questions contribute to construction of generally applicable theory, which serves as a base for decisions about practical matters. A wide range of educational questions have the nature of a need to know. They require a strategy of research to arrive at answers, therefore:

> A person is engaged in *educational research* when scientific inquiry about an educational question provides an answer that contributes an increase to the body of generalizable knowledge about educational concerns.

Since the field of education is broadly based in many contributing disciplines, educational research may contribute generalizable knowledge to closely related areas. The educational practitioner can be expected to use knowledge from those same areas to aid in making practical application of theory to school situations. For these reasons educational research is not as clearly delimited as the above statement might imply. The professional educator often goes to sociology, psychology, anthropology, or some other area that studies human action and/or behavior in society when making decisions about educational matters.

AN EARLY USE OF EDUCATIONAL RESEARCH

A pioneer in educational research, J. M. Rice, gave impetus to further study of educational practices through use of scientific methods in an early research study devoted to the investigation of the way that spelling was presented in the classroom.[1] He wanted to find out what teachers accomplished in different classroom situations and determine what the more successful teachers were able to attain. The results of the study showed that students learned no more in a 40- or 50-minute period than in a period of ten or fifteen minutes, and Rice concluded that since the compensation for spelling time is not appreciable past a minimum, the waste of time should be eliminated.

In a follow-up article the same year, Rice discussed professional criticisms of his research and also presented favorable reaction to his scientific approach.[2] Of particular interest is a letter received from a Dr. Euchen, Professor of Philosophy at the University of Jena. In his letter, Euchen indicated that his independent research in the same area of investigating conservation of pupils' time had resulted in the same findings as those of Rice. A small class of primary pupils met requirements of excellence with only five to eight hours of instruction per week. Euchen concluded that instruction, particularly at the lower grades, should be simplified. He opined that pupils spend far too much time in the classroom for the amount of learning accomplished and value received. The results of these early studies opened other areas to investigation of teaching practices.

EDUCATION AS A SCIENCE

Criticism of the Rice study continued to be heard from colleagues, although more and more educators began to see some value in scientific procedures. At a meeting of superintendents in the spring of 1897, Rice asked, "How can we tell at the end of eight years whether the children who have had forty minutes of spelling instruction are better spellers than those who have had only ten?" No one attempted to answer the question, but some replied that "the question could never be answered" or that Rice was wasting time by asking silly questions, and the meeting closed with most classing it "a failure."[3]

Nevertheless the early studies of Rice encouraged investigation of practices in other subject areas. By no means was the scientific approach widely accepted for education by the scholars of the early twentieth century, and the acceptance of scientific studies in education continued to be rejected by many educators at all levels. By 1902 Rice had this to say about the use of science in education:

> In view of the circumstances that during its long period of existence pedagogy has established no facts, that side by side with it, in other fields, facts have multiplied and developed into sciences, it is perfectly legitimate to ask whether pedagogy will admit of purely scientific treatment, whether it is possible for use to accumulate such facts as will lead to the discovery of certain fundamental pedagogical laws and certain methods and processes upon which all educators must agree.[4]

At the same time Rice developed two propositions:

> It may be that the nature of the child mind is so elusive, and the influence of natural endowments, heredity, and environment so varied, that all definite observation is ren-

---

1. J. M. Rice, "The Futility of the Spelling Grind," *Forum* 23 (April 1897): 163-72.
2. J. M. Rice, "The Futility of the Spelling Grind, Part II," *Forum* 23 (June 1897): 409-19.
3. J. M. Rice, *Scientific Management in Education* (New York: Hinds, Noble, & Eldredge, 1913), pp. 17-18.
4. Ibid., p. 2.

dered impossible, or it may be that we have not yet applied proper methods of observation.[5]

Paraphrasing Rice, the two propositions become:
1. The nature of a child's mind negates any scientific study through direct observation.
2. Proper methods of observation have not been applied to educational problems.

The best statement about present theory would be that probably each of the two propositions has some degree of validity. Personal facts are more difficult to obtain and interpret than public facts, making educational studies difficult to carry out. Also research methods used to study problems are at best in need of increased sophistication.

One of the basic premises used in early attacks on scientific studies was that education was an art and could not be approached in a scientific way. Many still view it as more of an art than a science. The difference between education as an *art* and education as a *science* can be explained as follows:

The art of education deals with the practical applications of knowledge to the educational scene.

The science of education deals with the facts and principles that build an organized body of knowledge about educational concerns.

Those problems that deal with building an organized body of knowledge about educational concerns through the scientific structure of inquiry are, unquestionably, research questions. Educational research is scientific in that knowledge of general truths and operation of general laws have been obtained and tested through a scientific approach to solving problems.

The knowledge is not presented or considered by educators as final in any sense. Rather, given more and better information, it stands to be tested and subject to change. Most of the knowledge is based on theories in various stages of sophistication. All fields of study have found it difficult to establish natural laws—those principles held to be derived from nature and being everlasting. The universe is certainly structured on a framework of natural laws, but as yet most of these have escaped humans. Few, if any, natural laws are proposed for the body of knowledge about educational concerns. However, through scientific investigation, the gulf of ignorance is hopefully narrowed.

APPLYING THE SCIENTIFIC METHOD TO EDUCATIONAL PROBLEMS

The educational problems that can be taken up scientifically are those that are *testable*. One assumption underlying this notion is that there are some educational problems that are metaphysical and are not amenable to empirical testing. Questions that depend on value judgments or beliefs are of this kind. Statements like the following are metaphysical in nature:

Sex education should be a part of the primary-grades curriculum.

Boys should take a course in homemaking before graduation from secondary school.

One year of military training between the ages of eighteen and twenty-one would build character for adult life.

Implied questions, such as:

Should sex education be a part of the primary-grades curriculum?

Should boys take a course in homemaking before graduation from secondary school?

---

5. Ibid., p. 3.

> Should one year of military training between the ages of eighteen and twenty-one be required to build character in boys and girls for adult life?

are not likely to be answered with a high degree of agreement from objectively obtained information. Consequently the scientist does not deal with them and others like them, since any results will remain indeterminate. The scientist is aware that questions like these must be dealt with but his or her concerns are with questions and hypotheses that imply the availability of objectively obtained data for observation and testing. Other kinds of questions can be approached through a structure of problem solving, and are discussed in the remainder of the chapter.

The taxonomy in figure 1.1 was developed to aid in the discussion of roles of those working to solve educational problems through problem-solving techniques. Like all models that attempt to abstract reality, it has some shortcomings. The sharp divisions made in the taxonomy are often less clear in reality because of the more complex nature of the real world settings. As the developers of the taxonomy state:

> . . . , this presentation recognizes that in a real life problem situation there may be a need to know, to choose, and to do merged. The recognition of the taxonomy is not an expectation that we can make every problem situation a "pure" application of research. The taxonomy should help us merge the research, development, and evaluative processes as we seek to solve real and complex problems.[6]

Any strategy utilized in problem-solving can be associated with one of the three strategies, but a person working with one problem may utilize more than one of the strategies. The point here is that they are different enough that the different roles are discernible based on the activities of the person working to solve the problem. A discussion of the three strategies follows in the next few pages to help those engaged in problem solving to communicate as clearly as possible.

EVALUATIVE PROCEDURES

Evaluative procedures are in the branch of the tree in figure 1.1 that deals with problems based on a need to choose. Since they are not research oriented, little will be said here except to help clarify the meaning attached to research processes. Evaluative procedures are those techniques associated with the gathering of information for judging alternatives when making decisions. Education utilizes evaluation in many ways, but the one most directly related to teaching-learning activities has to do with determining the extent of student learning. Other forms of evaluation are based in program appraisal, accountability questions, and fixing the effectiveness of teaching, teachers, and administrators.

A look at one of these areas may help orient us with evaluation and, in turn, help us to understand what belongs in the area of research. The direction of evaluation in education can be discerned from a view regarding this area in a comprehensive handbook on student evaluation:

---

6. William J. Gephart, "Toward a Taxonomy of Empirically-based Problem-Solving Strategies," in *Similarities and Differences in the Research and Evaluation Processes* (Bloomington, In.: Phi Delta Kappa, 1973), p. 43.

Educational Research as a Science

The intent of this book is to present a broader view of evaluation and its place in education. We are primarily concerned with its use to improve teaching and learning. Briefly, our view encompasses:
1. Evaluation as a method of acquiring and processing the evidence needed to improve the student's learning and the teaching.
2. Evaluation as including a great variety of evidence beyond the usual final paper and pencil examination.
3. Evaluation as an aid in classifying the significant goals and objectives of education and as a process for determining the extent to which students are developing in these desired ways.
4. Evaluation as a system of quality control in which it may be determined at each step in the teaching-learning process whether the process is effective or not, and if not, what changes must be made to ensure its effectiveness before it is too late.
5. Finally, evaluation as a tool in education practice for ascertaining whether alternative procedures are equally effective or not in achieving a set of educational ends.[7]

Educational evaluation serves the purpose of furthering valid decisions about a wide array of school problems. The evaluator gathers information and uses it to make judgments about school-related events, and to present alternatives to those making decisions in specific educational settings.

The many directions of educational evaluation tend to make a statement of the precise role of the evaluator difficult. Borich says that attempts to define the evaluator's role have been no more successful than definitions about the role and qualifications for corporation presidents.[8] Basic to an understanding of evaluative strategies is a view that evaluation is a feedback mechanism that is essential if school people are to learn from their experiences.

DEVELOPMENTAL PROCEDURES

Developmental procedures are in the branch in figure 1.1 that deals with problems based on a need to do. This aspect of education deals with the development of instruction, curriculum, and materials associated with the ongoing in-class parts of the process of education. Development of theories of instruction, test development, other material development, and broad and local curriculum changes belong in this type of scientific activity.

A technique of curriculum development, *action research,* utilizes a model of great interest to several disciplines. It is a well structured model that uses continuous feedback to attack specific problems in one particular school setting. Since the intent of the activity is not to produce generalizable knowledge and the orientation is to only one setting, this type of procedure is a tool of the curriculum specialist, *not* the researcher. Within the total model of action research is a part that utilizes research strategies. Specific subparts of the major question can be directed as questions to be answered by research when present knowledge is inadequate.

---

7. Benjamin S. Bloom, J. Thomas Hastings, and George F. Madaus, *Handbook on Formative and Summative Evaluation of Student Learning* (New York: McGraw-Hill, 1971), pp. 7-8.

8. Gary D. Borich, ed., *Evaluating Educational Programs and Products* (Englewood Cliffs, N. J.: Educational Technology Publications, 1974), p. 30.

Many of the problems of curriculum change are of a complex nature, and could merge the three areas. Usually the change will begin with some specific disturbing situation, but, as the particular problem area is investigated, it must be viewed in the context of the total school scene. In order to study the specific situation a comprehensive diagnosis and study must be made. The major task is one of curriculum change, which is classed as development. Each stage of development will use evaluation information of all types to defend and give feedback to the development work. Research techniques may be needed to study effectiveness in objective terms.

Although action research and curriculum change fall outside the sphere of evaluation and research, curriculum developers may need to call on these areas for their particular contributions. Development of instructional tools refers to activities devoted to production of appropriate textbooks, films, manuals, software for computer-aided instruction, and other devices to be used in the learning setting. Successful development of a product requires a wide knowledge of educational theory and utilization of evaluative information as a feedback about the product's effectiveness.

RESEARCH PROCEDURES

The third strategy is associated with the need to know. The purpose of the remainder of this book is to discuss at length research in education as it relates to the addition of knowledge about the educational process. Metaphysical questions, questions of evaluation, and development questions are considered to lie outside the area of educational research. The reader should remember that he or she will find the same person working in two or more of these areas at different times in different projects or, perhaps, within the same study. The researcher may find that he or she needs a particular type of test to gather data. If no standardized tests are available he may need to develop the needed test. When he does this he is functioning as a *developer* not as a researcher. What is important for the present discussion is that the reader becomes knowledgeable about the roles associated with each strategy. The distinction is also helpful when conversing with colleagues about professional activities.

Because of the wide range of problems in education, no one formula can be presented to guide the educational researcher. The seven-step model provided for the scientific method can serve as the general model which can be adapted to the solution of a particular problem and its unique set of circumstances. It should *not* be viewed as a "do it yourself kit," but, rather, a way to structure a logical approach to answer a researchable problem.

Although there is a general sequence of research steps, they should not be viewed as a staircase. The use of the steps on a stairway is quite different—each step is used in a sequence with all of the others, and, once utilized, is set aside and not used again until another trip is made on the stairway. The structure of research inquiry requires that several of the steps be considered at once so that the total of the procedures will present a logical sequence. One may skip ahead to a later step to consider a decision at an early point, in light of its effects elsewhere in the process. In most cases there will be a natural order for procedure that is unique to the problem under study, but the steps are not independent.

There can be little direction without a clear and concise presentation of the problem under study. When the problem has been reduced to a well-prepared question, the most important element needed to make the scientific method function for the educational setting has been isolated. If the question meets the criteria for a research study,

then the rest of the procedures can be fitted to answering the question. Keep in mind that the answer to this question is the product of the research study. The next chapter is designed to give direction to the total process of research by breaking the total research process into three general divisions:
1. Planning stage
2. Investigation stage
3. Generalization stage

In general each activity of research can be associated with one of the three stages, but the interdependent nature of the parts again precludes working in isolation from all of the others. Maybe this is the reason why those persons engaged in research are prone to make statements like:

I am confused.

I need to talk to someone about this.

or ask:

What do I do next?

If one finds himself asking a question similar to this one or making statements like those above, he may be experiencing the same feelings and frustrations that a long-time researcher was suffering when he said that research is *organized confusion.* The frustrations are *not* reserved for the newly initiated. At least one rewarding moment exists for every study—that occurs when it all fits together as a *structure of inquiry.* This occurs when the engineering provides a vehicle to answer the question and, in turn, adds to present knowledge.

DOES RESEARCH MAKE A DIFFERENCE?

The contribution of research to the process of education is widely debated by professional educators and other interested persons. Many of the negative comments have been directed toward the inability of research to give immediate answers that have permanent applicability. An understanding of research as a science should help the writers who are impatient and/or critical.

The nature of science does not allow answers to always be right. An integral part of the scientific approach is the correction factor that permits science to correct itself when it is wrong. The test of differences in the school setting brought about by educational research lies in the beliefs and how they change over a five- or ten-year period.[9] The facts that beliefs change should not be used as evidence against the scientific approach to educational problems, but as a strength for developing theory to bring about change within the school setting.

The nature of humans and their characteristics present many difficulties for the educational researcher that are not encountered by researchers in the physical sciences. Progress and differences can be made only through persistent, patient, and purposeful probing. The changes made in the past should give encouragement to present day educational researchers as they attack problems scientifically.

SUMMARY

In this chapter *educational research* has been defined as structured scientific inquiry of educational questions that provides answers which contribute to the generalizable

---

9. Ellis B. Page, "Accentuate the Negative," *Educational Researcher* 4 (April 1975): 5.

knowledge about educational concerns. A seven-step model based on the scientific method has been presented as a general model to be adapted to the unique set of circumstances of a particular problem to be researched. Educational problems that are testable are those which can be approached scientifically. Problems that are basically metaphysical and involve answers that are at best value judgments are not amenable to scientific inquiry.

The evaluation and development strategies have also been discussed briefly to help the reader develop the understanding that research in education is to be used when the problem is based on a need to know.

A well developed question generated by the problem is the most important element in a scientific approach. Research has been presented as being somewhat confusing and at times frustrating, but as a process which also has its rewarding moments. One such reward is received when a study fits together as a *structure of inquiry*. Another is received as changes in educational practices come from the development of educational theory.

3

Structuring Research Activities

> *Grasping the structure of a subject is understanding it in a way that permits many other things to be related to it meaningfully.*
>
> —Jerome S. Bruner

When presented with an obstacle or an indeterminate situation, a number of options are open as alternatives. One option is to turn it aside, avoid it, and give it no more consideration. Assuming that this choice is not made, a person must come face to face with the situation by taking some action designed to overcome the felt difficulty. Educational research provides the structure for the scientific investigation of problems based in establishing facts and principles about educational concerns. The structure for the research process is built around three sequential phases designed to answer the problem question. The first set of activities is devoted to planning the attack, the second is the implementation of the plan, and the third is intended to generate generalization from this study to the field of education.

PLANNING STAGE

The important decisions about procedures are made in the planning stage, and to a large extent they determine the worthiness and validity of the final product of the research process—*an answer to the problem question.*[1] The first major decision which must be made in regard to the problem is based on getting an answer to the question:

Is this a problem that is researchable?

Before the answer to this question can be obtained four other questions must be attended to:

---

1. The problem question refers to the refinement of the felt difficulty (the indeterminate situation) into a clearly presented question which the researcher wants to answer. That answer becomes the output of the research process.

1. Is the answer already known?
2. Can the solution to the problem be determined from objectively obtained data and/or information?
3. Is this a question that can be answered without checking established policy or using speculation?
4. Are there any ethical aspects which would preclude carrying out the study?

For an area to be researchable the first and last questions must be answered "no," and the second and third "yes." If the answer to the question is known, the time and money spent on a research project would be wasted. A scientific approach to the solution of problems assumes that the information needed can be obtained objectively and organized meaningfully for interpretation. An independent interpretation of the results is necessary if a contribution is to be made to present knowledge. The consideration of ethics is important because of the human subjects involved in most educational research. Inanimate objects can be studied in almost any way without fear of permanent damage, but studies of human beings must be carefully checked to see that the subjects under study are not affected adversely by any procedure or treatment that involves such subjects.

Problem Presentation

It is next to impossible to answer the above questions and to proceed with the process without a well developed problem to provide direction. Early clarification of the felt difficulty is best attained by writing a question, keeping in mind that the answer is the object of the research. Since it will be almost impossible to progress toward solution without direction, a major task associated with planning is to write a well developed and delimited formulation of the problem. When the question is established, the direction of the study becomes clearer.

Kerlinger has said that the researcher will not always be able to "formulate his problem simply, clearly, and completely,"[2] but that this difficulty should not allow him to avoid presenting the problem or to lose sight of the necessity to do so. Part II of this textbook deals extensively with problems and problem presentation through specific questions.

Literature and Research

Once the direction is determined, the researcher needs to investigate present knowledge to find an answer and/or to become more knowledgeable himself or herself about the problem area, other closely related problems, and theories that pertain directly or indirectly to the problem. The better informed the researcher, the better the research. Since almost everything that is known today has been recorded and can be found in some library, the researcher must become skilled in the use of the library—not to do his research but to do one of two things:

1. provide a ready-made answer to the problem, or
2. provide a context of knowledge for background of the problem.

Although libraries are physically different and are organized along diverse schemes, they all have the same basic function of storing knowledge. Students must develop library skills in order to find efficiently present knowledge related to a current study.

---

2. Fred N. Kerlinger, *Foundations of Behavioral Research,* 2nd ed. (New York: Holt, Rinehart and Winston, 1973), pp. 16-17.

Chapter 12 in part IV of this text is designed to aid students in developing these needed skills.

Hypotheses

The next section of the planning stage is sometimes called *analysis*. If the answer to the implied problem question is not found in what is presently known, the background knowledge acquired is used to state the most logically conceived answer to that question as a hypothesis. The hypothesis and possible subhypotheses are developed to be tested for validity. Objective data that will be needed and available to test the hypotheses are catalogued as a part of the analysis.

Definitions

Certain words, methods, and concepts which relate to the study should be carefully defined so that everyone understands just what each means. A special definition may be in order for one or more of the following reasons.

1. *Clarification of practice*—a carefully explained definition should overcome any ambiguity about practices. For example, an approach to learning that uses a heuristic form of learning should be explained carefully rather than saying that the investigation was conducted to study the discovery approach. Since what might be heuristic to one person might appear to be quite expository to another or what might seem to be exposition to one might be classed as heuristic by another, the researcher needs to specifically explain what he or she means by discovery. Carefully stated procedures help to define practices.
2. *Special meaning of a word*—if a commonly used word is given a special meaning this could create real ambiguity, especially for those who are not directly involved in the study. Special meanings of words should be avoided, if possible, but if one is used the meaning attached to the word in the particular study needs to be made clear.
3. *Newly invented terms*—if it becomes necessary in the course of the study to produce a new term it must be specially defined.
4. *Technical terms*—any word that requires special and/or unusual knowledge should be made clear. Words specific to an area would be considered technical terms.
5. *Major variables*—all major variables for the study need to be defined.

An authoritative source should be utilized whenever possible, at least as a basis for the definition. Modification can be added as needed. Remember when dealing with words that they can mean whatever the user chooses. As Lewis Carroll wrote:

> "Whenever I use a word," Humpty Dumpty said, in rather a scornful tone, "it means just what I choose it to mean—neither more nor less."

The best route to take is to use the word as it is commonly understood by the audience which will be interested in reading about the study. The implication is to choose a meaning as it is usually used in the discipline, unless there is good reason to do otherwise. A good source of word definitions for educational studies is:

Carter V. Good, editor, *Dictionary of Education*, 3rd ed. New York: McGraw-Hill Book Company, 1973.

Operational Definitions

Word definitions substitute conceptual representations for the expression which is being defined. One major enigma with definitions which use words is the fact that if one looks up the words used in a definition, then looks up the words used in those definitions, ad infinitum, eventually the word that was originally defined is used to define another word. A way to overcome this not-so-small vexation is to use what has come to be called an *operational definition*. The operational definition tells, in terms of performance, the outcomes that the word implies.

Rather than define the characteristic of "weight" as the "heaviness of the mass of an object," it might be better to define "weight" operationally as "the reading of the dial on a particular appropriate set of scales, giving the name and model number of the device." Assuming that the scales are available to all, there is no interpretation of words needed. Anyone could, within degrees of inaccuracies of measurement, read the dial the same as any other person. A definition that explains how a trait is to be quantified operationally, as was done with weight, is a *measured operational definition*.

An *experimental operational definition* tells how the researcher manipulates a variable under study. In behavior modification a researcher might give tokens to be cashed in for candy or toys. When the investigator tells how subjects will be tested under varying circumstances, he or she has defined the variable by using an experimental operational definition. In each case—measured and experimental—the operational definition is in terms of actions (operations) and tells how something will be measured or manipulated.

An example of a measured operational definition is:
> *Popularity* is the number of choices an individual receives from other classmates as indicated by the use of the sociometric device in Appendix A.

An example of an experimental operational definition is:
> *Treatment of the independent variable, counseling technique*—for one group of subjects the interviewer will face the subject and keep eye contact as much as possible and for the second group the interviewer will turn in the chair and look at the wall and/or the window while conducting the ten-minute meeting.

Many of the terms in education are at best only roughly defined. A term may be so global that it encompasses different ideas for different people, or it may merely mean something different to different people. There are some terms, such as "intelligence," to which there is common agreement about what it is generally, but disagreement about many of the aspects that must be dealt with when formally defining it. An operational definition explains specifically what the word means to the investigator and his study.

The researcher must make sure when planning the study that she or he understands the meaning of terms used, and that he conveys *his* meaning to others. It is true that the researcher can define in any way that he desires, but he should be able to defend his definition.

Assumptions

For each study there will be some underlying propositions that are taken for granted. Many must be assumed to be true whether they are clearly demonstrable or not. Although it is not necessary to make an exhaustive list of assumptions, the researcher looks carefully for these and lists specifically those that are basic to the study. Examples of stated assumptions are:

Creativity can be measured by use of a paper and pencil test.
Student behavior is a function of the specific setting in which it takes place.
Frustration is a product of anxiety.

Assumptions are listed to help provide a setting for the study and to better prepare for evaluation of the conclusions of the study. The decision to list or not to list lies with the investigator, and his/her guide should be that all assumptions which relate directly to the problem should be listed.

Methodology

A set of information gathered for the study is needed to base a conclusion about the answer to the problem question. This part of the overall plan structures the specific procedures about what or who will supply the data, how the data will be obtained, and how they will be analyzed.

The attention given to methodology focuses on the part of the scientific method called *experimentation* or *observation*. Methodologies for the three major research divisions are so diverse that each will be dealt with separately in chapters 8, 9, and 10.

INVESTIGATION STAGE

After all important decisions have been made and the plan has been deemed to be valid, the next stage is the implementation. Since the procedures have been determined, the implementation is a routine matter that follows specifically the directions of the methodology. Here the systematic execution of the design provides the data and/or information for analysis.

All sets of data hold many messages. It is the purpose of the investigation stage to provide clear messages and, through appropriate analysis techniques, to pick up the messages without distortion. The products of the investigation stage are usually referred to as *results*. Procedures include some or all of the following:

1. Ordering and/or tabulation of the gathered data[3]
2. Descriptive analysis[4]
3. Correlational analysis[5]
4. Inferential analysis[6]
5. Summary of results, including tables *summarizing* outcomes of data treatment. The summary should not include any evaluation of the findings, but should be an objective reporting of the analysis of data. Tables of raw data usually appear in the appendices.
6. The information of a historical study utilizing qualitative data will in general be organized along a dimension of time, geographic region, variables under study, or other appropriate factors. The analysis is an objective interpretation by the researcher.

---

3. Charles D. Hopkins, *Describing Data Statistically* (Columbus, Ohio: Charles E. Merrill, 1974), pp. 1-27.
4. Ibid., pp. 29-81.
5. Ibid., pp. 83-98.
6. George A. Ferguson, *Statistical Analysis in Psychology and Education*, 3rd. ed. (New York: McGraw-Hill, 1971), pp. 146-426.

Any contribution to the general body of educational knowledge will come from the data. The importance of careful presentation of these outcomes cannot be overemphasized. Logical organization and clearly presented summary tables will help determine what contribution the study makes. Without this organization, any contribution might be hidden and not be apparent to anyone, including the researcher who is conducting the study.

The summary should synthesize the results of the study to provide a basis for the conclusions. Findings that tend to contradict each other should be pointed up, as well as results that support each other. Findings can also be compared to findings of other studies to give a basis for the generalization stage. The investigation stage will be given more complete coverage in the several chapters in the remainder of the book.

GENERALIZATION STAGE

Although the investigation stage provided the pulling together of the data into a synthesis, the major reporting of conclusions is left for the generalization stage. The most important aspect to keep in mind in drawing conclusions is to *be sure that the conclusions represent what the data have demonstrated*. Of course, the way to do this is to base the conclusions on the data rather than on what the investigator would like to find.

The report must be scientific, and the investigator must follow the scientific approach to the finish. This means that he or she must view a conclusion, which does not support his best guess (the hypothesis), as equally important to pushing back the frontier of ignorance as an outcome that supports the hypothesis. It may be—and usually is—as important to scientists to know what is *not* true as to find an outcome that is positive to the research hypothesis.

Being right is usually viewed as much better than being wrong. There is something about the nature of human beings or our culture that says being right is OK and being wrong is not OK. Nevertheless conclusions should be straightforward statements about the relationships of the variables under study, which in turn relates the findings to the hypothesis. The conclusions will also relate the findings of this study to the current body of knowledge.

Statements about the implications of this study should be discussed and related to present theories, present educational practices, and anything else that seems appropriate. Although the researcher is free to write anything he/she believes relevant in this section, he must be careful that what he says is backed up and supported by the results. A statement should be made about further required research directly or closely related to the problem under study. This gives direction to others interested in the same problem area.

The importance of the generalization stage is evident when it is viewed as the section that presents the answer to the original problem question and ties it to present knowledge. Undoubtedly this is one of the most important aspects of scientific inquiry. More direct help in drawing conclusions will be found in chapter 11.

A STRUCTURE FOR THE PLAN

A device to aid the researcher in designing a plan that has come into wide use in recent years is the *research proposal*. It was created when students and those asking

Structuring Research Activities

for grants of money to fund research projects were requested to tell specifically what the research was about and how they intended to proceed through to the solution of the problem. The proposal has evolved to become as essential to research as a blueprint is to the construction of a building. The proposal has three essential elements:

1. Background of the problem
2. Problem presentation
3. Methodology

There is not one and only one format for a proposal, but all proposal guidelines should include the three aspects listed above. Some guides for proposal development ask for a complete review of the professional literature, while others ask that only enough be included to give necessary background to provide the context for the present study. A major section required for a proposal for research funding would be an additional section on the budget for fund expenditures. In general a bibliography would be included for all proposals to list references used in preparing the proposal or, at the option of the writer or thesis committee, an extensive bibliography including other related materials.

A well prepared proposal will cause the writer to consider all important details from problem formulation through the research design. The design should be presented in detail, with each part explained so specifically that another researcher would be able to repeat the study in exactly the same way that the originator would proceed. Chapter 13 in part IV of this book discusses at length the elements of a research proposal, and will provide more direction in actual preparation.

SUMMARY

The structure of inquiry has been developed through the three major areas of *planning*, *investigation*, and *generalization*. The procedures related to each area have also been briefly discussed, and the functions of each major area and its relationship to the others presented.

The planning stage is entered after a decision has been made to attack some obstacle. The researcher uses it to clarify the question and to find out if the answer is already a part of present knowledge. If it is not, a theoretical framework and design are developed to provide an answer.

The investigation stage is entered to implement the procedures presented in the proposal as appropriate to the problem question—identifying subjects, making observations, gathering appropriate data, obtaining the results, and synthesizing the results. A basis for drawing conclusions is provided by this stage.

The generalization stage evaluates the results of the study by (1) drawing conclusions and relating them to present knowledge, (2) stating implications for educational practices, and (3) proposing further research related to the study.

The research proposal has been briefly discussed as a tool for the researcher to use in structuring research activities into a well developed plan. It is a convenient method of communication between prospective researchers and other interested persons, such as representatives of funding agencies and doctoral committees.

When a final report of the research study is made, after implementation and completion, the three stages should be represented accordingly depending on the type of final report being prepared. Two organization types follow.

THESIS OR DISSERTATION FORMAT

Chapter number	Chapter Title	Structure
1	Introduction	Planning stage
2	Review of Related Research	Planning stage
3	Procedures and Techniques	Planning stage
4	Analysis of Data	Investigation stage
5	Findings, Conclusions, Implications, and Recommendations	Generalization stage

JOURNAL MANUSCRIPT

Section	Section Title	Structure
1	Not titled, but includes: title; author's name; institutional affiliation; and an abstract	Overview
2	Not titled, but includes: the introduction plus a summary of the related literature	Planning
3	Method: includes a description of the subjects, apparatus, and procedures	Planning
4	Results: summarizes the data and interpretive devices and techniques	Investigation
5	Discussion: includes conclusions, implications, and recommendations	Generalization

BIBLIOGRAPHY

Anderson, Scarvia B. et al. *Encyclopedia of Educational Evaluation.* San Francisco: Jossey-Bass Publishers, 1975.

Ary, Donald; Jacobs, Lucy Chesar; and Razavich, Asghar. *Introduction to Research in Education.* New York: Holt, Rinehart and Winston, 1972.

Becker, Carl. *The Heavenly City of the Eighteenth Century Philosophers.* New Haven: Yale University Press, 1932.

Best, John W. *Research in Education.* 2nd ed. Englewood Cliffs, N. J.: Prentice-Hall, 1970.

Bloom, Benjamin S.; Hastings, J. Thomas; and Madaus, George F. *Handbook on Formative and Summative Evaluation of Student Learning.* New York: McGraw-Hill, 1971.

Boas, George. *The Inquiring Mind.* LaSalle, Ill.: Open Court Publishing, 1959.

Dewey, John. *How We Think.* Boston: D. C. Heath & Co., 1910.

_____. *The Quest for Certainty.* New York: Minton, Balch, and Co., 1929.

_____. *How We Think.* Boston: D. C. Heath & Co., 1933.

Englehart, Max D. *Methods of Educational Research.* Chicago: Rand, McNally, 1972.

Ferguson, George A. *Statistical Analysis of Psychology and Education.* 3rd ed. New York: McGraw-Hill, 1971.

Gephart, William J.; Ingle, Robert B.; and Saretsky, Gary. *Similarities and Differences in Research and Evaluation Processes.* Bloomington, In.: Phi Delta Kappa, 1973.

Good, Carter V., ed. *Dictionary of Education.* 3rd ed. New York: McGraw-Hill, 1973.

Helmstadter, G. C. *Research Concepts in Human Behavior.* New York: Appleton-Century-Crofts, 1970.

Hillway, Tyrus. *Handbook of Educational Research.* Boston: Houghton Mifflin, 1969.

Hopkins, Charles D. *Describing Data Statistically.* Columbus, Ohio: Charles E. Merrill, 1974.

Jones, Ralph H. *Methods and Techniques of Educational Research.* Danville, Ill.: The Interstate, 1973.

Kerlinger, Fred N. *Foundations of Behavioral Research.* 2nd ed. New York: Holt, Rinehart and Winston, 1973.

Lehmann, Irvin J., and Mehrens, William A. *Educational Research—Readings in Focus.* New York: Holt, Rinehart and Winston, 1971.

McGrath, J. H. *Research Methods and Designs for Education.* Scranton, Pa.: International Textbook Co., 1970.

Manhelm, Theodore. *Sources in Educational Research: A Selected and Annotated Bibliography.* Detroit: Wayne State University Press, 1969.

Mouley, George J. *The Science of Educational Research.* 2nd ed. New York: Van Nostrand Reinhold, 1970.

Rice, J. M. "The Futility of the Spelling Grind," *Forum* 23 (April 1897): 163-72.

Rice, J. M. "The Futility of the Spelling Grind, Part II," *Forum* 23 (June 1897): 409-19.

———. *Scientific Management in Education.* New York: Hinds, Noble, and Eldredge, 1913.

Sax, Gilbert. *Empirical Foundations of Educational Research.* Englewood Cliffs, N. J.: Prentice-Hall, 1968.

Stufflebeam, D. L. et al. *Educational Evaluation and Decision Making.* Itasca, Ill.: F. E. Peacock, 1971.

Thompson, Stith. *Tales of the American Indian.* Cambridge, Mass.: Harvard University Press, 1929.

Travers, Robert M. U. *An Introduction to Educational Research.* New York: Macmillan Co., 1968.

Van Dalen, Deobold B. *Understanding Educational Research.* 3rd ed. New York: McGraw-Hill, 1973.

Worthen, B. R., and Sanders, J. R. *Educational Evaluation: Theory and Practice.* Worthington, Ohio: Charles A. Jones, 1973.

PART II

The Problem: A Question and Its Answer

The heart of any research project lies in the question. The output of a research project is the answer to the question. Each is needed as an integral part of the process. This part of the book is intended to provide an overview of the research process, from problem identification through development of a hypothesis. Attention is given to general planning of research and to a general structure for collecting, organizing, and treating data.

Part II is not designed as a *do-it-yourself kit,* and only general treatment will be given to some topics, which are developed in later chapters that are more appropriate for their coverage. In the next four chapters the steps of the scientific method are used to structure the inquiry of educational questions, and special attention is given to basic considerations of observation and measurement. Keep in mind the working definition of educational research as *a scientific structure of inquiry of educational questions that provides answers with generalizable knowledge about educational concerns for those questions.*

4

Problems and Hypotheses

> *But it is hard to conceive modern science in all its rigorous and disciplined fertility without the guiding power of hypotheses.*
> —Fred N. Kerlinger

The scientific approach exists as a problem-solving strategy, and, as mentioned in an earlier chapter, the *problem* is what makes the scientific method work. The central element is the problem. The solving of problems provides an output of knowledge, but there is general agreement that merely accumulating answers in isolation does little to create a working body of knowledge. The scientific approach to solving educational problems is structured to go beyond the simple addition of facts to known knowledge. It is directed toward developing a body of scientific principles about educational concerns.

In the past the trend of educational research has been to deal with practical problem questions having answers with specific application using what is called *applied research* techniques. Other kinds of problems may be of interest to researchers and important to education simply because something is unknown at this time. Research directed to answering questions of a fundamental theoretical nature rather than a practical nature is referred to as *basic research*. Exploration of the unknown can supply answers to questions of the practitioners and/or contribute to the body of scientific principles about educational concerns. Both types of research are to be encouraged for the field of education, because of their potential contributions to bettering the educational process used in our schools and adding to generalizable knowledge. Both types of research are used to answer questions posed by problems in all facets of the educational process. This chapter takes up the study of basic research, how problems are clarified, and how hypotheses are developed for testing.

SOURCES OF EDUCATIONAL PROBLEMS

The original sources of most problems in education are those large elements of the educational process which are most obvious to educators. Major questions such as the following arise as educators carry out their professional roles in education.

> How can the language arts subjects be taught so that reading retardation is no longer a problem in the secondary school?
> What procedures can be implemented to reduce the drop-out rate to a minimum?
> What type of counseling technique is best to use with elementary school students?

The above questions and others like them evolve from very important areas of concern for educators. The answers to questions like these would make a large impact to improve educational policies, but, in general, the very large questions are not researchable in that form. The major difficulty that researchers have when confronted with such questions is that the scope of the problem is too great. Educational research can contribute to improve education by providing ways to study significant parts of a large problem and thus make small additions to knowledge about the major problem. However to attack very large problems in one study is generally an attempt to perform the impossible. Each researcher needs to develop a mind set so that he or she is aware of the contribution to knowledge which is made through the study of specifics, rather than feeling that he must forge ahead into an all-out attack on the major problem.

The first two major questions presented above are probably not answerable in terms of a generalization that is likely to be widely applicable. However each has many aspects that can be investigated. Students of research need to develop self-discipline to avoid the attempt to reach answers for questions that are too large in scope. There is a tendency for those who are new to research to try to solve very large problems because they are the most visible. All researchers must keep in mind that all of the world's ills are not solvable through one research study. The choice of a problem is not only important, but becomes crucial when relevant answers are the desired output of the research process. Most researchable problems are based in some larger problem, and the answers to questions under study, in general, will be tied to educational theory about the principles relating to the large problem.

The third major question above is not one that can have one answer for all situations. It cannot be tested because not all possibilities can be investigated. By careful choosing of counseling theories for study, the researcher can make statements about particular theories in specific situations. The answers for these particular conditions will provide information for situations having the same conditions. Good counseling practices for students in post-secondary vocational schools may be quite different from good counseling practices for elementary school students. Successful counseling practices for elementary schools in one geographic location may be quite different from good counseling practices for elementary schools in another geographic location because each has a unique set of characteristics. At the same time, however, some practices could conceivably be appropriate for all counselors in all kinds of situations. The need is not to attempt to decide what is best but to find how varying practices work given different times and settings. Findings through research studies about counseling practices contribute to counseling theory and should be reflected in school settings as counselors improve their techniques.

What has been said about counseling, of course, holds for other areas as well. A question that asks what is best needs to be rewritten so that there is a plausible answer. For example, the first question below could be improved by modifying it into the researchable question which follows it.

> What is the best way to develop understanding and retention of mathematic principles?

Problems and Hypotheses

Which is more effective in developing understanding and retention of basic mathematic principles—the traditional drill approach or a contemporary mathematics program intended to develop meaning?

Research efforts are to be viewed as the pursuit of knowledge by teams. Even the individual working alone is probably part of a larger body of individuals and teams working to solve a large problem by pooling the results of a number of lesser studies which contribute knowledge about the large problem. Thus the body of knowledge about educational concerns accumulates. The problem may come from the experiential background of the researcher, an educational or psychological theory which interests the researcher, or a combination of both.

PROBLEMS GENERATED FROM PRACTICE

The direct experiences of practitioners of the educational process provide likely sources for much research study. A felt need or obstacle can appear very naturally from the day-to-day activities of those persons who are engaged in the teaching-learning process as they meet the tasks of selecting and sequencing pupil activities and other facets of the interrelations between teaching and learning. Need for inquiry becomes evident to practitioners when they are required to make a decision on the basis of incomplete information. In fact, the beginning researcher of educational problems will most likely choose problems from personal professional experiences. Although many of these studies will deal with immediate problems, the solutions of those problems often contribute to the larger body of generalizable knowledge.

The area of study will most likely be a part of the discipline that the researcher knows well, one in which he feels that his level of expertise will permit him to work with a high degree of understanding. A thorough knowledge of the field will provide the background needed to identify gaps in knowledge. Professional experience areas of educators, such as the following, are sources for problems.

1. Teaching methods of subject matter area—science, reading, language arts, mathematics, social studies, foreign language, home economics, business, or technical
2. Teaching at various educational levels—nursery school, kindergarten, primary grades, middle school, junior high school, secondary school, or higher education
3. Nonacademic area—recreation, extracurricular activities, or religion
4. Learning environment—nondirective; authoritarian; physical aspects, such as temperature or noise
5. Social interactions of the classroom
6. Nongraded elementary schools
7. Programmed instruction or self-study texts
8. Use of classroom time
9. Special education services
10. Teacher expectations of students
11. Teacher attitudes toward change
12. Nutrition and learning
13. Parent education
14. Continuing education or adult education

15. Learning activity packages
16. Educational media—print and nonprint

Of course, it is impossible to give an exhaustive list of places with researchable questions, and researchable problems lie in many areas not listed here. The preceding list is intended to give some direction to students who will, as a course assignment, be required to identify a specific problem for study. It will provide some direction into areas that provide researchable problems. Thus the researcher should choose to work in an area which he or she knows well, and should select a problem that holds genuine interest. Experience can provide an appropriate research problem for most course assignments.

A Problem from Practice

An elementary school teacher continually works to develop mathematical concepts for students. One topic which receives considerable attention is that of physical area. Very early in school experiences teachers present activities that provide opportunities for pupils to form the concept of area and later to develop formulas to quickly compute areas of two dimensional figures. The interpretation and understanding of the area for a circle is difficult for many young pupils.

A teacher might question (developed from the problem implied above) how practice in estimating areas of rectangles and squares would help students to estimate areas of circles. This problem could become the basis of a research study, and the question might evolve into:

> What effect does practice in estimating the area of rectangles and squares have on students' test scores on a test of the estimation of the area of circles?

By developing a hypothesis of the answer, in addition to specific procedures for collecting and interpreting data, the teacher could research this problem within the school setting. Although intended to answer the question for one setting, carefully planned research has value for possible generalization to other settings. For the above problem question the results of the study may shed light on the question of the transfer of learning and its implications, far beyond the limits of the immediate classroom where the question was researched. The answers to many closely related questions are valuable to the development of knowledge about educational concerns when they are brought together in a statement of an encompassing educational theory.

PROBLEMS GENERATED FROM THEORY

Another source of problems is found in deduction from theory. Theories are generalized principles, and application of theory to specific educational problems needs to be investigated. A theory is useful in educational settings if it is tested for possible classroom use before widespread adoption and implementation. The investigator may use theory to generate a specific hypothesis to be tested through the controlled and structured investigation of scientific inquiry. Some sources of educational researchable problems using theory to generate a hypothesis are:

1. Theories of learning—animal and human
2. Personality theories
3. Sociological theories
4. Theories of instruction

Problems and Hypotheses

5. Measurement theory
6. Theories of behavior change

The above list suggests types of theories that can generate hypotheses to be tested. One should not think of the two areas for sources of problems—experience and theory—as being mutually exclusive. Many difficulties that arise in education are based in both of these areas, and the resulting problem could be identified as a problem deducted from *both* theory and experience.

A Problem from Theory

In 1963 the Working Conference on Research on Children's Learning met in Cambridge, Massachusetts, for two weeks to study how children learn. The monograph written to report the conference indicates that an earlier meeting had been held in November 1962 and that the meeting ended with the development of three categories of questions relating to learning.[1] The first was based in attitudinal and affective skills, the second in cognitive skills, and the third in stimulus control. The group disbanded in 1962 with the expressed task of preparing working papers for the 1963 meeting. One such paper presented within the category "attitudinal and affective skills" suggested three possible investigations about how children learn.[2] These suggested investigations were considered first from the general area of human learning, then a category within that broad field, further broken down into a division within the category, and finally the specific study.

The narrative of the paper developed several hypotheses about how the indicated factors affected student learning based on accepted learning theory. The final section presented some specific investigations for possible study:

Suggested Investigations

These ideas contain implicit suggestions for several critical investigations. Let us make some of them explicit.

Project 1:

To study the effect of *similarity* between teacher and child on the child's receptivity to learning. In this investigation one would vary sex of teacher and the degree to which the child perceived basic similarities between self and teacher interests, class, and ethnic and racial membership, and then study differential learning in individual or classroom situations.

Project 2:

To study the effect of the sex-role appropriations of the material to be presented on ease of acquisition. One would create maximal and minimal congruence between the sex of child and content of material to be mastered and contrast the ease of learning.

Project 3:

To study the differential effectiveness of curriculum change on children high and low on initial motivation to master. In this study, one would assign children to groups high or low on initial receptivity based on indexes of their perception of school and intellectual

---

1. Jerome Bruner, ed., *Learning About Learning* (Washington: Government Printing Office, 1966), FS5.212:12019.
2. Jerome Kagan, "Motivational and Attitudinal Factors in Receptivity to Learning," in Bruner, *Learning About Learning*, pp. 34-39.

mastery. One-half of each group would be assigned to one of two curriculum treatments with the presumption that the effect of curriculum would be marked for high receptives but negligible for the lows. These are but samples of studies by which one might attempt to assess the importance of initial receptivity.[3]

Using this approach, many small studies, generated from throughout the major area of how children learn, can tie together the various aspects of learning, and, in turn, strengthen or reconstruct the original theory. The results of many separate studies can accomplish what would be impossible if the large problem were attacked in its entirety within one large question. Interrelated research is especially helpful in building the body of knowledge about education.

Another source of specific problems can be found in the concluding section of most reports about specific educational research projects. Every research study generates more questions, and it is the custom for the investigator reporting the research to colleagues to list problems related to the problem under study. Look in the final report of the research for a section titled *Recommendations for Further Study*. In general, this section will be a part of the concluding statement of the researcher's report of the study to interested persons.

SELECTION OF A PROBLEM

The first ideas about a problem will in most cases be global—too large for one study. At this point the prospective researcher may want to talk to someone else to help direct attention to a question that is more researchable, but still worthy of sudy. A colleague, an advisor, a major professor, or an expert in the field of study where the problem is based should be able to provide guidance and help in choosing a researchable problem that will also be of interest. Each will be able to raise questions for consideration in choosing a problem for study. Two basic questions that need to be attended to are:
 1. Can the problem be solved by a research strategy?
 2. Can it be carried to conclusion? (Time, money, available data, and knowledge of the field must be given consideration.)

Those who are consulted will be able to help decide if the problem is important enough for the answer to add to the body of knowledge about educational concerns. Or, perhaps more important, someone may be able to direct the questioner to readings of research already completed on the subject, which indicate general agreement within the profession as to the answer. This does not mean that one research study should be used as a basis for the decision. The prospective researcher must decide if and when the evidence is sufficient and valid enough to accept as factual.

The following list of problem questions was developed by one class of graduate students taking their first course in educational research. It is composed of the questions developed by the individual students. The questions are presented here as the students first presented them for review. Most were rewritten later in another form, for clarity and sophistication, before they were usable for the term's research project. They are included here to indicate the wide range of topics studied and to provide examples of different approaches to selecting problems. The list of research questions as first presented follows without editing:

---

3. Ibid., pp. 38-39.

Problems and Hypotheses

How are teachers' expectations of tall children reflected in those students' achievement?

What are the effects on reading achievement for two ways of grouping—flexible and rigid?

What are the reasons for parents encouraging apathy in their children toward art?

How are those students who need speech correction associated with those same students who also need remedial reading?

Is there a difference in attitude toward change for experienced teachers as compared to less experienced teachers?

How is the ability to speak a foreign language affected by two uses of classtime—pattern drills and informal conversation?

What effect does discipline have on creativity in elementary art?

What is the impact of malnutrition, associated with the child from low socioeconomic background, on the development of that child's reading skills and comprehension?

What is the effect of an individualized reading program on the reading ability of the disinterested reader?

What effect does the number of items on a mathematics test have on the measurement of mathematical skill at junior high level?

What effect does the lactose deficiency have on the achievement of the primary children?

What effect does student handwriting have on a teacher's evaluation of essay responses to items on a secondary home economics test?

What effect does verbal interaction between mother and child have on a child's verbal competence in the initial school years?

Which of the following methods of instruction for fourth year mathematics would be more effective in moving students to desired outcomes—a teacher in the classroom or the teacher on instructional television?

What is the effect of short-term parent education on the behavior of the parent toward the child?

How are the two characteristics—college grade point average and on-the-job counseling effectiveness—related?

How does melodic presentation of subject matter affect the length of attention span for preschool children?

What is the effect on achievement in the basic business class in the time spent when a workbook is used for a wide range of planned activities?

*How does the degree of women's liberation in developing Southern Asian countries compare to the liberation of United States women?

*How can the special needs of graduate students be met by on-campus housing?

*To what degree do influencing factors determine the clothing purchases of teenage students?

*What is the effect of weight lifting on the performance of distance runners?

*What are the differences in the child's growth as determined by different infant feeding formulas?

---

*Some students were not teachers and those students chose topics appropriate to their professional fields.

Selected problem questions gathered from other students' papers that pose questions in other areas of education are:

> Which is more effective in developing motor skills—part or whole learning?
> How does a prepared learning sheet, given to students before they read the assignment, affect the student's performance in a high school United States history course?
> What effect will quiet background music have on the aggressive behavior of emotionally disturbed children?
> What effect does IVTC program #732 have on skill development in an automotive program at the post-secondary-school level?
> What are the parental attitudes regarding the use of male teachers in early childhood education?
> How do coloring books affect the child's visual perception?

Looking through these two lists of problem questions, one can see the wide range of problems that confront teachers. These are not presented as models for writing questions for research but, rather, as illustrations of areas of concern. Each student was asked to check his question with the criteria that Kerlinger set for presenting a research problem:

1. The problem should express a relation between two or more variables.
2. The problem should be presented clearly and unambiguously in question form.
3. The problem and its presentation should be such as to *imply* possibilities of empirical testing.[4]

The reader might like to check some or all of the students' problem questions to see (1) if the variables being studied in each question can be identified, (2) if the writer has presented it clearly and unambiguously (Can it be improved? How?), and (3) if it implies empirical testing.

A good research question *cannot* be answered *Yes* or *No*. Answers for good research questions are not dichotomous, that is, the answers are not clear-cut yes or no answers. After a research question is written it must be checked to see if it can be answered yes or no. Generally direct questions asking for a yes or no answer can be answered without invoking the research process. The question "Can listening skills of second grade pupils be increased?" implies an answer that is already known. Many questions about how to do it and effective procedures for developing listening skills are still unanswered.

Usually the question to ask should be one that requires an answer in terms of degree, or how to accomplish already determined goals. A question should generate a generalization which can be supported or not supported by the critical experiment and observations made in the research investigation. The question "Does the method of teaching reading affect the reading achievement of first grade students?" has the obvious answer "yes." The basic question is—what differences in achievement are brought about by different methods of teaching reading to young children?

---

4. Fred N. Kerlinger, *Foundations of Behavioral Research* (New York: Holt, Rinehart and Winston, 1973), pp. 17-18.

Problems and Hypotheses

After the research question is written check to see if it can be answered yes or no. If it can, rewrite it in terms of effectiveness or degree of contribution of a particular factor or an existing relationship. The following question may be checked for quality, using the guidelines suggested:

> Do perceptions of the women's movement differ among college women?

The most obvious fault with the above question is that it asks for a yes or no answer. One way of overcoming that difficulty is to place the word "How" before "do," thus reading "How do perceptions...?" Another fault is based in the fact that a very large question remains to be answered. The question is stated in such broad terms that it might be difficult to decide when it has been answered. The third criterion—implications of empirical testing—may be violated because of the scope of the question. There is no need to attempt more than what can be handled in one research project.

A suggested improvement would be to break it down into smaller parts and look at a specific factor or selected factors. A study might focus on the different perceptions in regard to age of the student.

The question then might become:

> How do college women perceive the women's movement as a function of the differing ages of the students?

Other variables associated with the original question that can be isolated for study include class rank, major area, and marital status. These variables and others could be viewed in isolation by separate studies and the information pooled, or, given enough support in the way of time and financial help, it could conceivably be developed around the more general question modified to the following form:

> How do perceptions of the women's movement differ among college women?

When selecting a problem for study the researcher is well advised to write a question that he or she would like answered, and check it against the listed criteria. If at this point the project seems to be feasible, the investigator turns to further developing the clarification of the problem so that his mind is clear as to just what the study entails.

PROBLEM CLARIFICATION

The question gives the direction to the study—a well developed problem question will clarify for both the researcher and the interested reader just what the study is designed to do. The answer that is being sought is the product of the research. When planning the study the researcher can receive guidance in methodology. If his/her plans help to answer the question then they are appropriate research procedures.

A distinction is now made between the purpose of a study and the problem of the study. If the purpose of the study is stated, it does not replace the problem question. In general the purpose is not the same as the problem. The purpose of a study might be to contribute information about how students learn, and the problem might be to determine how the similarity of teacher and pupil affects the child's receptivity to learning. (See Kagan's "Suggested Investigations," in Bruner, *Learning About Learning*.)

A technique that has been used successfully is to state the purpose of the study as an investigation of the problem question, such as:

> The purpose of the study is to investigate one aspect of learning by answering the following question—How does similarity of teacher and pupil affect the child's receptivity to learning?

The researcher may find it convenient to add a short paragraph that delimits the scope of the study. The question does leave much detail unsaid, and a short addendum to the question directed to specific points will provide the opportunity to take care of any ambiguity within the question.

A narrative for the above question might indicate *what* teachers and *what* pupils will be a part of the study. The paragraph might be something like this:

> Specifically for this study teachers and pupils of the first three grades of the elementary school are investigated for discernible relationships of likeness or difference and how they reflect in the student's ability or inclination to receive learning through classroom activities.

Definition of terms will also help to clarify the direction of the study. Any term that is defined for the study will delimit the study. After the problem has been chosen and carefully delimited into researchable form, a search of what is now known (present knowledge) should be made to discern an answer to the problem question. If the answer is not found in present knowledge the researcher should develop a research hypothesis. Development of the hypothesis is given attention in the next section.

THE HYPOTHESIS

Speaking informally, the research hypothesis is the researcher's best guess as to the answer to the problem question. The hypothesis is a statement about the relationship of the variables under study in the research. It may be stated in different ways, but each hypothesis should (1) be in the form of an answer to the proposed question, (2) include an expressed relationship, (3) be testable through empirical investigation, (4) be stated clearly using the simplest terms to convey the thought, (5) be consistent with what is known, and (6) if possible, be based on a commonly accepted theory. Some examples of hypotheses for educational research problems are:

> Melodic presentation of subject matter increases the attention span of young children.
>
> Strict discipline reduces students' creativity as reflected in art objects.
>
> Poor handwriting reduces the evaluation of students' papers for an essay test in a secondary home economics test, and good handwriting will increase the evaluation.
>
> Quiet background music reduces the aggressive behavior of emotionally disturbed children.

These hypotheses were developed from specific problems presented previously in this chapter. Try to write a hypothesis for other problem questions given previously. If you find that it is difficult to write an acceptable hypothesis, check the problem question. A poorly presented question that does not meet the desired criteria may be difficult to

Problems and Hypotheses

answer with an acceptable hypothesis statement. Try rewriting the question, keeping the same implied question but checking carefully against the three criteria for problem questions. It should now be easier to write the hypothesis. An exception to this approach to writing hypotheses is given in the next paragraph.

One type of question does not appear to meet the criterion of a direct relationship, and, therefore, the hypothesis must be stated differently. The previously stated question, "What are the reasons for parents encouraging apathy in their children toward art?" is of this type. The hypothesis should be a listing of those factors which contribute to apathy. The research hypothesis could be stated thus:

> There are two reasons why parents encourage apathy toward art in their children: (1) lack of a personal appreciation of art and (2) a feeling that school time should be spent in the content subjects.

The hypothesis that meets the three criteria is a very powerful tool of educational inquiry (it has been said to be *the most powerful tool*). This power is based in the purposes that hypotheses serve:

1. Hypotheses give statements of relationship that are empirically testable and can be found to be either probably true or probably false.
2. Hypotheses give direction to the study and the experimenter. An unending accumulation of data without preconceived ideas or anticipation of outcomes would not only be inefficient but fruitless.
3. The hypotheses are evidence that the researcher has a sufficient background of knowledge to propose explanations to extend the body of educational knowledge.
4. Hypotheses give continuity to the study by providing a basis for drawing conclusions for study.

A study may have more than one hypothesis. It might have a major hypothesis that is too broad to be tested in that form but other testable subhypotheses could be derived from it and tested separately. The major hypothesis will not be tested directly, but the design of the study will test each of the subhypotheses. Thus the researcher will draw conclusions from them and, in turn, conclusions about the major hypothesis. It can be said that the subhypotheses, although each is tested separately, are used to test the major hypothesis.

Research problems are not directly testable. A problem must be tested indirectly through the hypothesis that it generates. The best way to answer the question "How does noise level which exists while students are taking a history test affect their scores?" requires a hypothesis in order to be tested. *Possible* hypotheses are:

1. A high noise level causes a reduction in history test scores while a low noise level causes history test scores to increase.
2. A high noise level causes history test scores to increase while a low noise level causes a reduction in history test scores.
3. Different noise levels have no effect on history test scores.

Each of the listed hypotheses is a statement of a proposed relationship of the two variables—noise level and test scores. A research hypothesis may be stated in different ways, but each statement should meet the three criteria. It is likely that a thorough review of present knowledge about effects of noise on performance of human beings would tend to support one of the above three hypotheses. Studies of the effects of noise on performance in offices, factories, homes, and other environments, including classrooms, would give information about what to expect in the history testing session. Of course the researcher must choose only one of the hypotheses to test. At this point he or she makes a commitment in the form of an educated guess about the outcome, and tests his conjecture (this is the hypothesis). He now has something to test. Without it he does not give the study an opportunity to support or not support anything.

Scientifically speaking it makes no difference in the outcome whether the researcher has *guessed* correctly or incorrectly, since the results will be the same. Of course if the hypothesis is tied to a theory positive results for the study will strengthen an already developed theory. A scientific investigation uses ground rules to remove the researcher emotionally from the study and provide opportunities for objective decisions. This is a place where one of those ground rules is used.

The hypothesis must be formed before the data are gathered.[5] To be useful, information gathered must be for or against something or it serves no purpose. However, it is not necessary to guess correctly to add knowledge to the bank of information about educational concerns. The tendency for the researcher to associate failure with a study that does not support the hypothesis needs to be wiped out of the minds of those engaged in attacks on problems utilizing scientific approaches.

The researcher has not placed his or her professional reputation at stake when testing a hypothesis—he should be content to feel that a well developed and conducted study adds to the body of knowledge, regardless of the results. Only through the hypothesis can the investigator tell positive from negative evidence, and thus push back the frontier of ignorance. Even negative evidence should be viewed as negative only in relation to the hypothesis under study—not to the science of education generally or to the researcher specifically. Positive results merely support the hypothesis, and negative results merely indicate that the gathered data fail to support it. Either result gives valuable information about educational concerns.

PROOF WITHIN RESEARCH

Two words that should *not* be used with hypothesis testing are *prove* and *disprove*. It is not the purpose of research to set aside for all time the answer to a problem with a proof, since that is a goal that is impossible to attain. There must always be room to change a decision given more and/or better information on the problem. Any proof within the context of hypothesis testing must be qualified as being based on present knowledge.

At one time the atomic chart had places for ninety-two elements. Not all had been identified, but there was general agreement among scientists that there could be only ninety-two elements and secondary school students were told (at least this author was told) that it could be proven that there could not be more. The atomic chart is now beyond one hundred elements, and probably more will be isolated in the future.

---

5. The betting windows at race tracks are closed before a race is run. The management finds that this works much better than leaving the windows open for, say, thirty minutes after the completion of the race. Research studies do much the same thing, and people in research tend to view their studies in much the same way. The game, of course, is the gathering of information to be organized for interpretation and reporting of results. After the game is played and results reported, conclusions are objectively drawn.

Problems and Hypotheses

It would have been much better to have said that it is *unlikely* that there could be more than ninety-two, but given more information on this subject more might be found. People can make decisions only from present knowledge—more knowledge might prove us wrong but rarely, if ever, will it prove us right.

Better terms to use with hypothesis testing are *support* and *nonsupport*. The results of a study either support the hypothesis or they do not support it. If there is proof within the research process, it is within the context of convincing evidence. Evidence may compel acceptance of a fact as truth, but not as an unyielding commitment by the researcher to his or her decision. The hypothesis that the researcher uses to direct the study and tests with empirical data is known as a *research hypothesis*.

THE UNHYPOTHESIS

A discussion of the research hypothesis would be incomplete without reference to a part of research methodology that is often erroneously associated with research hypotheses. There is a term, *null hypothesis,* that causes much confusion in the area of research, especially for those who are working in this field for the first time. This author chooses to call it the *unhypothesis* because it has nothing to do with what the researcher expects to find as an answer to his question. Research designs that use a test of significance in the statistical treatment of data use what is unfortunately called a null hypothesis. It is unfortunate because it has nothing to do with conjecture. There is no guessing, no background of information to support it, and no connection with theory. It exists as a part of the statistical treatment for some descriptive studies, but more often as a part of the statistical treatment design of experimental studies.

The statement of a null hypothesis is *not* a negative statement in terms of treatment effects, for example:

Research hypothesis:

Melodic presentation of subject matter will increase the attention span of young children.

Not a null hypothesis:

Melodic presentation of subject matter will not increase the attention span of young children.

Either of the above could be used as a research hypothesis for the problem question:

How will melodic presentation of subject matter affect the attention span of young children?

The null hypothesis is *not* just a statement that is negative of a positively stated research hypothesis. It is not used in the development of the researcher's hypothesis of expected outcomes of the study (his guess or conjecture). It *is* used as a part of statistically based decision-making procedures. If a statistical test were used for a study of the effects of melodic presentation of subject matter on young children's attention span, it could read as follows:

There is no significant difference in the mean attention span of third grade pupils when subject matter is presented in a traditional way and when it is presented in melody.

The use of the null hypothesis will be discussed at length with tests of significance and statistical design where null refers to no statistically significant difference. It exists because present statistical procedures cannot test the research hypothesis directly (a few special cases excepted). Since the term *null hypothesis* is in wide use, the tests of significance discussed later will be presented with a null hypothesis to test. The relationship between the research hypothesis (the researcher's best guess for an answer) and the null hypothesis (the unhypothesis—a part of a statistical test which is not a guess) will become more clear when statistical methodology fully explains the role of the null hypothesis.

THEORY DEVELOPMENT

Scientific approaches to problem solving go beyond the solving of problems in isolation. Although the solution of a problem generated by a felt need is important for the individual experiencing the need, two major purposes of all true scientific activities are *explanation* and *prediction*. The individual project hypothesis that is developed from present knowledge and experience is intended, through testing, to predict as well as explain. Theories developed from scientific activities are intended to form generalizations which can be used to make predictions for events of the future.

A theory explains and predicts phenomena through established relationships among variables using the theory's antecedent-consequence (cause and effect) knowledge for prediction bases. A theory is intended to integrate, organize, and classify the many facts supplied by isolated studies and provide meaning in the way of contributions to a body of knowledge. Kerlinger sums this in a definition. A theory is:

> *A set of interrelated constructs (concepts), definitions, and propositions that presents a systematic view of phenomena by specifying relations among variables, with the purpose of explaining and predicting phenomena.*[6]

Theory development is concerned with those results of observation in which the processes symbolized by the constructs interact such that deductions are permitted. Theories are formulated by fitting together results of observation and study. Theory is not vague conjecture: conjecture—yes; vague—no. The hierarchy of guesses goes in this order: blind guess; educated or rational guess; hypothesis; theory; and law.

The hypothesis is developed to be tested—
The theory is developed to explain and predict.

Theories get started and they grow through revision. Some theories get started and must be aborted. Scientists deal with false starts, and theories that need to be revised. The whole process of theory development involves a continual sophistication of the knowledge about interaction of processes to allow deduction for explanation and prediction. The inputs for theory development are results of the research activities of observation, study, and experimentation. They provide the information needed by educators to form and sophisticate theories, and contribute to the development of science through theories that:

---

6. Kerlinger, *Foundations of Behavioral Research*, p. 9.

1. Organize existing knowledge in particular areas. A theory brings together and gives deeper meaning by connecting the results of individual studies.
2. Explain adequately for *today* the results of research studies. The scientist's explanation is never ultimate and must be left open given more data.
3. Predict future phenomena. Although not established as an absolute truth a theory allows prediction with a high level of accuracy.
4. Provide new leads for inquiry. Rather than being terminal a theory generates further investigation.

One step above theory is law—*natural law*. With adequate confirmation some theories lead to establishment of a principle that is accepted with little question, thus becoming a natural law. The regularities among phenomena can be explained by laws, and the search of science is the way to express these regularities. Science premises that if the conditions of any given situation could be reproduced in total the phenomenon would be duplicated. Given different conditions, the phenomenon may or may not occur. Theories provide working tools for the researcher as he/she seeks to discover conditions leading to a given phenomenon. Enlightenment as to why it does not occur in what appears to be similar conditions establishes regularity in prediction and in turn results in establishment of natural laws.

The ultimate goals of science are discovery of the natural laws. A theory can be viewed as a bridge between the hypothesis and the natural law. Progression to the laws commences with the problems. Formulation and testing of a hypothesis related to the problem provide knowledge for development of theories. The well developed theory that is accepted with little question becomes a law. To keep this status a law must explain every case that it is intended to explain—no more, no less. Failing to do this, the law must be rebuilt or discarded depending on its ability to fit with the new evidence. The difference between a theory and a law is sometimes based in the person viewing the interpretation given to explain phenomena, and what might appear to be a natural law to one may be something quite different for someone else. Although they both are supplied with the same information, the interpretation may be quite different. However each discipline has certain generalizations that have withstood the test of time, which are widely accepted by experts in the field and are considered to be natural laws.

FROM A PROBLEM TO HYPOTHESIS

From the early 1900s,[7] through the 1930s[8] and 1960s,[9] to the present time, there has been a question of how to use classtime to best meet objectives of elementary school mathematics programs. Early evidence seemed to support the use of drill to meet stated objectives, but later evidence indicated other techniques to be equally or more successful in meeting objectives. Most contemporary elementary mathematics programs divide

---

7. Edward L. Thorndike, "The Effects of Practice in the Case of a Purely Intellectual Function," *American Journal of Psychology* 19 (July 1908): 374-84.

8. William A. Brownell, "Psychological Considerations in the Learning and Teaching of Arithmetic," *The Teaching of Arithmetic,* Tenth Yearbook (Washington, D.C.: The National Council for Teachers of Mathematics, 1935), pp. 1-31.

9. Charles D. Hopkins, "The Emerging Elementary Mathematics Program," *The Teachers College Journal* 36 (January 1965): 151-52.

classtime so that both drill and meaningful activities are used in the classroom program. The question generated by the problem of how to present mathematics is: What is the best way to present a program of elementary mathematics?

As usual the first question is too large to research in total, and probably belongs to the areas of curriculum development. Based within the very large question are many smaller researchable questions that can be asked.

A more limited area of the larger problem of how to best present the mathematics program is the use of classtime. A research study could be based in an investigation of two different uses of arithmetic classtime as they related to the students' achievement in arithmetic computation and understanding of basic arithmetical principles. The following researchable question could evolve from this aspect of the large problem:

> What are the effects on arithmetic computation and arithmetical understanding when the classtime used for drill is replaced by informal investigations of problems involving large mathematical concepts?

The above question meets the three criteria set for reasearchable problems.

1. It deals with a relationship between the variable of "use of classtime," and the criterion variables "computation" and "understanding."
2. It is in the form of a question.
3. It implies the possibility of empirical testing.

Basically there are two questions asked—one deals with the effects on computation and the other deals with the effects on understanding. Two research hypotheses will be needed to direct the investigation. Three possible research hypotheses can be developed for the question of computation effects, namely:

1. The ability to compute is facilitated by replacing drill with informal investigation of problems.
2. The ability to compute is lessened by replacing drill with informal investigation of problems.
3. The ability to compute is not affected by replacing drill with informal investigation of problems.

Three possible research hypotheses can be developed for the question of understanding effects, namely:

1. Arithmetical understanding is increased by replacing drill with informal investigation of problems.
2. Arithmetical understanding is lessened by replacing drill with informal investigation of problems.
3. Arithmetical understanding is not affected by replacing drill with informal investigation of problems.

Of course, in an actual study the hypotheses would be stated in more specific terms than those used here, to insure clear and unambiguous statements. The researcher would choose one hypothesis from each set of three, as presented above, to serve as his research hypotheses about treatment effects on the two variables — computation and understanding. Also in an actual study the terms would be defined so that it is clear to the reader what the researcher means by "drill" and "informal investigation of problems," "computation" and "understanding." The choice of research hypotheses would be determined by information available and/or theory that applies to this particular question. A researcher might choose the following statements of research hypotheses to test, basing his or her decision on all information available:

Problems and Hypotheses

1. There is no difference in computational ability between a class of students taught with the drill approach and a class where the time spent for drill is replaced by informal study of problems dealing with large mathematical concepts.
2. The understanding of basic elementary principles is increased for a class where drill has been replaced by informal study of problems dealing with large mathematical concepts.

Other pairs of hypotheses would be chosen by other researchers depending on their view of present knowledge and theory and their own past experiences.

After the researcher has clearly delimited his problem, presented it unambiguously, and developed the research hypothesis, he next turns to the task of answering the question. The next chapter, "Planning the Study," deals with procedures for selecting subjects to study, collecting data, and treatment of data that provide results which either support or refute the researcher's hypothesis.

SUMMARY

This chapter has covered the parts of the scientific approach that deal with formulation of clearly delimited problems and development of research hypotheses. Personal experiences and theory have been suggested as possible sources for researchable problems. Some specific sources from experience and a problem deducted from theory have been used to provide examples of how problems can be chosen.

Aspects to consider in selection have been listed, with questions that students have written being presented for the reader to evaluate, using three criteria for presenting a research problem. The hypothesis has been presented as an educated guess as to the researcher's answer to the problem question, and the relationship of the hypothesis to theory has also been established. Further, the null hypothesis (unhypothesis) has been discussed as a part of statistical procedures with the student being admonished not to confuse the null hypothesis with the researcher's conjecture about outcomes.

Finally an indeterminate situation has been developed into a problem, with researchable hypotheses generated, as an example of how a researcher might function when working with scientific approaches to problem solving. This chapter has dealt with the problem question and the researcher's proposed answer. The next chapter takes up the matter of testing the proposed answer empirically.

5

Planning the Study

> *The fact is that the major effort in the undertaking of research should be devoted to the planning stage.*
> —Robert M. W. Travers

After a problem has been clearly delimited and the hypothesis has been developed from related information, the researcher needs to develop procedures and techniques to test that hypothesis. To do this he or she must put together a planned strategy designed to select subjects, to observe and/or measure them, and to develop ways to interpret the observations as support or refutation of the previously stated hypothesis. All research studies need a plan or design to direct the attack on a problem question. The word *design* has two meanings in research. In experimental research, design is used to refer to the selection of the proper statistical tools for treating the data. The plan or design of a study to be dealt with in this chapter is much more encompassing and refers to the total methodology of:

1. Selection of subjects, or other sources of information[1]
2. Choice of a sample to study
3. A basic framework to:
    a. gather the information
    b. organize the results
    c. interpret the results.

Keep in mind that the design referred to here is the master plan, and that, within this framework, experimental research will utilize as a part of its overall design a section referred to as *statistical design*. The use of the term should be clear in context. The major purposes of this stage of research are to develop a way to gather data that deliver clear messages and to choose proper techniques to pick up those messages while

---

1. Anything that is used by the investigator to make a decision about his hypothesis. It includes facts from documents, relics, observation, measurement, and so forth. A synonym is data.

keeping an eye open to ways of interpretation. It may seem strange to the reader to refer to a set of numerals as having messages, but the researcher gathers the data to tell something about variables under study. The success of the research depends on being able to establish a plan to acquire clear, concise, and detailed facts and techniques to organize the information and transcribe it into the results of the study.

The importance of the study rests in the procedures set up as the design. It becomes important to gather the appropriate data from the correct sources in such a way that they will relate to the proposed answer (the hypothesis) and, in turn, to the problem question under study. The plan should be a logical sequence of procedures that has the means of providing interpretable results. The products of the plan are results to be used to develop the conclusions of the study and to connect them to present knowledge and implications for alteration of present practice.

The type of information gathered determines whether the research study is judged to be a qualitative study or a quantitative study. The distinction between the two is made on the basis of describing observation on a numerical scale (quantitative) or a nonnumerical scale (qualitative). The difference rests in being able to assign meaningful numbers (those that can be treated mathematically) for quantitative studies. Any use of numerals for identification or labeling would not be mathematically meaningful and would not constitute a quantification. The quantification would come from the counting of occurrences within categories. Refer to the section on scaling in chapter 7.

The degree of adequacy in a study is, in general, the ability of the design to provide a way to answer the question in specific terms which are generalizable beyond the sources of the information. The rest of this chapter is devoted to expansion of the points listed above, discussion of methods for obtaining appropriate facts for a historical or other qualitative study, and appropriate data for a quantitative study.

SELECTING SOURCES OF INFORMATION

The problem question will give direction to the type of data needed and the source or sources of information needed, but specific decisions must be made as to exactly what primary and/or secondary sources will be utilized in a historical study, or what phenomena or human subjects will be observed or measured for a descriptive or experimental study. The question becomes:

Where and how can data that relate to the problem be obtained?

For the qualitative study the data will be found in documents, relics, and/or accounts of firsthand witnesses. For the quantitative study the data will be created by the study of designated objects or subjects. In either case the need is to obtain all of the information required for the study but no more, since it is inefficient to use the researcher's time and the subjects' time to gather data not needed for the study.

A qualitative study—usually based in a question best answered by a study of the past—may examine closely an institution, a movement, an idea, a person or persons, and their interrelationships. It becomes necessary in the planning for a historical study to use the focus of the clearly delimited problem question to indicate the type of data needed to answer the question under study. The source of information should be made clear by the question asked. If the question asks why an idea about student learning was tried and discarded, the answer will probably be found in written materials. The

Planning the Study

researcher needs to identify specifically what materials would be most likely to have pertinent information. The decision to use particular journals for specific time periods and names of authors most likely to write to the point under study, or other specific sources, needs to be a part of the planning. Searching through written materials needs as much direction as any other study. Of course the decision to look in certain places does not preclude the use of other sources or rule out information found by chance. The structuring of the attack should in no way be a limiting factor, but a well planned attack will reward the investigator by the time saved in the search.

A qualitative study that asks about the type of materials included in physics textbooks in the years 1930 through 1939 would send the researcher in a specific direction. The source would be the actual textbooks that could be located. Some studies will utilize combinations of written material sources, relics, and eyewitness accounts. Much of the planning for the historical study lies in making decisions about where to look for the needed information. Conclusions are then made, based on the information, and presented as the answer to the proposed question. If a hypothesis is used, a statement of the conclusions will be made in regard to whether the study supported or refuted the hypothesis. The chapters on historical research (chapter 8) and the library (chapter 12) give more attention to this matter and to the use of a hypothesis in qualitative studies.

The sources of data for a quantitative study are more a product of the study itself, and the data are created through procedures designed for that one particular research study. Although there are designs of a general nature, each study is unique unto itself and the planning for a quantitative study will create a specific design for answering a specific question. Studies of a quantitative nature will utilize *devices* to gather data. Checklists, rating scales, tests, and surveys are all examples of data-gathering devices. These are not to be thought of as sources of data, but rather as instruments to aid in observation and measurement of whatever is being studied. The source of the data is found in the subjects of study. A class of biology students may be studied through the use of a biology achievement test. The test is not the source of the information—the biology students taking the test are.

The research question will dictate the type of data needed and, most likely, the possible sources of data. All available sources should be considered, placed in an order of priority, and a decision made as to which will be used in light of how well the data relate to the problem under study. A study that is based in explaining conditions as they presently exist (a descriptive study) will, in general, utilize different types of data from a study that manipulates conditions (the experimental study). Since in a descriptive study the only manipulation by the researcher is in the methods of observation and the analysis, he is limited to data that are available through normal events—anything that he studies would have happened without his observation or measurement. In general, data for descriptive studies will be collected through the survey, case study, documentary analysis, and job analysis; for correlational studies data will be collected from measurement.

Experimental studies will use data of a more technical nature since the study is based in a study of the manipulation of one or more variables by the experimenter. The plan utilizing quantitative data must specify the kinds of data needed and the best sources of those data. The chapters on experimental research, descriptive research and the proposal each cover the selection of sources as they relate to each type of study.

SELECTION OF SUBJECTS

Since education deals primarily with human beings, a large proportion of studies gather data about characteristics of designated human populations. The study itself will generally be directed to a particular population, but the researcher must decide which specific individuals (the sample) will provide the data. In research the term *population* means any clearly defined aggregate or set of people or things. The term *sample* means a subaggregate or part of the population. In most cases total populations will be too large to permit a contribution from each member, since studies are limited in time and financial support available. In planning for the study the researcher must decide
1. what population is being studied and
2. which particular elements of that population (the sample) will provide data for the study.

A sample that has the same characteristics as the population is very important to generalization. It allows for inferences and generalizations from the sample that is being studied to be applied to the population.

It may be that because of some limiting factor, such as a small number of subjects geographically convenient or some other administrative difficulty, the researcher will not be able to have a sample that meets all of the characteristics needed to allow generalization from the sample to the parent population (or what the researcher perceives to be the parent population). All studies should attempt to approach as closely as possible the methods described in the next section, where desirable sampling procedures for providing representativeness are given attention. A representative sample is needed to reduce sampling error to a minimum. Sampling error is the difference between a measure of a characteristic in the sample and the true measure of the same characteristic in the population. A sample that has nearly the same characteristics as the population allows generalization from the sample to the population. A few studies will be conducted in which all of the procedures are ideal, and some studies will be conducted in which most all the procedures violate the set of ideal procedures. Most studies will fall somewhere in between.

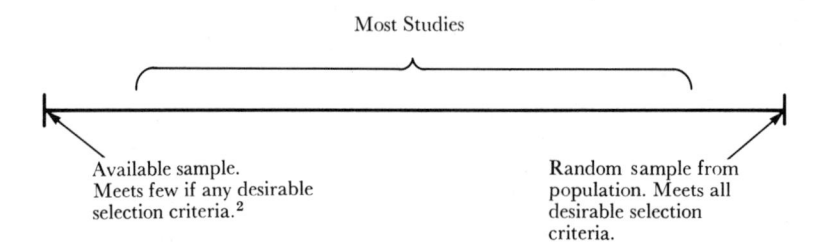

Most Studies

Available sample. Meets few if any desirable selection criteria.[2]

Random sample from population. Meets all desirable selection criteria.

The available, incidental, or grab sample simply uses intact classes or groups for study and is to be avoided if possible. The preceding sentence indicates that the grab sample can be used. If that is the best sample that can be obtained, it must be used. The use does not make it more desirable nor does it give the confidence that better procedures provide, but all questions should be attacked, which justifies even undesirable procedures.

---

2. An exception to this is the situation where the class or group which is used represents the total population. With this situation, sampling is not used, and there is no problem with sampling error.

Planning the Study

The Swiss psychologist Jean Piaget studied the development of children's thinking for more than fifty years. Until recent years little attention was given to his writings because his studies were of individual children or relatively small numbers of children. For a period of about fifteen years he studied mostly his own children. Today studies of large numbers of children are supporting many of his conclusions derived from his small samples. Since 1960 scholars of American psychology and education have recognized that Piaget is one of the giants of developmental psychology.[3] Much of what Piaget has contributed to education would have been lost if he had restricted his studies to ideal research situations. An example of his procedure follows:

> The second period of Piaget's investigations began when, in 1929, he sought to trace the origins of the child's spontaneous mental growth to the behavior of infants; in this case, his own three children, Jacqueline, Lucienne, and Luarent. Piaget kept very detailed records of their behavior and of their performance on a series of ingenious tasks which he invented and presented to them. The books resulting from these investigations, "The Origins of Intelligence in Children," "Play, Dreams and Imitation in Children," and "The Construction of Reality in the Child" are now generally regarded as classics in the field and have been among the major forces behind the scurry of research activity in the area of infant behavior now current both in America and abroad.[4]

Ferguson speaks to this point when he says:

> In practice, experiments are clearly not always conducted in the way our statistical preconceptions suggest they should be conducted. Experienced experimentalists are frequently aware of this. Much of the art of the experimentalist is concerned with reading conclusions from data which do not satisfy some conditions necessary for rigorous inference.[5]

What holds for the experimentalist is also true for researchers using results of surveys and other data-gathering devices used in descriptive studies. The individual chapters devoted to the types of research will expand on how the researcher can function with less than ideal conditions. The next section discusses desirable criteria for sample selection.

SAMPLING TECHNIQUES

When the scope of a quantitative study, either descriptive or experimental, does not permit use of information from every subject in the population, the planning procedures must include decisions about how the subjects in the sample will be chosen. Procedures of sample selection should not provide any bias between characteristics of the sample and characteristics of the population. If the elements of the population can be individually identified, a *random sample* can be obtained. To obtain a strictly random sample the sampling selection procedures must provide equal probability that each element in the population can appear in the sample and also that each choice of a sample element be independent of all other choices.

---

3. David Elkind, *Children and Adolescents. Interpretive Essays on Jean Piaget*, 2nd ed. (New York: Oxford University Press, 1974), p. ix.
4. Ibid., p. 16.
5. George A. Ferguson, *Statistical Analysis in Psychology and Education* (New York: McGraw-Hill, 1971), p. 123.

The procedures determine whether the sample is random. Some procedures which at first appear to be random are *not* random. The usual use of the term *random,* meaning haphazard or without order, is not the definition used in sampling for research. A definite rule for selection controls the procedures to assure equal probability and independence thus generating a random sample for statistical procedures.

An example that comes close to meeting the above restrictions but technically falls short is the procedure of drawing names from a hat. Assume that a sample of 60 is to be chosen from a population of 400. The names are placed in a container so that the folded papers are all the same size and mixed well. Without looking, a first name is chosen for the sample, then a second name, and so on. What is the probability that any one of the 400 would be selected on the first choice? (Answer: 1 in 400) What probability is associated with the second choice? (Answer: 1 in 399) Next? (Answer: 1 in 398) The probability is *not* constant, as required, and therefore the sample is not random. An attempt to overcome this problem of unequal probabilities is made by replacement of each paper into the container before the next paper is drawn thus keeping the probabilities equal. If the condition that a paper will not be used if drawn a second time is used, the conditional model has the same probabilities associated with it as the model that does not use replacement.[6] Although either procedure of sampling—with or without replacement—falls short of meeting the required criteria, either would in most cases not inject bias to sample characteristics when compared to the population characteristics.

If a roster is alphabetical or listed in some systematic arrangement, every *n*th name could be chosen for the sample. Called *systematic sampling,* this procedure can be viewed as having, in most cases, no bias, although the possibility does exist that the characteristics may not be independent of the ordering. Thus again the sample is not a strictly random sample.

A more acceptable, and the most commonly used, procedure when each element can be identified as described above is to use a table of random numbers. A table of random numbers (see figure 5.1) consists of several (many) pages of columns of digits that have been generated in such a way that there is no pattern to the sequence. In other words there is the same probability of any digit following any other, and the selection of each was independent of all other choices. Such tables can be found in statistics books or other similar sources.[7]

Figure 5.1 illustrates a page from a table of random numbers. To use a table of random numbers, assign consecutive numbers to the elements of the population being studied, perhaps using the alphabetical order of surnames. Start at any point in the table and proceed down (or up) the table, using the appropriate number of columns to identify enough tabled numbers to satisfy the chosen sample size. For a sample of 60 out of 400, three columns are needed. The first sixty numbers that appear indicate the elements for the sample and the sixty names associated with those numbers become members of the sample.

Using figure 5.1 to choose a sample of ten random numbers from a population with

---

6. J. L. Hodges and E. L. Lehmann, *Basic Concepts of Probability and Statistics* (San Francisco: Holden-Day, 1970), p. 92.

7. See Rand Corporation, *A Million Random Digits with 100,000 Normal Deviates* (New York: Free Press, 1955); also see *Table of 105,000 Random Decimal Digits.* Statement no. 4914, file no. 261-A-1. Interstate Commerce Commission, Washington, D.C., May 1949.

Planning the Study

```
77513 03820    86864 29901    68414 82774    51908 13980    72893 55507
19502 37174    69979 20288    55210 29773    74287 75251    65344 67415
21818 59313    93278 81757    05686 73156    07082 85046    31853 38452
51474 66499    68107 23621    94049 91345    42836 09191    08007 45449
99559 68331    62535 24170    69777 12830    74819 78142    43860 72834

33713 48007    93584 72869    51926 64721    58303 29822    93174 93972
85274 86893    11303 22970    28834 34137    73515 90400    71148 43643
84133 89640    44035 52166    73852 70091    61222 60561    62327 18423
56732 16234    17395 96131    10123 91622    85496 57560    81604 18880
65138 56806    87648 85261    34313 65861    45875 21069    85644 47277

38001 02176    81719 11711    71602 92937    74219 64049    65584 49698
37402 96397    01304 77586    56271 10086    47324 62605    40030 37438
97125 40348    87083 31417    21815 39250    75237 62047    15501 29578
21826 41134    47143 34072    64638 85902    49139 06441    03856 54552
73135 42742    95719 09035    85794 74296    08789 88156    64691 19202

07638 77929    03061 18072    96207 44156    23821 99538    04713 66994
60528 83441    07954 19814    59175 20695    05533 52139    61212 06455
83596 35655    06958 92983    05128 09719    77433 53783    92301 50498
10850 62746    99599 10507    13499 06319    53075 71839    06410 19362
39820 98952    43622 63147    64421 80814    43800 09351    31024 73167

59580 06478    75569 78800    88835 54486    23768 06156    04111 08408
38508 07341    23793 48763    90822 97022    17719 04207    95954 49953
30692 70668    94688 16127    56196 80091    82067 63400    05462 69200
65443 95659    18238 27437    49632 24041    08337 65676    96299 90836
27267 50264    13192 72294    07477 44606    17985 48911    97341 30358

91307 06991    19072 24210    36699 53728    28825 35793    28976 66252
68434 94688    84473 13622    62126 98408    12843 82590    09815 93146
48908 15877    54745 24591    35700 04754    83824 52692    54130 55160
06913 45197    42672 78601    11883 09528    63011 98901    14974 40344
10455 16019    14210 33712    91342 37821    88325 80851    43667 70883

12883 97343    65027 61184    04285 01392    17974 15077    90712 26769
21778 30976    38807 36961    31649 42096    63281 02023    08816 47449
19523 59515    65122 59659    86283 68258    69572 13798    16435 91529
67245 52670    35583 16563    79246 86686    76463 34222    26655 90802
60584 47377    07500 37992    45134 26529    26760 83637    41326 44344

53853 41377    36066 94850    58838 73859    49364 73331    96240 43642
24637 38736    74384 89342    52623 07992    12369 18601    03742 83873
83080 12451    38992 22815    07759 51777    97377 27585    51972 37867
16444 24334    36151 99073    27493 70939    85130 32552    54846 54759
60790 18157    57178 65762    11161 78576    45819 52979    65130 04860

03991 10461    93716 16894    66083 24653    84609 58232    88618 19161
38555 95554    32886 59780    08355 60860    29735 47762    71299 23853
17546 73704    92052 46215    55121 29281    59076 07936    27954 58909
32643 52861    95819 06831    00911 98936    76355 93779    80863 00514
69572 68777    39510 35905    14060 40619    29549 69616    33564 60780

24122 66591    27699 06496    14845 46672    61958 77100    90899 75754
61196 30231    92962 61773    41839 55382    17267 70943    78038 70267
30532 21704    10274 12202    39685 23309    10061 68829    55986 66485
03788 97599    75867 20717    74416 53166    35208 33374    87539 08823
48228 63379    85783 47619    53152 67433    35663 52972    16818 60311

60365 94653    35075 33949    42614 29297    01918 28316    98953 73231
83799 42402    56623 34442    34944 41374    70071 14736    09958 18065
32960 07405    36409 83232    99385 41600    11133 07586    15917 06253
19322 53845    57620 52606    66497 68646    78138 66559    19640 99413
11220 94747    07399 37408    48509 23929    27482 45476    85244 35159

31751 57260    68980 05339    15470 48355    88651 22596    03152 19121
88492 99382    14454 04504    20094 98977    74843 93413    22109 78508
30934 47744    07481 83828    73788 06533    28597 20405    94205 20380
22888 48893    27499 98748    60530 45128    74022 84617    82037 10268
78212 16993    35902 91386    44372 15486    65741 14014    87481 37220
```

FIGURE 5.1 A Table of Random Numbers

Source: R. P. Runyon and A. Haber, *Fundamentals of Behavioral Statistics*, 2nd ed. (Reading, Mass.: Addison-Wesley Publishing Co., 1971), p. 320. Reprinted by permission of the publisher.

200 elements, the procedure would go like this. For this example the middle three digits from the sets of five digits are used. The table is entered in the second set from the left side, and this sample will be the names associated with the first 10 numbers less than 200. The table entry looks like this:

77513   03820   86864   29901
              37174
              931

The first number for the sample will be 034, second will be 113, giving the sample numbers of 034, 113, 066, 026, 097, 137, 046, 023, and 170, from the second column, and 130 from the third column. Given a different rule and starting place, a different sample would be obtained. All samples chosen in this way are random—each element of the population has equal probability of inclusion in the sample and the choice of one element for the sample has no bearing on any other choice, giving randomness to the selection. The sample is also a random sample of all possible samples of 10 that could be chosen from the 200 population elements.

With random sampling there is no control on sample characteristics beyond probability and independence. Statistical procedures are dependent on random selection, and they are basically a study of what can happen when samples are drawn at random. A mathematical model which uses a sampling distribution compares what a researcher sees in his experiment with what could be expected when abstracting from the model. A technique that may be used to give added control to sample characteristics when the population can be divided into strata on one or more variables is called *stratified* random sampling. The method of stratifying a random sample allows equal allocation from each population class stratum to the sample, and retains randomness through equal probability. The strata are the different levels or categories of a characteristic,

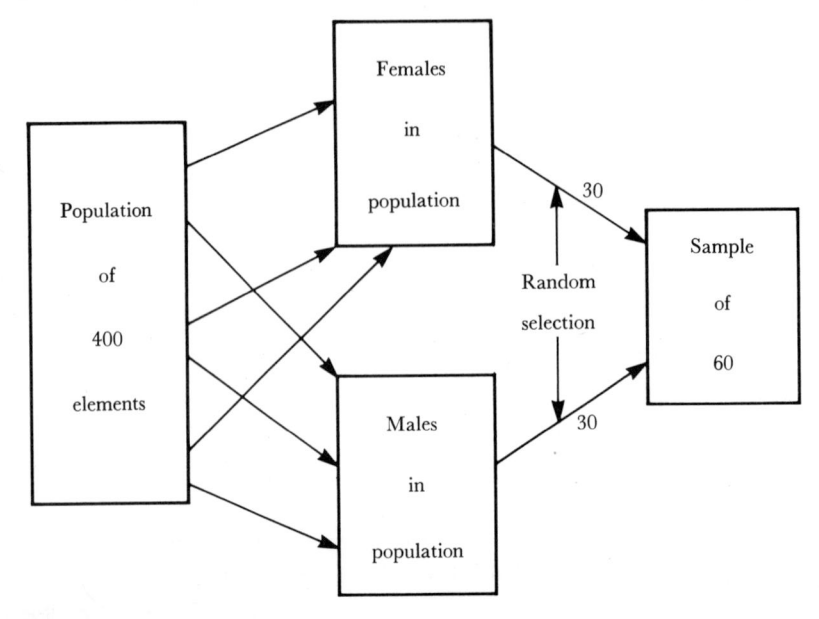

FIGURE 5.2   Selecting a Random Sample of 60 Elements from a Population of 400

Planning the Study 61

e.g., the strata for the characteristic of hair color could be black, brown, blond, and red. To stratify a human population on the variable *sex*, the population is divided into two classes based on *sex*. One half of the cases for the sample are chosen from the class female and one half from the class male, using random procedures for selection from each class. Graphically it looks like figure 5.2. Selection from identified strata of male and female controls for any bias on the sex variable. Stratification on two variables, sex and past achievement levels, would be developed as figure 5.3 shows.

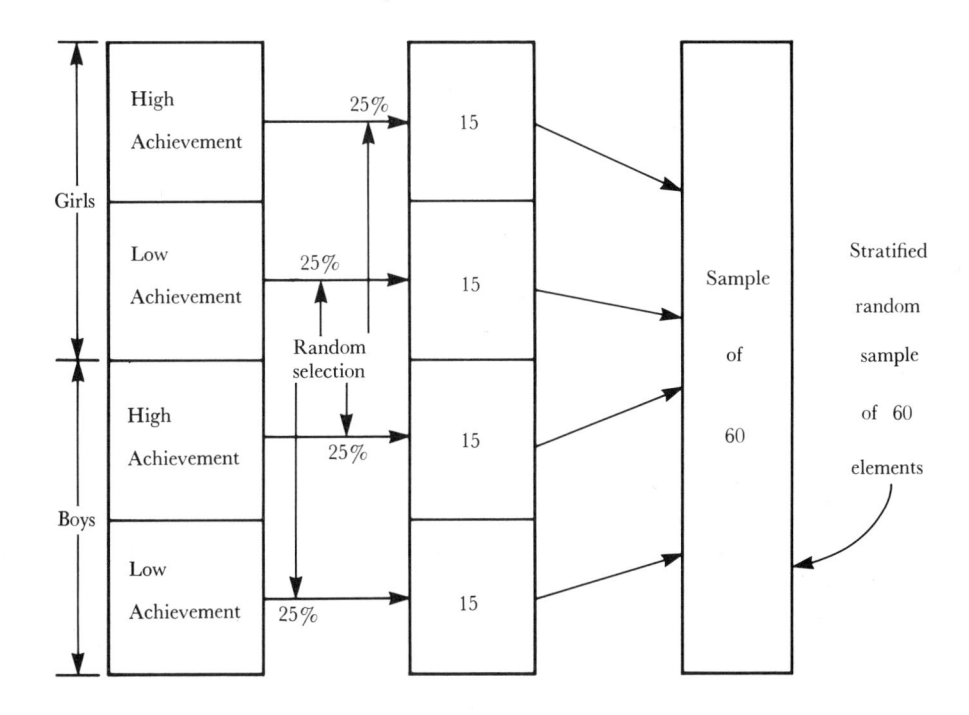

FIGURE 5.3 Stratification of a Sample on the Variables of Sex and Achievement

The procedure to create a proportionally stratified random sample requires information about proportions within populations. The only added feature to this technique is the selection from cells in the same proportion that the cell has within the population and looks like figure 5.4.

The researcher constantly strives to make his/her sample representative of the population characteristics. Stratification of samples gives the researcher control of important variables in order to give a sample more accurate representation of the parent population. His sampling techniques are directed toward providing a representative sample. Theoretically a population of elements which can be listed could be stratified on all variables. However, practically, this could not be done for a human population, since the number of subjects within each cell used for selection would be too small. (If stratified for all variables, the cells would probably consist of one member each since no two human beings are exactly the same on all variables.) In practice, stratification should be limited to the two or three variables that the researcher feels are most important to control. When deciding about stratification, it becomes most

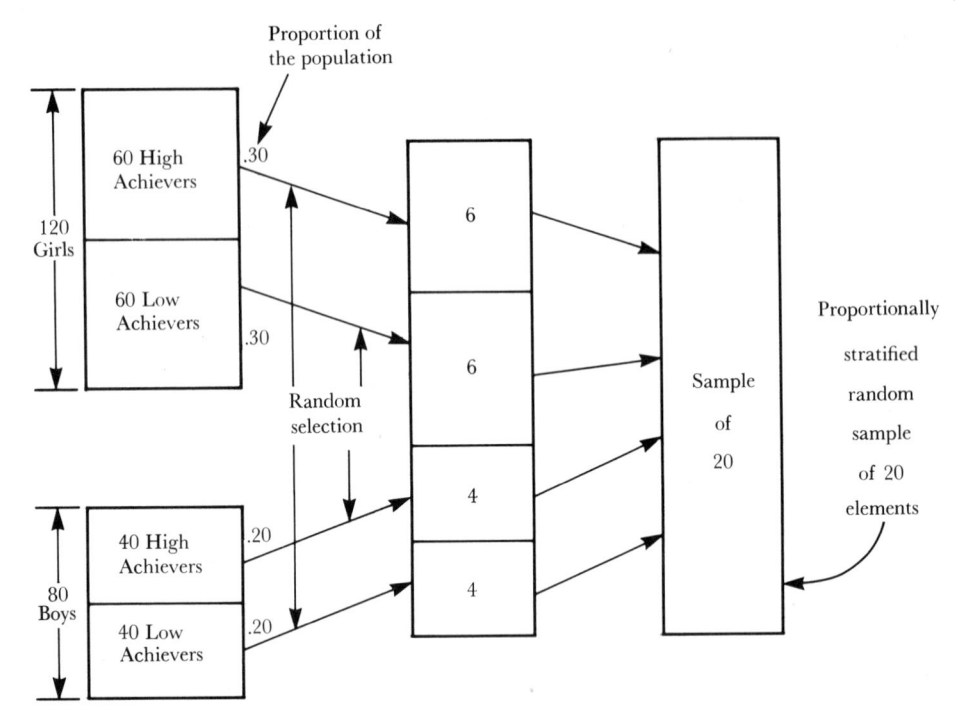

FIGURE 5.4 Proportionally Stratified Random Sample Procedures

important that the characteristics of the entire population be considered in relation to the problem under study before undertaking the sampling techniques.

Selection of a sample that is representative of the population is a difficult task. Many populations are too large to allow the researcher to make the list required for the above techniques. Where possible, procedures that generate a random sample should be used, but it is recognized that other procedures must often be used in practice. Designs that are constructed without regard to real world conditions must, in many instances, be altered when it is necessary that the study be performed under real world conditions. When planning the study the researcher must make decisions in terms of how close he can expect to find or create conditions that fit the abstracted ideal design. How can the medical researcher of a particular ailment be sure that the subjects with ailments who are admitted to one clinic for study are like others who go to other clinics across town, in another state, or country, for the same ailment? How can a basketball coach generalize from one player who is seven feet tall to all other human beings who are seven feet tall? How can a researcher of educational practices generalize from Harlan, Kentucky, to Harlem, New York? The next section deals with problems of generalization from samples that do not meet the criterion of equal probability in assignment. *Equiprobability* means that the sample is representative for statistical procedures and further generalization. When equiprobability is not possible, other steps must be undertaken.

Sampling without Randomness

This section attends to the use of generalization from samples that are not obtained randomly. Students probably think that this cannot be done, since equiprobability is

Planning the Study

needed for generalization. Where possible, random sampling is to be used; however much research would be impossible if the investigator were restricted to those studies amenable to random sampling. Much of the art of researching is being able to put together a workable plan where actual conditions do not allow all of the stated criteria to be met. One condition that is often difficult to meet is that of drawing a sample from a population *at random*. The task becomes one of putting together a plan that is acceptable by colleagues who are considered to be experts or authorities in research procedures. It is too much to hope (or expect) 100 percent agreement from everyone, since many times a single choice must be made from one of several alternatives. Others would make other choices—thus the disagreement. A plan should be thought through logically so that each choice and each part can be defended as the best choice within the framework of acceptable research practice. The best rule of thumb follows these guidelines:

1. Consider all alternatives
2. List relative strengths and weaknesses
3. Weigh carefully the alternatives
4. Make the best rational decision on these bases.

Where the choice is not ideal, it must be the compromise which provides more advantages than any one of the others. Criticism of research in all fields is based on unacceptable practices—where acceptance means what is accepted generally in the field. Unacceptable may be in the eye of the beholder, especially if all authorities do not agree as to what is acceptable practice. An attack on research procedures may mean that the person criticizing would have made a different choice than the researcher did at one or more places in the design. This attack may, in some instances, be an arbitrary decision based on personal biases, and, in others, it may be based on violation of what are widely accepted procedures of research. The plan cannot control for arbitrary attacks but can do much to control for attacks based on accepted practice.

A frequently heard attack is in regard to sample representativeness, since in most cases random procedures for the study exist at only the abstract level. Sampling procedures should approximate as closely as possible the theoretical assumption of equiprobability. If sampling procedures assure approximately equal probability, then theory based on that concept can be used in sampling for the study. Two examples of approximate equal probability have been mentioned—systematic sampling and drawing names from a container. In each of these methods of obtaining a sample the list used for the population must be exhaustive. Samples drawn from lists that do not provide a complete record of the elements of the population may reflect a bias within the sample. A list of registered automobile owners might be considered as representative of the total population, and be used to draw a sample to generalize about the total population. If the public transportation office of a large city were studying habits of people using the city bus lines, they would find that the list of licensed car owners would not be appropriate for sample selection since the ownership or nonownership of an automobile is probably not independent of use of city buses. A study based in the characteristics of car owners' use of bus lines could use the list of registered owners because the list would include all owners—it is exhaustive. Make sure that the list used for selection of a sample is, in fact, the appropriate listing of the population under study.

The above methods have little relevance if the population elements cannot be listed. A special education teacher may have four autistic pupils in an entire school district. An experimentalist may study fifty white rats in a T-maze. A study may be made of all kindergarten pupils in a school district, in regard to creativity exhibited in art objects. How can results of research on any of these three groups be considered generalizable? A posteriori investigation of sample characteristics may show that the sample does not differ greatly in important traits from the population. For the autistic children, the characteristics that class them as autistic identify them with others classed the same way, and allow them to be representative of other children with like characteristics. The sample of white rats could be compared to other rats on physical characteristics and, possibly, on some performance tests.

Other variables of sex, age, aptitudes, socioeconomic background, and the like can be given attention and reported for subjects in a study. The conclusions drawn for that study on subjects with certain traits can then be generalized to other subjects with like traits. Carefully reported research lets those reading about the research have a basis for drawing their own generalizations and, in turn, the implications for other subjects.

The kindergarten children may be studied and compared with respect to sex, age, mental measurements, socioeconomic background, and other variables that the researcher would consider important for the study of creativity, as exhibited in art objects. If the sample shows no bias on important variables, the researcher may consider the sample as representative and use it as if it were a random sample. The use is based on the assumption that the conditions closely approximate the results expected from equiprobability sampling. The acceptance of the results of the study will rest primarily on how well others agree about how closely this assumption is met.

For studies where information is lacking about the parent population, the researcher is forced to rely on past personal experiences, colleagues, and/or intuition to avoid biases in sampling. The difficulty with agreement is magnified many times in studies of this kind, and the researcher must be ready to defend his or her procedures.

A very useful technique in studies in which random sampling cannot be used lets the reader generalize from information provided in the report of the study. In addition to data used in the study, the investigator can provide demographic information about sample characteristics. For example, by giving the average IQ, a measure of the variation of IQ scores, the socioeconomic breakdown, age range, and other pertinent data, the researcher provides the reader of the research an opportunity to make generalizations to similar groups. The results of a study on subjects with particular characteristics will be generalizable to groups with like characteristics. A difference on only one variable might cause the study's conclusions to not be generalizable to another situation. Two sets of sixth grade students might be very much alike on all variables except geographic location. There is probably enough difference reflected among individuals growing up in a rural midwestern community and individuals growing up in the inner-city schools of a large metropolitan district to preclude generalizing from one to the other, even though all are much alike on variables like age, sex, and IQ.

Check Your Understanding

See how the following situations vary and how a researcher would be open to possible criticism for each. Which of the following selection procedures would give a sample that would be considered representative for research purposes? Which would be suspected of possible bias because of selection procedures?

Planning the Study

Population	Sample selection procedures	Representative (Yes-No)	Bias (Yes-No)
A. all of the 5,000 students at Zee University	Choose the first 50 students who enter the Business building after 10:00 A.M. on May first.		
B. all of the 5,000 students at Zee University	Choose the first 50 students who enter the bookstore after 10:00 A.M. on May first		
C. all of the 5,000 students at Zee University	Choose every 100th name from the registrar's alphabetical student list.		
D. all of the 5,000 students at Zee University	Use a table of random numbers to choose 50 names for the sample.		
E. all students enrolled in courses offered by the English Department	Use those students enrolled in English 479 — Literary Criticism.		
F. all sixth grade students in the United States	Use all sixth grade students in Terre Haute, Indiana, schools.		
G. all psychology textbooks published between 1930 and 1940	Use all psychology textbooks published in 1935.		

A. Probably *not* representative because the sample would most likely be heavily loaded with business-major students. The bias would be an overrepresentation of business students in the sample when compared to the proportion in the population.

B. Probably a better representation of the several schools than in (A) but there are many selection factors that determine who goes to the bookstore and who does not. The bias could come from several sources. Those living close to the bookstore are more likely to shop there than those who live farther away. Those on close budgets may not visit the bookstore as often as more affluent students. Try to think of other possible selection factors that might bias the sample.

C. This is what is called *systematic sampling* and would in most cases not be suspect of creating a biased sample. It is usually an acceptable procedure, although it does not provide equal probability in sample selection. Sample should be representative with no bias.

D. This procedure would provide a representative sample for all statistical procedures, and it should *not* be a biased sample.

E. Not representative because those enrolled in English 479 are probably more sophisticated English students than all but a small segment of those enrolled in all English classes. Bias is toward English majors being overrepresented in the sample.

F. Students from any one limited geographic area are not likely to be representative of a much larger area because of differences in important characteristics. There is much room for bias, thus the importance of listing sample characteristics for the reader.

G. Although the chosen date was the middle of the decade, the books of 1935 probably would *not* be representative of books from the ten-year period because of the amount of change over the ten years. Bias would be toward those topics of most concern in 1935.

Random Assignment

In many research plans groups are compared to identify differences between the groups after different treatments. To look for differences after treatment, it is necessary to be able to say something about differences before treatment is applied. The best way is to start both groups at the same level. The selection of two samples from the population at random defines two samples that are considered to be the same on all variables. If the two are the same when the study starts and the difference at the end is appreciable, the difference can be attributed to treatment effects.

When the population being studied does not permit random selection of subjects to allow for equal groups, *random assignment* of subjects to groups can be used to equate the groups for statistical tests. When subjects have been chosen for the study and all are to be assigned to treatment groups, random assignment will control for all variables between (for two groups) or among (more than two) groups. For the two-group study each subject can be assigned a number and, by random procedures, can be assigned to one of the two groups by alternating the assignment according to the sequence of appearance in a table of random numbers. A modification of this procedure will allow assignment to *any number of groups* under study.

A combination of random sampling *and* random assignment can be used to select and assign subjects to groups. A selection of subjects can be made randomly, and then those subjects can be assigned to groups randomly.

If a research study involves only two groups and the number of subjects to be assigned is not large, a coin flip method can be used when a table of random numbers is not available. Procedure: write the name or identifying number for each subject to be assigned on a separate piece of paper; fold all papers to the same size; place all papers in a container; and mix well. Draw two papers from the container and place them on a table so that one is to your left and the other is to your right. Set a ground rule for a coin flip. Example: if heads comes up, the one to the left goes to group A, if tails comes up, the one to the right goes into group A. Of course the remaining one will always go to group B. Continue drawing pairs and flipping the coin until all have been assigned. Equiprobability in *assignment* is assured. This assignment generates equally sized groups and equates the groups for statistical tests of significance.

Further randomness in assignment can be used when *assigning treatment* to the two groups. Devise a rule when assigning the treatment to the two groups. Example: if heads comes up when flipping the coin, group A will get treatment C, or if tails comes up when flipping the coin, group A will get treatment D. Group B will then be assigned the other treatment. To assign thirty students to two treatment groups when using the coin-flip procedure to assure randomness:

1. Write the names (or numbers) of subjects on like pieces of paper, fold and mix well in a container.
2. Draw two papers with names (or numbers) and place one to the left and one to the right.
3. Devise a rule for a coin flip.
4. Flip the coin and assign each to a group.
5. Continue drawing pairs and assign to groups until papers are exhausted.
6. Flip a coin to assign treatment to a group.

Random *sampling* procedures are utilized to control for bias externally in sample characteristics as compared to population characteristics. Random *assignment* controls

Planning the Study

for bias internally in that each subject has equal probability of appearing in either of the two groups.

Check Your Understanding

Which of the following selection procedures would give samples that would be considered equal for research purposes? Which would be suspected of possible bias because of selection procedures?

Subjects to be assigned	Assignment procedures	Equal Groups (Yes-No)	Bias (Yes-No)
A. 30 white rats to two groups	The first 15 caught go to group A, and the last 15 caught go to group B. A coin is flipped to assign treatment to the two groups.		
B. 40 students to two groups	Each student is assigned a number, and a table of random numbers is used to divide the 40 by alternating assignment to the two groups. Group A is then assigned the experimental treatment.		
C. students in two introductory speech classes to two groups	The treatment was assigned randomly by flipping a coin, and the 8-o'clock class became the control group and the 11-o'clock group became the class to receive the experimental treatment.		
D. 40 students to two groups	Each student is assigned a number and a table of random numbers is used to divide the 40 by alternating assignment to the two groups. A coin flip is used to assign the experimental treatment to group A.		

A. The first fifteen were the easiest to catch and may be more passive — less active and/or less aggressive. Bias would be in regard to the variables that might contribute to them being caught first. The assignment of treatment to groups would introduce no *new* bias.

B. Equality acceptable for statistical procedures. Arbitrary assignment of treatment could violate equal probability but probably not a serious error. Flip a coin to assign treatment for the two groups.

C. The assignment of treatment by a coin flip is OK. The bias would result in selection to the two class periods. Time, instructor, meeting place, and type of class organization could be contributing bias.

D. Randomness has been used in both assignment to groups and assignment of treatment, therefore representing equal groups and *no* bias in the sample.

Other Sources of Bias

A source of bias for some quantitative studies is found when volunteers are used to respond to a survey for a descriptive study or to receive treatment in an experimental study. The fact that some persons volunteered and were used for data gathering and others did not volunteer introduces bias into any study based on volunteers. In most cases the bias is based in the fact that the subjects are self-selected. The subjects may be more outgoing, more gregarious, or more highly motivated than those who did not volunteer, thus providing a nonrepresentative sample.

When the study utilizes a questionnaire to gather the information, the elements of the population chosen to receive the questionnaire may be a representative sample, but the responding individuals—the ones actually supplying the data—may be a poor representation of the population. A question based in a controversial issue may trigger responses from those either strongly for or strongly against. For example, one individual strongly against a proposal for future action may, through influence and/or effort, see that others also against it return the questionnaire and thus weight the sample data — so that the sample has a disproportionately large number of "against" votes when compared to the number in the total population who are "against." The same may happen if the eager one is "for" the issue. Ways of coping with these problems are presented in later chapters.

Sampling Qualitative Data

The plan for a study that uses qualitative data for analysis may also include sampling procedures for collecting the information. The problem of sampling may be based in a situation where the amount of material to be examined is overwhelming. If the material is printed in journals or documents, decisions about which ones to use must be made in light of how to get a representative sample without laboring through every scrap of evidence. With modern retrieval methods using data storage and computer disk files, this is not the major problem today that it was in the past. Nevertheless specific procedures must be decided in the plan and sampling techniques included, if needed.

The analysis of the problem should include consideration of the dimensions to be used and, in turn, assist in sampling. The sample could be taken in terms of time intervals, events, writings, issues, persons, or such. The plan should indicate clearly the way that the material will be sampled and the data required to answer the question.

In view of the preceding discussion of selecting subjects to be sources of information for the study, procedures for selecting a sample which permits generalization becomes essential. All parts of the plan must contribute to assure that the sample is representative of a clearly defined population, and that the reader is aware of procedures used for selection. Difficult problems associated with sampling arise when the elements of the population to be sampled cannot be listed. Acceptable procedures for experimental studies are expanded in chapter 10, and methods of validating data from surveys are taken up in chapter 9.

FRAMEWORK FOR A STUDY

The choice of the basic framework for a study will be made in light of the question asked. When an event or events has already occurred, the framework for the plan will use historical research techniques for structure. The important steps include location of remains and records, their criticism both internally and externally, and the interpretation of information found to bear on the case in point.

Whenever the researcher sets out to study a situation as it now exists, the framework of the study will be descriptive. Descriptive research, in addition to merely describing, *interprets* present conditions. Included with study of conditions is study of relationships, present practices, attitudes, and trends that seem to be developing.

Planning the Study

Conclusions for descriptive studies are based on results of data analysis which interpret by comparison, contrast, and cause-effect relationship.

When the researcher studies cause-and-effect relationships by manipulating one or more variables and studying the effects on one or more variables, the study will be framed in a structure of experimental research. The role of science to explain, control, and predict requires conditions that (1) permit manipulation of the independent (experimental) variable and (2) allow employment of techniques that eliminate or equalize effects of associated variables.

Contemporary scientific thought judges *the experiment* as the *best* strategy approach to research, and its use is to be encouraged in educational studies even though laboratory-like conditions are difficult to obtain in most educational settings. All questions are worthy of study. The decision to use one strategy rather than others will be made by taking into consideration the nature of the question and the availability of usable data from appropriate subjects.

DATA COLLECTION

All research studies, whether qualitative or quantitative, need information about variables that are being studied. The information may come from documents, objects, animals, or human beings. The information in first form requires organization before it becomes meaningful enough that its hidden messages about questions under study can be interpreted. The organization might be as simple as listing a set of scores in order of magnitude. The largest value is listed first and other values arranged so that each succeeding value is larger than all of those falling below.

One major function of data processing is to organize qualified data so that interpretations may be made. The organization of qualitative data may be as complex as providing a structure to interpret large amounts of factual data that cannot be reduced to numbers. Data collection procedures must be chosen and implemented to supply data which are easily organized. The manner of collection can facilitate the organization of the data if the plan projects the appropriate way to organize the data. For example, a survey questionnaire can many times be arranged so that computer cards can be keypunched directly from the returned forms. Without preplanning, an intervening step may be required to put the data into interpretable form. The use of bibliography cards to record data from a historical study allows arrangement of material through an ordering of the cards. This many times saves at least one organizational writing of the material. Other equally time-saving procedures can be incorporated if the researcher coordinates data collection procedures with an appropriate organizational scheme.

Traditionally the complexities of collecting information obtained from relics, documents, and bibliographical materials has been so time consuming that many important investigations were either scaled down in scope or not attempted. Many of the questions left untouched by researchers in the past are now open to investigation through the use of computers that utilize disk files for storing nonnumeric information. Techniques have been developed that turn the previously limited coverage given bibliography and government data into comprehensive coverage, and much of what in the past was left to accidental uncoverage can now become routine.

Researchers have always been cautious about researching questions that overextend the capabilities of handling the data. Present researchers must be aware of limitations attached to treating data but, at the same time, must be aware that many questions unanswerable in the past are researchable today.

Computers have reduced hand calculation that requires hours, to machine calculation that requires a few seconds. Even more valuable to inquiry is the fact that now previously unanswerable questions dealing with such subjects as astronomy and education come under investigation because calculation with large quantities of nonnumeric data can be handled routinely. Do not limit a study unnecessarily by assuming that a question remains unanswerable for all time. What was unanswerable yesterday may be treated routinely today.

Descriptive research uses observational techniques such as surveys — both interview and questionnaire — to gather data, and the nature of the data will require different techniques to organize. The data gathering techniques for descriptive studies should be developed to provide quantified data that are amenable to appropriate treatment. In general, experimental studies generate data in quantified form, and the organization is easily made for data treatment. If unusual procedures require special collection tools such as a checklist or scorecard, the collection instrument should be arranged for easy organization of the data.

The best rule of thumb for directing the choice of data gathering techniques it to fit together a plan that utilizes the most appropriate kind of data and that supplies them in sufficient quantity to provide results for making valid conclusions. The following points should be considered when planning procedures to collect data.

1. *What data and how much?* The necessary data must be gathered and steps must be taken to avoid gathering unnecessary information. To gather unneeded data can be expensive in money and time. Time of both researcher and subjects is wasted if gathered information is not used. In experimental studies, a careful look must be taken to see that required data do not violate any ethical rights of the subjects. The data required must in no way demand procedures that would affect the subjects negatively.
2. *Where can the data be obtained?* In many educational studies the data are gathered from subjects in the school setting. In most cases permission must be obtained from proper administrative persons. They need to know specifically what data are wanted, how they will be used, and how results will be disseminated. For historical studies, documents and school records need to be examined. Written permission should be obtained early to avoid developing a research plan and discovering that, for some reason, the information is not available.
3. *How to collect and record the data.* For most experimental studies this is not a major difficulty, but for descriptive and historical studies this may be the major decision of the design. Many sources may be opened only through the willingness of individuals to open document files or to reveal information—personal or public—that they possess. For historical study, the availability of primary sources is crucial, since reliance on secondary sources reduces the validity of the study. The data should be recorded in such a way as to be interpretable in that form.
4. *When to collect the data.* The researcher should make special efforts to avoid any time period that would be considered atypical in regard to general conditions. If test scores are being gathered, the time of day, day of week, or place on the school calendar all may cause conditions to vary. Such atypical times as the day before or after a vacation, first or last period of the day, Monday, or Friday should be avoided

Planning the Study 71

for data gathering. Surveys and other requests for information should be timed to avoid any conditions that would bias the information gathered.

For each study the appropriate methods of gathering data developed will contribute to the unique design for that study. Particular data gathering instruments will be identified or created to provide the exact data needed to provide an answer to the question. The tools for gathering the data are discussed in the three chapters devoted to historical, descriptive, and experimental research. Attention is now given to expedition of the process of analysis by careful organization of data.

ORGANIZATION OF DATA

The gathered data must be assembled in some way other than by haphazardly recording bits and pieces to be fitted together at some later time. A very important aspect of the plan must give attention to how the facts will be organized for interpretation. The organization should be directed by:

1. type of information needed for the study and
2. how the data will be analyzed.

Careful coordination between data-gathering procedures and data treatment will be based in the organization procedures. Efficiency can be built into the methodology by recording the original raw data into an easily interpretable form, and the design can do much to expedite analysis. Certainly qualitative studies using words will need a much different arrangement than a quantitative study, where the facts are sets of numbers. Quantitative data should be organized for treatment and presented to readers through the use of tables and graphs. For hand calculation or desk calculators, the frequency-distribution table and contingency tables provide tools for organization. If a computer is to be used, the data will be organized through a deck of properly punched computer cards or in a form that can be easily transferred to cards. The results should be reported in appropriate tables.

There are no rigid guidelines for organizing qualitative data. The final organization is done as the narrative of the report is composed. While gathering nonnumerical data it would be well to keep in mind the following suggestions to help organize the prose into a well presented and logical sequence for valid interpretation:

1. Use bibliography cards to record the information extracted from sources.
2. Record comparative study information fact-to-fact, and leave interpretation until later.
3. Keep factual the documentary evidence and the information gained from relics to avoid interpretation at recording time.
4. Keep a time line to place the gathered information chronologically.
5. Be objective in deciding the emphasis to be given to gathered information.

When planning for the study be sure to structure your data organization with an eye to the type of data gathered and the interpretation procedures to be employed. Specific techniques for organizing data are discussed within the chapters devoted to the three types of research activities.

TREATMENT OF DATA

To provide interpretable results, the data gathered must be organized and examined carefully. The planning of the research must include definite direction for treatment of the data, since much of the success of data analysis rests on the ability of the data gathering procedures to provide interpretable data and on the choice of appropriate methods for the analysis. The treatment of the data is intended to provide a solid basis and support for the conclusions drawn about the study. Any valid decision about the research hypothesis rests on the researcher's ability to show that the treatment of the data for the study is appropriate and that the results are adequate for forming valid conclusions.

The treatment of data for a historical study can best be viewed as the evolution of an outline that the researcher develops, as his theme takes shape in his mind. The plan for a historical study should include a tentative outline based on the types and sources of data being used and how the data will be validated through formal criticism. Development of a working outline encourages thoughtful review of gathered data and should provide a logical sequencing to an objectively obtained decision about the proposed question. By the time the material is collected, the arrangement of the data should be in close conformity with the way that the final report will be made.

The validity of the decision will be enhanced by (1) a mastery of the information, (2) clearly perceived relationships, and (3) conclusions based on objectivity rather than researcher bias. The original outline from the plan and the evolved outline from data treatment should build as much objectivity as possible in what is, at best, more subjective than most would like research studies in education to be.

Educational research based in the historical view is intended to obtain facts (information) with historical authenticity and to derive valid conclusions (interpretation). The relationship between the two is well expressed as follows:

> Information, as such, is not Interpretation. Interpretation is revelation based on information. But they are entirely different things. However, all interpretation includes information.[8]

For historical research studies the treatment of the data is the interpretation given to obtained data.

For descriptive studies requiring documentary analysis, much the same treatment procedures will be used as for the typical historical research study:
1. a tentative outline;
2. a working outline developed as the information is being gathered; and
3. a written narrative for basing conclusions.

A descriptive study based in a question that asks about present conditions utilizes data of a different nature. Information from surveys, interviews, checklists, rating scales, and other data-gathering devices utilized in gathering data about present conditions can, in most cases, be expressed as descriptive statistics to assist in analyzing the data. Correlational techniques can be utilized to investigate for relationships between variables, and Likert scaling provides ways for treating data that the researcher can assume have been generated by a scale that has approximately equal intervals.

For many studies in the behavioral sciences, the data gathered may not meet all of the assumptions required for parametric tests of significance. The data from many

---

8. Freeman Tilden, *Interpreting Our Heritage* (Chapel Hill: University of North Carolina Press, 1957), p. 18.

descriptive studies are frequencies, ranks, or values, obtained where the assumption of normality of distribution of scores cannot be assumed or tested. Today nonparametric techniques of hypothesis testing are suited to data of this nature and should be used when the more powerful parametric tests are not appropriate. The two names used with these tests allude to the reasons for their suitability. They are often called *distribution free* since they assume nothing about the distribution of the population or, alternatively, many nonparametric tests are called *ranking tests,* suggesting their other advantage: they may be used with scores which are not exact in a numerical sense but may be ordered in ranks.[9]

The investigator should become aware of the techniques available for interpretation of data with the above characteristics. Computational simplicity is an advantage as is their usefulness with small samples. Siegel's coverage of nonparametric tests is a classic, as it was the first book to attempt to gather many nonparametric techniques under one cover, and is still widely used by researchers. The student of research is well advised to spend some time in becoming familiar with ways to treat these kinds of data by reviewing *Non-Parametric Statistics for the Behavioral Sciences.*

In addition to the descriptive analysis and data analysis, the element of interpretation of meaning must be covered by the researcher. Conclusions are interpretations that consist of generalizations, formed through reasoning, and judgments by the researcher. Careful coordination of treatment procedures provides the needed bridge between the gathering of data and the conclusions.

Descriptive studies falling between the documentary analysis, utilizing strictly qualitative data, and studies of present conditions, utilizing quantitative data, use both sorts of data. Types of descriptive studies using both are case studies, community studies, antecedent-consequence studies, trend studies, and studies that compare the present with the past—*comparative studies.*

As used in research, the term *experimentation* refers to inquiry activities in which laboratory, or near-laboratory, conditions allow a variable, or variables, to be manipulated with strict control over the other remaining variables. The research investigates the effects on certain clearly identified dependent variables. Since the researcher has strict control of the situation, most of the treatment for data from experimental studies uses statistical techniques providing precise answers to aid in interpretation and for basing conclusions. The data are quantitative and, if properly gathered, will provide what most researchers feel is the best basis for making decisions. The plan for an experimental study must identify the appropriate statistical procedures to analyze the data. Interpretation in the form of conclusions is needed for experimental studies, and it takes much the same form of generalization as the conclusions for historical and descriptive studies.

For the descriptive study and the historical study the interpretation of the data is, in general, left largely to the researcher, but in the analysis of quantified data statistical models are available that allow the researcher to remove himself or herself from making decisions at certain places in the process, thus providing more objectivity to the results. Do not interpret this to mean that experimentation in education is 100 percent objective—it still remains much an art. Light gives us a step into this idea when he says:

---

9. Sidney Siegel, *Non-Parametric Statistics for the Behavioral Sciences* (New York: McGraw-Hill, 1956), p. vii.

My colleagues and statistics students sometimes seem a bit startled when I share with them my belief that data analysis is an art as much as it is a science. It must seem to them a bit incongruous that the same fellow who on one day interprets significance levels and suggests specific statistical techniques such as two-stage least squares should on another day question how "scientific" such a process is.[10]

Light speaks on the importance of data treatment and sums up his argument with, "A good analyst, who has insightful judgment both in selecting a model and scaling responses for different variables, can draw useful inferences from his research. A poor analyst, of course, cannot."[11] The reader of the research should go beyond the reported results and make a judgment of the particular design. The researcher should go beyond using a model simply because someone else used it in a somewhat similar situation or because it is simple. Contrary to what many believe, even quite sophisticated statistical designs do not in themselves provide ready-made conclusions to research studies.

The two specific areas of gathering and treating data are so closely related that it is difficult to separate them except for formal discussion such as the preceding. The subjects to be studied make up an integral part of the decisions made in the basic plan for the study. In practice, the researcher must consider each facet in regard to how it relates to and affects the others. A person observing someone functioning as a researcher would find it difficult to sort out activities of plan development precisely enough, so that it would be clear where each activity would fall, because all of them are being fitted together at the same time.

SUMMARY

After a problem has been isolated and delimited and hypotheses developed from extended reading and experiential background, a specific plan of attack is necessary to answer the research question. Referred to as a *design,* the plan structures, through specific procedures, ways of gathering specific data from specific sources of information, and ways of interpreting the obtained data.

Sources of data come from attributes of objects, animals, and human beings. The source of the data will, in most cases, determine the type of data gathered and, in turn, limit and/or direct interpretive procedures. It becomes important that the interpretation be as objective as the situation will permit, but lack of objectivity should not limit what is researched. Inquiry procedures can be developed to answer educational questions of all kinds. Very difficult situations demand that the researcher function as an artist as well as a scientist keeping in mind that it is:

> Far better an appropriate answer to the right question, which is often vague, than an exact answer to the wrong question, which can always be made precise.[12]

The research plan, including methodology, is concerned with the following points:
1. Procedures associated with identification of sources of information and/or selection of specific elements to supply data.

---

10. Richard J. Light, "Issues in the Analysis of Qualitative Data," in Robert M. W. Travers, ed., *Second Handbook of Research on Teaching* (Chicago: Rand McNally, 1973), p. 318.
11. Ibid., p. 319.
12. J. W. Tukey, "The Future of Data Analysis," *The Annals of Mathematical Statistics* 33 (1963): 13-14. (Quoted in Light, "Issues in the Analysis of Qualitative Data," p. 318.)

Planning the Study

2. Techniques to be used to collect and process the data.
3. Organization of the results in interpretable form.
4. Summarization of the results to provide a basis for drawing conclusions.

In this chapter coverage has been given to the above topics as they relate to research generally, and a brief overview was given for each area of historical, descriptive, and experimental research. The topics related to sampling have been developed at greater length than others because of their close relationship to both descriptive and experimental research. The other topics are treated at greater length, where more appropriate, in the chapters that follow.

For guidelines to writing an overview of the complete study, see chapter 13, "The Research Proposal." This structure for proposed studies for funding agencies or committees for candidates seeking advanced degrees serves as an excellent model for other research studies. The next chapter takes up the important topics of observation, and chapter 7 covers measurement. These are two closely related topics that contribute much to the ability of finding valid answers to educational questions.

6

Observation

> *Without a constant and alert exercise of the senses, not even plays and games can go on; in any form of work, materials, obstacles, appliances, failures, and successes must be intently watched.*
> —John Dewey

"Keep your eye on the ball." Why is this an often repeated phrase directed to the beginning tennis player? Is it so that the player will hit the ball in the precise center of the racket face? Probably not, since the well constructed racket will return well within a large area of the strings. Why does the batting coach for a baseball team admonish his players in the same way? Certainly it is important that the bat come in contact with the ball within limits; however, even with some error associated with the way the ball hits the bat, the swing can result in a hit.

The phrase, "Keep your eye on the ball," can usually be interpreted as, "Focus carefully on what you are doing," or "Concentrate." The coaches are saying — if you are to succeed in the task at hand you must give undivided attention to what you are doing. Much of athletics takes place above the shoulders, and if the player is to be successful he or she must not let a series of thought processes get in the way of the one important swing of the racket or bat. Many coaches will tell a player to let the subconscious take over the task and to not focus on trying to remember all of the small tasks involved, but to keep a "mind set" on the overall task at hand.

The art of researching is much different from playing tennis or baseball, but the meaning behind "Keep your eye on the ball" is just as important to the task of research as it is on the tennis court or ball field. The researcher must learn to develop conditions within himself that allow him to focus on the task from that moment when, through observation, he meets his problem, to the drawing of conclusions, which also involves observation. *He/she must develop skills to aid him/her in observation throughout the research study.*

Everyone has skill in observation — skill used to interpret, through the senses, the environment. The researcher must push beyond the simple task of direct observation into more complex observation, requiring more than mere sense reaction. The following section, based on four psychological factors associated with techniques of observation, is directed to helping the researcher develop awareness of the importance of observation.

PSYCHOLOGICAL FACTORS OF OBSERVATION

Much of the activity associated with answering questions takes place in the real world. Although a large amount of the educational researcher's time is spent in the "ivory tower" abstracting, planning, and theorizing, he or she must at some time move into the real world to test his theories with objectively obtained information. Much of the success of research rests in the researcher's ability to collect data which are relevant to the study. A scientist uses the term *observation* somewhat differently from the way it is usually used. Any data about subjects that are used as bases for drawing conclusions are called observations, but procedures of observation do not necessarily incorporate techniques of observation by human beings. A reading on the Brain Wave Analyser, developed by Dr. J. P. Ertl, is an observation, although the only direct observation by the investigator is in recording readings from the dial. Data gathered from a machine that records on a magnetic tape are observations. Tests provide data that are observations. Direct observation by human beings also generates observations. Valid conclusions depend on objective data, so it becomes important for the human observer to develop skills within himself/herself to obtain reliable facts, much as a machine provides its objective data.

Observation and its interpretation include four psychological factors that must be considered: *attention; sensation; perception;* and *conception.*[1]

Attention

Attention is a condition of readiness requiring a selective narrowness of receptivity. Successful observation demands that the many stimuli constantly assailing the senses be carefully screened, since the mind is not capable of attending to all of them. The skill that the tennis coach was developing for the student when he said, "Keep your eye on the ball," was the selection process that here is called attention. The mind set requires that the researcher be attentive to selecting from all received stimuli only the specific ones that are relative to the task at hand.

Learning to concentrate becomes an important part of observation. The research observer must put himself in the position of focusing on that portion of stimuli which pertains to the problem and to tune out or ignore the portions that do not relate to the problem. However the concentration of attention on a specific area of concern must not cause the researcher to miss pertinent data. He/she must avoid any selection within that area. He must be sure that the selection does not force him to ignore facts that are relevant to the study. The researcher's attention should be so objective that he or she does not knowingly or unknowingly bias the information. He must attend to data that do not support, as well as data that do support, and must also notice all pertinent data, without being distracted from his structured selective attention.

---

1. Diobald B. Van Dalen, *Understanding Educational Research,* 3rd ed. (New York: McGraw-Hill, 1973), p. 37.

Observation

Sensation

Awareness of the world comes through the senses. Sense organs can distinguish sounds, smells, physical feelings, sights, and tastes. The researcher uses his/her senses to provide an awareness of that part of the world's phenomena which pertains to his question and search for the answer. *Sensation* is the stimulation of the sense organs to allow the person to experience an event. Many times a person must assist the senses by using instruments like eye glasses and hearing aids. Even with these helps, many sounds and sights are not picked up because they are outside the limits of human capabilities, and these limitations place a restriction on stimuli that can be used in interpretation. Other instruments are needed to help pick up stimuli and extend the range of observation. Microscopes and telescopes, scales, thermometers, and tests are examples of tools used to extend human senses to extend awareness of stimuli not otherwise apparent.

A researcher must give thought to the quality of the signals, and take steps to utilize techniques that provide clear and undistorted impressions on the senses. Any instruments used must be of the highest sophistication available or, as in the case of data-gathering testing instruments, they may have to be produced for the study.

A special problem arises when human behavior is being studied directly—the observation procedure itself may introduce a new factor not present in a more normal situation. When observing human subjects, the observer must take steps to remain as inconspicuous as possible—visibility of the observer and/or his tools must not change conditions of the subjects or affect the situation appreciably.

Perception

Observation is more than paying attention to a circumstance and picking up the stimuli—what has been picked up must be interpreted. Anything that is viewed must be linked to the past through experience. Sensations are perceived in light of past experiences. A sound is merely a noise until the one who receives the sound identifies and categorizes the sensations by comparing it to like sounds of the past. The interpretation is the *perception*. Since meanings are the products of individual minds, various interpretations come from different persons although the sensations or physical stimuli that they receive are all the same. A sound that comes from a distance on a clear summer evening may sound like a train to one person, a truck to another, and a plane to another, although they all receive the same waves of sound.

A person's perception of received stimuli is reflected also in the interpretation of what are called optical illusions. An optical illusion is a figure that appears to change, although the configuration of the figure does not change. Of course the change in the figure is the interpretation or perception given the figure by the viewer. A classic example is the "face or vase" illusion, where a figure changes appearances from face to vase and back to face. The researcher does not have this same problem with his stimuli but it does point up the importance of the interpretation made through his perception. What something *appears* to be, compared to what it *really* is, may be quite different, but to the beholder it is what he or she sees in it.

Optical illusions can be psychological rather than visual. Rooms have been built in which all the objects appear to be the wrong size. However an awareness of this may depend on a background of experiences and on knowing that an adult is larger than a child, regardless of how near or far away the child is standing.

Another difficulty in perception is that the sensations received may not be interpretable in the received form. The light rays, which an eye receives, of a pencil partially submerged in water show the pencil to be bent. The eyes are picking up the correct stimuli because the refraction bends light rays. The question of whether the pencil is bent or straight requires viewers to perceive this in terms of what they know about pencils. An early research study involved the study of refraction of light and how the study affected subjects' ability to shoot at targets under water. The question was based in applying a learning to a real-world situation.

Messages that researchers receive from their data and/or information are as difficult to work with, or more so, as the previously mentioned physical sensations received by the five senses. Development of procedures to provide valid interpretation for research studies, in the form of conclusions, requires integration of the sensations into interpretable form. Perception of data about human behavior and/or information of all types requires a high level of observational skill.

Conception

When past experience does not give the necessary information to interpret received signals, the mind must turn to something else. When the person creates an answer through some intellectual process beyond past experience, he or she is working at the level of *conception*. When he hears a noise on a summer evening that he has never heard before, he may interpret it as, "I have never heard a noise like that, but it sounds more like a truck than anything else I can think of." He has bypassed the limitation of experiences and has developed an imaginary concept to explain the unknown, and the conceptualization permitted visualization of what could not be perceived directly from experience. Conception moves beyond perception by building imaginative concepts.

Hypothesis development is, in general, at the level of conception. Most problems and resulting questions in education occur because of a lack of knowledge about a situation. By building a conceptual scheme, the researcher moves beyond mere experience to solve problems by testing the scheme in a real-world setting.

OBSERVATION AND HYPOTHESES

The art of conceptualization is a special area of observation that requires the researcher to depend heavily (almost exclusively) on his or her own ability to integrate informal observations about relationships to formulate hypotheses that make statements about cause and effect. If a hypothesis is too broad to be tested as formulated, observation can deduce testable hypotheses from within it. Since this is the level of abstraction from outside past experience, hypotheses may be difficult to develop.

Difficulty in formulating hypotheses about human behavior is magnified many times by the fact that any behavior is the result of many contributing variables. Early study by research and many present research studies are univariate—*if-then* statements that involve only one variable for the *if*, or antecedent, and one variable for the *then*, or consequent, part of the sentence. Most problems and hypotheses are actually multivariate.

In most cases, separating the variables for study is somewhat artificial and must be accounted for in the conceptualization of the hypotheses, the interpretation of conclusions drawn from studies, and in theories developed. More advanced studies involve multivariate hypotheses that allow a higher level of conceptualization for research

Observation

hypotheses and, in turn, more sophistication of both formal and informal observational techniques.

OBJECTIVITY IN OBSERVATION

Humans' attempts to interpret their sensations are frequently made more difficult by a number of intervening human characteristics. Most of the obstructions to observation are associated with one, or combinations, of the following:

1. *Personal interest.* A strong personal commitment may cause the observer to see what he or she wants to see.
2. *Early decision.* A quick association may not provide time for all the needed information to be collected.
3. *Anticipation.* A mental set of what is expected may result in a faulty inference.
4. *Personal knowledge.* If a person knows little about an area he/she may draw on what he does know from another area to erroneously explain sensations.
5. *Emotions, prejudices, values, physical condition, and other personal constructs.* Faulty inference can come from these unknowingly and may be difficult to identify.

Most of the above difficulties arise from the fact that observers are human beings. Mark Twain has been credited with saying that the worst thing that can be said about someone is that he has human characteristics. Since researchers are human beings they must take steps to overcome these built-in difficulties.

The most effective approach is to build as much objectivity into research procedures associated with observation as is possible. The following research procedures can help to reduce errors in perception and conception. A researcher:

1. Develops a wide background of knowledge in the area where the problem is based. Anyone works better in a situation where he or she has much knowledge, so the researcher builds his knowledge to a high level.
2. Studies other views that are different from his own. Some investigators even try to support a view opposite of their own through the gathering of information.
3. Writes in words that have common meaning or makes clear how he/she is using words by giving his definition.
4. Writes about specific acts rather than about judgments or interpretation of the acts.
5. Examines data with a questioning mind. Rather than accepting any data at face value, he/she develops techniques, invents or constructs new instruments, and uses available tools to provide the most clear signals to interpret the data.
6. Develops a system of recording data. Since any delay in recording data may contribute to inaccuracies, a system of precise data recording is developed to provide a means of quick and accurate recording of the facts to produce a permanent record.
7. Uses quantification of data whenever possible. Numbers provide more exactness in reporting and help to avoid ambiguity associated with vague statements about size, numbers, and so forth.

All aspects of the researcher's observation can be improved by building objectivity into procedures of research. Especially important for research is the direct observation used in gathering information of a qualitative nature. A structure or frame of reference for the observer must be developed by the researcher for every study that requires this kind of data. It is not enough to view a situation and report what was seen in a narrative report. Methods for educational observation depend on actions of individual observers in the presence of sensations. Some reasonable technique for translating the received stimuli into interpretable observations or data is necessary for transmitting the behaviors into interpretable results. The next section is intended to provide ways to structure observation, using the seven points listed above as bases for objectifying human observation.

TECHNIQUES OF DIRECT OBSERVATION

All research procedures include direct observation at some time in the process. The involvement may only be to gather background material or may be an inspection of results of a study. At other times the major data-gathering techniques will be procedures of direct observation of those subjects under study. Direct observation is especially valuable when studying very young children, laboratory animals, or processes, but it is not limited to these uses. Direct observation should be a larger part of research activities, but it is many times forgotten when planning such activities. This section discusses checklists, rating scales, scorecards, and ranking as tools to aid direct-observation techniques for collecting data.

The most important part of developing techniques of direct observation is the preparation provided in training the observer. Training for the particular task involved in each study should be developed so that observations by different observers are consistent. Such preparation should include actual hands-on observation by the observers so that they can become accustomed to the mechanics and be able to compare the results to see how well between-observer differences have been eliminated. General suggestions for preparing observers for a particular study are:

1. Observers should be included in the planning of the structure to gather data.
2. Observers should know the purpose of the study, but if a comparison of subjects or groups of subjects is involved they should not know which subjects are in each of the different groups.
3. Observers should have the opportunity to test the techniques in practice before making observations for the study.
4. Cultural differences between the observer and the observed should be investigated for possible effect on the validity of the data being collected.
5. Effects of the observer on the observed situation should be investigated. The natural conditions should not be appreciably altered.

When planning the structure for observation, particular techniques or combinations of techniques will develop a unique design for the study. The material in the following sections covers some traditional ways of observing for educational research that have withstood the test of time. A researcher may need to use one or some of these or he/she may need to develop something unique to provide valid data. As a well known comedian once said, "What you see is what you get." Carefully thought-through procedures will let the researcher see and get what he needs to answer the question under study.

Checklists

The observer of behavior needs a well devised instrument to record observations. Some tally sheet in the form of a checklist (see table 6.1) facilitates recording by avoiding the need for writing a narrative. A checklist has two major contributions to observa-

Observation

TABLE 6.1 Checklist for the Return of Service in Tennis

DIRECTIONS: Below are definable aspects that are important to successful return of serve. Check each one for each service return for one set. Determine the percentage of attainment for the set.		Percentage
Number of returns	~~1~~ ~~2~~ ~~3~~ ~~4~~ ~~5~~ ~~6~~ 7 8 9 ~~10~~ ~~11~~ ~~12~~ ~~13~~ ~~14~~ ~~15~~ ~~16~~ ~~17~~ ~~18~~ ~~19~~ ~~20~~ 21 22 23 24 25 26 27 28 29 30 31 32 33 34 35 36 37 38 39 40 41 42	
Back straight	ＩＩＩＩ ＩＩＩＩ ＩＩＩＩ ＩＩＩＩ	100
Knees bent	ＩＩＩＩ ＩＩＩＩ //	60
Watch ball come off server's racket	ＩＩＩＩ ＩＩＩＩ ＩＩＩＩ	75
Correct backswing	ＩＩＩＩ ＩＩＩＩ ////	70
Lean into stroke	////	20
Get the ball while it's rising	/	5
Contact the ball before it gets to you	ＩＩＩＩ ///	40
Stroke fluidly through the stroke	ＩＩＩＩ /	30
Racket head above the wrist	ＩＩＩＩ ＩＩＩＩ ＩＩＩＩ /	80
Recover position for next return	////	20

tion: (1) it is an efficient (time-wise) method of recording, and (2) the data are objective. Time is of the essence when observing ongoing events that do not allow special time-out periods for data recording. Checklists provide a way for the recorder to "keep up" with happenings. In addition the checklist avoids requiring the observer to make considerable judgment while performing the observation. The list assures that the observer gives attention to those important facts while avoiding unimportant aspects.

Checklists which are customarily used in judging musical performance and gymnastic competition furnish those judges with a record for evaluation. Thus they avoid an evaluation after the fact with no way to reflect other than through memory. Many products are evaluated through a structure provided by a checklist. Researchers use them for the facility that they provide and also for their ability to provide well organized objective data for interpretation.

Rating Scales

Many variables of importance to the teaching-learning process can be quantified to some degree or intensity, but do not lend themselves to closer degrees of measurement. If some sort of order can be established to quantify amounts of a variable, a rating scale can be constructed to differentiate varying degrees of the variable. A rating scale could be devised to record the degree of cloudiness of the sky. To the author's knowledge there is no precise measuring instrument to do this, but the problem could be approached through a rating scale that would provide categories that vary from a completely clear sky to a completely cloudy sky. A "cloudy sky scale" might look like this:

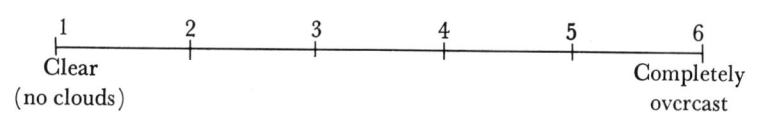

```
   1         2         3         4         5         6
   |---------|---------|---------|---------|---------|
 Clear                                          Completely
(no clouds)                                      overcast
```

The scale units for the cloudy sky scale have been rather arbitrarily set at six. There is no established rule about the number of units to use in a rating scale but observance of the variable may give direction to the appropriate number of categories. Too few points on the scale result in only a crude measure with little meaning, and too many points make discrimination by the observer too difficult. Three points on the scale to measure cloudiness might look like this:

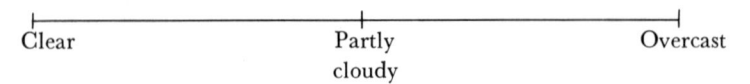

|―――――――――――――+―――――――――――――|
Clear   Partly   Overcast
                     cloudy

The points here have been named rather than numbered. This technique is used in rating scales where statements describe varying degrees of that being observed. Three points on the above scale are probably of little use in recording sky conditions for scientific study, although it is quite useful in prediction of weather conditions.

A scale with many points may or may not be of help to the observer. It is questionable whether the fine divisions in the following scale would provide more usable data about sky conditions than the six-unit scale.

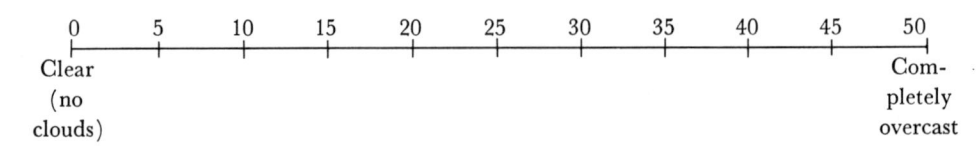

0   5   10   15   20   25   30   35   40   45   50
|―――+―――+―――+―――+―――+―――+―――+―――+―――+―――|
Clear   Com-
(no   pletely
clouds)   overcast

For observation of human behavior a statement that describes specifically a point in relation to other points will, in general, increase the reliability of observations. Studies of the numerical power of words used to describe observations indicate the importance of choosing the correct descriptors. Relationships of adjectives—such as *disgusting, inferior, ordinary, pleasant,* and *admirable*—have been studied as to favorableness and the effect on the favorableness when the words are modified by a particular adverb—such as *decidedly*.[2]

Descriptions for points on a scale should be used to help objectify scaling techniques. An example of a rating scale for judging a particular behavior might look like this:

―+―――――+―――――+―――――+―――――+―――――+―
Admirable Charming Good   Bad   Disgusting Contemptible

If the researcher has reason to believe that the distance between all adjacent pairs of points is equal or nearly so, then for statistical treatment he/she could assign numbers for the points. The numbers may or may not appear on the original scale.

    1   2   3   4   5   6
―+―――――+―――――+―――――+―――――+―――――+―
Admirable Charming Good   Bad   Disgusting Contemptible

Some guidelines for developing scales are as follows:
    1. Do not have too many or too few points on the scale. Too few result in a crude

---

2. Norman Cliff, "Adverbs Multiply Adjectives," in *Statistics: A Guide to the Unknown*, ed. Judith M. Tanur et al. (San Francisco: Holden-Day, 1972), pp. 176-84.

measure. Too many make discriminations difficult and time consuming for the observer.
2. Use an even number of points on the scale. This forces the observer off the center of the scale—that happy medium that everyone wants to hit.
3. Allow reactions at only the listed points. If the observer marks between points, interpretation must be made arbitrarily by the interpreter. Even if he is the one who observed, reflection will be difficult.
4. Select meaningful descriptors for the categories. Careful selection of adjectives and modifying adverbs give direction to the observer. (See Cliff.)

The important objectives for rating scales are (1) to do away with reflection on what happened through memory, (2) to develop a structured recording procedure that is efficient for the observer and that does not interfere with what is being observed, and (3) to get a detailed record of the original behavior.

Scorecards

A numerical rating scale called a scorecard can be used to structure observation of a complex entity. Though rarely used for observing human behavior, the scorecard is frequently used to evaluate school buildings, communities, textbooks, and school programs. Scorecards have also been designed to categorize socioeconomic status of individuals, families, and groups. Each important contributing factor is listed on the scorecard, and a predetermined number of points is assigned for each one in relationship to its importance among the others listed. A total for the scorecard is intended to be an indication of the overall evaluation. A major problem arises when the validity of the data is investigated. Since the observation rests primarily on *reported* information, the value here is questionable. Other questions arise about the use of scorecards when important intangibles make contributions to the entity, but the scorecard does not allow for their contributions. Nevertheless scorecards can help structure observation for some research studies and can be used to gather particular kinds of data.

A scorecard for elementary school physical education programs provides a model that can be adapted to other special uses for research purposes since the general procedures are the same, although the purposes might be different.[3] Any use of the scorecard would be to get a total picture of some complex entity.

The Neilson-Arnett scorecard lists four major divisions: Instructional Staff; Facilities; Program (organization); and Program (activities). Each of these divisions has from four to seven subcategories, giving twenty-three aspects, each having a subscore. The final page of the scorecard and the subdivision of Division IV, the Intramural Athletic Program, are shown in figure 6.1. The total for subdivision 4C is recorded in the summary sheet for the division, and the total Division IV total is recorded in the master scorecard. The total for the four divisions is the total for the master scorecard. The master scorecard also provides for a percentage score for the school's physical education program.

Rankings

Observation may require comparing those subjects being studied to each other, rather than to some absolute scale. An ordering by ranks provides an opportunity for the

---

3. N. P. Neilson and Glenn W. Arnett, *A Scorecard for Use in Evaluating Physical Educational Programs in Elementary Schools* (Salt Lake City: University of Utah Press, 1955), p. 53.

4C. *Intramural Athletic Program*		
General Standards	Points Possible	Points Scored
Adult supervision is provided for the program	3	
Detailed management and leadership are supplied by pupils	3	
Competition is among teams of pupils classified by age, height and weight	3	
Pupils are used as umpires, referees, judges, and scorers	3	
Intramural activities are not held during the daily instructional period	3	
Round-robin and ladder tournaments are held in intramural play	3	
Activities Used in Competition		
Bat Ball	3	
End Ball	3	
Long Ball	3	
One Old Cat	3	
Pin Soccer	3	
Softball	3	
Prisoner's Ball	3	
Soccer Dodgeball	3	
Triangle Ball	3	
Basketball Throw	3	
Captain Ball	3	
Circle Soccer	3	
Corner Kickball	3	
Handball	3	
Feather Ball	3	
Rotation Soccer	3	
Shinney	3	
Square Soccer	3	
....	3	
....	3	
....	3	
Total Points Allowed	60	

Scorecard Summary Sheet

Division IV—Program (Activities)	Points Possible	Points Scored
A — Activity Emphasis (Instructional Period)	58	
B — Activities Taught (Instructional Period)	342	
C — Intramural Athletic Program	60	
D — Achievement Tests in Individual Athletic Events	40	
Total	500	

Total Scores	Points Possible	Points Scored
Division I—Instructional Staff	500	
Division II—Facilities	500	
Division III—Program (Organization)	500	
Division IV—Program (Activities)	500	
Total for Scorecard	2000	
Divide Score by 2	1000	
Percentage Score for School (Divide by 10)	100	

FIGURE 6.1 Section of a Scorecard used to Evaluate an Elementary School Physical Education Program

Observation

researcher to give serial numbers to the elements being studied.[4] A rank order assigns a position number for each number in a distribution of values, so that all of the values greater than any one value are on one side of it and all values smaller than it are on the other side of it. All values that are the same as it are assigned the same number.

An example of a ranking is:

> A judge is asked to evaluate a set of paintings by assigning a one (1) to the painting that he judges to be the best, a two (2) for the next best, and so on. For five paintings—AB, AC, AD, AE, and AF—he might judge them this way:
>
> | Paintings | Ranks |
> |---|---|
> | AD | 1 |
> | AE | 2 |
> | AB | 3 |
> | AF | 4 |
> | AC | 5 |

Each position indicates the judge's ranking of the art object in relation to all of the others without assignment of definite quantities to the attributes being judged.

Ranking allows the researcher the opportunity to differentiate within groups where the observation is within a limited range of a continuum, and to handle quantitatively data that cannot be more exactly discriminated. Assignment of ranks on a variable under study may assist the observer in building objectivity into a stubborn situation where more refined techniques cannot be used.

SUPPLEMENTING DIRECT OBSERVATION

Direct observation may be supplemented in two ways:
1. By devices that extend the human senses in areas where the senses alone fail to provide data with the desired degree of validity. These are in most cases mechanical devices, such as movie cameras, television cameras, and sound recorders, that provide permanent records of events for careful study, and devices used to extend the senses, such as microscopes, telescopes, and listening devices.
2. By testing instruments. Tests are used to gather data through an instrument of measurement where physical measuring devices such as rulers, yardsticks, weighing scales, odometers and such are not appropriate. These tests are used primarily to measure constructs associated with achievement, aptitudes, and personal-social growth.

Mechanical Instrumentation

Movie cameras, television cameras, sound tape recorders, counters, timers, and hundreds of other mechanical devices are available to aid in observing. Some provide a record that can be studied intensely and repeatedly by teams of observers. Instruments that record mechanically are not affected by human biases, emotions, or selective and capricious memories. Of course the human element will enter into interpretation, but it should contribute only minimally if readings are carefully checked through viewing by other researchers. Other devices provide an extension of human senses and provide

---

4. Charles D. Hopkins, *Describing Data Statistically* (Columbus: Charles E. Merrill, 1974), pp. 5-7.

observations not possible within the human limits. Instrumentation serves three major purposes in observation:

1. It provides a purely objective record of what happened as the events occurred; however each record is limited to the scope of the recording device. A movie camera does not give a complete view of a classroom so the record is limited to what is on the film. A tape recorder picks up only sounds within its range — no more and sometimes less.
2. It provides a way to gather sensations not available through the human senses. This contribution is limited to the extent of the sophistication of the devices. Some are very refined, but some are relatively crude.
3. It provides a way to quantify many variables under study. The noise level of a situation can be recorded in decibel units; the speed of electrical impulses within and between parts of the brain can be measured; and other characteristics can be quantified.

A major limitation of mechanical devices is that these instruments are more easily used in the laboratory than in natural settings. The use of any instruments should be carefully checked for any change of the natural environment under study as a result of their introduction to the situation. Any alteration of the setting may change the measure of what is being studied.

The researcher should find out about mechanical devices available for use in the study, investigate carefully how they could contribute to his needs, and utilize them for their value in the refinement of his observations. The researcher may decide that the television camera could provide information for the study, but upon introduction to a classroom he or she may decide that it changes the environment and interacts with the setting so much that it cannot record the usual or natural interactions which take place when it is not a part of the scene.

Tests

A large portion of psychological and educational data consists of observations made by testing devices used as measuring instruments. When possible, the sophistication provided by well developed and validated tests should be utilized for research studies. Since this technique is widely used in research it is discussed as a topic in the next chapter on measurement.

A rather arbitrary decision has been made by the author to discuss measurement as a separate topic. Much of educational measurement involves an observer as a part of quantification techniques of assigning categories, symbols, or numbers to observations. A measurement procedure requires a clearly stated operation or rule that can be applied by a well trained observer. In this sense the separation of measurement from observation is artificial and has been made only for pedagogical reasons.

Other Techniques

Less used techniques for aiding in observation will be discussed as tools for specific uses in either historical, descriptive, or experimental research. Several of these are the inventory, problem lists, skill measurement, questionnaire, opinionaire, and blank.

OBSERVATION IN EDUCATIONAL RESEARCH

The educational researcher uses observation to identify problem areas. He/she uses observation to acquire a background of knowledge pertaining to the problem and uses this knowledge to develop a hypothesis. He uses observation to gather data that can be used to test the hypothesis, and conclusions are developed after observing the results of the data collection. Each of these situations utilizes observation in different ways. The first use of observation may be at the level of looking and seeing while studying an obstacle in education. At this level the use of *attention* and *sensation* would help establish the problem and its limits. *Perception* is used when organizing present knowledge and especially when interpreting results of data gathering and treatment. *Conception* is used when the researcher must go beyond his or her present knowledge to develop hypotheses and theories.

Observation is used throughout the animal world, and the skills of observation in both the hunter and the hunted have evolved to a very high level. Even the eye-set for animals contributes to increasing the power of observation. In general those animals that hunt have the eyes set in the front of the head for intense observation of prey, while those hunted have eyes set on the sides of the head to give a wide-range view of the surroundings. The researcher cannot rely solely on personal-animal instincts for his observation. He/she cannot depend on the everyday observation that serves most of us very well, and must be dissatisfied with uncontrolled observation. The process of merely looking at phenomena does not provide the reliable data needed for valid inferences. Useful description of observed events must be put in a frame of reference, and the observer must describe events in interpretable categories.

For educational studies based in human behavior, two methods of observing the behavior are (1) observation of people in a natural setting or a devised setting and (2) questioning of subjects about their behavior. When using observation in behavioral research a decision must be made about how and when the sampling of the behavior will take place. Procedures should be made up to build a representative sample much the same as representativeness is built into any sample.

SAMPLING OBSERVATION

Two sampling plans used with direct observation are event sampling and time sampling. The answer to the question, "Can the behavior best be recorded and interpreted on the basis of division by units of behavior or units of time?" will be influenced by the research problem. Creative ideas about using checklists, ratings, scorecards, mechanical devices, tests and such can be found in research literature or be developed especially for the present research study.

Event sampling makes use of behavior occurrences in individuals or interactions between and among individuals in the setting being observed. Examples of individual behavior would be temper tantrums, teacher questions, student questions, errors in a tennis match, and acts of creativity. Examples of interactions are quarrels, voluntary in-class debates, and incidents of submission and domination. Event sampling has the advantages that natural settings provide by giving a closeness to reality and continuity to an integral occurrence, not possible in time sampling.

Time sampling selects different points in time for recording observations. The observer may record on a checklist what is happening every so many seconds — say, ten or fifteen—over a predetermined time span. The sampling might be at ten-minute intervals for time periods through a day, week, or other appropriate time block. Time blocks should be chosen at random over a long enough time period to assure a representative sample. There are many ways to set up selection of samples. Decisions about the length and frequency of the blocks will be influenced by the study and type of data required. Behavioral observation systems from past studies give direction to the researcher using direct observation, but new and creative approaches for present studies will provide the most valid data and may contribute new methodology for observation techniques. Those working in this area are encouraged to try new methods of observation and report on the results. Continued refinement of methods of observation will permit the educational researcher to function better in the important areas of human interrelations in the classroom and other group interaction. Data-gathering instruments and schedules that organize observation work are necessary for complex situations that will produce data which can be treated with some form of systematic analysis.

Research activities for considering a question and producing a subsequent answer cause the researcher to be engaged in observations of many kinds. The educational researcher dealing with human behavior will need to rely heavily on direct observation to provide valid answers for his or her questions, and the value of the outcomes (conclusions) rests heavily on being able to develop skills in quantifying through observation. The next chapter on measurement extends observation techniques to methods of quantification through more direct means of using measuring devices for assigning number values.

SUMMARY

Valid conclusions for research studies rest on valid and interpretable information in the form of data. To get data of this kind the researcher must utilize techniques of observation to obtain data which have clear and undistorted signals for analysis procedures. Observation has been used in a very broad sense to include all information gathering techniques, e.g., visual (through the senses), mechanical instruments, and educational tests. Any bit of data is called an observation.

Four psychological factors of observation — attention, sensation, perception, and conception — have been discussed: *attention* being a condition or preparation for readiness to receive selected stimuli; *sensation* being the actual receiving of the physical impulses; *perception* being the interpretation of received stimuli in light of past experiences and knowledge; and *conception* being the creation of an interpretation in the form of a proposed answer through some intellectual process.

Human beings' obstructions to observation are based in the limitations and frailties provided by human nature. The scientific approach to researching furnishes procedures designed to reduce human errors associated with perception and conception by objectifying observation by supplying background knowledge of the problem area, studying different viewpoints, communicating in clearly understood or defined words, examining data with a questioning mind, recording data in a system, and quantifying data when possible.

Personnel should be trained specifically for each data-gathering procedure used in a research project, so that they may become accustomed to the mechanics of gathering techniques. They should be prepared to use one or more of the following to assist in observation: checklists; rating scales; scorecards; mechanical instruments; tests or one of the less used techniques of inventory; problem lists; skill measurement; questionnaire; opinionnaire; and blank.

Problems in getting a representative sample from direct observation can be overcome by carefully planning the observation through either event sampling or time sampling.

Observation

Event sampling utilizes behavior occurrences, and time sampling chooses time units for recording observations. Previously reported research studies provide traditional, unique, and creative approaches to the very important area of observation, but each new research study requires a structure tailored especially for the question under study. A researcher must be prepared with knowledge about how others have functioned, but must also be ready to be creative in his or her own right, to bring out new observational techniques.

7

Measurement

> *Any scientific investigation uses measurement, if only at the nominal-scale level, and certainly it behooves the investigator to think very carefully about the level of measurement he is using.*
> —William L. Hays

What is measurement? It is the process of measuring. Simple enough? No—not really. Lyle V. Jones reports that the word *measure* has forty different meanings, and may refer to any of the following uses: the process of; the result of; the instrument for; and the units used in measuring.[1] Agreement on one meaning of *measurement* appears unlikely within the above context especially when one realizes that measurement serves so many different purposes.

The major purpose of all measurement is to observe by providing information about specifically indicated characteristics of objects, organisms, or events, where that information will be numerical representations of the attribute being studied. The outcome of measurement is a set of observations.

The subjects of measurement are not objects, but some property of the objects. A "room" itself is not measurable, but its variables of length, width, height, and volume can be measured. These can be determined in quantitative terms. Human subjects are *not* measurable, but they too can be measured on such characteristics as height, physics achievement, motivation, creativity, or any other trait that can be isolated. Since the characteristics of most concern in education are not quantifiable by simple mechanical devices, like rules, scales, and odometers, special problems are associated with educational measurement. This chapter has the major objectives of (1) introducing those measurement principles most directly related to educational research and (2) presenting selected topics of practical use.

---

1. Lyle V. Jones, "The Nature of Measurement," in *Educational Measurement,* ed. Robert L. Thorndike (Washington, D. C.: American Council on Education, 1971), p. 335.

MEASUREMENT: A DEFINITION

Since the words *measure* and *measurement* are used in so many ways, a working definition is needed for communication in this book. For our use measurement will be defined as *a process of assigning by rule a numerical description to the observation of some attribute of an object, person, or event*. The rest of this chapter is designed to help the reader investigate the *process* of measurement as used by the educational researcher.

The process of measurement is basically the same for the many sciences—physical, social, and behavioral—but the techniques used to assign the numerical descriptors and the precision with which they can be assigned are quite different for each of the techniques. All measurement is made according to rules. The rules for measuring characteristics of physical objects, such as boards, desks, and doghouses, are much better than rules associated with such attributes as motivation, creativity, and biology achievement. Kerlinger says:

> Measurement is a game we play with objects and numerals. Games have rules. It is, of course, important for other reasons that the rules be "good" rules, but whether the rules are "good" or "bad," the procedure is still measurement.[2]

To understand attempts to quantify traits of intelligence, creativity, motivation, and so forth as measurement requires an understanding that the assignment of the number constitutes the measurement. Any property that can be isolated can be measured. The property may be complex and the rules for dealing with it may not be "good" at this time, but the scientist continues to refine the rules. He or she is encouraged by the thought that if something exists it must be measurable through assignment of a numerical description.

It is possible to satisfy our definition of measurement with poor procedures—poor procedures develop from lack of knowledge about setting up an isomorphic relationship between the structure of measurement (the rules) and some numerical structure which includes the same rules. For example, if a researcher collects a set of data and wants to find an arithmetical average (mean) he/she must be assured that the data are amenable to the two processes of addition and division. If the data were the carefully measured heights of twenty-five first grade children, the average would be meaningful if the rules were isomorphic to the structure of arithmetic. If the data were hair color of the same twenty-five students, and the researcher assigned numbers of 1 for brown, 2 for blond, 3 for black, and 4 for red, the data could not be averaged, since the rules of assignment would not be isomorphic to the structure of the arithmetic processes. The arithmetic for averaging one blond at 2 and one redhead at 4 can be performed, and $(2 + 4) \div 2 = 3$. The problem now is one of interpretation of the resulting "3." It has no real-world meaning because our measurement rules do not permit the arithmetical operations of addition and division needed for a meaningful interpretation of the 3.

The idea of distinct levels of measurement is important for the educational researcher when he/she must treat collected data. The operations that can be performed on a given set of scores depend on the rules used in the numerical assignment. The next

---

2. Fred N. Kerlinger, *Foundations of Behavioral Research* (New York: Holt, Rinehart and Winston, 1973), p. 427.

Measurement

section discusses four distinct levels of measurement and their relation to the research process.[3]

FOUR LEVELS OF MEASUREMENT

The discussion of the levels of measurement will be presented in hierarchical order, beginning with the lowest level. A limiting factor to the level will, as mentioned before, be the rules used in assignment—the rules being limited by either (1) the nature of the variable or (2) our lack of ability to develop appropriate rules.

Nominal Scales

Measurement at its lowest level involves numerical assignment to simply classify characteristics into broad categories. In the preceding example of the attribute of hair color, the classes brown, blond, black, and red, which were described numerically, could have been described just as easily with some other set of symbols. In fact the symbols—brown, blond, black, and red—would serve as well as any numerical expression for the categories except for conveniences of recording. Any set of symbols used to categorize an attribute into distinct classes constitutes a *nominal scale*. Since other symbols besides numbers can be used to classify nominal variables, some experts in measurement exclude as measurement the process of assigning numerals for identifying categories of classification where the numerals *cannot* be treated mathematically. If this procedure were excluded from measurement, it would prevent many educational procedures for quantification from being called measurement.

There are two rules for nominal measurement—(1) all the members of a level of an attribute are assigned the same numeral and (2) no two levels are assigned the same numeral. The numeral used to identify the level (class) cannot be treated mathematically, but since the elements assigned to each class can be counted and compared mathematically it seems for our purposes that procedures for nominal scaling are measurement.[4] The only relationship that can be found and given attention is that of equivalence or the lack of equivalence. After the subclasses have been counted, a statement can be made about the frequency count in each class. Statements can be made about the class with the highest frequency of occurrence, the class with the lowest frequency, and classes that have the same number of frequencies.

Statements about results of nominal scaling can only be statements regarding same or different. In a running race the finishers can be compared as finishing in the same time (tied) or different times. If the results were reported with only the information about ties and differences the reported data would be at the lowest level, or nominal. Reported in this way, the operations that can be performed on the data about running ability are limited by the rules of assignment, not by the nature of the attribute itself. The importance of using the "best" rules for assignment of numbers is pointed up by the use of a "poor" rule above.

Some variables are amenable only to the measurement scale of nominal. Examples include sex, race, eye color, hair color, and such, where criteria can be set up only

---

3. Paul Leslie Gardner, "Scales and Statistics," *Review of Educational Research* 45 (Winter 1975): 43-57. (A historical and contemporary consensus.)
4. Kerlinger, *Foundations of Behavioral Research*.

for broad categories with no order as to relative number values for numerals used for assignment. The members of each category can be counted and comparisons made among frequencies for the categories.

Ordinal Scales

The next higher scale of measurement results when the rules of assignment involve rank ordering. Ranking is possible whenever the classes, in addition to being different, are in some relation such that a is greater than b, and b is greater than c through all of the classes. The result is an *ordinal scale*.

The basic difference between a nominal and ordinal scale is that, in addition to the relation of equivalence, the relation of *greater than* has been incorporated in the rules of assignment of the numerical descriptor. The numbers assigned as ranks are quantitatively relative in regard to the trait being measured, but they do *not* indicate quantity in absolute terms nor are the intervals between the numbers to be equal.

If a running race is assumed to measure race-running ability, then in addition to categorizing only same or different in regard to the trait, a ranking will permit statements about how the runners compare relatively. The runner finishing first has more race-running ability (at least for the one race) than all other runners, the second finisher has more than all others except the one who finished first, and so forth. Statements of less than can also be made. The rule for assigning numbers to ranks utilizes a numerical scale which allows, in addition to statements of same or different, a comparison of relative quantity between the numerical description of ranks.

Interval Scales

The next higher scale of measurement results when the rules of assignment involve numerical description, such that numerically equal distances on the scale represent equal numerical distances on the attribute being measured. If the assignment of numbers is made such that it can be determined how large the distance between objects is by the scale values then the measurement is *interval scaling*.

Equal distances on the measuring scale must represent equal distances on the property being measured. This permits statements about differences *within* the scale. The thermometer is an example of a measuring instrument that measures at this level. A difference of five degrees any place on the scale is the same as a difference of five at any other place on the scale. If the unit is the degree, then the two 5s represent the same quantity. ($15 - 10 = 5$ and $175 - 170 = 5$.) If the unit is a rank, then the difference of five ranks does not necessarily represent the same absolute difference. If assignment of a numerical descriptor is characterized by use of a constant unit and an arbitrary zero point, then the measurement is interval scaling.

In addition to ordering the finish of a running race, timers could measure the times with a stopwatch. Assume that the first three finishers had the following times: 54 seconds; 56 seconds; and 60 seconds. Statements could be made about intervals between pairs of runners—the interval between second (56 sec.) and third (60 sec.) is two times as long as the interval between first (54 sec.) and second (56 sec.).

$$(60 - 56) = 2 \cdot (56 - 54) \text{ or } \frac{60 - 56}{56 - 54} = \frac{4}{2} = 2.$$

The rank order of one, two, three associated with first, second, and third place does not give this information.

The rule for assigning numbers on an interval scale permits statements about a distance on the measuring scale and the equal interval on the attribute being measured, and allows intervals to be added or subtracted. Statements about ratios of differences

Measurement

within the scale can be made, but a restriction is placed on ratio statements comparing original measurements because the rule of assignment involves an arbitrary zero point. The temperature of fifty degrees (either centigrade or Fahrenheit) is only twice as much as twenty-five degrees when speaking of measurements within the scale and not in absolute units, e.g., a reading of fifty degrees does *not* represent twice as much heat as a reading of twenty-five degrees since the zero on the thermometer does not represent a total absence of heat.

Ratio Scales

The highest position of measurement is obtained when the rules of assignment include an absolute zero for the scale. The zero for this scale represents a total lack of the attribute which is being measured. If assignment of the numerical descriptor includes all of the rules for assignment of the lower scales plus a true zero point, the measurement is on a *ratio scaling*.

Numbers on a ratio scale represent absolute amounts of that being measured. Jimmy, who weighs 86 pounds, is twice as heavy as his brother, who weighs 43 pounds. Compare the measurement of weight with the measurement of temperature. A temperature of 86 degrees does not represent twice as much heat as a temperature of 43 degrees.

Return now to the running race described earlier. What can be said about the running ability of two brothers, the older being the first place finisher (54 seconds), if the younger brother ran the race in 108 seconds? These statements can be made about the differences in the times for running the race:

1. they have different amounts of race-running ability (nominal);
2. the winner of the race had more race-running ability (ordinal); and
3. the difference $(60 - 54 = 6)$ between first and third place is only one-ninth of the difference $(108 - 54 = 54)$ between the two brothers (interval).

TABLE 7.1 Scales, Defining Relations, and Appropriate Statistics

Scale	Defining Relations	Type of Statistical Test Parametric	Type of Statistical Test Nonparametric	Examples of Appropriate Statistics
Nominal	1. Equivalence		✓	Mode Frequency of occurrence Contingency coefficients
Ordinal	1. Equivalence 2. Greater than		✓	Median Percentiles Spearman rho Kendall r Friedman Anova by ranks
Interval	1. Equivalence 2. Greater than 3. Known ratio of any two intervals	✓		Mean Standard deviation Pearson r Analysis of variance t-test
Ratio	1. Equivalence 2. Greater than 3. Known ratio of any two intervals 4. Known ratio of any two scale values	✓		

Can it be said that the winner at 54 seconds has twice the race-running ability of the brother who ran the race in 108 seconds? Obviously the answer is *no* because of the absence of an absolute zero for the variable being measured—race-running ability. It can be said that the younger brother took twice as long to run the race as his brother did, since the elapsed time is measured on the ratio scale, but the rules of assignment of the numerical descriptors do not allow statements of race-running ability at the ratio level of measurement.

Since most of the educational questions are based in psychological factors rather than physical factors, the educational researcher will only rarely be involved with variables which permit measurement on the ratio scale. From our viewpoint of educational research the distinction between interval and ratio scale is not important, and it becomes convenient to think of three scales rather than four when choosing statistical designs for studies. Table 7.1 shows the relationship among scales, defining relations, and statistical procedures appropriate for each scale.

MEASUREMENT IN EDUCATIONAL RESEARCH

Although the educational researcher deals with objects and persons, he or she does not measure objects and persons. In general the concerns of measurement are with properties or traits of objects and persons. Thus are we to assume that he/she measures properties and traits? In most cases *no,* since the attributes of concern do *not* allow direct measurement as a carpenter measures a board with a steel rule. Studying the trait of creativity, or measuring the trait of creativity, does not involve direct observation or measurement. The property of creativity for a human subject cannot be measured directly, as the property of length for a table may be. Physical characteristics are, in general, open to direct measurement while personal characteristics must be measured indirectly.

The properties of human subjects which are of interest to educators are not open to public inspection. The educational researcher will usually be looking for effects that indicate the trait being studied. Thermometers are used to indicate the effect of temperature differences on a liquid (alcohol or mercury) in a tube. The thermometer does not measure temperature directly, but a scale along the side of the tube indicates differences in temperature *indirectly*. The achievement test in physics is intended to measure achievement in physics *indirectly*.

Only rarely will the educational researcher measure characteristics directly. He or she will be looking for certain signs that indicate the trait and the amount. A major problem to the researcher is the quantification of the trait. He is involved with questions like, "What am I measuring?" "How do I measure it?" and "How do I know that I am measuring what is to be measured?" Valid answers to these questions and others like them are going to be much more difficult when making inferences indirectly than when directly observing (or measuring) physical properties, such as hair color, height, and skin color. The validity of the answers depends heavily on (1) developing the ability to define what is being measured, (2) finding or inventing instruments to measure, and (3) establishing a relationship between that being measured and the measuring instrument.

Researchers use operational definitions (see chapter 3) to describe what they are measuring. The person defining the trait tells what activities are necessary to indicate

Measurement

the trait (not the amount—just the activity). Popularity can be indicated by a choice on a sociogram. The number of choices a person gets is a measure of the trait. Popularity could be defined as: Popularity is the number of choices a pupil receives on the "Some Name Sociogram."

This clarifies for the researcher what he/she means by popularity and communicates to a reader how it will be measured. However it does not answer the question, "How do I know that I am measuring what is to be measured?" There is no way to assure this, and usually the validity of the answer will vary in degrees among individuals. Researchers have situations where agreement with an operational definition is 100 percent, and other situations where disagreement is 100 percent; most studies fall somewhere between.

The scale of measurement, in large degree, determines what statistical procedures are appropriate for treatment of the data. (See table 7.1.) Further development of the relationship between measurement procedures and statistical procedures is presented in a later section. Suffice for the present that the level of measurement in the hierarchy will determine and/or limit the statistical techniques that can be used. Nominal and ordinal data will be treated with a class of techniques labeled *nonparametric,* and interval and ratio data will use *parametric* procedures. In appropriate sections, attention will be given to problems of how data are to be treated when questions arise concerning the level of measurement.

CHARACTERISTICS OF MEASURING INSTRUMENTS

An overview of the properties of measuring instruments will be given here, and each will be considered in relationship to other aspects of the research process. Included for discussion are validity, reliability, and usability. Ten characteristics for judging tests are presented as a check on test quality, and as direction for developing tests to measure attributes under study.

Validity

The most important property of any measuring instrument is the validity. Validity of a measuring device is the degree to which the device measures what it is supposed to measure. A measuring stick that is marked in feet can be used to measure the width of a table (length also) and the measurement will be listed to the nearest foot. Is the device valid? Yes, it measured the characteristic of table width. How accurately it did it is another question. Could a furniture maker in a distant city use measurements that are given in feet for width and length to build a table to fit neatly into an alcove in a dining room, also reported to the nearest foot? He might do this by good luck, but not by good management. The measurement rule that is needed for the assignment of table measurements is not present in the unit of a foot. *A measuring device is valid to the degree of accuracy with which it measures that property to be measured.* The result of a measurement should quantify *what* it is supposed to measure and do it accurately.

In measurement of physical characteristics, establishing validity is not a large problem. To convey the size of the table to the furniture maker the unit of measure could be made as small as necessary by dividing the measuring stick into smaller equal parts. The directness of physical measurement also contributes to establishing a high degree of validity in the measurements for physical properties. Many of the properties that the educational researcher deals with allow only indirect measurement and questionable definition of the traits. Questionable definitions mean that the validity of the measurements is also questionable; therefore it becomes necessary to state validity in terms of *degrees* of validity.

The degree of validity for each measuring instrument (mechanical or test) used in research must be determined and reported. Included are establishment of (1) general validity, (2) specific type of validity, and (3) appropriateness for use in the present study. Validity for mechanical instruments is largely a matter of showing appropriateness for present use—*usability*. Test validation is more difficult to establish and will be covered when tools of researchers are discussed in the next three chapters.[5]

Reliability

The ability of a measuring device to do whatever it does consistently is known as reliability. For a measuring device to have high reliability it must do whatever it does in the same manner all of the time. The definition of reliability makes no reference to a device being able to do what it is used to doing—only whether it performs its function with consistency. A school dismissal bell that is set to ring at 3:00 P.M. each day and rings at 2:50 P.M. each day has a high degree of reliability. Is this valid? No! To be valid the bell must do consistently what it is used for and, of course, that is ring each day at 3:00 P.M. To ring consistently at 2:50 P.M. is enough to establish reliability, but validity has one more attribute to be considered—that of doing what it is being used for.

The degree of reliability will be less than perfect, since all measurement contains some amount of variability. Variability associated with measurement is referred to as *error*. The school bell that rings at 2:50 P.M. each day does not ring at exactly the same time since the triggering mechanism is affected by factors of temperature, humidity, and such chance errors or factors of the mechanism itself that cause it to vary the time that it rings. The error is likely to be small since mechanisms set to ring bells tend to perform much the same each time. As the amount of error associated with measurement increases, the reliability of the measuring instrument is lessened, and in turn our confidence in the measurements is correspondingly lessened. The measurement lacks reliability to the degree that error is associated with assignment of the quantification.

Exact measurement of continuous variables does not exist because any recording by units involves the concept of nearness, thereby building some error into the measurement. Most variables of educational concerns are continuous, although the most important element of the educational process—the human being—is a discrete variable. When quantifying a human population, only positive whole numbers can be used. Most traits—like motivation, history achievement, or scholastic aptitude—can take any values on scales used for measurement at the choice of the person who decides the rules for measurement. Even measurement of variables by assignment to categories includes nearness when the variable is continuous. Not all eyes that are assigned to the class of "blue" are exactly the same shade, and some in that class may be very close to another assignment.

Additional error is involved in reading dials and marks on measuring devices. The readings on the dials and scales of measuring devices will vary, depending on the person

---

5. For more information and bibliography see Lee J. Cronbach, "Test Validation," in *Educational Measurement,* ed. Robert L. Thorndike (Washington, D.C.: American Council on Education, 1971), pp. 443-507.

reading them and the different relative positions of the readers. Differences in interpretation of scoring responses on tests contribute to the variability of those scores. As previously mentioned, instruments used to measure are themselves a source of variation through imperfections within themselves. Chance errors reduce the reliability and in turn the validity of measurement. The sources of chance errors are:
1. Imperfections of the measuring instrument itself.
2. Interpretations—reading or scoring—of the instrument information.
3. Inconsistency in the subjects being measured.

The chance error referred to here is *not* to be confused with a mistake. Error in measurement has more to do with variation. The *more variation* associated with the quantification, the less the reliability or the *more the unreliability*. "The degree of reliability of a set of measurements is a very important consideration, both in the practical day-to-day use of tests and in empirical research."[6]

Prediction is a part of all scientific work. If one is to make predictions the data used as a basis for the predictions must be generated by reliable measurement procedures. Reliable conclusions are based on reliable data. Low correlation coefficients in studies of association (correlation) can be the result of data that are not reliable.

Reliability is a contributing factor to the degree of validity for measuring instruments. A test is not able to do what it should do (validity) without doing it with consistency. The relationship between validity and reliability is best stated formally as:

Reliability is a necessary but *not sufficient* condition for validity.

Of course a test may do what it does with high reliability but may not be doing what it should. Reliability for a test instrument is usually established by a statistical procedure of correlation or internal consistency methods. Several sections of Stanley's[7] discussion of reliability are devoted to what he calls "logical and empirical aspects" of reliability determination as he expands our discussion of sources of variation that affect reliability, namely:

  I. Lasting and general characteristics of the individual
 II. Lasting but specific characteristics of the individual
III. Temporary but general characteristics of the individual
 IV. Temporary and specific characteristics of the individual
  V. Systematic or chance factors affecting the administration of the test or the appraisal of test performance
 VI. Variance not otherwise accounted for (chance)[8]

These topics are especially important for the researcher as he/she views measurement within the study and in how it affects research conclusions. Building high reliability into measurement procedures contributes to increasing the validity of the measurements and, in turn, the accuracy of the conclusions. The researcher must keep in mind that establishment of reliability for measurement is necessary but that establishment of validity, which includes the condition of reliability, is more important.

---

6. Julian C. Stanley, "Reliability," in *Educational Measurement*, ed. Robert L. Thorndike (Washington, D.C.: American Council on Education, 1971), p. 356. Excellent coverage of reliability and a bibliography.
7. Ibid., pp. 359-69.
8. Ibid., p. 364.

Usability

The usability of a measuring device refers to its practicality for the situation in which it is being used. Major concerns for the researcher are administration, collection of data, interpretation of data, and cost of time and money. Each of these must be considered in light of the others. A movie camera might provide an excellent way to observe a situation, but to be assured that the introduction of the camera is having no effect on the interaction may take special attention. The cost of concealing the camera and related logistics may be too expensive for the budget and/or not practical for the natural setting. An individually administered test might provide the best data, but the length of time involved in gathering data with few testers used for test administration might affect the validity of the data. An individually administered test might be too expensive for the budget. In most cases if the use of mechanical devices is feasible, cleared for use by the administration and not too expensive, they should be used because the data are easily obtained and, in general, easy to interpret.

Special problems arise with use of paper and pencil tests. In administration, factors to be considered are recording of responses, time required and number of sessions needed, and standardized instructions for both those administering and subjects taking the test. If the test will be used in different places with different groups, the conditions must be as similar as possible to make valid comparisons. Scoring procedures should be sophisticated to provide data which can be meaningfully organized and treated for results. For research purposes raw scores are usually used, but standard scores provided by standardized tests may be used if appropriate for treatment procedures. With a large number of subjects, machine scoring services for standardized tests or hand scoring procedures, using scoring masks, can be utilized. Either of these can be used to efficiently score and organize the data for treatment and to report results for interpretation.

Proper administrative procedures are important to the reliability and validity of the measurement. It is unfortunate that many otherwise excellently planned research studies are rendered invalid or their validity reduced because of measurement obtained through casual approaches to use of the measuring devices and/or scoring. Scoring problems are created mainly when responses must be subjectively judged by the scorer. Reliability and, in turn, validity of measurement are enhanced by carefully administered measuring devices and attention to detail in all scoring procedures. Both later chapters and educational measurement books will help the researcher establish appropriate procedures for particular problem areas.

Other Characteristics

Obviously measuring instruments have other characteristics. They are important in varying degrees depending on how the researcher will be using the scores. Ebel lists ten important characteristics for classroom tests that researchers can *also* consider as important to other measurement procedures for research.[9] They are *relevance, balance, efficiency, objectivity, specificity, difficulty, discrimination, reliability, fairness,* and *speediness*. Each is important in its own right and should be considered to the degree that it relates to the measurement being used for the study, regardless of whether the measuring instrument is a test or some other measuring device. Ebel's list of ten characteristics for a classroom test is especially important for the study requiring that

---

9. Robert L. Ebel, *Essentials of Educational Measurement* (Englewood Cliffs, N. J.: Prentice-Hall, 1972), pp. 359-82.

a test be developed. Selection of a test from standardized tests is covered in the next section.

At this point in our discussion of test characteristics, mention should be made of a very valuable source of information for ready-made standardized tests available for research use. Much time can be saved if an *appropriate* testing instrument has already been created. The emphasis must be on *appropriate* because what might be an excellent measuring device (test) in one situation may not be so in what appears to be a similar setting. Information about most standardized tests is available in *The Mental Measurements Yearbook* series. These include data about each test, critical reviews of each test, list of books about tests and testing, a periodical directory, a test publishers directory, and indices. They are recognized as indispensable guides to standardized tests. The latest edition, *The Seventh Mental Measurements Yearbook,* is in two volumes.[10]

More complete information can be found in the manuals published to be used with the tests. The final decision should be made only after checking the items and tasks that the test provides. The items on a test provide an operational definition of what the test measures. The researcher must decide whether it is measuring the variable which is to be measured in his/her study.

WHAT TEST TO USE

Although not all data for educational research are generated by tests, the paper and pencil test is widely used for educational measurement. The researcher who decides that he can best obtain needed data by testing must decide between (1) an existing test or (2) a test he develops for his particular study. Large amounts of time and effort are required to construct a high quality test. Considerable skill is also required to accomplish the task. For these reasons researchers, in general, look to existing instruments first. Instruments developed for other research studies may be appropriate for similar studies, but the most likely source will be found in a completely standardized test. A *standardized test* is a measuring instrument which has been developed such that the administration, scoring, and score interpretation have been made uniform for all testing situations. Thousands of tests have been "standardized" for use in the broad areas of achievement batteries that cover a very broad coverage of several subject matter areas to tests so specific as to measure "marital communication."

As mentioned earlier, *The Mental Measurements Yearbook* series is a source of information about most existing standardized tests. The researcher can find the following information about listed tests, (1) test name, (2) author, (3) publisher, (4) appropriate age (or grade levels), (5) date, (6) cost, (7) references for information about its use, and (8) one or more critical reviews of the test, in addition to other pertinent information. In addition to the achievement batteries covering several areas of the curricula, tests on specific subject matter are listed. Character and personality tests are divided into projective and nonprojective. Intelligence tests are divided into group and individual tests, with a special listing for tests that measure specific areas thought to relate to intelligence. In addition to multiaptitude batteries, areas such as mechanical ability, vocations, and interests are given separate attention. Miscellaneous tests listed range from "computer programming" to "courtship and marriage."

---

10. Oscar K. Buros, *The Seventh Mental Measurements Yearbook* (Highland Park, N.J.: Gryphon Press, 1972).

Careful selection is the key to choosing an appropriate standardized instrument. Several tests should be identified that may be usable, then compared on their important characteristics. The one that provides the most valid measurement for study should be selected. If a test cannot be found to meet the needs of the study, then development of a special test is better than using an inappropriate test merely to save time.

The following guidelines should aid the researcher in organizing data about several tests to help in making comparisons for selection.

Guidelines for Evaluating
a Standardized Test

1. Name of test, date, and author
2. Publisher and cost
3. Purpose of the test
4. Grade levels or ages
5. How many equivalent forms?
6. Test content
7. Administration time and directions
8. Validity
9. Reliability
10. Norms provided
11. Test format
12. Scoring procedures available
13. Manual (complete and usable?)
14. Review(s) from Buros, *The Mental Measurements Yearbook*
15. Personal evaluation

The guidelines can, of course, be modified by adding more categories or deleting any that appear here that are not particularly important to *your* investigation. Sources for the needed information are *The Mental Measurements Yearbook*, test manual, the test itself, and professional journals, such as *The Journal of Educational Measurement* and *Educational and Psychological Measurement*. An excellent way to tell what a test measures is to take the test yourself. Tests are on file in libraries and available in specimen sets from test publishers.

DEVELOPING A TEST

As mentioned earlier, test development falls outside the scope of research and belongs to the strategy based in the "need to do." Then why is it being discussed in a research book? Because (1) research people need to know how a test is developed to be able to use tests properly and (2) the researcher may have to assume the role of a test developer and create his or her own test instrument. This section is *not intended to prepare you to develop a test* but to indicate those aspects that need to be considered when building a test and characteristics to consider when selecting a test. Many good texts are available to assist in building a test, and much of *Educational Measurement* is devoted to building high quality measuring instruments. A document published by the American Psychological Association proposes standards for standardized tests, gives guidance to selection of tests for research, and aids in test development.[11]

---

11. Robert M. Guion et al., *Standards for Educational and Psychological Tests* (Washington, D.C.: American Psychological Association, 1974).

Measurement

When building a test, the test maker must keep in mind that he/she is developing a measuring device. A test instrument is as much a measuring device as a ruler, yardstick, or weighing scales. He must decide what is to be measured, how to *best* measure it, and a way to validate the measuring device. A test is a "general term used to designate any kind of device or procedure for measuring ability, achievement, interest, and other traits."[12] The purpose of a test is to quantify the amount of the trait being measured by assigning a numerical descriptor to each individual being considered. The test maker must decide what tasks will be best for measuring the characteristic. Tests utilize many different types of tasks for subjects being measured. Essay, short answer, and completion types of test items place different demands on the student than do true-false, multiple-choice, classification, and matching items. The first set requires the test taker to supply the response, while the second set asks the test taker to select a response from possible responses that are provided by the instrument. Each has advantages and disadvantages that must be considered. Major consideration must be given to the reliability of responses and interpretations made from the scores.

Construction of a high quality test for research purposes will include these steps:
1. Plan specifications of the test including item type, number of items, which specific items, and format.
2. Write items of appropriate difficulty to allow the device to distribute the quantification along the measuring scale (discrimination).
3. Pretest the items and analyze the data.
4. Rewrite the items according to indications provided by the item analysis.
5. Prepare a preliminary form of the test.
6. Administer the preliminary test to a second group as a pilot to (a) check mechanics of administration, (b) see if time limits are appropriate, and (c) provide more data to analyze about the items themselves.
7. Make changes to put the test in final form.

After the general purposes of the test have been established and the specific area to be measured by the test clearly fenced in, decisions about specifications must be made.

Within any specific area there are a large number of tasks which could be provided to quantify the amount of the trait being measured. In most cases the test maker has an uncountably large number of individual tasks available that can be used in the test instrument. Test time is limited. Which ones will be used, and how will they be chosen? Most test makers find that a blueprint in the form of a table of specifications is helpful (most consider it necessary) in building a valid test. The next section is devoted to a technique that will define the scope and emphasis of a test. In addition to helping in test building, the table of specifications can be used to guide test selection. By working back from the test itself, the table can be built by identifying topics covered in the items and the emphasis given each topic, which will help the one looking for a test for a particular use to relate test emphasis to needs.

Table of Specifications

One of the most important aspects of establishing validity is to define what is being measured. Since what is being measured is defined through the tasks provided, selecting appropriate tasks in proper relationship to the total test is extremely important. The content of the test must be a reflection of subtopics in their respective importance, and

---

12. Ebel, *Essentials of Educational Measurement*, p. 566.

must elicit the desired behavior. The *table of specifications* is built in two dimensions to coordinate into one matrix the aspects of (1) topics covered in the test and (2) behavior needed to react to test tasks.

A table of specifications may take many different forms, but the skeleton in table 7.2 points up the basic components needed to build one for a specific test.

TABLE 7.2 Basic Components for a Table of Specifications

Topics \ Behaviors	1.	2.	...N	% of test	No. of items
1.	?% / ?			?%	?
2.	?%			?%	?
3.					
N				total 1	total 1
Totals Totals	?% / ?	?% / ?		100%	100%

The descriptors for the behaviors (across the top of table 7.2) are usually taken from taxonomies of educational objectives, which have been written by Bloom and Krathwohl. Some possible divisions are knowledge, comprehension, application, analysis, synthesis, and evaluation for the cognitive domain; receiving, responding, valuing, organization, and characterization by a value or value complex for the affective domain. Examples of both follow:

Cognitive Domain[13]

    I. Knowledge
       A. Specifics
          1. Terminology
          2. Facts
       B. Ways and means of dealing with specifics
          1. Conventions
          2. Trends and sequences
          3. Classifications and categories
          4. Criteria
          5. Methodology
       C. Universals and abstractions
          1. Principles and generalizations
          2. Theories and structures
    II. Intellectual abilities and skills
       A. Comprehension
          1. Translation
          2. Interpretation
          3. Extrapolation

---

13. Benjamin S. Bloom, ed., *Taxonomy of Educational Objectives: The Cognitive Domain* (New York: David McKay, 1956), pp. 201-7.

        B. Application—use of abstractions in particular situations
        C. Analysis
            1. Elements
            2. Relationships
            3. Organizational principles
        D. Synthesis
            1. Production of a unique communication
            2. Production of a plan or proposed set of operations
            3. Derivation of a set of abstract relations
        E. Evaluation
            1. From internal evidence
            2. From external criteria

Affective Domain[14]

1.0 Receiving (attending)
    1.1 Awareness
    1.2 Willingness to receive
    1.3 Controlled or selected attention
2.0 Responding
    2.1 Acquiescence in responding
    2.2 Willingness to respond
    2.3 Satisfaction in response
3.0 Valuing
    3.1 Acceptance of a value
    3.2 Preference for a value
    3.3 Commitment (conviction)
4.0 Organization
    4.1 Conceptualization of a value
    4.2 Organization of a value system
5.0 Characterization by a value or value complex
    5.1 Generalized set
    5.2 Characterization

The descriptors which are used are determined largely by the characteristic being measured. The use of specific behaviors depends largely on how the test maker feels about specific behavioral objectives. Regardless of bias (either for or against) in regard to how valuable specifics are, some sort of classification should be built along the dimension of behavior—the behaviors being expected on the test.

Topics are based in some kind of content. The dimension of topics is listed in content to be covered. The amount of detail to be employed must remain a decision for the test maker as he or she considers the material to be covered.

In general the number of behaviors to be elicited should not exceed three, and topics should be limited to not more than five. With too many cells the distribution of items becomes difficult. After deciding what behaviors to include and the topics to cover, the relative importance of topics can be distributed through the cells, providing a crude but effective method of balancing a test.

To illustrate the process, consider the home economics teacher who wants to measure achievement in a unit on textiles. She may have the following general objectives:

1. The student can name and describe the natural and synthetic fibers used in clothing construction.

---

14. D. R. Krathwohl et al., *Taxonomy of Educational Objectives: The Affective Domain* (New York: David McKay, 1964), pp. 176-93.

2. The student understands the properties of pilling and shrinking of textiles.
3. The student can apply knowledge and understanding of textiles and their properties to clothing selection.

Using these broad objectives, the test maker should decide the relative importance of behaviors and topics. The decisions might look like this:

A. Behaviors
  1. Recall of information (knowledge)   20%
  2. Understanding (comprehension)   50%
  3. Ability to apply knowledge and
     understanding (application)   30%
B. Topics
  1. Natural fibers   15%
  2. Synthetic fibers   20%
  3. Pilling   10%
  4. Shrinkage   10%
  5. Choosing casual clothes   45%

The decisions on behaviors and topics, with associated percentages, are next incorporated into the table of specifications, and the cells are filled in based on the best judgment of the test maker, as indicated in table 7.3.

TABLE 7.3 A Table of Specifications for a Test on Textiles

Topic \ Behavior	Recall (Knowledge) % / items	Understanding (Comprehension) % / items	Apply (Application) % / items	% / No. of items
1. Natural fibers	6 / 3.6	9 / 5.4	0 / 0.0	15 / 9
2. Man-made fibers	4 / 2.4	16 / 9.6	0 / 0.0	20 / 12
3. Pilling	0 / 0.0	5 / 3.0	5 / 3.0	10 / 6
4. Shrinkage	0 / 0.0	5 / 3.0	5 / 3.0	10 / 6
5. Choosing textiles for casual clothes	10 / 6.0	15 / 9.0	20 / 12.0	45 / 27
TOTALS % / items	20 / 12	50 / 30	30 / 18	100 / 60

Obviously the test maker cannot write fractions of test items, such as 3.6 or 2.4. Some adjustment must be made as the test is finally formed, but the table of specifications, in spite of its roughness, is necessary to direct the construction of a test instrument that provides valid data. The next step in test preparation provides an opportunity to further clarify some of the objectives and utilize specific educational objectives.

Writing Test Items

A full-blown discussion of the task of writing items for a test is beyond the scope of this book, but a few suggestions as to what is involved may be helpful to provide direction in the choice of good tests. Basically, item writing consists of these steps:

1. Choose the appropriate type of item.
2. Write items that relate to the objectives.

Measurement

    3. Plan the difficulty level of each item and the test instrument as a whole.

    4. Write items that discriminate levels of differences.

Choice of a task that is relevant to measurement of the trait being considered is especially important in testing. Different types of items are available to the test maker and he or she should choose carefully the task that best fits the topic and behavior being measured. At times, either of the two types will do equally well and then the decision is rather arbitrary; at other times, the decision is crucial.

Relating items to general objectives is handled adequately with a well developed table of specifications. The more specific objectives must be reflected in specific items and, in turn, fit to the appropriate cell of the table.

Decisions about item difficulty require more test theory than can be presented here, but they can be made only after consideration of whether the testing is for mastery or testing with a sample intended to distribute scores along a scale. For research purposes, measurement is needed to show differences of characteristics. Two ways are employed to do this. The first uses what is called a *power* test, where the test provides tasks of varying difficulty from very easy to very difficult. The assumption is that if the test starts with easy items and the tasks are each progressively more difficult, each student will drop off at his or her level. The second way utilizes only those items that fall in the middle of the scale and omits very easy items and very difficult items, including only what is referred to as *medium difficulty* items. The medium difficulty item is one for which the proportion of test takers getting the item correct is approximately halfway between that proportion associated with chance and the proportion where all get the item right.

For an easiness index a true-false item would have a medium difficulty level of 75 (halfway between 50 and 100), while for a difficulty index a true-false item would have a medium difficulty level of 25 (halfway between 0 and 50).[15]

For most tests used in research Formula B (see footnote 15), which gives a direct measurement of difficulty, is better. Although it may seem plausible that varying levels of difficulty for the items would be best, research shows that the desirable characteristics to allow for discrimination are best met by providing tasks of medium-difficulty level. Very difficult items that are missed by nearly all test takers contribute little to the variance or scattering of the scores along the measurement scale. Very easy items that are answered correctly by nearly all test takers also contribute little to increase the variance and scattering of scores along the scale. To show differences among subjects the scores should be distributed along the scale, not grouped together at one point.

Tests used for such purposes as diagnosing, screening, and ascertaining characteristics, such as interests and the like, are not intended to be used for comparison purposes,

---

    15. The two formulas below are presently used to indicate how easy or difficult an item is. Formula A gives a percentage of those responding who answered correctly, thus an "easiness index." Formula B gives a percentage of those responding who answered incorrectly, thus a "difficulty index."

                        Formula A.   *Formula B.*

$$P = \frac{N_R}{N_T}(100) \qquad\qquad P = \frac{N_W}{N_T}(100)$$

P = difficulty level   P = difficulty level
N_R = no. getting item right N_W = no. getting item wrong
N_T = no. who tried the item N_T = no. who tried the item
(Gives an easiness index)   (Gives a difficulty index)

thus different approaches to item difficulty will be used. Be aware of the importance of giving attention to item difficulty when building tests for research—look to educational measurement books for specific types of tests.

The discrimination power of test items is, of course, especially important for tests used in research. If the instrument is to provide valid measurement and to identify differences, the test must accurately measure the trait being measured. Highly discriminating items provide test scores that vary widely and provide more valid measurement.

Preparing the Final Test Form

After the items have been written they must be pretested, analyzed, and rewritten for the final form of the test. Careful administration is important for pretesting since the final form of the item rests on decisions made from the pretest data. The last step is to develop the final test instrument that will be administered to the subjects. Decisions must be made about the kind of reproduction, directions, page format, item format, and art work.

Chapter 5, "Gathering, Analyzing and Using Data on Test Items," in *Educational Measurement*, is an excellent source of information on how to pretest and how to use the data for rewriting items.[16] Chapter 6, "Reproducing the Test," is an excellent source for the final decisions of developing the final form. Other educational measurement books will expand these and other tasks associated with test development for the test maker.

WHAT KIND OF DATA?

Once data are obtained they must be interpreted. Interpretation procedures rest on the type of scale that generated the data. Kerlinger says the scales in behavioral and educational research are "mostly nominal and ordinal . . ., though the probability is good that many scales and tests used in psychological and educational measurement approximate interval measurement well enough for practical purposes. . . ."[17] There is general agreement among researchers and statisticians that most of our data are not interval (as we would like them to be), but there is no general agreement as to what to do about it. In general Kerlinger's preceding statement is accepted and most persons use ordinal data as interval data with the assumption of equal intervals in scaling. To follow the rules rigidly would deprive the researcher of many analysis techniques that have proven to get satisfactory results. On the other hand, ordinal data which are used as interval data interpretations may be in error. The paradox is not easily resolved but those who oppose the use of the assumption of equal intervals apparently decrease in number each year.[18]

Nunnally agrees with Kerlinger when he says that those who oppose the use of the assumption of equal intervals "will have to admit that deviations from those assumptions usually have scant effects on the analyses which are performed."[19] He feels that

---

16. Robert L. Thorndike, ed., *Educational Measurement*, 2nd ed. (Washington, D.C.: American Council on Education, 1971), pp. 130-59.

17. Fred N. Kerlinger, *Foundations of Behavior Research*, 2nd ed. (New York: Holt, Rinehart and Winston, 1973), p. 438.

18. Paul Leslie Gardener, "Scales and Statistics," *Review of Educational Research* 45 (Winter 1975): 43-57.

19. Jum C. Nunnally, Jr., *Introduction to Psychological Measurement* (New York: McGraw-Hill, 1970), p. 21.

most psychological data except (1) nominal data and (2) data obtained by ranking are meaningfully expressable as interval data. He adds:

> The real issue does not concern whether or not to use the intervals on measurement scales in mathematical analysis — if they are there, why not use them? The issue is one of which calibration of intervals will prove more useful in the long run. Consequently, there is nothing wrong with performing mathematical operations that take seriously the intervals of measurement when investigating intelligence tests, personality tests, and other measurement methods employed in psychology. With the foregoing considerations in mind, it would be foolish of psychologists not to employ those powerful methods of mathematical and statistical analysis which assume interval scales, *unless the data were originally obtained from ranking methods.*[20] (Italics added.)

The condition of measurement in education seems to be: when characteristics are described in categories, measurement is *nominal;* when characteristics are described through assignment of ranks or ordered, measurement is *ordinal*; when the scale that assigns the numbers has equal intervals, measurement is *interval*; when equal intervals can be assumed for ordinal data without serious error, the data can be considered as *interval* for statistical treatment; and, of course, any measurement from absolute zero with equal units in the scale is *ratio* measurement. Discussion of statistical procedures requires consideration of the condition of measurement and will be very important to the selection of the statistical design.

SUMMARY

The basic problem in educational measurement is based in the question: how can a measurement scale be related to important behavioral factors of persons or attributes of objects and events? Measurement has been presented as a process of assigning a numerical description to observations according to a rule. In general educational measurement assigns the number through an indirect approach of looking for indications of a factor's influence, rather than measuring the factor directly as might be done in most physical measurement.

Four levels of measurement—nominal, ordinal, interval, and ratio—have been presented in an order of hierarchy, and each discussed as it relates to measurement practices. Measurement in educational research involves questions of: (1) What am I measuring? (2) How do I measure it? and (3) How do I know that I am measuring what is to be measured?

The characteristics of validity, reliability, and usability are important to consider when building or choosing a high quality measuring device for research purposes. Special attention has been given to test selection and test development, since tests are widely used to provide information for educational research. The use of a table of specifications can direct the test builder's efforts to construct a test that samples the behaviors and topics deemed important in the measurement. The tasks provided by the test instrument should be of medium difficulty to allow the discrimination needed for fitting the trait being measured to the measuring scale.

When choosing appropriate statistical procedures for data treatment the scale of measurement must be considered. Most data in the behavioral sciences—excepting

---

20. Ibid.

those obtained by nominal assignment or by ranking—can be treated as interval data.

It should be obvious to the reader that discussion of measurement and scaling methods in this chapter covers but a small part of the body of knowledge about educational measurement. Those individuals who devote full time or a portion of their time to research are constantly developing their skills in measurement to enhance valid research conclusions. In addition new and better methods are being developed, and as theoretical and practical knowledge grows researchers will be provided with new tools to attack important problems in education. The educational researcher must keep abreast of these new tools and utilize them to sophisticate the state of educational research.

BIBLIOGRAPHY

Bloom, Benjamin S., ed. *Taxonomy of Educational Objectives: Cognitive Domain.* New York: David McKay, 1956.

Borich, Gary D., ed. *Evaluating Educational Programs and Products.* Englewood Cliffs, N.J.: Educational Technology Publications, 1974.

Brownell, William A. "Psychological Considerations in the Learning and Teaching of Arithmetic." In *The Teaching of Arithmetic,* tenth yearbook. Washington, D.C.: The National Council for Teachers of Mathematics, 1935.

Bruner, Jerome, ed. *Learning About Learning.* Washington, D.C.: Government Printing Office, 1966. FS 5.212:12019.

Buros, Oscar K. *The Seventh Mental Measurements Yearbook.* Highland Park, N.J.: Gryphon Press, 1972.

Cliff, Norman. "Adverbs Multiply Adjectives." In *Statistics: A Guide to the Unknown,* edited by Judith M. Tanur et al. San Francisco: Holden-Day, 1972.

Cronbach, Lee J. "Test Validation." In *Educational Measurement,* edited by Robert L. Thorndike. Washington, D.C.: American Council on Education, 1971.

Ebel, Robert L., ed. *Encyclopedia of Educational Research.* New York: Macmillan Co., 1969.

Ebel, Robert L. *Essentials of Educational Measurement.* Englewood Cliffs, N.J.: Prentice-Hall, 1972.

Elkind, David. *Children and Adolescents. Interpretative Essays on Jean Piaget,* 2nd ed. New York: Oxford University Press, 1974.

Ferguson, George A. *Statistical Analysis in Psychology and Education.* New York: McGraw-Hill, 1971.

Gage, Nathaniel Lees, ed. *Handbook of Research on Teaching.* Chicago: Rand McNally, 1963.

Gardner, Paul Leslie. "Scales and Statistics." In *Review of Educational Research* 45 (Winter 1975): 43-57.

Guion, Robert M. et al. *Standards for Educational and Psychological Tests.* Washington, D.C.: American Psychological Association, 1974.

Hays, William L. *Statistics for Psychologists.* New York: Holt, Rinehart and Winston, 1963.

Hodges, J. L., and Lehmann, E. L. *Basic Concepts of Probability and Statistics.* San Francisco: Holden-Day, 1970.

Hopkins, Charles D. "The Emerging Elementary Mathematics Program." In *The Teachers College Journal* 36 (January 1965): 151-52.

_____. "Mathematics in the Elementary School—Why?" In *Educational Perspectives of the Elementary School,* edited by Ralph H. Jones and Benjamin F. Walker. Dubuque, Iowa: William C. Brown, 1969.

_____. *Describing Data Statistically.* Columbus, Ohio: Charles E. Merrill, 1974.

Jones, Lyle V. "The Nature of Measurement." In *Educational Measurement,* edited by Robert L. Thorndike. Washington, D.C.: American Council on Education, 1971.

Kagan, Jerome. "Motivational and Attitudinal Factors in Receptivity to Learning." In *Learning About Learning*, edited by Jerome Bruner. Washington, D.C.: Government Printing Office, 1966. FS5.212:12019.

Kerlinger, Fred N. *Foundations of Behavioral Research*. New York: Holt, Rinehart and Winston, 1973.

Krathwohl, D. R. et al. *Taxonomy of Educational Objectives: The Affective Domain*. New York: David McKay, 1964.

Light, Richard J. "Issues in the Analysis of Qualitative Data." In *Second Handbook of Research on Teaching*, edited by Robert M. W. Travers. Chicago: Rand McNally, 1973.

Neilson, N. P., and Arnett, Glenn W. *A Scorecard for Use in Evaluating Physical Education Programs in Elementary Schools*. Salt Lake City: University of Utah Press, 1955.

Nunnally, Jum C., Jr. *Introduction to Psychological Measurement*. New York: McGraw-Hill, 1970.

Page, Ellis B. "Accentuate the Negative." In *Educational Researcher* 4 (April 1975): 5.

Rand Corporation. *A Million Random Digits with 100,000 Normal Deviates*. New York: Free Press, 1955.

Schwab, Joseph J. "Problems, Topics, and Issues." In *Education and the Structure of Knowledge*, edited by Stanley Elam. Chicago: Rand McNally, 1964.

Siegel, Sidney. *Non-parametric Statistics for the Behavioral Sciences*. New York: McGraw-Hill, 1956.

Stanley, Julian C. "Reliability." In *Educational Measurement*, edited by Robert L. Thorndike. Washington, D.C.: American Council on Education, 1971.

Table of 105,000 Random Decimal Digits. Statement No. 4914, File No. 261-A-1. Washington, D.C.: Interstate Commerce Commission, May 1949.

Thorndike, Edward L. "The Effects of Practice in the Case of a Purely Intellectual Function." In *American Journal of Psychology* 19 (July 1908): 374-84.

Thorndike, Robert L., ed. *Educational Measurement*. 2nd ed. Washington, D.C.: American Council on Education, 1971.

Tilden, Freeman. *Interpreting Our Heritage*. Chapel Hill: University of North Carolina Press, 1957.

Travers, Robert M. W. *Second Handbook of Research on Teaching*. Chicago: Rand McNally, 1973.

Tukey, J. W. "The Future of Data Analysis," *The Annals of Mathematical Statistics* 33 (1963): 13-14.

Van Dalen, Diobald B. *Understanding Educational Research*. 3rd ed. New York: McGraw-Hill, 1973.

PART III

Inquiry Methodologies

The broad base of inquiry in education is reflected in the wide range of methods used to answer educational questions. Inquiry, part III, has been divided — admittedly arbitrarily and artificially — into three very general classes of inquiry: *Historical, Descriptive,* and *Experimental.* Questions based in the past require historiographical approaches to collect and interpret data. Questions that ask about current conditions require descriptive, sometimes called correlational, techniques. Questions involving manipulation of variables in laboratory-like conditions require experimental procedures.

In practice this division may or may not be clearly evident in the on-going activities of the researcher. Each inquiry class is to some degree based in the past. Each inquiry class is also related in some way to a current problem.

Historical inquiry is limited to data collected from the past. Descriptive research utilizes data from the past as background for a problem based in current conditions. However experimental research uses data from the past as background for a problem, data about the present for further guidance, and data created for the study. Because of the nature of each class to be progressively inclusive, the order of presentation will be: first, historical research; second, descriptive research; and third, experimental research. Keep in mind that events for historical and descriptive research would have happened even though the research had not taken place, while events for experimental studies have been created for the study and would not have happened without it.

8

Studies Based in Historical Inquiry

> *The dominant characteristics of our schools today are the product of a long history, and those who hope to alter those characteristics need to know their origins and enduring functions in order to act effectively.*
>
> —Stephen Ternstrom

What is historical research? Is there a discipline of historical research? These are questions without generally accepted answers, and debate continues as to whether scientific investigations based in the past can be conducted. For the discussion here the assumption is made that educational questions *can* be attacked through a scientific approach, although any structure of inquiry based on selection of information obtained from the past is necessarily limited. The limitations are based in the type of question that can be asked, the information that can be used, and, in turn, the validity of the answers derived. These limitations do not escape the eyes of historians and others who are involved in historical analysis as evidenced by a quotation of one who writes about educational concerns:

> No historian can entirely divorce the categories with which he approaches the contemporary world from those with which he studies the past. Our concerns shape the questions that we ask and, as a consequence, determine what we select from the virtually unlimited supply of "fact." That state of affairs remains submerged and implicit in most historical work.[1]

Since the researcher works in the context of present knowledge, special care must be taken to avoid "presentism," or the imposition of modern thought patterns on an earlier era, when making judgments about the past.

Other matters for consideration include the collection of needed evidence, its validation through historical criticism, and its interpretation into usable conclusions.

---

1. Michael B. Katz, *Class, Bureaucracy, and Schools* (New York: Praeger, 1971), p. xxv.

The key to valid historical research in education rests in the use of acceptable procedures to deduce the answers to educational questions from vast amounts of potential data.

The body of knowledge known as "History of Education" is now undergoing what Sloan refers to as "demythologizing."[2] He says that the writers of recent works on educational history have "repudiated the older tradition, exemplified by Cubberley, of writing the history of education as the progressive and triumphant evolution of the public school," and replaced it with "determination to probe underlying motives and interests, to relate ideas to social and institutional structures, and to consider how theory is transformed in practice." Although the purpose of educational research does not include writing the history of education, the new direction for historical writing is closely related to the products of historically directed educational research.

The goal of historical research in education is to clarify present day practices and problems by providing a historical knowledge base. The technological revolution and the resulting new conditions of the present have brought about challenge of institutions and, in turn, caused beliefs and values to be reconstructed. It seems that education has been especially susceptible to widespread discussions of practices and associated problems. Knowledge gained through historical inquiry can provide the foundation for better understanding of questions under current consideration, and can contribute to a better understanding of educational concerns.

This chapter is devoted to a study of acceptable procedures needed to provide valid conclusions to historically based questions. A recently reprinted and augmented edition of the classic *Guide to Research in Educational History* updates a valuable aid for anyone engaged in historical research in education.[3] The *Guide* and other references listed later should be consulted regularly by those persons engaged in answering questions about the past.

NATURE OF HISTORICAL RESEARCH

The historical method of research utilizes acceptable procedures to determine the accuracy of statements about the past, to establish relationships and, if possible, the direction of cause and effect. Good says:

> Viewed as research, history may be defined as an integrated narrative or description of past events or facts, written in the spirit of critical inquiry, to find the whole truth and report it.[4]

The process of educational research about the past generates facts and, in turn, conclusions using techniques to help interpret the remains of the past. It also evaluates and verifies statements of others since the historian cannot use direct observation or create his/her own data. For these reasons the historical researcher works under greater handicap than other researchers. He must use existing information in its present form. He has no control over what information remains for study, thus he cannot assume that something did not exist or take place simply because no record can be found.

---

2. Douglas Sloan, "Historiography and the History of Education," in *Review of Research in Education,* ed. Fred N. Kerlinger (Itasca, Ill.: F. E. Peacock, 1973), p. 246.
3. William W. Brickman, *Guide to Research in Educational History* (Norwood, Pa.: Norwood Editions, 1973).
4. Carter V. Good, *Essentials of Educational Research* (New York: Appleton-Century-Crofts, 1972), p. 148.

Studies Based in Historical Inquiry

Although the above limitations cause the historical researcher to function differently from researchers engaged in other types of inquiry procedures, historical research techniques take an approach to inquiry similar to the steps of the scientific method, with necessary adaptations for taking into consideration the uniqueness mentioned above. Historical inquiry begins when an indeterminate situation raises a question where the answer can be found in the past, continues as a critical search for truth, and ends with a defensible conclusion.

STEPS IN HISTORICAL RESEARCH

Historical inquiry uses a process similar to that of other scientific inquiry. The historical researcher's activities can be identified with the following steps:

1. Identification and isolation of the problem.
2. Development of a research hypothesis.
3. The accumulation of source materials, their classification and criticism, and determination of facts.
4. Organization of facts into results.
5. Formation of conclusions.
6. Synthesis and presentation in organized form.

There is some question about how the historian uses a research hypothesis (step 2 above). Some historical studies do not explicitly state research hypotheses before gathering source materials. Investigators often imply by their interests and the stated or implied questions that hypotheses are implicit, if not explicit, to the investigation. It seems that even narrative history designed to merely report facts is in some way based in implied hypotheses.

The use of the hypothesis in historical research has been attacked because the test of the hypothesis is in some ways different from the test used in experimental research and, therefore, less acceptable within the rules of science. Whether one accepts that the research hypothesis can be used in historical studies and whether or not the hypothesis statement is testable in principle is a matter of individual interpretation. A question also arises as to whether data gathered from the past can be used as empirical data. Hempel says:

> But if a statement or set of statements is not testable at least in principle, in other words, if it has no test implications at all, thus it cannot be significantly proposed or entertained as a scientific hypothesis or theory, for no conceivable empirical finding can then accord or conflict with it. If a study is to add to the knowledge of educational concerns then the hypothesis provides a way of bridging from data gathered to theory proposed.[5]

There does not seem to be a clear division between statements that are not testable and hypotheses that are testable. The probing of new areas, relating ideas to social and institutional structures, and consideration of how theory is transformed into practice causes educators to ask new questions about the past. The recent focus on investigating different kinds of questions based in the past broadens the scope and gives rise to questions about relationships among phenomena. The research hypothesis is likely to

---

5. Carl Hempel, "The Test of a Hypothesis: Its Logic and Its Force," *Philosophy of Educational Research,* ed. Henry S. Broudy et al. (New York: John Wiley, 1973), p. 364.

be used more and more in historical research as questions about motives, interests, and relationships of institutional structures are asked in historically based questions.

Identification and Isolation of the Problem

Bernard Bailyn's *Education in the Forming of American Society* "has been accorded a firm place in the historiographical canon as virtually the manifesto of a new movement."[6] Bailyn and other writers of recent articles about the impact of education on all social institutions have changed the range of historical inquiry from merely a study of formal pedagogy to include the investigation of more dynamic questions about relationships among ideas and their social environment. Important educational questions stem from the study of social issues which are based in the past. Historical research is especially useful to obtain knowledge about previously unexamined areas, to reexamine questions where the answers are not as definite as desired, and where present accounts are inadequate.

Historically based problems can be delimited or isolated along any of four dimensions: time; geographic area; person involved; and activities. The scope of the study may be expanded or reduced by control on one or more of these categories. When too broad a question is asked, the researcher is likely to be forced to decrease the scope. The tendency to ask questions which are too broad results in research studies being decreased in scope more often than increased. Unlike other research questions the historically based topic may need to be widened as the data collection takes place.

Since the researcher begins a historical study with only a general idea as to the scope, he or she proceeds differently in this particular area of inquiry. When looking for data about the question he may find that the answer is based in an area that was not apparent before starting, or that what appeared to relate to the problem was not efficacious. Nevertheless one should commence the project only after a clearly stated question has been formed to give the needed direction for the research.

The identification and delimitation of historical problems is exceedingly important in order to avoid an endless collection of data with no expressed use for the information. A vague idea about some not-too-clear task does little to provide direction for the study and procedures of inquiry. The question can be used to clarify the problem and, at the same time, be a sounding board for the activities of the researcher. If what he/she is doing relates to obtaining an answer to the proposed question, then it is pertinent to the study; if it does not help answer the question, then it is not appropriate methodology for the study. When all of the accumulated information of the past is opened to study, the importance of the above guidance to direct the researcher in his or her quest for answers cannot be overestimated.

Since all research studies have a historical base and the investigator for any study must place his or her study in context with the past as well as the present, every study is to some degree a historical study. The techniques of the historical researcher will serve the correlationalist who studies present conditions, as well as the experimenter who studies effects of manipulation of variables, especially in gathering data as background for a study and development of a research hypothesis. In this sense both the correlationalist and the experimenter are, in part, practicing historians.

---

6. Sloan, "Historiography and the History of Education," p. 240.

Studies Based in Historical Inquiry

The Hypothesis

A certain amount of knowledge is needed to develop a question that is specific enough for research purposes. Given more knowledge the investigator can develop his/her hypothesis as a proposed answer to the question which is being asked. Since there is no way to test the historical hypothesis directly, the answer to the question must be based on facts as they are collected for the study. For these reasons some historians prefer to work without a hypothesis. For the same reasons, what are conclusions in some historical studies take the form of hypothesis in other types of research. When the researcher has some knowledge to provide a historical context for a proposed answer to the question being studied, a hypothesis should be developed. The value of the historical hypothesis rests in its faculty to provide something to refute or support, and its contribution makes the drawing of conclusions more objective. For these reasons the use of the historical research hypothesis is to be encouraged. For further discussion of the historical hypothesis see Good.[7]

Accumulation of Source Materials

All of the information recorded in the past plus everything else which remains of the past is available for historical research. The task of the historical researcher is to gather appropriate information, place it in the context of the historical period under study, and interpret its relationship to the logically conceived hypothesis in regard to support of the hypothesis. Knowing where to look is important to the study of the past. The type of question that has been asked helps the researcher decide where he or she might find data that will contribute to solving the problem. A question based on prayer in public schools might utilize the *Encyclopaedia of Religion and Ethics* as an overview of the problem area, while a question in a closely related area of moral education would need sources of L. Kohlberg's writings, such as *Religion and Public Education,* and their bibliographies. Another question may send the researcher to try one of the sources listed below. A classification of sources for data to be used in historical research follows:

1. Physical remains: historic sites, roads, aqueducts, pyramids, fortifications, buildings ruined or whole, furniture, human remains, clothing, food, utensils, pottery, implements, weapons, machinery, industrial processes, and fine arts and museum pieces of many kinds.
2. Orally transmitted material (sometimes in writing), such as folklore, legends, ballads, tales, anecdotes, sages, traditions, customs, manners, burials, ceremonials, social institutions, and language.
3. More elementary and durable kinds of representative or artistic materials, not written in the ordinary sense, such as inscriptions baked upon clay, chiseled stones, monuments, stamped coins, woven tapestries, vases, scenic or portrait sculptures, historical paintings, and portraits.
4. Hand-written materials (sometimes in print), including papyri, bricks bearing cuneiform writing, vellum or parchment manuscripts, and such more recent documents as chronicles, annals, biographies, memoirs, diaries, and genealogies.
5. Printed books, papers, and literature.

---

7. Good, *Essentials of Educational Research,* pp. 98-102.

6. Motion-picture film, microfilm, and recordings, including radio and television.
7. Personal observation (by the writer or by people whom he interviews).[8]

For educational studies, school related records, documents, buildings, furniture, equipment, textbooks, examinations, student work, and oral reports of school officials, students, and parents first come to mind as likely sources of information. Historical evidence from other areas is needed for studies involving social issues and institutional structures and must be considered in identification of possible sources. Although all possible sources cannot be listed here, professional journals and newspapers should be included in most investigations of questions about education based in the past. Each study taxes the creativeness of the researcher to come up with every possible source of data.

The major task of the historian is to obtain the best information available from the several sources listed in the above classification. A further classification of historical sources sorts the data into two major categories — *documents* and *relics* — according to whether the source was created for the expressed purpose of making a record, or whether it is merely an artifact. Examples of documents of record are: The Congressional Record; minutes of meetings; university registrar files; school attendance and grade records; diaries; memoirs; laws; charters; maps; and such.

Relics are those physical objects which have been preserved, either by plan or by happenstance, but were not created to transmit deliberately a record for future consultation. Examples of relics are furniture, implements, utensils, art objects, portraits, literature, buildings, roads, clothing, and so on.

Each of these sources is valuable to the researcher in different ways: the documents for their objectivity and directness in reporting and the relics for their transmission of information in interpretation. Documents present data directly in a straightforward manner that requires no interpretation. Relics have given scientists an opportunity to reconstruct past civilizations with accuracy although many people of the past left no documents. For example, the daily activities of inhabitants can be reconstructed through the utensils they used to obtain and prepare food. Also games of skill indicate something about the amount of leisure time. Other glimpses into early cultures are provided by what they left in the way of relics.

Each of the sources is limited in some ways. A record may be in error because the record was deliberately falsified or an event which occurred was incorrectly interpreted by the recorder. Documentary evidence about an event of the past may be recorded in the impressions of an eyewitness, but the recorder may knowingly or unknowingly record incorrectly. Documents are further limited by the change in meanings of words over a long span of time.

The use of relics is limited since their meaning must be interpreted by the investigator. Recently created objects may be incorrectly accepted as relics of the past and erroneously used as evidence. Newly created objects of art, engravings of famous figures, and other objects have been passed as originals and later discovered to be products of modern creation.

Errors in recording frauds, hoaxes, and forgeries have been perpetrated for many years. Motives of material gain, enhancement of the state or church, and the practical joke contribute to the problems of dealing with the past. A stone figure, The Cardiff Giant, was accepted by experts in several fields and validated as a fossilized figure of

---

8. Good, *Essentials of Educational Research,* p. 155.

an ancient giant, but was later disclosed by a reporter as a well planned hoax to make money from its display to the public.

A twenty-year running account of the activities of a Bill Edwards, which took him from college graduation to the grave, was uncovered as a practical joke. The following newspaper account gives the details:

21-Year Hoax Revealed by Davidson Grads

DAVIDSON, N.C. (AP)—Bill Edwards, whose name and image are enshrined in a memorial at Davidson College, will be dropped from the alumni rolls of his alma mater. It seems he never existed.

The storied young bachelor, whose exploits appeared for a decade in the college alumni bulletin, was a hoax perpetuated by members of the class of 1953.

Over the years, the alumni bulletin reported Edwards as a "real estate pioneer" at Metuchen, N.J., and a researcher on "the zero gravity platform" in Singapore.

In 1973, it was reported that he had died mysteriously while investigating a drug ring operating between Hong Kong and Metuchen.

Classmates contributed some $20,000 to the college's new library and a bronze plaque and photo of Edwards were mounted on the memorial bookdrop, which was dedicated last month.

On Monday, members of the class said the reports were arranged from Metuchen by a classmate who lived there. The photo was of a former Navy buddy of one of the hoaxers.[9]

Carefully prepared records that have been checked, e.g., minutes of meetings, after being submitted by the recorder for acceptance are in most cases easily validated for evidence. After a long time lapse, other recordings, e.g., memoirs or events, are many times more difficult to validate.

It has been pointed out by experts in the areas of anthropology and historiography that many times people may reveal more valid evidence through physical objects than through documents. A judgment of gathered facts serves as an evaluation of the worth of the information for forming conclusions for inquiry. The next three sections give direction to classifying and validating evidence for basing conclusions.

Determination of Facts

The use of information as fact depends on the source of the information and how well it withstands a test of its authenticity and trustworthiness. The best evidence about the past is provided by *primary* sources: (1) the relics that remain of the past; (2) documents; and (3) reports of eye-witnesses to happenings of the past. Also useful to the historian are *secondary* sources: accounts of events that were not actually experienced by the one reporting. Primary sources are considered as original or underived. The records or relics that remain have only the observer or eye witness coming between the information and the user of the information (the historian). A secondary source is a derived source in that the mind of a nonobserver has intervened between the information in its original form and the user of the information (the historian). If a newspaper reporter attends a city council meeting and writes a report of the meeting in an article, the article is a primary source. If he interviews those who participated

---

9. *Indianapolis Star*, November 6, 1974, p. 65, col. 4. Reprinted by permission of the *Indianapolis Star* and the Associated Press.

in the meeting and writes an article, the article is a secondary source since the information is interpreted and reported from the mind of a nonobserver.

The same relic may be a primary source for one investigator and a secondary source for another investigator with a different question. Material in students' textbooks would be classed as secondary evidence for most studies. The researcher who asks the question, "What topics were covered in textbooks written for the fourth-grade science classes between the years 1960 and 1965?" will use the material in fourth-grade science texts as primary material. The classification of the data as primary or secondary depends on:

1. how the record was made, and/or
2. how the information is being used.

It becomes important for the researcher to look closely at both aspects as he or she classifies data as primary or secondary, remembering that what might be secondary for one study, may be primary for another study. Sometimes there is no way to determine which parts of a source are primary and which are secondary.

Both primary and secondary sources are valuable for the historical researcher — primary sources because of their directness and nature of being underived, and secondary sources because of their contribution when primary sources are not available. Primary sources always carry more weight than secondary sources because of their directness and significance as authentic accountings.

A necessary part of the process of historical research is the subjection of the material to *criticism*. Criticism is a scientific investigation of collected information in regard to matters of origin and validity. Criticism is conducted to detect unintentional errors or any deliberate falsification in order to establish the validity of the data. The historian must determine (1) the authenticity and (2) the credibility of his information. Without the test of criticism of the data, the hypothesis cannot be tested, and, in turn, the conclusions have little basis for contribution to a body of knowledge. The tests of criticism use both external and internal criticism.

External criticism concerns the authenticity of the information — is it genuine? The focus of external criticism is *not* on the meaning attached to the evidence, but rather with establishing why, where, when, how, and/or by whom the document or relic was created.

Internal criticism concerns the meaning and trustworthiness of evidence. What meaning can be attached to the isolated facts? The focus of internal criticism is *not* on the object or evidence itself but on the meaning attached to it. After the process of external criticism has established the authenticity of information, the credibility of the information is checked by internal criticism of the contents. Together the two types of criticism provide a technique to establish the degree of validity to be attached to each bit of data used in a study. A historian remains skeptical of evidence until he/she has applied criticism to the information, and is satisfied that it is usable data. Although the researcher can never have complete confidence in the data, those data which are deemed to be factual are accepted for use. Some techniques used to establish validity of the data are discussed next.

Data Validation Techniques

Validation for physical characteristics of documents and relics, whether print or nonprint, is aided by the use of many tests. Very old artifacts can be tested for age by carbon dating, and physical characteristics of objects can be compared to what is known about similar objects from the same time and region. The type of ink, age and composition of the paper, and watermarks can be used to investigate the authenticity of documents and other printed matter. Other techniques using photography, ultraviolet rays, fluoroscopes, and such are also available for use in external criticism. These are used essentially to detect fraud or to establish parameters of time and physical makeup of the evidence. In addition to physical authentication the historian must give attention to questions such as:

1. Did personal gain, interest, practical joke, or pride cause the creation of the object?
2. Did the report closely follow the event?
3. Does the information include anything that could not have been known at that time?
4. Does it include everything that a person should know at that time?
5. Has anything been lost in translation?
6. Is this evidence typical of the author and of the time period?

After the process of external criticism has established the authenticity of the information, it becomes necessary to analyze the documents or remains as to their meaning and then to establish their meaning, accuracy, and trustworthiness. Even genuine information from formally recorded records must be checked for flaws, errors it might contain, and mistakes of fact, since even competent recorders are fallible. Tests of credibility are applied to determine actual meanings, losses through translation, contamination of statements by writer bias, phobias, illogical deduction, and/or inaccuracies in reporting. The question of credibility involves any aspect which would stand in the way of true reporting of an event or any involvement with outright hoax, fraud, or forgery. A list of "guiding principles" about historical methods gives direction for external and internal criticism used to establish authenticity and credibility:

> Since neither antiquity, nor memory, nor written characters are truly incorruptible witnesses, historians must approach all of them with critical doubt. Certain general principles, to be observed in reading and judging sources, may be briefly put: (1) do not read into earlier documents the conceptions of later times; (2) do not judge an author ignorant of certain events, necessarily, because he fails to mention them (the argument ex silentio), or that they did not occur, for the same reason; (3) underestimating a source is no less an error than overestimating it in the same degree, and there is no more virtue in placing an event too late than in dating it too early by the same number of years or centuries; (4) a single true source may establish the existence of an idea, but other direct, competent, independent witnesses are required to prove the reality of events or objective facts; (5) identical errors prove the dependence of sources on each other, or a common source; (6) if witnesses contradict each other on a certain point, one or the other may be true, but both may be in error; (7) direct, competent, independent witnesses who report the same central fact and also many peripheral matters in a casual way may be accepted for the points of their agreement; (8) official testimony, oral or written, must be compared with unofficial testimony whenever possible, for neither one nor the other is alone sufficient; (9) a document may provide competent and dependable evidence on certain points, yet carry no weight in respect to others it mentions.[10]

Van Dalen lists seventeen questions which historians use to check validity externally, and fourteen questions to check validity internally, that extend the principles listed

---

10. Thomas Woody, "Of History and Its Methods," *Journal of Experimental Education* 15 (March 1947): 170.

above.[11] When writing about "problems of evidence that center on the issue of validity" Beach said:

> Most of them fall within one of two domains: given specified ideas or events, (1) how representative were they of larger groups of people or series of events and (2) what impact did they have, if any, upon subsequent human thought or behavior? The first is a question of correlation, the second a question of cause.[12]

Verification can be obtained by one of the several ways, but the researcher must determine what is *fact*. A rule of thumb used to guide historical research is to accept information in documents as fact whenever there is no reason to suspect inaccuracy or fraud. Even careful verification is no guarantee of the truthfulness of the information, but the historical researcher feels more confident with the use of these accepted procedures of historical research than with uncritical acceptance of any evidence in explaining the past.

Validation of evidence through criticism becomes more and more important as historical research is asked to do more than provide a narrative of past events. The narrative of history requires merely location and verification of data. Historical research methods, which primarily focus on the drawing of conclusions, require the highest level of sophistication of techniques for validating information gathered about the past to assure valid conclusions. The output of validation procedures are *facts*. A fact as used in research is any bit of information that can be used in an investigation. A scientist does not claim that a fact he used will remain a fact to eternity, and revision may be necessary given new or better information. However for the present he/she has data which have been verified as usable in the present study.

Organization of Facts into Results

The several facts that have been validated for a study must be placed into some logical arrangement to allow for the collective meaning to be ascertained. This component of the process allows the researcher to objectively form the results of the study.

The notes and established facts should already be on bibliography cards—only one fact per card. The facts are now ready to be fit into some organizational framework. They could conceivably be ordered in a time sequence from early to present. They could be organized by topics, geographic location, or some other logical division. The possible relationship being investigated might provide a natural division by the variables of concern. If the major emphasis of the study is to identify cause and effect, the division could be made between the presumed cause variable and the criterion (dependent) variable.

After the logical arrangement has been made the cards will be used in two ways. First the interpretation of the collective meaning will be made, and second the final writing will be developed from the cards.

Interpretation of Facts

Since facts by themselves have little meaning, after they are determined and organized, they must be interpreted. The interrelationships of all of the gathered facts must be

---

11. Deobold B. Van Dalen, Ph.D., *Understanding Educational Research*, 3rd ed. (New York: McGraw-Hill, 1973), pp. 167-70.

12. Mark Beach, "History of Education," *Review of Educational Research* 34 (December 1969):566.

viewed globally to determine their significance to derivation of an answer to the research question. The interpretation of the facts is the *analysis of the data*. The data for historical studies may be analyzed in one of two ways:
1. If the research hypothesis is stated, then the analysis is a study of the facts in regard to how they support or refute the hypothesis. The interpretation tests the tenability of the research hypothesis.
2. If a research hypothesis is not used, the analysis takes the form of hypothesis development, and the output of the study is a hypothesis which serves as a conclusion.

Testing the tenable position of the historical research hypothesis consists of weighing the supporting evidence against the refuting evidence. The final decision is that the evidence either does or does not support the research hypothesis. If a research hypothesis is not used, the interpretation or analysis of evidence gathered about the question leads to early speculation about the overall meaning of the data first gathered. As more data are accumulated the early speculation evolves into a tentative hypothesis. The researcher continues to form generalizations and to sophisticate his or her conjectures by testing the tentative hypothesis against consistency and agreement with the facts. The hypothesis developed from the investigation serves as the conclusion for the study.

The task in either of the above approaches is one of taking obtained information about the past and determining its significance by interpretation to find the whole truth. In each case the hypothesis is intended to order the bits of information into a meaningful statement which serves as an acceptable answer to the posed question. Since the historian (or any researcher) works with less than all of the data, his/her analysis of the data must be, at best, tentative, and given more information he may need to revise the concluding hypothesis. Since the stopping point for any historical research is the researcher's decision, the conclusions for one study might provide a starting point for another study.

The interpretations drawn from the evidence are based on *what* happened in the past but, more importantly, also include *why* and *how* it happened. The historian must deal with the representativeness of his limited data in interpreting ideas and events—are they unique or are they representative? A popular test for representativeness of an *idea* is the measure of consumer receptivity to an idea. An idea is not in itself noteworthy without the test of how it was accepted and/or used by contemporaries. The importance of the contribution of an idea is best tested by how much the idea influenced history over a time span, and this, in turn, measures its representativeness. The question of whether *events* are unique or representative is not easily resolved and is based in one's concept of the nature of historical phenomena. If each sequence of events is seen as unique, then representativeness will be difficult to claim, and any sequence of events will be viewed as being built on that unique set of circumstances. If historical phenomena are viewed as being continuously correlated, the establishment of relationships becomes more realistic.

To show a causal relationship the researcher, in addition to showing a relationship, must establish its direction through cause-effect, antecedent-consequence implication of evidence. This is the most difficult task for the historian, and a major reason why the research hypothesis is used as a causal statement to be tested. *If-then* hypotheses are to be encouraged as a way to establish direction of cause and effect. In the *if-then* hypothesis statement, the independent variable is the presumed cause and the dependent variable the presumed effect. The task of historical inquiry is to establish cause through a direct relationship among the variables under study. The historian has the same problem as investigators in other areas—an event is usually the function of many contributing factors and, for this reason, a study of cause is exceedingly complex. For a listing of specific procedures to assist interpretation, the reader is directed to sixteen points presented in *Understanding Educational Research*.[13]

Research Conclusions

The outputs of the analysis of the facts are the research study's conclusions. The conclusions for most historical research are presented, for acceptance by the reader, on the basis of faith in the researcher's knowledge. Is this different from any other type of research procedure? No, not in essence, only in degree. Even the most convincing and well written report of an experimental study can be built on fictitious data. The type of research guarantees nothing in the way of the validity of a study—historical research is possibly more exposed to error because of the problems that have been discussed. It is the author's opinion that there is no reason to believe that historians have a larger share of swindlers than any other group, and that, with good procedures, they can indeed draw scientific conclusions from their data. If the historian can (1) avoid presentism, (2) make clear and plausible interpretations of appropriate evidence, (3) span the knowledge with established relationships, (4) show cause-effect, and (5) show his/her grasp of the field through his report of the study, then he is established in the scientific community.

Conclusions are drawn to show the reader what the study has revealed. The conclusion goes beyond the simple statement of support or lack of support of the hypothesis. Since the final products of scientific inquiry are the laws and generalizations which form the framework that unifies relationships established in isolation, the conclusion should be a generalization tied to theory within the context of the accepted relevant body of knowledge about educational concern.

Synthesis and Presentation in Organized Form

The overall chain of reasoning of the many separate but related parts of the process must be synthesized and presented in a logical argument supported by validated facts. Most writers find that an integrated outline fosters the needed continuity.

The actual construction of the narrative develops the synthesis. The rough draft will expand the outline, paragraph by paragraph, into the final presentation. The number of rewritings will vary among writers. Some writers attempt a final writing the first time through, but few succeed. A more realistic view of the task would probably reveal several rewritings and revisions.

To achieve clarity and naturalness in the synthesis and its presentation, the writer is well advised to write paragraphs and/or sections after reading contributing material but not taking narrative directly from cards. After the first draft, points which have been missed can be inserted and any errors of fact can be corrected in rewritings. Do not be discouraged by the need to rewrite and revise material—all writers encounter the same experience as they build their narrative.

HISTORICAL WRITING

The historical novel is created within the mind of someone who has excellent knowledge about a particular time period and particular geographic location. Historical

---

13. Van Dalen, *Understanding Educational Research,* pp. 177-78.

Studies Based in Historical Inquiry

writing can, on the other hand, be merely an objective reporting of what has happened. Somewhere between these two extremes is the writing of historical research. The writer of the historical novel is expected to fill in any gaps in his or her knowledge and to create anything that the story needs, using historical knowledge as a guide. No reader expects that every reported happening actually occurred, or that the characters actually existed. Historical writing at the other extreme requires that the reporting be only at the highest degree of confidence, and stated without interpretation.

The writer of historical research must walk the line between writing a novel and writing a historical narrative. He/she must deal only in established facts but, at the same time, must build continuity through insight. He must also establish relationships, try to identify causes, and be able to build relationships with data that lack the conclusiveness that the researcher would like without distorting the truth. Producing a report of historical research requires the highest level of writing expertise.

The research hypothesis can give direction to what is relevant to the study. It also furnishes a basis for analysis and for conclusions, provides an agent for the synthesis that follows the criticism and validation of the evidence, and serves as a vehicle to build continuity into the writing. Documentation, decisions about the arrangement of topics, the relative importance of the facts, and the interpretation can be fit into the general model for a scientific approach to inquiry, as presented earlier.

The organization of the material may be by a time line (chronological), by regions (geographical), or by subject (topical). As Good states:

> A topical or thematic grouping of historical materials has been recommended as a functional organization to meet the criticism that older histories of education and courses in this field were a mass of comparatively unrelated facts, with little consideration of the pertinent social forces and the activities and problems of schools and professional workers.[14]

How the writer develops the logical chain of reasoning from the raw data is more of an art than a science. It is enough to say here that it should be presented in an effective style utilizing literary skills to build a report which is accurate and maintaining interest without damaging the truth. The personality of the writer will be reflected in his or her method of presentation of a logical conclusion to the question. The narrative will include (1) a well defined question, (2) a review of the literature as background, (3) the research hypothesis, (4) methodology for testing the hypothesis, (5) presentation of the evidence, (6) results, and (7) conclusions and implications. Further help in writing historical research will be found in *The Modern Researcher*.[15]

TOOLS FOR HISTORICAL RESEARCH

Since the historian deals with documents and relics, the world is his or her workshop. His tools will include anything which will uncover evidence, ranging from shovels and bulldozers to the latest computer. Unlike other researchers the historian must be prepared to go where the evidence is rather than choose where to gather it or how to create it. With modern transportation the historian's increased mobility provides added opportunity to gather needed evidence from both documents and relics. The historical

---

14. Good, *Essentials of Educational Research*, p. 177.
15. Jacques Barzun and Henry F. Graff, *The Modern Researcher* (New York: Harcourt, Brace and World, 1970), Part 3, "Writing," pp. 255–378.

researcher has all of the tools of archaeology available to him for physically uncovering evidence, and can use them in much the same way that they are used by archaeologists. However most of the work of the historical researcher in education is conducted by using other aids, like libraries, bibliographies, and school-related records.

The Library

To classify a library as an aid may seem strange, but the answer to many questions asked about education requires a synthesis of knowledge already recorded in bits and pieces. Unless needed information is in school records the evidence is likely to be found in the library. Since the use of the library as an aid is presented later as a separate topic (chapter 12), it will suffice for now to say that skill development for library work is most important for the historical researcher as he/she works through the catalogues, indexes, and reference shelves toward the information that is needed.

Guides and Handbooks

The American Historical Association's *Guide to Historical Literature* is an excellent starting point for any historically based study.[16] The *Guide* gives bibliographical entries for selected historical literature to the date of its printing. Items from 1957 to 1960 are not systematically covered, but considerable coverage is given. The table of contents lists: Part I, "Introduction and General History"; Part II, "Historical Beginnings"; Parts III through VIII, "Geographic Areas"; and Part IX, "The World in Recent Times." Examples of coverage: the *Guide* gives sixty-four entries for the topic "The Doctrine and Practice of Historiography," and the index covers 112 pages. The *Guide* is not specific to education but will be a valuable tool to use early in an investigation. Other more specific guides are available and listed in the index of *The Historian's Handbook—A Descriptive Guide to Reference Works*.[17] This is an invaluable tool for "both students and scholars of the social sciences." The contents pages read like *a list of specific tools* available for the historian to use. The *Handbook* serves as a source for sources. Its main headings are:

1. The Library and its Catalog
2. National Library Catalogs and National and Trade Bibliographies
3. Guides, Manuals, and Bibliographies of History
4. Encyclopedias and Dictionaries
5. Almanacs, Yearbooks, Statistical Handbooks, and Current Surveys
6. Serials and Newspapers
7. Geographical Aids
8. Biographical Materials
9. Primary Sources and Dissertations
10. Legal Sources
11. Government Publications

Census Data and Depositories

Recent census information covers wide areas and is particularly valuable when quantification can be used in data analysis. Breakdown on many factors provides data that

---

16. American Historical Association, *Guide to Historical Literature* (New York: Macmillan Co., 1961).

17. Helen J. Poulton, *The Historian's Handbook — A Descriptive Guide to Reference Works* (Norman: University of Oklahoma Press, 1972).

are otherwise impossible to obtain for one study. The United States Census Bureau conducts a census on the population of the United States each decade. *The Statistical Abstract of the United States* reports a summary of statistics annually to supplement the ten-year report.

Depositories are particularly good sources of facts because the collection is usually kept as a "collection of record." *Research in Archives: The Use of Unpublished Primary Sources*[18] is a reliable guide dealing with American archives and provides a way into materials available in archives and other special collections not generally catalogued. For guides to manuscripts and archives of special kinds of materials see *The Historian's Handbook.*[19]

An example of special collections which are available is the extensive collection of more than 4,500 dictionaries that is a part of the Rare Books Department at the Indiana State University Library. The Cordell Collection of Dictionaries represents the entire history of Western Lexicography, and continued efforts of acquisition add to its numbers yearly. Other equally complete collections are available for other special areas and can be located through the above sources.

A number of libraries throughout the United States have been named as depositories for government publications. Government publications cover almost every field and are especially valuable for educational research. An aid to finding material in these publications has been prepared and is kept current by revisions.[20] A guide to serials and periodicals published by the federal government includes extensive listings for education.[21]

Computers

From the time that Herman Hollerith invented machine-punched cards and Frederick Jackson Turner used the data generated by their use in the 1890 census, historians have seen the need for new methods to tabulate not only quantitative data but qualitative information such as occupation, years of formal education, and other demographic features.[22] Each new advance in data processing gave additional encouragement to the possibility of (1) reducing the drudgery associated with gathering evidence for historical studies and (2) assuming the task of interpreting data.

Following World War II the "mechanical brain" that was being developed seemed especially adaptable to the type of research done by historians. The "brain" evolved into what is now called a computer. Several generations and families of computers are now history. A study of their contribution to historical research at this time falls mainly in the area of reducing human drudgery by doing those things that computers do best—the routine menial tasks. They have not evolved to the level where they can take over thought processes needed for interpretation, but that does not deny it as a possibility in the future.

---

18. Phillip C. Brooks, *Research in Archives: The Use of Unpublished Primary Sources* (Chicago: University of Chicago Press, 1969).

19. Poulton, *The Historian's Handbook,* pp. 177-91.

20. Laurence F. Schmeckebier and Roy B. Eastin, *Government Publications and Their Use* (Washington: Brookings Institution, 1969).

21. John L. Androit, *Guide to U.S. Government Serials & Periodicals* (McLean, Virginia: Documents Index, Box 195, 1969).

22. Arthur H. Moehlman et al., *A Guide to Computer-Assisted Historical Research in American Education* (Austin: University of Texas Press, 1969), p. 7.

That the computer is making a contribution is evidenced by the increasing size of the volumes of the journal, *Computers and the Humanities*. Current issues of that journal and *Computer Studies in the Humanities and Verbal Behavior* will bring the reading about the impact of computers on history up-to-date as current articles survey computer use in the special areas.[23] The present status of the computer's popularity is difficult to ascertain because the enthusiasm of historians varies—the swing is from the claim that computers will solve all (or nearly all) of the problems to the claim that they will contribute little (if anything) to solving problems based on history. There seem to be fewer and fewer of the latter assertions as time moves on.

Computer technology has advanced indexing, building of checklists, bibliographology, library cataloging, and other techniques used to organize bare facts. Such assistance has released the historian from tasks of drudgery and given him more time to think. In this way the computer *has* contributed to the aspect of thinking. Presently a combination of machine and humans, each doing what it does best, seems the best way to utilize the strengths of each to answer questions based in the past and, thus, to add to present knowledge.

The major contribution of the computer to historical research is the vast storage available through the random-access disk files. If the data are in computerized files, then the files allow the researcher, who is accustomed to spending many long hours searching bibliographies and other listings of sources, rapid retrieval of information needed for an investigation. Materials filed in Educational Resources Information Centers (ERIC) are carefully catalogued for a manual search, but when several different subject headings (descriptors) are involved the manual search can be impractical. Progress can then be expedited by a computer search of the entire ERIC files. More than 100 information services are available to search ERIC holdings, *Abstracts of Instructional Materials in Vocational and Technical Education, Psychological Abstracts,* and others. A list of currently available information services can be obtained by writing to ERIC, National Institute of Education, Washington, D.C. 20208.

How computer storage and retrieval systems can be developed and used has been recorded by Professor Arthur H. Moehlman and his colleagues, who use an illustration of the legislative activities bearing on education in Texas to explain the model. In 1969 the authors saw the need for three "essential aids to research in American educational history":

1. *A Guide to Computer-Assisted Historical Research in American Education* with special computer-associated capabilities in a Remote File Management System (RFMS) as delineated in the present volume.
2. *A Guide to American Educational History* should provide a chronological and structural bibliographical guide to the various categories of education and should also be linked into the vast bank of computer-stored and retrievable information of FRMS level as a data bank.
3. *Guides to Source Materials and Bibliographies for State Educational Systems*, are essential to definitive, substantive research in the history of American education. These guides may well be based on the computer-assisted research procedures developed

---

23. See Charles Tilly, "Computers in Historical Analysis," *Computers and the Humanities* 7 (September-November 1973): 323-35; and Robert Whallon, Jr., "The Computer in Archaeology: A Critical Survey," *Computers and the Humanities* 7 (September 1972): 29-45.

in the *Guide* just completed with its functional hierarchical classification system from the Morphology of Categories.[24]

Since the publication of Moehlman's *Guide* advancements have been made in coordinating efforts to computerize data. For example, Educational Information Networks (EDUCOM) is designing and implementing an international computer network which has the purpose of sharing many educational computer resources. By learning how to use the computer services the researcher who studies the past can avoid much of the drudgery and frustration of manual searches and free himself for the more important aspects of analysis and interpretation. As an aid to the researcher:

> The computer can be an [*sic*] competent servant of the researchers, but maximum use of its capabilities depends upon the researcher's accuracy, academic background, and above all of *what they ask*, the way in which the "data base" is structured, and its relative completeness and detail. The computer may be regarded as a "black box" which will enable the historian to investigate great masses of data much more rapidly than by conventional means.[25]

Regardless of advancements in computer technology the above statement will probably hold for some time in historically based educational research. More creative uses of the computer in historical research go beyond decreasing drudgery of hand procedures and

> ... a few investigators are demanding more of the computer: building complex files with extensive cross-referencing, testing complex mathematical models against large bodies of data, stimulating social processes in order to rule out assumptions which produce implausible results, performing content analyses of texts.[26]

Others are finding means of validating data through linguistic analysis, literary analysis, principal component analysis, and such.

SUMMARY

Historical research is the branch of the scientific method that looks to the past to answer questions. Although the question of scientific status is attached to historical inquiry it has been assumed that scientific approaches to historical inquiry meet the criteria of scientific status. The most scientific decision which has been made (whatever it was) was built from a framework of knowledge available at the time of the decision. Historical research using available data and accepted principles and practices makes decisions scientifically. All decisions, historically based or not, are open to alteration given more information, whether the decision is in the physical sciences, behavioral sciences, or the humanities. Differing degrees of confidence are attached to decisions in all sciences.

The footsteps of historical research have followed those of the general scientific method with some differences evident in special problems dealing with collecting,

---

24. Moehlman et al., *Guide to Computer-Assisted Historical Research,* p. 2.
25. Ibid., p. 74.
26. Tilly, "Computers in Historical Analysis," p. 334.

criticizing, and interpreting data and forming the conclusions. The importance of primary materials has been pointed up, and historical criticism of evidence has been discussed as being external criticism, dealing with authenticity, and internal criticism, dealing with credibility. From the validated evidence the researcher must draw his/her conclusions through interpretation and then write the findings in a scholarly narrative.

The major tool of historical research has been found to be the library, with other sources of public school records and relics associated with education also contributing evidence. Special tools for historical research are guides, handbooks, census data, reports, depositories, and the computer. These tools all contribute to finding available evidence, with the computer supplying ways to locate and interpret data with new and creative procedures.

9

Descriptive Studies for Inquiry

> *A survey of present conditions is an essential guide to one's thinking, whether in evaluating the course he is now following, or in embarking on a new venture. For any purpose, the starting point is important.*
> —Carter V. Good and Douglas E. Scates

Historical studies are designed to answer questions based on the past, and certain procedures were discussed in chapter 8 to aid in historical inquiry. Questions that concern present conditions require different techniques to arrive at answers. These techniques are designed to describe existing conditions, and the term *descriptive research* is generally used to classify procedures used to generate knowledge by studying conditions as they currently exist.

The term descriptive research has been chosen to refer to this section only after much thought was given to other possible titles. The label is not wholly appropriate because this type of research does much more than describe. Writers point out that all research is involved in describing—historical research describes the past, experimental research describes what has happened to certain variables given certain manipulation of other variables, and descriptive research explains the present through description of what now exists.

All educational questions which ask about the state or condition of what now exists require the strategy of description. Two basic uses are made of description of the present: one is to assist administrators and other education personnel in making decisions within the limited scope of a politically defined school geographic area, while the other generates generalizable knowledge and adds to the body of knowledge about educational concerns. A distinction is made here to clarify practices.

The study of descriptive research as a process to create new generalizable knowledge places the study of conditions within a geographically limited region in a special category. A gathering of information about school conditions for administrative uses falls in the class of a *status study*. Since status studies are important in making valid

Inquiry Methodologies

decisions a short section is devoted to it. An understanding of the status study should also help clarify the role of descriptive research.

THE STATUS STUDY

Most researchers study existing conditions as a preliminary step into the investigation of questions that they want to answer. Each researcher establishes the current status of the field under study, to the degree that information is available to him or her. A study that *terminates* with a reporting of the status of current conditions is called a status study. In this sense each research study is in part a status study; however, to develop a research study, the investigator must go beyond mere description and utilize techniques that allow for conclusions and implications generalizable to education in general. Procedures that are designed to gather the information needed to make administrative decisions for one school district help administrators make informed choices about limited school settings.

Description, per se, is used in all branches of inquiry. A description of the present state of the educational institution in the Zee County School District is important to those people who are directly affected by that institution's level of functioning. It is important to society as a whole only indirectly, so a determination of its condition will not, in most cases, contribute to the body of generalizable knowledge about education in total.

Information gathered from a school district may show that the first grade enrollment for the next year will be about 10 percent less than this year. A closer look at the data may show that one elementary school in the district will have 15 percent more pupils next year, while another may have 20 percent less. This is important information in planning for the next year, but the procedures used to gather and compile data for purposes similar to this are basically a study of status, not research procedures. Activities to provide data for use in making these kinds of administrative decisions should be associated with evaluation, not research.

Procedures designed to describe a school district's educational system for evaluative purposes have been assigned to the inquiry strategy of evaluation. The exclusion of this type of activity of gathering and tabulating data as a research procedure is not to be interpreted as an indication that the activity is not important; it is, but it should not be confused with studies intended to apply to education in general.

Status studies are important in reporting existing educational practices and in gathering facts about school facilities, equipment, personnel, curricula, and such. The study may be merely to establish the ratio of teachers to pupils. The study may be about aspects of a particular school and/or the community that it serves. Very large surveys are conducted by the United States Government Bureau of Census, and also by educationally oriented organizations, which report the status of special topics in very large geographic regions. Tables of facts are available from the Bureau of Census. In any case the status study merely reports conditions without making judgments, and refrains from any attempt at discovering relationships, making predictions, or establishing cause and effect.

Status studies are most valuable when used as vehicles to gather data for specified practical purposes. They are not intended to add to present knowledge about educational concerns, but they serve in a unique way to improve education in our schools.

Descriptive Studies for Inquiry

Although status studies do not require involvement with generalizations in the same way research studies do, careful attention must be given to sampling, questionnaire construction, and interviewing when they are involved in the accumulation of facts. The important decisions based on data supplied by status studies require that the person charged with carrying out the study be informed of acceptable techniques. The separation of status studies from research studies is not to be interpreted as downgrading them. The division has been made as a pedagogical device to separate the two for discussion and to point up the major difference.

The somewhat arbitrary divisions have been made primarily to facilitate communication about some very closely related procedures. A good grasp of the differences helps to separate for inspection many different activities that have been and, at times, still are carelessly thrown together under the loosely defined term *research*. Students may wish to review again the earlier discussion of the divisions of scientific strategies in chapter 1. The basic difference between *to know* and *to choose* is again used to separate research activities and evaluation activities as we meet questions based in a context of *what is*.

NATURE OF DESCRIPTIVE RESEARCH

Traditionally techniques of evaluation and the activities used to gather data to supply information for administrative decisions about facilities, staffing, and budgeting have fallen under the scope of descriptive research. Confusion resulted when too many different things were included under one broad strategy, thus the decision to place those procedures used to provide information for a specific decision situation under the strategy of "need to choose."

The following types of inquiry are specifically *excluded* from the scope of descriptive research:
1. questions based in the past;
2. questions to be answered by manipulating variables in laboratory-like conditions;
3. questions based in development of programs, tests, and such; and
4. questions based in the present but directed to a specific school situation for evaluation or administrative decisions about facilities, staff, and budget.

What is left for descriptive research? Descriptive research deals with those questions that are based in the present state of affairs which have implications beyond the limits of the subjects or other elements studied. Questions which generate answers that contribute to principles and theory about educational concerns are many times answerable through study of current conditions and existing relationships.

Descriptive research can be viewed as having two distinct parts. First, the study by description provides the data about the present conditions. In research mere description is not a goal but a means to the end. Statements of individual facts are not intended to be scientifically interesting nor to be valuable in developing new generalizable knowledge. Second, the establishment of the meaning takes the data and forms conclusions by comparing, contrasting, or identifying relationships. The first part could be viewed as *descriptive approaches* and the second as *correlational techniques*. The first part is much like a status study, while the second involves the research aspect of the process.

The Correlator

The educational inquirer who uses descriptive research as defined here would be a *correlator*—one who "studies the variation which already exists in nature."[1] In a correlational study, "the particular values of the variable, and the frequency of their occurrence are not fixed, or controlled by the investigator."[2]

That all of the occurrences observed would have happened without the study makes the correlational study particularly valuable for the field of education, since many educational questions are either difficult to answer or unanswerable through laboratory manipulation of variables. If the effects of different treatments applied to subjects might be harmful and/or unethical, a natural setting must be used. A descriptive study also seems to be a logical choice when the interaction of numerous independent variables and their effects on several dependent variables are to be studied. When isolation of variables for laboratory-like studies does not provide answers that are directly generalizable to the natural setting, descriptive techniques must be used.

Since the descriptive study can be used so widely in education, the social sciences, and the behavioral sciences, it is likely to remain a major strategy for answering educationally based questions. With the development of multivariate statistical techniques, educational researchers are turning to descriptive research techniques more frequently for analysis of complex situations.

The correlational study and the experimental study can be used jointly. The correlational study can be used to establish a relationship that can be developed into a cause-and-effect hypothesis, and the carefully controlled experiment then can be used to test that hypothesis. Investigators using descriptive research, as well as investigators using the experiment, hope to establish how variables are related through carefully executed procedures. Experimental evidence which supports the conclusions of descriptive studies adds strength to accepted theory and is encouraged when conditions permit a controlled experiment.

Descriptive Data

The ongoing world with all of its components provides the source of information about present status. There are three ways to get the information: through direct observation; by measuring attributes of the elements of the world; or by asking the elements, if they are human beings, for information that may be difficult to observe or measure. At times, combinations of the three will be used. To study a student's attitude toward a new method of teaching a foreign language through use of a laboratory carrel, one might use direct observation to see how he reacts, through his willingness to use the laboratory and actions while there; ask him to respond to a device designed to measure attitudes toward the laboratory; and directly ask him to give his reaction in a narrative or a structured device.

The descriptive approaches appear to be relatively simple, but many difficulties are associated with developing appropriate techniques to obtain the needed information from subjects. Unfortunately much of the information about human beings is personal and not readily available to the researcher. The needed information may be difficult to obtain since the cooperation of the subjects may be difficult to acquire.

---

1. George A. Ferguson, *Statistical Analysis in Psychology and Education* (New York: McGraw-Hill, 1971), p. 17.
2. Ibid, p. 16.

Special attention must be given to all available tools, their use, and their possible effects on subjects, to assure that needed data are obtained.

A major problem associated with descriptive research is the interpretation of the data. Since the researcher has no control beyond choosing what data to gather, interpretations are highly subjective and open to some of the criticisms attached to conclusions for historical studies. A major difference between historical and descriptive data is that the study of current conditions does have available all of the data and does not have to rely on only a portion that remains, as is true of historical research. A comprehensive study of the needed data, and possible methods to obtain them, allows the researcher to give the topic total coverage by using objective methods. Conclusions to well planned and executed descriptive studies seem to be more readily accepted than conclusions to historical studies because the data are more easily validated.

STEPS IN DESCRIPTIVE RESEARCH

Well designed studies for descriptive research follow the steps of the general scientific approach to inquiry. As in all inquiry the problem question is the major component that makes the descriptive research process function satisfactorily. On the surface the descriptive study may appear to be simply a matter of gathering much information and looking to see what one has. The veteran researcher knows the importance of planning exactly what data are needed, how best to secure the data, and how to interpret them.

Problem Presentation

After an indeterminate situation or barrier is met and the decision to attack it has been made, the researcher needs to place the problem into a clearly written question that he or she wants answered. A carefully prepared question gives needed direction for the study. If the question is research-oriented, it will give attention to comparison, contrast, or relationship. Descriptive research will give attention to those questions that can best be answered by studying present conditions. It will not give attention to a purely description-oriented problem, best answered by a status study.

To say that the aim of a study is "to explain through description the drop-out problem at Zee High School" is not a researchable problem. To qualify as a research problem the purpose would have to be expanded to bring in the scope of comparison, contrast, or relationship, to allow generalization to other settings. To qualify as a logically proposed investigation of a local problem, it would need either to be delimited to set bounds for the inquiry or divided to study the problem in parts, since it is too broad in this form. For example, the larger problem could be investigated by specific areas. Possible questions are: What effect does tracking of students through the high-school grades have on the drop-out rate? What are the effects of an intramural program of athletics on the drop-out rate? Answers to these and similar questions can be used to direct local decisions. The answers may be generalizable beyond that particular high school, but the research is not specifically designed to do that.

Background

A thorough knowledge of the background of the topic for a descriptive study allows the investigator to place the conclusions of his or her study within the context of educational theory. By reading widely he can attain a thorough understanding of investigations and opinions about closely related aspects of his question, which allows him to generate conclusions that contribute to the body of knowledge of educational concerns.

Decisions about all important aspects of the study become more valid when they are made in the context of a good understanding of closely related topics. Definitions of variables under study can be carefully framed and, when possible, placed in operational terms. Techniques used in other studies may give direction to the present study.

Status reports and tables of data from the Census Bureau and other agencies are useful as background information. When the overview of the literature is combined with all other data the basis for developing a hypothesis is obtained. The importance of background information for a study cannot be overemphasized, but this part of the research process is one that is often passed by too lightly.

Hypothesis

Although descriptive studies lack the control by manipulation of one variable while other variables are held constant, the hypothesis is useful in descriptive research. The hypothesis gives direction for the study by providing something for the data to support or refute. A framework to gather data, analyze them, and draw conclusions uses the hypothesis as a vehicle to organize the answer to the original question. Techniques of testing hypotheses for descriptive studies tend to be more objective than those used to test historical hypotheses, and statistical techniques are available to supplement the researcher's subjective judgments about what the data indicate.

Gathering and Analyzing the Data

After the hypothesis is clearly stated the researcher must decide what information will be needed to test it and how best to obtain it. He or she must select and/or construct the data-gathering instruments to provide the needed data, and must choose the elements to supply the data. Finally he/she must decide how the data will be organized, validated and/or tested for statistical significance, how they will be interpreted, and how they will be presented in the final report.

With careful planning of procedures to gather the data and adequate training of persons needed to carry them out, the actual gathering of the data is routine. Pilot studies are often used to identify mechanical or procedural difficulties in gathering information from human subjects. A *pilot study* is a scaled-down version of the full-blown study. It uses a small number of subjects who will not be used to provide data for the major study, and it gives the researcher, and any aides who will be participating in the study, an opportunity to see how well the plan fits together logistically to correct any difficulties encountered with procedures or mechanical devices. Sampling techniques need not be a part of the pilot study since the data will not be analyzed and reported.

Conclusions

The researcher should interpret the results of the study by drawing conclusions about what the results imply for education generally and/or specifically. An alternative to a statement of conclusions drawn by the researcher is used extensively in some sciences. In these fields, the conclusions are not specifically attended to by the investigator but

Descriptive Studies for Inquiry

are considered to be implied by the results and left for the reader to interpret. Some possible reasons for including a statement of the researcher's conclusions in educational studies are found in the following lines.

> Just why the behavioral scientist traditionally is expected to present his own interpretations and conclusions as well as the results of his investigation is not entirely clear. Perhaps it is because there are so many possible misinterpretations to avoid with behavioral data; perhaps it is because the behavioral scientist is lazy and wishes the interpretations made for him; perhaps it is because, working with people, he is more aware of the problems of communication; or perhaps it is because he has so often been required to justify what he is doing (as contrasted with the physical, and to some extent the biological, sciences where enough concrete and immediately useful results have been produced so that the public no longer questions efforts in those areas).[3]

SOURCES OF DATA

Many of the traits and characteristics of most concern in educational research are tied to objectives of the educational process—those instructional outcomes of the teaching-learning relation. For the educational activities of a school program to be effective they must move students toward the desired goal or aims that form the basis for educational objectives. These traits and characteristics that appear in educational objectives become criterion variables in research studies. Many objectives relate to student achievement. Research studies consider effects of variables on student achievement. However to study the effects of variables on student achievement the researcher must have a measure of such achievement. In general the data for descriptive studies will be information supplied by measurement of criterion variables, e.g., student achievement in biology. In the cognitive domain student achievement in subject matter stands out as a particularly important criterion variable, thus the study of related variables makes up a large part of educational research.

The affective domain of personality and social development is increasingly becoming more a part of the educator's concern. The constructs of creativity, motivation, aspiration, and the like become sources of data as they appear as criterion variables. Development of motor skills is also important, and variables that indicate skill development become criterion variables.

Since the educational process is so complex and encompassing, the above examples make up a small part of a wide spectrum of possible attributes measured for data in descriptive studies. The sources of data for descriptive studies are, in general, a sample of subjects selected to be measured on the criterion variable of the study. An appropriate sampling technique chosen from among those already discussed in chapter 5 should be used to select those subjects that will supply, through measurement of some psychological or sociological construct, data for the study. In most descriptive studies the sample is observed or measured on the criterion variable. When this cannot be done directly, indirect effects deemed to indicate presence of the criterion variable are studied. To study the impact of an intramural sports program on school attitudes the researcher may use a sample to study the absence rate, tardiness, and so forth as

---

3. G. C. Helmstadter, *Research Concepts in Human Behavior* (New York: Appleton-Century-Crofts, 1970), p. 68.

indicators of attitude toward school. In this example, school attitude is the criterion variable, and the other characteristics are investigated and quantified to indirectly indicate and measure attitude.

The source of information for descriptive research studies, as defined for our use, is found primarily in the attributes of human beings. They are studied by comparing, contrasting, and investigating to establish relationships. Information for status studies is provided by a greater range of sources, such as school buildings, classroom materials, and supporting services, although it does not exclude the student population from study.

TYPES OF DATA

Both qualitative and quantitative data are used in descriptive research studies; however as newer and better ways of quantifying attributes are developed qualitative data are used primarily as background for the study and to build hypotheses. An attempt to study a problem by a descriptive narrative alone would, at present, be inappropriate as a technique for descriptive research.

Qualitative Data

Qualitative data that the researcher obtains are important to him or her as background for a problem and as information to help arrive at a hypothesis, but should not be used as data for results of a study or as a basis for conclusions. If a trait or characteristic is considered as a variable for study then it is quantifiable,[4] and to do less than supply objectively obtained quantities is not acceptable research procedure. The suggestion has been made that information about nominal variables should be considered as qualitative data and that they should be called qualitative variables, but this limitation seems inconsistent with the contemporary use of measurement in educational research and our earlier discussion of types of data generated by nominal variables. A very powerful tool, multiple regression analysis, is used to study variables that can be broken into distinct subdivisions. To consider nominal variables as traits that can be studied only through a narrative analysis would deprive the researcher of much objective treatment of data.

Quantitative Data

A variable that serves as a criterion variable or independent variable generates data that can be categorized as either nominal, ordinal, interval, or ratio depending on the nature of the variable. The type of data determines to a large degree the statistical procedures that can be used to help interpret the data.

Studies that use nominal variables will be limited to quantifying by counting frequencies of occurrence. Since there is no order to the set of classification categories, the only values that can be used are the counting numbers associated with the category frequencies. Meaningful mathematical treatment is limited to comparing those counting numbers directly, by percentages in the several categories, ratios within the counting numbers, certain nonparametric statistical tests of significance, and appropriate correlational and regression techniques.

---

4. Fred N. Kerlinger, *Foundations of Behavioral Research*, 2nd ed. (New York: Holt, Rinehart and Winston, 1973), p. 40.

Descriptive Studies for Inquiry

A rule of measurement for nominal variables can be viewed as a function describing how subjects are assigned to categories of the trait being measured. A set of junior high school students can be assigned to categories using a rule of measurement for the trait of "favorite color." The rule of measurement is: assign to the category "blue" each member who states a preference for blue; assign to category "yellow" each member who states a preference for yellow; and so on for each student being studied. Of course the categories must be exhaustive, which means that the variable "color" has enough categories to accommodate all possible choices of colors. Frequencies of occurrences for the categories are the counting numbers associated with the categories after the set being studied is completely assigned. This is an often used method of assignment for studies that are designed to study conditions as they exist, when the variable under study cannot be classed higher than nominal or when a higher level variable is treated within categories.

Given information that permits a rule of measurement including at least ordering, the researcher has additional statistical techniques that he/she may use to interpret the data. He can use additional correlational techniques, other nonparametric tests, and additional statistics for describing the data. Of course this type of rule also allows treatment in distinct categories as well. The order of finish of a race of nine runners has the added property of order that was lacking in the nominal assignment. For analysis, the nine runners could be categorized into three classes consisting of (1) the first three finishers, (2) the second three finishers, and (3) the last three finishers. In this assignment the order of the three categories is retained, but the order within categories is lost.

At times researchers assign subjects to categories on the basis of a measurement of a particular attribute. When this is done the variable is called an assigned variable, and it takes on the characteristics of an independent variable—one that can be manipulated by an investigator. Descriptive studies use combinations of types of variables when studying relationships and cause-effect. The assigned variable may be nominal and the criterion variable ordinal, for example. A study could be made of the running ability of philosophy majors compared to anthropology majors. The two categories on the variable of college major were chosen by the researcher and the assignment made on that basis. The criterion variable, running ability, could be ordered by rank, giving the combination of an assigned variable that is nominal and a criterion variable that is ordinal.

Other quantitative data will be either *interval*, if the rule of measurement has a scale with equal intervals, or *ratio*, if it has the added rule of assignment from absolute zero. Since these types of data contain more information than nominal and ordinal, more procedures are available in the form of parametric techniques. Descriptive studies that include testing or measurement using equal intervals may obtain interval data from time to time but only rarely will the data be classed as ratio. Any interval or ratio data can be ordered or categorized for data treatment when appropriate, but some of the information is lost when a lower rule of assignment is used. (See chapter 7.)

TOOLS OF DESCRIPTIVE RESEARCH

Descriptive research tools are needed to gather data about present conditions and to interpret those data through contrast, comparison, and relationships. The tools are of two kinds—those that are used to collect data and those that are used to interpret the data after they have been obtained. Since the technique of descriptive research is correlational, it deals with the real-world setting without manipulation by the researcher. The researcher must take special precautions to see that neither his presence nor the study itself changes the existing conditions in a way that the results are confounded by a condition not present in the real-world situation being studied.

Tools for gathering the data are designed to quantify, or allow for quantification of, the variables being studied—primarily the criterion variable. Tools for interpretation will, in large, be statistical procedures applied to the data. The results of the statistical interpretations will then be used by the researcher to reach conclusions about the study. The importance of choosing the set of tools to utilize in the gathering of data and in interpreting them cannot be overemphasized. Such choice is a major concern when planning the study.

Several aspects of the plan must be fit together, and decisions must be made in the context of what kinds of data can be obtained, what rules of measurement can be used, and, in turn, the proper statistical techniques. The interdependence of these aspects excludes decisions about one without giving due consideration to the others. For example, the nature of a question places limitations on the type of appropriate data which would in turn set limits on the proper tools to gather the data. Additional limitations on the proper statistical procedures used to interpret the data are imposed by the rules of measurement used in gathering the data. Since the study must be made within existing conditions without manipulation, circumstances may limit the plan that is being developed, but the overall attack should combine the best combination of procedures for this situation which is unique.

Earlier discussion has brought us through the taxonomy to the fourth level (see figure 1.1), where specific plans are formed through a methodology designed to answer the specific question asked. The study started in the trunk of the tree representing the scientific method used in inquiry, passed through the first set of branches that stand for three major strategies, and through the next set of branches representing types of research. The original question sets the direction for the study and affects decisions at all levels, especially at the fourth level where specific plans are made for each individual study. Our decisions now will be made with an eye to gathering appropriate data and selecting proper procedures to interpret them for the question under study.

Tools for Gathering Data

The tools for obtaining data about present conditions are intended to give objective information in quantitative form. Techniques must be chosen to give the best basis and input for the interpretive tools, and a close relationship must be established between gathering and interpreting procedures to see that a logical and functional sequence is developed. The tools that are discussed in this section are those most often used in studies of present conditions—those that are most likely to provide data that can be studied for contrasts, comparisons, and relationships.

Direct observation is especially valuable to establish the present condition. Since all science is directed toward understanding the world around us, the beginning of all scientific endeavors is based in direct observation. First attempts to discover regularity are nearly all based in what one sees directly. The use of direct observation has fallen into disfavor with some researchers as being unscientific and subject to distortion by the observer. Problems associated with direct observation are in most cases based in the frailties of humans (see chapter 6), and when these are overcome through objec-

Descriptive Studies for Inquiry

tive procedures which use checklists, scorecards, and extension of the senses by mechanical devices, direct observation becomes a valuable tool for descriptive research.

The *questionnaire* provides a way to get personal information from subjects that may not be readily obtainable in other ways. In recent times the mailed questionnaire has been heavily criticized and, as a result, has fallen into some disfavor as a device for gathering data. The misuse of the questionnaire, rather than its nature, has been the cause of its poor reputation. To write down a set of questions, reproduce them in sufficient numbers, and mail them to subjects who are expected to complete and return them seems an easy way to gather research data. However without careful attention to important details such a plan will do little to shed light on researchable problems.

Preparation of an instrument capable of delivering the necessary data involves three aspects. The researcher must first learn how to ask a question that is definite and clearly presented, and one that generates an answer that is also definite and quantifiable. Second, the format of the questionnaire must be structured so that the respondent will have no difficulty in recording his response and will not miss any item entirely, and it must be composed of a logical sequence of questions. Third, the instructions must be sharpened so that all ambiguity is eliminated, and the final plan for reproduction is completed.

Questions should be asked in a way that will allow the answers to be easily organized for reduction in data processing. *Close-ended* questions which ask that the respondent choose from a provided list will, in most cases, provide more easily processed data than *open-ended* questions that permit the responding person to create an answer. The answer to an open-ended question must be interpreted, thus reducing the reliability of the data.

After the questions have been refined they should be presented to a few persons similar to those who will receive the questionnaire, to check that the questions can be read quickly, the implied task is clear, and an answer can be easily obtained. An overview of the questions should be made to assure that all of the needed data will be obtained and that the respondent is not asked to take time to give information that is not needed for the study.

Since a respondent cannot ask questions to clear up any ambiguity, the instructions and format determine to a large degree the success of the questionnaire and the usefulness of the collected data. An instrument with inadequate instructions and a confusing format that is discarded by a large proportion of those sampled will lower the validity of the data and may cause the project to be abandoned or a new set of questionnaires to be mailed. This can happen even to a set of excellent questions.

General instructions should include how the answers are to be given for close-ended questions and whether a long or short answer is to be given for an open-ended question. An excellent guide for the respondent answers can be given by placing a box by each listing for a close-ended question, and a line or lines to limit the response to an open-ended question. (See figure 9.1.) Another useful format to use when a particular answer generates another question is shown in figure 9.2. The format of the questionnaire should include a logical ordering of the questions according to content and the contingency of one item on other items.

After the questions have been refined, the directions written, and the format developed, the copies for mailing must be prepared. The method of reproducing the questionnaire is important to achieving a high rate of return for the mailing. A

```
┌─────────────────────────────────────────────────────────────────────────┐
│ 7. Which one of the following cities would you consider to offer the best environment for a
│    promising young violinist to advance professionally?
│           New York                                                    1 ☐
│           Boston                                                      2 ☐
│           Philadelphia                                                3 ☐
│           Chicago                                                     4 ☐
│           Dallas                                                      5 ☐
│           Houston                                                     6 ☐
│           Los Angeles                                                 7 ☐
│           San Francisco                                               8 ☐
│           Other (specify)_____ 9 ☐
│
│                                    OR
│ 7. Which American (United States) city do you consider to offer the best environment for a
│    promising young violinist to advance professionally? _____
│ 8. Why did you choose the particular city that you listed in number 7? _____
│    _____
│    _____
└─────────────────────────────────────────────────────────────────────────┘
```

FIGURE 9.1   Two Different Structures for Responses to a Questionnaire

questionnaire will look best and be received best if set in type; however this is the most expensive method and requires the most time for preparation. Copies made by multilith or photo-offset processes are a close second to type-set copy and will generally be of acceptable quality for a mailed questionnaire, require less preparation time, and be less expensive. Dittoed or mimeographed copies are to be avoided unless the costs of the others are prohibitive. Enough copies should be prepared in the first run to cover for staff use and final reports.

Demographic data for a questionnaire should be obtained in a section at the end of the instrument. Remember to ask for only that information that the study requires.

A decision about whether to make the reply anonymous will have to be made. If validation of the data calls for a follow-up interview for a portion of the responses or if efforts will be made to learn characteristics of the nonrespondents, the inclusion of a name or at least an identifying number will, in most cases, not have a major influence on returns. If the questions are of such a nature that the request to supply a name would affect the returns, the respondents should be assured of anonymity. Anonymous returns do not allow validation of data, and, since low returns cannot be supplemented by a follow up without a mailing to the complete sample, returns may be confounded by second returns from some. As with most aspects of research procedures the most important decisions must be made in context with all other aspects.

```
┌─────────────────────────────────────────────────────────────────────────┐
│ 12. Have you attended any of the meetings of the Educational Psychology Lecture Series
│     this school year?
│         YES_____ if yes, check here ─────────────┐
│         NO_____                                  │
│                                                                 ▼
│                     1. Professor Clouse   . . .  _____
│                     2. Professor Jerse    . . .  _____
│                     3. Professor Sullins  . . .  _____
└─────────────────────────────────────────────────────────────────────────┘
```

FIGURE 9.2   A Contingency Question Format

Descriptive Studies for Inquiry

The researcher should prepare a highly refined device to gather the data necessary to answer the research question. The above general directions can be supplemented for more refinement by consulting a more expanded discussion of questionnaire development.[5]

Having developed an appropriate device to gather the needed data the researcher must identify the subjects who are to receive the questionnaire. The recipients may be all of the names on a previously prepared mailing list, such as all of the members of an organization, all citizens in a geographic region, or some other list that is appropriate. Many times the ones to receive the questionnaire constitute a randomly selected sample of subjects from a larger population. Generalizations are made to the population based on information obtained from the sample. The usual procedures for drawing representative samples should be made to assure randomness and independence in selection. A major point to consider (but often overlooked in early planning) is the need for current addresses. An out-dated mailing list or a list without addresses is of little value to a current study.

Since sample data are used for generalizations a major concern for all questionnaire studies is the rate or percentage of return. The rate is crucial to the success of the study. Imaginative techniques have been designed to encourage questionnaire returns. A return envelope that requires no postage or addressing is essential. As further inducement to the recipient a small monetary reward is sometimes effective. A statement that makes the recipient aware of the importance of the study for him could increase returns.

If feasible, mailed questionnaires can be scheduled for pick up by the researcher or an assistant to increase the rate of return. The questionnaire can be hand delivered, explained, and left with the understanding that the mail will be used to return it. The less effort required from the respondent, the higher the rate of return. Follow-up mailings, telephone follow ups, and personal calls can be scheduled to increase the number of returns.

A question often asked about a set of data that has been gathered through a mailed questionnaire is, "What is an adequate percentage of returns to allow conclusions to be drawn?" Any generalization from returns to the original sample or to the larger population assumes that each element of the sample returned a questionnaire. Of course only rarely, if ever, will the returns be close to 100 percent. More important than percentage of returns is the study of possible bias in returns when considering the body being generalized to. If a return of 10 percent from a large sample had no bias, then the 10 percent return would be adequate. Let us hurriedly say that any 10 percent return is highly likely to be biased, and that percentage of return would generally be unacceptable. A 10 percent return probably means that the device was poorly prepared, and only the 10 percent who felt very strongly about the issue would take time to return the questionnaire. A very conservative set of figures for rate of return is given by Babbie as: 50 percent is adequate for analysis and reporting; 60 percent is good; and 70 percent is very good.[6] He also points out that "a demonstrated lack of response bias is far more important than a high response rate." However lack of response bias is associated with high response rate. If there is a question about response bias, a

---

5. See A. N. Oppenheim, *Questionnaire Design and Attitude Measurement* (New York: Basic Books, 1966); and Earl R. Babbie, *Survey Research Methods* (Belmont, Cal.: Wadsworth Publishing Co., 1973), pp. 140-56.
6. Babbie, *Survey Research Methods*, p. 165.

comparison of answers for early respondents can be made to answers of late respondents. The assumption here is that responses of the very late returns will, in general, be much like the nonrespondents. Comparison can also be made in terms of demographic data for respondents and nonrespondents.[7]

An accepted practice when figuring the rate of return is to reduce the potential sample size by the number of undeliverables and figure the percentage by dividing the number of returns by the net sample size (number mailed, less those undelivered). If a mailing of 172 had 8 that were not delivered and 128 returns, the rate of return would be:

$$\frac{128}{172-8} = \frac{128}{164} \quad \text{or } 78\% \text{ return.}$$

This procedure of taking net sample size for the denominator assumes that the undeliverables represent a random sample of the original sample. Any independence from bias would be difficult to establish because of the characteristics of a population that is not locatable.

The *opinionnaire* or *attitudinal scale*[8] can be used in conjunction with a questionnaire or as a device by itself to gather data not possible to obtain through a questioning process. Rather than asking the respondent a question, the researcher can ask him to respond with the extent to which he holds an opinion or attitude. Most attempts to determine attitudes and opinions take the form of scaling. Scaling techniques (see chapter 6) are based on formats that give order to response classes. Sometimes referred to as the Likert Technique, since Rensis Likert[9] used such a scale in an early study of attitudes, scaling is used widely to measure personal characteristics. Scaling can be used with statements to which the respondent can indicate his agreement or disagreement and in addition weight his response by marking a point on an ordered scale. The original Likert Scale used five categories—strongly agree, agree, undecided, disagree, and strongly disagree. Other numbers of categories and descriptors can be used to modify the general model to a specific need. Point values can be assigned for categories with an order from low to high scoring: 1 for the least favorable response, to a high of 5 for the most favorable. (Favorable may be "agree" or "disagree" according to the opinion of the researcher.)

Good procedure for scale development suggests that the favorable end of the scale be varied so that the respondent must give careful attention to each item rather than merely responding without weighing the statement for himself/herself. If he is expected to agree (or disagree) to all items, the validity of the measurements may be questioned. It is not necessary to provide numbers on the questionnaire since this can be done in the scoring procedures and the indication of the correct (favorable) response can remain hidden. The score for the scale can be a composite or total for all of the items. For a six-point scale for twenty statements the highest score would be 120, and the lowest score would be 20. An average derived by dividing the total by the number of statements gives a position on the ordinal scale as an indication of the measure of the opinion or attitude under study. A high score or high average would indicate an attitude favorable to the one held by the constructor of the scale.

---

7. Oppenheim, *Questionnaire Design and Attitude Measurement*, p. 34.
8. Ibid.
9. Rensis A. Likert, "A Technique for the Measurement of Attitudes," *Archives of Psychology* 140 (1932): 1-55.

Since respondents' reactions to items on Likert-type scales are much like those for a multiple-choice examination, total scores for scales can be treated much as other test data. If needed, a cross section of the sample through each item can be determined by averaging all responses to each individual item. An average response for item one could be obtained from responses to the first item and so on for all the statements or a selected sample of statements.

Careful refinement of each statement is very important to make this technique function properly. True opinions or attitudes are sometimes difficult to obtain through scaling because the desired (by the researcher or society) response is usually apparent to the respondent. He/she may tend to give the "obviously correct" response rather than his/her true feeling about the statement. A backlash against an obviously correct answer results when a respondent gives an obviously wrong answer. Referred to as the "boomerang effect" the subject may for personal reasons give answers other than true feelings as a way of revenge.[10] Time given to learning about how others have used scaling to measure attitudes, to careful preparation of statements, and to attention to detail including scoring is well spent for enhancing the probability of getting high-quality data.

The *personal interview* is a face-to-face meeting of a questioner and a responder, or an oral presentation of an opinion or attitude scale. In most cases the interview is organized around a structure much like a mailed questionnaire. However the interview has a number of advantages that stem from the personal contact of the direct meeting that the questionnaire lacks.

The response to an interview can be expected to be greater than to a questionnaire, with returns of over 90 percent not being uncommon. The interview permits an interaction not readily available within the usual structure of the questionnaire—allowing the respondent to clarify the question asked and the questioner to probe for the specific meanings of answers. A structure can be developed which allows for branching of questions based on the respondent's answers. A question that asks for a response of *agree* or *disagree* could have different follow-up questions for different responses, or have a follow-up question for one response but none for another.

Since quantitative data are needed, the directness of the interview provides a way of obtaining objective data about some variables of a personal nature that may be difficult to obtain any other way. The interviewer also has the opportunity to get answers by direct observation, which is not possible for a response taken from a mailed questionnaire. Major disadvantages of the interview result from the time involved in gathering data. Also interviews are expensive in terms of money and time expended, so the interview should not be used if a more economical way of gathering the data will be equally effective. Most of the procedures for preparing a questionnaire apply equally to the interview, and the previous discussion can be used as a guideline for structuring the order of questions and the recording of responses.

As a rule the interviewer should dress about the same way he or she expects the persons to be interviewed to dress. He/she should assume a neutral position so that the validity of the responses is not affected by the way the interview is conducted. To increase the reliability of the data each question should be asked exactly the same way each

---

10. Joseph Masling, "Role Related Behavior of the Subject and Psychologist and Its Effects upon Psychological Data," *Nebraska Symposium on Motivation* (Lincoln: University of Nebraska Press, 1966).

time, and the responses should be recorded immediately in a previously structured recording sheet. (The sheet could be in the form of a checklist. See chapter 6.)

Practice interviews will assist in the development of a thorough understanding of the total interview and its parts as well as the specific procedures of administration. If more than one person is to be used to do the interviewing, practice sessions allow comparison of results and agreement as to what reaction should be made, given certain conditions while interviewing. The procedures should be checked to see that sufficient and accurate information is provided for interpretation. By gathering demographic data first, rather than last as in the questionnaire, the interviewer has an opportunity to build rapport with subjects.

As we have learned to expect from human involvement, interviewer bias may be difficult to overcome when steps are made to objectify the interaction. Preparation for the interview and well planned procedures for recording responses do much to keep objectivity in the process.

Testing instruments are the most widely used measuring devices for characteristics of concern to education. Well prepared and validated tests yield descriptions of behavior that can be used to explain (1) present status, (2) changes over a time interval, (3) future expected performance, and (4) to make comparisons between individuals and groups of subjects.

Scores on tests allow the researcher to make comparisons between groups being studied. If tests have norms (reported averages) for groups with known characteristics, then comparison of like groups or individuals can be made to the norming groups. An appropriate test can be a powerful tool for the correlationist who studies conditions as they exist by establishing relationships and indications of cause and effect.

Proper use of the psychological test in research requires an understanding of test theory, even though a test is not developed primarily for a study. Attention should be given to earlier sections devoted to tests and suggested sources beyond this text to aid in proper selection and use of existing tests and development of new instruments.

In selecting a test for a research study the researcher needs a thorough understanding of a well-defined construct to fit the measuring instrument (the test) to that being measured (the construct). Researchers have, in general, found contributions from testing of achievement and aptitudes to have more utility for educational research than work done in the area of personality. Study of personality and related constructs are, at least for the present, best left to clinicians who have made special study in this important area. Anyone planning a study in this area should at least have close touch with the specialist.

Inventories, blanks, and *lists* are useful self-reporting devices in gathering information from subjects about their likes and dislikes. The information can be compared in terms of known likes or dislikes for particular groups. It can be used to compare two or more groups, an individual at different times, or groups at different times.

Any self-report device is intended to get at the wealth of information that a subject has about himself or herself, especially inner feelings that may be difficult to identify in other ways. The validity of the data rests heavily on the subject's ability and willingness to report true feelings. If the right information is asked for and accurately given by the individual, then the self-report is a valuable tool in describing and studying real-world conditions.

Facts about a person's past can be very helpful in making predictions about the future. Self-report inventories that ask a series of questions such as the following may

Descriptive Studies for Inquiry

help to explain the expected future through prediction, or be used in studies of relationships.

How many movies have you attended in the last 7 days?
None	1_____
One	2_____
Two	3_____
Three or Four	4_____
Five or Six	5_____
Seven	6_____
More than seven (specify_____)	7_____

Other questions can be asked to determine interests through use of time: How would you spend a rainy afternoon if you could do anything you wanted to? A sunny afternoon? Or a cold winter afternoon?

Another technique, *forced choice*, is used to identify groups of interests by subjects' responses. In a forced choice the subject being inventoried chooses, from various situations, the one that he/she would most enjoy and the one he/she would least enjoy. Choices might include fishing, wrestling, hiking, and so on. Patterns in a series of responses are indicative of interests.

Two standardized inventories are good examples of how self-reports can be used in vocational guidance. Both *Strong's Vocational Interest Blank* and the *Kuder Preference Record Form* use a grouping of interests, as reported by subjects, to fit with groupings of known interests of people actively engaged in particular occupations. Chemists tend to like to do the same things and used car salesmen tend to have common interests, as do all job-alike people, but the *sets* of interests for each are different. A set of interests for an individual can be fit to a like set for a specific occupation to give guidance for selection of a vocation. Research studies find self-reporting devices a valuable help when data about inner feelings are needed.

Mechanical devices should be given consideration when deciding how best to gather needed data. In most cases the introduction of a mechanical measuring device will not significantly affect the ongoing activities of the real world being studied. The aspect of change must be given careful attention when making a final decision to use or not to use a mechanical device.

A mechanical device that introduces no new variable to a situation can be valuable to one studying the world the way that it exists because that is what any mechanical measuring device is designed to do. A thermometer, carefully concealed to measure temperature changes within a schoolroom, is not likely to confound the usual classroom situation, but the introduction of a TV camera or an extra observer writing on a clipboard may change the setting so much that information gathered would lose its validity for the usual situation.

Sociometry establishes the social structure of a defined group. In most cases a situation is established, and each subject chooses one or more other subjects according to a hypothesized relationship. In a sociometric design each subject could be asked to identify one member of the group to take him/her to the first-aid room to have a cut administered to. From the responses a network of relationships could be exhibited on a sociogram. A *sociogram* is a figure that shows each of the choices and points up the most popular, the isolates, and other relationships of interest to the investigator. Sociometric techniques allow the researcher to obtain the social structure of a group as

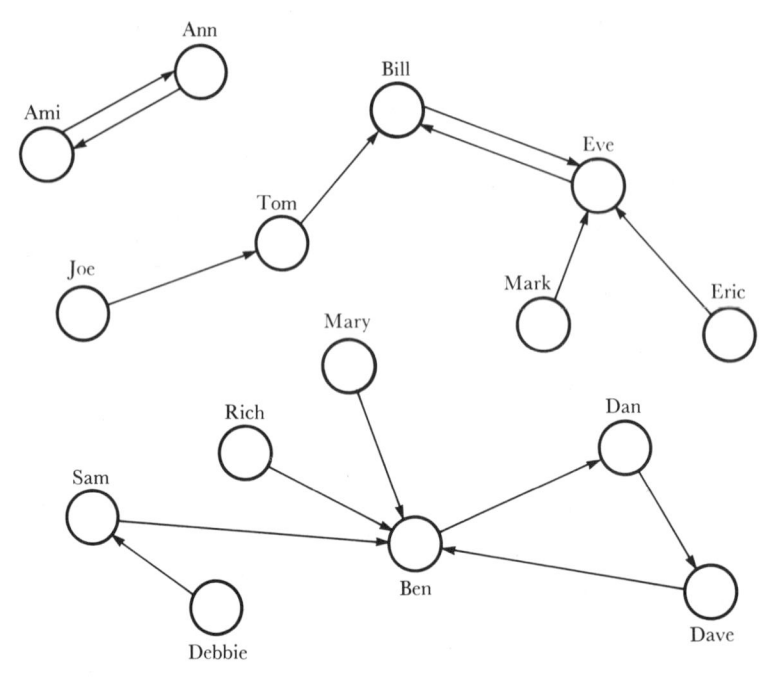

FIGURE 9.3 Sociogram for a Second Grade Class

determined by peers. What the sociogram or other device does is give an exhibition of the social structure for one situation at one point in time as illustrated in figure 9.3. It is a way of describing present status. Social interaction is so complex that direct observation does little to detect the relationships. Of course this structure is in constant change. A study that looks at two structures with a time interval between can be used to study effects of what happened in the interval.

Q methodology is well suited to the study of one individual. In its simplest form Q methodology uses a rank ordering of statements. The rankings of an individual can be compared by a correlational technique to a ranking of one or more other individuals. A set of individuals can be grouped by finding clusters of individuals that are much alike in their reactions to the statements.

If three registered Republicans and three registered Democrats were asked to rank eight persons seeking the office of governor, the Republicans would tend to rank Republican office seekers higher than Democratic candidates while the Democrats would tend to rank Democrats higher than Republicans. Using a rank of one as high and eight as low, the ranking might look like the data in table 9.1. The data show that Democrats did rank Democrats higher than Republican candidates and vice versa, as we expected. Q techniques extend to more complex studies that are not as obvious as the well managed example in table 9.1. Any set of objects, statements, art objects, words, and such can be ranked by an individual, with comparisons made individual to individual, individual to group, or group to group.

The *Q sort* is a modification of the ranking used above. The principle of ordering could be used for placing cards with statements from a large deck in a predetermined distribution according to criteria. A large number of statements—50 to 100—about

Descriptive Studies for Inquiry

TABLE 9.1 Rankings of Candidates for Governor

		Republican Voters			Democratic Voters		
		A	B	C	D	E	F
Democratic	G	8	7	8	1	2	1
Candidates	H	7	8	7	2	1	4
	I	6	2	4	3	4	6
	J	5	6	6	4	5	2
Republican	K	4	5	3	5	8	3
Candidates	L	3	4	5	6	7	8
	M	2	3	1	7	6	7
	N	1	1	2	8	3	5

something could be placed in a scale from *agree* to *disagree*. The arrangement for seventy statement cards might ask for the distribution in table 9.2. A study of the placement of cards in the extreme three compartments is usually used in interpretation. Q methodology is especially useful to the correlationalist's study of real-world conditions. His or her discovery techniques often need the heuristic quality of the Q in opening up new areas. More specific uses and a more detailed discussion of Q can be found in chapter 34 of *Foundations of Behavioral Research*.[11]

TABLE 9.2 Q-sort Distribution of Seventy Cards

	Disagree							Agree
Value of category	8	7	6	5	4	3	2	1 0
Number of statements to be placed in each category	2	4	7	13	18	13	7	4 2

Analysis of existing data may be a source of information for descriptive studies. Objective use of data already collected can be used in special cases to test hypotheses developed from data other than those used in the study. Of course, one *cannot* develop a hypothesis from certain data and then test the hypothesis by use of the same data or even part of it.

Two major disadvantages attached to the use of existing data should discourage this technique if any other method is available. First, the data available are limited to those that have been collected and recorded—they may or may not represent an adequate sample of what is being studied. The second disadvantage rests in what is called the *ecological fallacy*.[12] It is difficult and dangerous to conclusion making to assume a direct relationship between variables studied in this way. However the art of researching and use of innovative methods permit the use of existing data, if this is the only way to attack the question under study. In this technique the methods are more important than the data.

The *anthropological approach* not only is gaining much support for educational research but it is also being identified as a technique to overcome some of the problems of the limitations of coverage and accuracy of psychological data. New techniques are being created and older ones are being given new life by updating. Attention to impacts of social climate and use of naturalistic observation to supplement tests are becoming more and more a part of psychological research especially in the areas of infants,

---

11. Kerlinger, *Foundations of Behavioral Research*, pp. 582-600.
12. Babbie, *Survey Research Methods*, p. 36.

mentally retarded, and brain-damaged persons. Although not as extensive as the field-study approach of the anthropologist, the new approaches are moving toward the nature of anthropological field studies.[13]

Many educators feel that the time is long overdue for another approach in educational research and that anthropological procedures should be used more in educational research. The anthropological field method is seen by some writers as an excellent way to develop a hypothesis since "development of hypotheses is the special province of anthropological field method."[14] The writers feel that educational researchers are "often led to a 'quick and dirty' hypothesis, at best armchaired after some library search of appropriate literature and study of theory and that the field methods add a new dimension to hypothesis development."[15]

Anthropological field research studies a complete socioculture system to study humans. In our area of interest the system studied would be the educational system or one of its subsystems. This methodology is more than writing a description of something that happens in a school setting. Field research and statistical studies must be carefully designed. Those without carefully thought-out procedures "are worth the amount of conceptual thought that has been put into them—nothing."[16] Educational researchers who think that field study could best answer their questions are encouraged to go to the original works listed in references for the Lutz and Ramsey article, to prepare and execute a valid field study using anthropological methods. Also see an article by Peter Snidell, which has an extensive bibliography.[17] With additional excellent studies using this method, the field study may become an accepted and valuable tool for studying educational questions.

Summary of Data-Gathering Tools

The following tools have been presented as having utility in collecting data for the correlator who is studying existing conditions. A short description of each has been given, along with some possible uses. The reader is encouraged to better understand any tool that seems to be appropriate for gathering the information needed to answer his or her research questions by locating a more in-depth accounting of the techniques.

Direct observation	Questionnaires
Interviews	Scales
Tests, psychological	Tests, achievement
Self-reports	Mechanical devices
Sociometry	Q methodology
Study of existing data	Anthropological field-study approach

Investigators of educational questions will select from these tools and others when developing the methodology of descriptive studies. Other less used tools that can be used to obtain information include the semantic differential, projective methods, con-

---

13. Paul McReynolds, ed., *Advances in Psychological Assessment III* (San Francisco: Jossey Bass, 1974).
14. Frank W. Lutz and Margaret A. Ramsey, "The Use of Anthropological Field Methods in Education," *Educational Researcher* 3 (November 1974): 58.
15. Ibid., p. 5.
16. Ibid.
17. Peter S. Snidell, "Anthropological Approaches to the Study of Education," *Review of Educational Research* 39 (December 1969): 593-605.

Descriptive Studies for Inquiry

tent analysis, developmental approach—cross-sectional or longitudinal, case study, and social distance measures. Combinations of the above and creative designs provide almost limitless means to approach collecting data for descriptive studies.

Tools for Interpreting Data

Information-gathering tools provide data. Careful planning of the study will assure that the manner of gathering information will produce data that are interpretable. For assistance in interpreting data the researcher turns first to the broad field of statistics. Statistics can aid in interpretation of information in the form of empirical data by:

1. Reducing the data. Organization of the data puts it in a form for statistical treatment as well as providing tables and graphic representation.
2. Studying variation. Generalizations must take into account differences as well as typicalness. Although science is continually looking for typicalness within natural phenomena, much of science begins and ends with a study of difference —Darwin, Galton, and others.
3. Studying relationship. Techniques study how variations of two variables are concomitant. An identified relationship allows for hypothesis development and theorizing. Advanced techniques allow for study of more than two variables.
4. Allowing the researcher to make predictions. A high relationship between two variables may provide information and allow for highly probable predictions. One of the functions of science is prediction, which is valuable for research.
5. Allowing the researcher to make inferences. A study of one part of a population allows, through proper sampling, procedures statements about the population in general.
6. Testing how well obtained data fit with expectations (goodness of fit). This provides a means of testing the agreement of the hypothesis and observation.

The interpretive tools to be discussed in this section fall within the broad field of statistics. The scope of this book does not include a full-blown development of each topic discussed, therefore the intent of the present coverage is to show where these tools can be used and to some extent how they can be used. The mathematical understandings of statistics are left for the most part to books devoted to accomplishing that task. The more often used techniques get more coverage than the less used. In either case any technique to be used in a study should be further studied. The coverage here should permit the selection of a proper tool and if the prospective researcher does not already understand how to use it he/she should turn to a statistics book or to someone more knowledgeable about statistics to provide help in developing proficiency in its use.

Organization of the obtained information is the first task of interpretation. Descriptive studies tend to have large amounts of data that need formal processing, especially if the questionnaire, interview, or direct observation has been used. If the planning of the study fits a logical chain of reasoning and all the steps fit together, questionnaires, checklists, and such will be organized with interpretation in mind.

For large amounts of data the punchcard that is machine readable reduces a very large volume of data about a subject to a series of holes that can be read by a computer or other data-processing equipment.[18] In fact, good management permits a keypunch operator to work directly from returned questionnaires and other types of data sheets.

---

18. Babbie, *Survey Research Methods*, pp. 187-203.

If the type of data does not allow the needed organization, another step must be included to get from the original form to a form that is key punchable.

For smaller amounts of data, tables may be sufficient to present the data and/or to allow for calculation. With hand and desk calculators able to handle raw data easily, pure hand calculation is little used today.

Tables will be needed in most studies. They are used to present data in the final report and may aid in the statistical calculations. Formats for setting up tables vary from one style of book to another, but they all include basically the same components and perform the following major function—to arrange and present statistical data in a form that enables a reader to extract with little effort the meaning of the raw data. To do that the tables should:

1. Be self explanatory. The title and contents should convey the meaning without reference to the text.
2. Be in rank order or other logical sequence. This makes comparisons easy.
3. Be broken when they contain long columns by leaving space after every five or ten rows.
4. Have all necessary columns. This is especially important if the table is used for computation.
5. Be in the format of the chosen style.

Frequency tables are used to report frequencies of occurrence of reported values for one variable. Tables can also be used to report data and the logic of bivariate analysis (two variables) and multivariate analysis. Contingency tables (see figure 9.4) report for more than one variable, just as frequency tables report univariate analysis. Con-

Table 4.2 "Did you attend the book exhibit in the public library during the week of September 16 to 23?"

	Boys	Girls
Yes	27%	54%
No	73%	46%

FIGURE 9.4 Table of Bivariate Analysis

tingency tables for analysis divide variables into subgroups and report in cells the frequencies, proportions, or percentages of observations. Two variables, each divided into two parts, can be shown as in figure 9.4, and for more than two subgroups the contingency would look much like figure 9.5. For variables that are not dichotomous more than two subgroups can be formed.

Table 4.2 "Did you attend the book exhibit in the public library during the week of September 16 to 23?"

	Boys			Girls		
Grades:	7th	8th	9th	7th	8th	9th
Yes	45%	15%	20%	46%	51%	64%
No	55%	85%	80%	54%	49%	36%

FIGURE 9.5 Table of Bivariate Analysis

Descriptive Studies for Inquiry

Well constructed tables of data can add much to the understanding of a study by bridging the gap between sets of raw unorganized data and the manuscript text. Tables and figures, including graphs, can add much to help the researcher to analyze data and readers to understand the research.

Graphs provide a way of giving a very quick look at a set of data through pictorial representation of important characteristics. Either a table or graph, or both, can be used to represent a frequency distribution made up of frequencies of occurrences in sets of data. Creative uses of graphs and other figures provide additional ways to present data. Figures 9.6 and 9.7 illustrate how these can be varied for different uses. Different

			Interval Limits				
Interval	Tally	f	Apparent	Exact	f	cf	cpf
63-65	/	1	63-65	62.5-65.5	1	34	100
60-62	/	1	60-62	59.5-62.5	1	33	97
57-59	//	2	57-59	56.5-59.5	2	32	94
54-56	////	4	54-56	53.5-56.5	4	30	88
51-53	//// ////	9	51-53	50.5-53.5	9	26	76
48-50	//// /	6	48-50	47.5-50.5	6	17	50
45-47	////	5	45-47	44.5-47.5	5	11	32
42-44	//	2	42-44	41.5-44.5	2	6	18
39-41	/	1	39-41	38.5-41.5	1	4	12
36-38	//	2	36-38	35.5-38.5	2	3	9
33-35	/	1	33-35	32.5-35.5	1	1	3
		34			N=34		

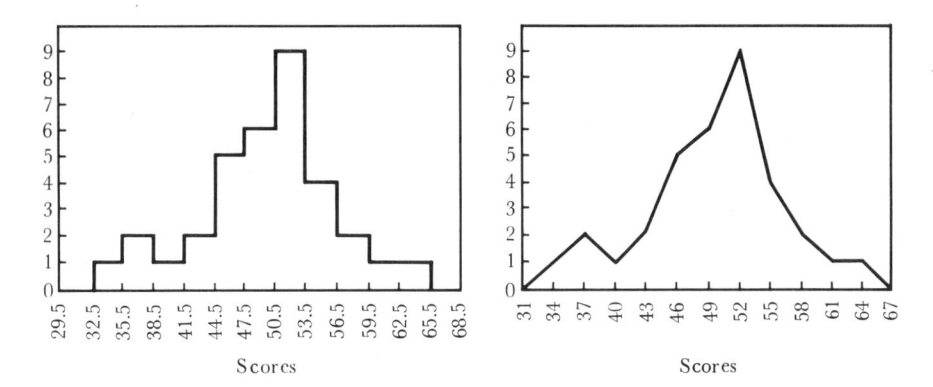

FIGURE 9.6 Use of Tables and Graphs

SOURCE: Charles D. Hopkins, *Describing Data Statistically* (Columbus, Ohio: Charles E. Merrill, 1974).

purposes direct the construction of graphs and vary the final product. The following principles should be considered when building a graph.

1. Label both axes.
2. The sequence of data should be low values to the left and high values to the right, and on the vertical axis low values at the bottom and high values at the top.
3. The zero points for the two axes should be the intersection of the axes. Attention to violation of this guideline can be pointed up by a break in the axis line.

4. The ratio of height to width should be about 3:5 or 2:3, and the units should be chosen so that no extreme distortion takes place.

A table for the computation looks like this:

Score X	Mean $\overline{X}$	$(X-\overline{X})$	$(X-\overline{X})^2$
64	60	+4	16
63	60	+3	9
62	60	+2	4
59	60	−1	1
57	60	−3	9
55	60	−5	25
		0	64

Graphically it looks like this:

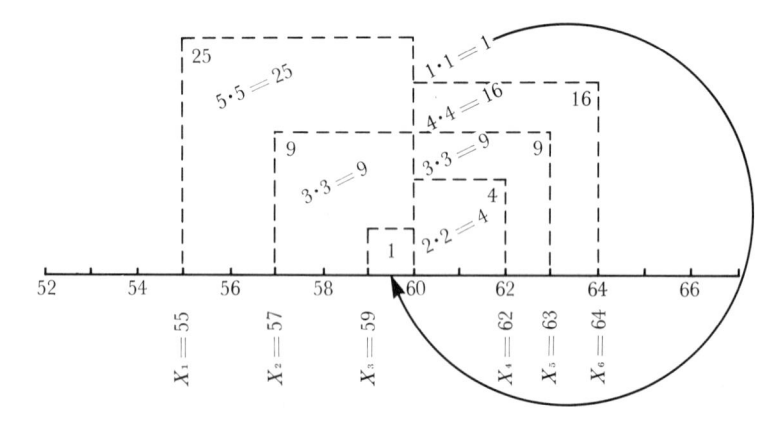

FIGURE 9.7 Use of a Table and Figure

SOURCE: Charles D. Hopkins, *Describing Data Statistically*.

The *scatter diagram* (scattergram) is a very important interpretive tool for a correlationalist. Since the scattergram gives a quick pictorial view of the relationship between two sets of data, it serves two major purposes for a researcher. It gives him/her a quick portrayal of a relationship without deriving a correlation coefficient, and it is a vehicle to display relationship in graphic form.

The scattergram is constructed on a two dimensional graph by plotting points that represent measures on two variables. In most cases the measurements will be pairs of values on a common subject. The relationship is revealed by patterns in the scattergram. The following scattergram in figure 9.8 reveals no discernible relationship between two variables. The dotted lines for one point (A) for subject A show how the scattergram is built. Each of the other points represents two measurements for one subject.

Patterns of linear relationship take shape when the data form along an imaginary line. In figure 9.9, a pattern, as in *A*, shows a positive or direct linear relationship, and *B* shows a negative or inverse linear relationship for the two variables being investigated for relationship.

The closer the dots approach to forming a line the greater the relationship—if the line moves up as the values on the *X* variable increase (left to right), the relationship

Descriptive Studies for Inquiry

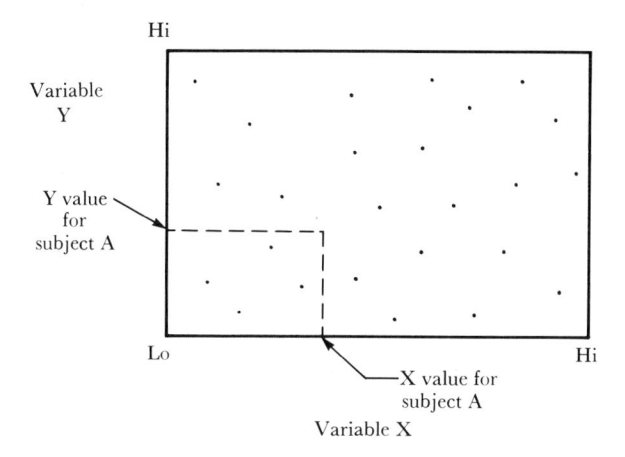

FIGURE 9.8 Scattergram Reflecting No Relationship

is positive, and if the line moves down as the values on the X variable increase (left to right), the relationship is negative. Correlational techniques discussed later in this chapter give an index for quantitative measure of the relationship between variables. Many lesser-used types of graphs and figures can be helpful for special needs of interpreting data.

The preliminary overview of most sets of data is facilitated through the use of diagrams—tables, graphs, or figures. Diagrams also aid the researcher and reader in bridging the gap from raw data to conclusions and provide a convenient way to shorten the narrative of research reports through data organization. Diagrams are not a substitute for statistical tests, but are an integral part of the interpretive phase of research.

The study of a *frequency distribution* can reveal some very important facts about the data. The four characteristics—central location, variability, skewness, and kurtosis—give the correlationist an opportunity to get information that is hidden in sets of raw data. The frequency distribution can be in either tabular or graphic form (see figure 9.6) and comparison of a number of frequency distributions indicates how they are different. Frequency is abbreviated as f. A characteristic that one becomes aware of is that the scores of each distribution fall within a limited interval of the scale, and that one value could be chosen as a value to indicate how the scores tend to center around a central point. The following question could be asked, "What one score could be

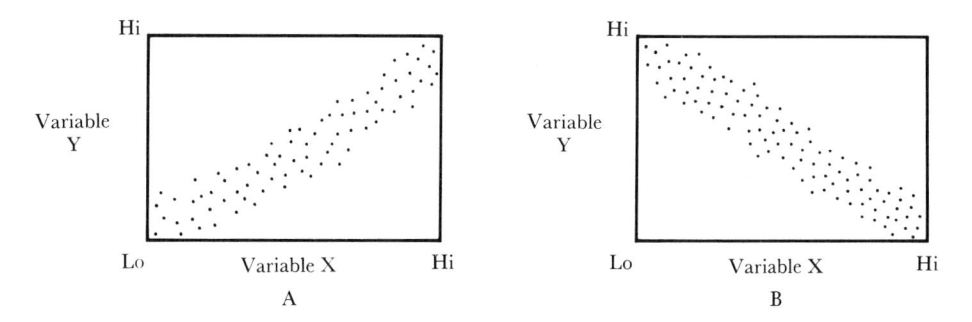

FIGURE 9.9 Positive and Negative Relationships for Variables X and Y

chosen to represent the distribution well?" This could be answered by giving the value that appears most often (the mode), by giving the arithmetical average (the mean), or by giving a point that divided the number of values into two equal parts (the median). The rules used to assign the numerical descriptors determine to a large degree the type of central tendency that can be used to describe the frequency distribution. Central tendency for nominal data can be shown only by the mode, for ordinal data the mode or median can be used, and for interval and ratio data the mode, median, or mean may be used.

Another characteristic that comes to one's attention is that of variability. Although a measure of central tendency is important it gives no information about the dispersion of scores. Widely used measures of dispersion are range, variance, and standard deviation, and lesser used measures are quartile deviation and average deviation. The question could be asked—"How are these scores scattered or dispersed?" This could be answered by giving the difference between the highest value and the lowest value (the range); by finding how each score differs from the mean, squaring that difference and getting an arithmetical average of the squared differences (the variance); or by finding the square root of the variance (the standard deviation).

The concept of variation with *nominal data* cannot be formally summarized because the numerical descriptors were assigned without magnitude. The variation rests in the occurrence of values in the mutually exclusive categories used for assignment. A little used measure of dispersion for ordinal data, the quartile deviation, is reported as one-half of the interval determined by the middle 50 percent of the values. A little used measure of dispersion for interval data averages the absolute values of deviation scores (average deviation). The most mathematically useful measures (variance and standard deviation) for interval data use the mean square of the squared deviations of a set of scores from their mean. Figure 9.7 represents pictorially the idea of a mean square. The *mean square* for the squares with areas of 25, 9, 1, 4, 9, and 16 is determined by adding the areas of the six squares and dividing by the number of squares, 6. $(25 + 9 + 1 + 4 + 9 + 16)/6$ equals $64/6$ which equals 10.67. The *mean square* or *variance* for the six listed values is 10.67 units. This is a two dimensional description of the dispersion of scores. The square root of the variance, $\sqrt{10.67}$ or 3.27, is the dispersion expressed in one dimension and is called the *standard deviation*. The large part played by the study of differences and sources of differences or variation in research makes these two statistics very valuable to all researchers. The analysis of variance is a study of the sources of the differences, and makes up a large part of statistical procedures. Properties of the standard deviation make it valuable in interpreting distributions and in tests of significance.

A study of the symmetry of a distribution can be reported by giving any *skewness* associated with the scores. If there is no indication of highly deviate scores (scores not like the rest) the distribution will be nearly symmetrical and therefore not skewed. Deviate scores at the end with high values of the variable being measured result in a positively skewed distribution, while deviate values at the end with low variable values result in a negatively skewed distribution. Skewness is associated with only those variables measured as interval or ratio, since equal intervals are needed to develop a concept of being deviate (see figure 9.10).

A characteristic closely related to variability is *kurtosis*. A graphical representation of a frequency distribution that is peaked in the center is called *leptokurtic* and results from measurements on subjects that are homogeneous (much alike) on the variable being measured. A graph that is very flat is called *platykurtic* and results from measure-

Descriptive Studies for Inquiry

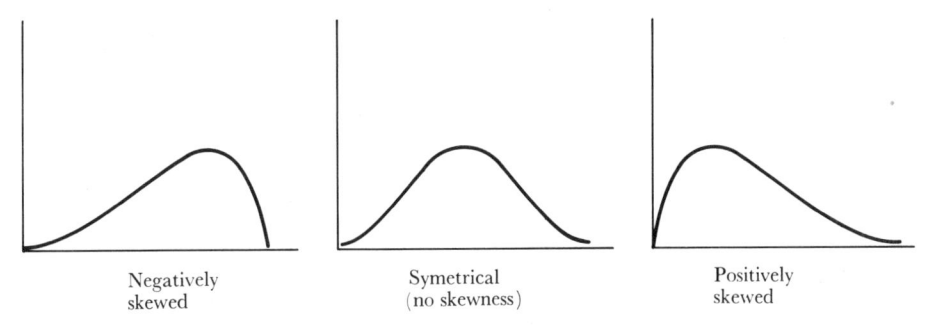

FIGURE 9.10 Three Frequency Distributions with Different Skewness

ments on subjects that are heterogeneous (much different) on the variable being measured. A graph that is bell-shaped (neither leptokurtic nor platykurtic) is called *mesokurtic*. Illustrations that show the characteristics leptokurtic, platykurtic, and mesokurtic are shown in figure 9.11. Kurtosis is associated only with data that have equal intervals in the assignment of numerical descriptors.

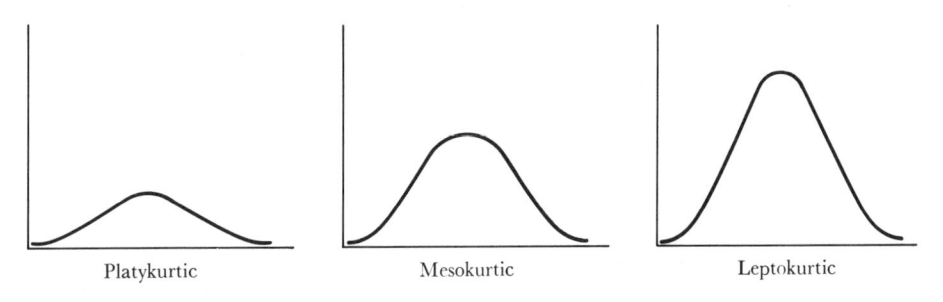

FIGURE 9.11 Three Frequency Distributions Differing in Kurtosis

The properties of central tendency, variation, skewness, and kurtosis, are used to describe sets of values (frequency distributions). A descriptive study is usually based in interpreting observations through the study of relationships within a set of scores and, more importantly, relationships between sets of observations using these properties as a basis for comparison.

A convenient way of presenting data (especially nominal) for inspection is to change numbers of cases to *percentages* and report the percentages in tables. Further interpretation of the percentage data usually includes some statistical test about differences.

The usual procedure for testing for differences for nominal data is to use chi-square tests. However, percentages can be tested directly by a technique that uses a *nomograph* to aid in the inspection of differences between percentages. A nomograph is a scale that interprets differences between two percentages for statistical significance. Although the nomograph lacks the precision of chi square it is accurate enough for an initial test. Where the differences border on significance, the usual chi-square technique can be used. For tables and more information about the use of nomographs see Oppenheim's presentation.[19]

Measures of relationship. An extension of the concept of variation of scores on one variable is the study of simultaneous variation of two variables. Many techniques of

---

19. A. N. Oppenheim, *Questionnaire Design and Attitude Measurement* (New York: Basic Books, 1966), pp. 287-92.

correlation (covariation) are available to assist the researcher in identifying relationships more precisely than the scattergrams are able to do. Measures of relationships are direct indexes[20] in that they reveal both the direction (nature) and the degree (magnitude) of how the two variables are related. The numerical descriptors of correlation range from -1.00 through 0 to $+1.00$ with -1.00 and $+1.00$ indicating respectively perfect negative correlation and perfect positive correlation; 0.00 indicates no relationship between the two variables.

The position of correlation is central to research based in observation of real-world conditions and cases where experimental studies are not feasible. In general the calculation of the index (coefficient of correlation) is straightforward by formula. Any correlational technique produces a coefficient that stands as an estimate of the covarying of the variables. The question "How do rankings of famous paintings by elementary school children compare to rankings given by college art majors?" implies a study of the relationship between sets of rankings from two groups with wide differences on important characteristics. If the two groups tend to rank the art objects much the same, that relationship will be reflected in a positive coefficient, the higher the relationship the closer to $+1.00$. If the two groups disagree in the rankings the inverse relationship will be reflected in a negative coefficient—the higher the relationship the closer to -1.00.

Since the preceding numerical descriptors (ranks) are ordinal in nature, an appropriate technique must be chosen. Spearman's coefficient of rank correlation is appropriate where the measurement has been made on two sets of ordinal data. The formula used is a derivation of a product-moment coefficient where the assignment of ranks assumes equal intervals. The basic formula for the Pearson product-moment coefficient (r) is a mean of the products of score deviations put in a standard score (z) form.

$$r = \frac{\Sigma(z_x \cdot z_y)}{N}$$

Σ means to sum
N is the number of paired measurements
z_x is equal to $\dfrac{X - \overline{X}}{\sigma_x}$
z_y is equal to $\dfrac{Y - \overline{Y}}{\sigma_y}$
X is a raw score on the X variable
Y is a raw score on the Y variable
$\overline{X}$ is the mean of the X distribution
$\overline{Y}$ is the mean of the Y distribution

The Spearman coefficient (rho) is obtained by the formula:

$$\rho = 1 - \frac{6\Sigma D^2}{N(N^2-1)} \text{ where}$$

ρ is rho (the correlation coefficient)
D is the difference in ranks
ΣD^2 is the sum of squared differences
N is the number of paired measurements. (In this special case the number of art objects.)

---

20. An index is a number that is made up of two or more numbers. The *cost of living index* is a weighted mean of typical prices of requirements of life, weighted according to the amount needed. The Dow-Jones average is an index of the price of several stocks.

Descriptive Studies for Inquiry

The data could be recorded as follows:

Art Object	Ranks given by: Elementary Students	Ranks given by: Art Majors	D	D²
One				
Two				
.				
.				
N				

$\Sigma D^2 = $ _____

Nearly all correlation formulas (exception: Kendall's T, which is a study of disarray)[21] are based on the Pearson product-moment rationale.

The choice of which correlational technique to use is based on the scales of the data for the two variables. Table 9.3 is provided to help the student identify appropriate techniques for combinations of scales of measurement of the two variables. Nominal variables suitable for correlational techniques have been further classified as dichotomous (true dichotomy) and dichotomized (forced dichotomy). An example of a dichotomous variable where the division is natural would be *male-female*, and an example of a dichotomized, where the division is artificial and gives up some information, would be *greater than median height* and *less than median height*.

Prediction

One aim of science is to be able to make reliable predictions of the future from information available in the present. Theory building deals with explaining and predicting and much of the utility of theory is being able to predict. Some scholars are ready to say that prediction is all important and that explanation is not needed if prediction gives the needed control. Explanation becomes important when dealing with generalizations. To discover that students do less well in a testing situation when the noise level is very high will allow prediction about student performance in noisy testing environments, and will in turn give direction to control of testing conditions. More important to development of theory would be an explanation of the inner workings of all of the interrelated variables to explain why the noise affected the test scores.

Prediction and correlation are closely related topics. The level of confidence of predictions depends on the degree of linear relationship between the predictor variable and the predicted variable. The following equation is basic to all discussion of regression (the statistical procedures used to make predictions):

$$Y' = a + bX$$

This is a general formula that describes a line when values are given to a and b, where X and Y' are values on the X and Y axes.

Y' is the predicted criterion score
a is a regression constant (the point where the line crosses the Y axis, figure 9.12)
b is a regression constant (amount of increase in Y given a unit increase in X, figure 9.12)
X is the predictor variable

---

21. Maurice G. Kendall, *Rank Correlation Methods*, 3rd ed. (New York: Hafner Publishing Co., 1962).

TABLE 9.3 Appropriate Correlational Techniques for Combinations of Different Measurements

Measurement Characteristics		Coefficient and symbol	Statistical Examples
Continuous (Interval, ratio, or combination)	Continuous	Pearson Product Moment r	Relationship between height (X) and weight (Y) of a set of subjects
Continuous	True dichotomy[1]	Point Biserial r_{pb}	Relationship between history test scores (X) and the answer (true or false) for item no. 1 (Y)
Continuous	Forced dichotomy[2]	Biserial r_b	Relationship between mental ability test scores (X) and above or below the average score on a reading comprehension test (Y)
Forced dichotomy[2]	Forced dichotomy[2]	Tetrachoric r_t	Relationship of position on two tests when subjects are rated as being above or below the median of IQ test (X) and a measure of hand grip (Y)
True dichotomy[1]	True dichotomy[1]	Phi ϕ	Relationship of married/unmarried students (X) and working/nonworking (Y)
Ranks (or capable of being ranked)	Ranks	Spearman rho ρ	Relationship of ranks for a set of paintings by art majors (X) and ranks by business majors (Y)
Ranks (or capable of being ranked)	Ranks	Kendall's Tau τ	Relationship of ranks for a set of paintings by art majors (X) and ranks by business majors (Y)
Ordinal	Dichotomous	Rank biserial r_{rb}	Relationship between untied ranks of order of finish of mile race (X) and training with or without weight lifting (Y)
Nominal	Continuous	Nonlinear n^2	Relationship of hair color (natural) (X) and scores on a test of creativity (Y)
Nominal (or categorized)	Nominal	Contingency Coefficient (C)	Relationship of socioeconomic status background $(X$ or $Y)$ and choice of favorite color $(X$ or $Y)$
Three or more sets of ranks		Kendall's Concordance (W)	Relationship among ranks of art majors (X), business majors (Y), and philosophy majors (Z) on art objects

[1] A true dichotomy results from measurement that is made on mere presence or absence of the variable.
[2] A forced dichotomy results when an assumed normal distribution is artificially divided into two parts. (Test scores above 75; Test scores below 75)

Descriptive Studies for Inquiry

Prediction is based on fitting a line to a set of scattergram points so that the sum of deviations squared of points from the line is less than that sum would be for any other line (see figure 9.12). When values are determined for *a* and *b* a regression equation

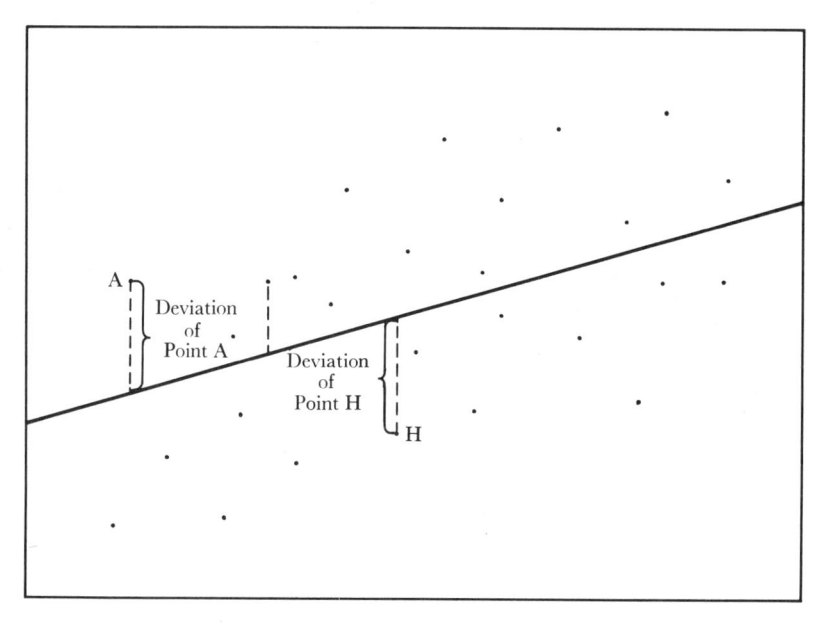

FIGURE 9.12   A Scatter Diagram Showing a Line of Best Fit

based on the preceding equation can be built for prediction between X and Y. If *a* equals 3 and *b* equals .5 then the equation for predicting Y' from X would be Y' = 3 + .5 (X). The prediction (Y') for a score of 7 on X would be Y' = 3 + .5 (7) = 3 + 3.5 = 6.5. For all scores of 7 on X, a Y' prediction of 6.5 would be made. Predictions for a scattergram where the points fall closely to a line (high relationship) the confidence of prediction will be very high and as the dots spread farther from the line (less relationship) the confidence of being close in the prediction becomes less and less. If you understand the principle involved above (not the statistical procedures—just the idea) you have the basis for all studies of regression since the concept is the same for all procedures. The concept carries through to multiple regression (more than one value used in prediction) to multivariate techniques and factor analysis. Most important for this discussion is an understanding of how research can use it to further inquiry in education. As relationships are identified prediction becomes possible, and studies can be made to investigate for an explanation for observed phenomena.

Variance

Statisticians have been criticized because they treat a large population as all being the same when representing all the values with a mean. If that is all that were done to interpret the scores in the distribution, then the criticism would be well founded. What the critics are saying is, "You have forgotten to look at differences." A number of jokes have been circulated about people who put too much confidence in one statistic. There was the nonswimming statistician who drowned in a lake that had an average depth of two feet because he put too much confidence in a mean value. There was also the statistician who had his head in the refrigerator and his feet in the oven and, on the average, felt very comfortable. Nevertheless statisticians do spend a considerable amount of time looking at variability.

A considerable part of statistics is devoted to comparing variances and to determining sources of variance. The variance (mean square) for a set of scores is a measure of the dispersion of the scores (see figure 9.7) and is used to explain one of the characteristics of a frequency distribution. If two or more groups are being examined and/or compared, the measure of variability gives a basis for comparison of the degree of scattering of the scores between groups. If the property of the groups being examined has much the same variance in each group, they tend to be much alike on that property. If the variances are much different, then the groups are not alike on that property.

Differences in variance can be very important in research. Visualize two highways that have these characteristics: average (mean) speeds of the cars on highway A and highway B are very close and the variance of the speed of cars on highway A is much greater than the variance of car speeds for highway B. How will the traffic flow be different? Which highway would you predict to have fewer accidents? Probably most important to the traffic researcher is: why do the speeds vary so much for highway A? *What is the source of the variance?*

The analysis of variance and related statistics give much attention to identifying sources of the differences or variation. For some reason(s) the drivers on highway B drove much the same (the variance was small) while those on highway A, though the average speed was about the same as highway B, had large differences among the speeds. Possibly the source of variance was in the cars—maybe some were very old and could not travel very fast while others were newer and more difficult to drive slower. Possibly the difference was in road conditions—curves and hills on highway A might cause variation in speeds. Maybe the source of variance was in the drivers—older drivers who drove very slowly and younger drivers who drove very fast could explain a large variance for highway A. Some of the variance would be attributed to other causes and possibly some would result from chance and remain unexplained.

Techniques of analysis of variance are used more widely in experimental research, but the study of sources of variance is still much a part of the correlational studies, as evidenced by the use of analysis techniques by Sir Ronald A. Fisher.[22]

Multiple regression is an extension of previously discussed correlational techniques, and is basic to the understanding of situations involving complex contributions of several variables.

> Within the decade [written in 1973] we will probably see the virtual demise of one-variable thinking and the use of analysis of variance with data unsuited to the method. Instead, multivariate methods will be well accepted tools in the behavioral scientist's and educator's armamentarium.[23]

Multiple regression is basic to multivariate methods. Multiple regression allows the investigator to view the contribution of two or more variables to one dependent

---

22. Sir Ronald A. Fisher, *Statistical Methods for Research Workers*, 14th ed. (New York: Hafner Publishing Co., 1970), pp. 213-339.

23. Fred N. Kerlinger and Elazar J. Pedbazur, *Multiple Regression in Behavioral Research* (New York: Holt, Rinehart and Winston, 1973), p. v.

Descriptive Studies for Inquiry

variable. Theoretically the number of variables that can be studied is unlimited, but in practice for the researcher the number *is* limited.

Educational questions are for the most part based in a complex situation where the integrands are complex. A study of the relationship of two variables in isolation has been proposed as artificial and not particularly meaningful. The techniques of multiple regression are for the most part too complex to be a part of one's initial study of research methods. Since this is a textbook to introduce students to educational inquiry, multivariate methods and factor analysis are mentioned only to familiarize the student with the terms and what they do. A logical first step to research fundamentals is through the question suggested earlier where a relationship between two variables is investigated (bivariate rather than multivariate). With adequate groundwork in bivariate research the extension to more complex conditions becomes a logical next step.

Multiple regression is, in principle, like predicting from one variable (X) to another variable (Y'). An added factor of more than one independent variable requires a weighting of each independent variable on a basis of its contribution to the dependent variable. The regression equation $Y' = a + b(X)$ used a partial regression weight (b) which reflects the increase in Y for each unit increase in X. Multiple regression formulas are built much the same way except the contributions of the several independent variables are weighted to explain the variability of the dependent variable.

> Multiple regression analysis is especially helpful to the correlationalist attempting to establish causes but it is also used in prediction. The basic analytic techniques of regression analysis are the same when used in studies primarily concerned with prediction or with explanation. The interpretation of the results, however, may differ depending on whether the emphasis is on one or the other.... Some applications of multiple regression analysis are of course appropriate in either a predictive or an explanatory framework.[24]

Other multivariate techniques that are useful to the area of descriptive research include canonical correlation, discriminant analysis, and factor analysis.

Canonical correlation extends multiple regression to include more than one dependent variable, allowing study of a set of independent variables and a set of dependent variables.

Discriminant analysis includes both predictive and inferential multivariate statistical techniques. It focuses on the analysis of groups of a population one from the other. A study of corporate bankruptcy found that firms that failed and firms that remained in existence had statistically significant different financial ratios.[25] A classification rule was formed to predict potential corporate failure.

Factor analysis is used to identify components by noting clusters of variables, for studies of human behavior factors have come "to be thought of as hypothetical variables which in various combinations accounted for or explained the variations in various kinds of human behavior."[26] Factor analysis attempts to identify strands or components that account for observable human behavior. "Many would insist that they are attempting to get at the fundamental realities and truths of mental activity or

---

24. Ibid., p. 282.
25. Edward I. Altman, "Financial Ratios, Discriminant Analysis and the Prediction of Corporate Bankrupsy," *Journal of Finance* 23 (September 1968): 589-609.
26. Paul Horst, *Factor Analysis of Data Matrices* (New York: Holt, Rinehart and Winston, 1965), p. 3.

human behavior, or perhaps even more philosophically fundamental concepts."[27] Factors (artificially created for study) are highly related to a cluster of variables while independent of other clusters, and therefore factors are shown to be independent of one another. Factors are created without real meaning and are at times misinterpreted. The fact that factor analysis always generates factors makes the outcomes difficult to interpret but does not indicate that factor analysis should not be used.

Development of tests intended to measure the construct of intelligence led psychologists to investigate theories based on factors. The need to operationally define intelligence through tasks in the test resulted in theories of intelligence involving factors. Manuals that accompany tests of intelligence, mental maturity, and so on are filled with information about how the authors view factors of intelligence.

Summary of Data-Interpreting Tools

The tools listed to this point are important to descriptive research for their ability to aid in analyzing present real-world conditions and relationships. Compilation and presentation of data in readable form are early steps to interpretation. Characteristics of frequency distributions and percentages can be used to further interpret, and comparisons between distributions can be made, by looking at differences among groups on specific measures of central location and variability. Correlational and prediction techniques including multiple regression and related multivariate techniques can be used to study relationships. Factor analysis is a special statistical procedure of computation used to study contributing factors for human constructs.

Goodness of Fit

A set of procedures based on a comparison of what one observes, as compared to what one expects to observe, given certain information and assumptions is called *goodness of fit* and is based on the chi-square (χ^2) distributions. It is beyond the scope of this book to explain chi square mathematically, but the concept and uses of goodness of fit as related to descriptive studies will be developed. Introductory statistics books give the mathematical development and computational procedures. Important to our concern here is for students to understand chi square well enough so that they will know when to use it in research procedures, especially for descriptive research strategies of inquiry.

The common element to all tests of goodness of fit is a comparison of numbers actually observed in any number of classes (categories), compared to the number expected to fall in the classes, based on what an *a priori* hypothesis says should fall in the classes. Goodness of fit techniques can be used to check characteristics of a sample with known values for a population. For example, an anonymous survey of a sample of university students could be checked for representativeness of class standing of those returning questionnaires, compared to proportions of students in the four undergraduate classes at the university. A researcher finds in the returns for questionnaire A the following numbers: 73 freshmen; 18 sophomores; 10 juniors; and 9 seniors. The registrar's list reveals the following enrollment percentages for the classes: 35 percent freshmen; 25 percent sophomores; 21 percent juniors; and 19 percent seniors. Table 9.4 gives the data for the observed and expected frequencies of occurrence in the classes. For some reason far more freshman students returned the questionnaire than the other classes. What we have observed certainly does not "fit" with what we expected

---

27. Ibid., p. 4.

Descriptive Studies for Inquiry

TABLE 9.4 Class Rank of Students Returning Questionnaire A

Class	Observed Frequencies	Expected Frequencies
Freshman	73	38.5
Sophomore	18	27.5
Junior	10	23.1
Senior	9	20.9
TOTAL	110	110.0

when the 110 students were distributed into proportions of enrollees, but neither would the data for table 9.5, which are the numbers for each class returning form B of another researcher's questionnaire. Again the freshman students returned more than expected, and our observed frequencies do not "fit" the expected frequencies. Careful inspection of the expected values reveals that under no conditions could we get perfect fit. Since the responding questionnaire totals will be positive whole numbers, there is no way to get a cell frequency for observed as 23.1, 32.5, or such.

TABLE 9.5 Class Rank of Students Returning Questionnaire B

Class	Observed Frequencies	Expected Frequencies
Freshman	47	45.5
Sophomore	31	32.5
Junior	28	27.3
Senior	24	24.7
TOTAL	130	130.0

The basic question for this test of goodness of fit is: are the returns for the questionnaires typical of class proportions except for small errors expected to be associated with any set of observed values? Some differences are not surprising. Goodness of fit techniques tell the researcher when to be surprised (or when to view observed differences as a very unlikely event by chance). It is not likely to find returns for questionnaire A in this proportion by chance alone, while the proportions for the returns for questionnaire B would result often just by chance.

The computation procedures for obtaining χ^2 values vary with the structure of the problem. For our two examples above the computation looks like this:

$$\chi^2 = \Sigma \frac{(f_o - f_e)^2}{f_e}$$

Where: f_o = observed frequency for a given cell
f_e = expected frequency for that cell
Σ = means to add

f_o	f_e	$\frac{(f_o - f_e)^2}{f_e}$	f_o	f_e	$\frac{(f_o - f_e)^2}{f_e}$
73	38.5	30.92	47	45.5	.05
18	27.5	3.28	31	32.5	.07
10	23.1	7.43	28	27.3	.02
9	20.9	6.78	24	24.7	.02
		$X^2 = 48.41$			$X^2 = .16$

Questionnaire A   Questionnaire B

Each χ^2 value would then be compared to a table prepared with the values needed to show significance (when the event is unlikely to happen by chance). For these tests χ^2 values of 7.815 *or more* show significance at the .05 level. The significance level is set by the researcher in the planning stages as a part of the ground rules for his or her study and represents the probability of saying that the difference is significant when in fact it is not (see chapter 10, "Null Hypothesis").

The decision for returns of questionnaire A is that the proportions of returns for the four classes were being affected by something other than chance fluctuations (null hypothesis rejected). Possibly the basic question was of more direct importance to the first-year student, or the freshman students might have thought that they were required to return it while the more sophisticated upper levels knew that the return was not required.

The decision for returns of questionnaire B is that the proportions of returns for the four classes were *not* affected by anything other than chance fluctuations (null hypothesis not rejected). The observed values *fitted* well with what was expected. The test of goodness of fit showed that questionnaire A returns *did not* fit with what would be expected from chance differences.

The concept of goodness of fit permeates much of the statistical work done with nominal data. The *test of independence* for contingency tables investigates the extent to which frequencies of one variable depend on (are contingent on) frequencies of the second variable. Other nonparametric tests can be used to test for goodness of fit for nominal data or higher ordered data that the researcher wants to treat as nominal data.

Goodness of fit tests extend into ordinal data where the sums of ranks for two sets of data can be tested for significance. Introductory statistics books include simple straightforward explanations of nonparametric tests.[28]

The relatively simple statistics associated with the types of tests discussed above make them particularly helpful to studies in descriptive research. They allow the dimension of adding to our knowledge rather than merely describing without generalization. There seems to be a tendency for someone to want to apply the highest level of statistics that he/she can to research problems. The inclination is to apply a complicated model when a simpler model may be more appropriate, and the complicated may actually inhibit logical reasoning about the problems. Inner relations among variables may be revealed by simple devices while more complex devices could in fact conceal them. A rule of thumb for researchers is to use the simplest device available that will reveal the messages contained in the data, keeping in mind that the problem should dictate the procedure rather than a statistical procedure dictating the problem.

Inference in Descriptive Research

The idea of creating knowledge through descriptive research is distasteful to some persons. The tendency to associate knowledge generation with only experimental procedures has resulted from and is based on the very powerful procedures of the carefully

---

28. Three books devoted to nonparametric tests are: Eugene S. Edgington, *Statistical Inference: The Distribution-Free Approach* (New York: McGraw-Hill, 1969); Sidney Siegel, *Non-Parametric Statistics for the Behavioral Sciences* (New York: McGraw-Hill, 1956); and W. J. Conover, *Practical Nonparametric Statistics* (New York: John Wiley & Sons, 1971).

Descriptive Studies for Inquiry 171

controlled experiment. As a researcher loses this control the tendency is to discount the results for any use other than a description.

With the above restriction to research procedures there appears to be no hope of inquiry into many important areas—not only in education and associated social and behavioral sciences but in physical health and other areas. The contention here is that, given properly designed research with appropriate procedures to provide results based on valid data, conclusions for descriptive studies are valuable in all areas where experimental control is difficult or impossible to obtain.

The art of the correlator may be of a higher level than that of the experimentalist if obstacles to completion are considered as criteria for evaluation. The book on statistical inference by Edgington can provide much support for the position that is taken here. He says, "Many ideas in this book will be of general interest not simply because they are new but because they are in direct opposition to commonly held beliefs about statistical inference."[29] Without detracting from the contribution of experimental research, which is not here questioned, a position of support for more descriptive research that is generalizable is encouraged.

SUMMARY

Descriptive research is based in studying conditions as they exist without intervention or manipulation by the investigator. In addition to a study of present status, descriptive research (1) investigates the meaning of what is being observed, (2) interprets through detected relationships what is viewed, (3) establishes a climate for predictions, and (4) investigates for cause-effect direction of identified relationships.

Being scientific in nature, descriptive research follows the scientific approach to problem solving, utilizing information about criterion variables that represent characteristics or traits of human beings important to the teaching-learning process. Quantitative data are generated to provide information that can be treated mathematically.

The tools to be used in descriptive research have been divided into those used to collect data and those used to interpret the data. Appropriate tools to gather the data are to be chosen through articulation with the problem, and tools for interpretation are to be selected in regard to the characteristics of the data that have been generated.

A study that is closely related to descriptive research—the status study—reports the present conditions without interpretation. This fact-finding and reporting study is the beginning for most research studies and also serves the question based in a practical situation where the outcome is not intended to be generalized into a theory or the body of present knowledge.

Descriptive research is used widely in education, and in the broadest sense all studies are in part descriptive since description is involved in all research in one way or another. Although the control of those variables under study is lacking, through a descriptive study many opportunities exist to study questions that are, for one reason or another, not researchable by careful manipulation of variables involved in the question.

---

29. Edgington, *Statistical Inference,* p. vii.

10

Use of the Experiment in Inquiry

> *Whenever a new discovery is made, crowds are ready with suggestions that this or that technique should now be used, but no one could have advised Fleming to discover penicillin or Columbus to look for America.*
>
> *Still the techniques of experimental design are extremely important because few discoveries are immediately useful as such. Indeed, most of them are soon forgotten unless their ingredient elements are meticulously analyzed according to a well-conceived plan.*
>
> —Hans Selye

The goals of science to explain, control, and predict lead to theory development about natural phenomena. To use theory as a means to the goals requires that empirical investigations be conducted to discover how well theory explains observed phenomena and to what extent it permits predictions and control. The most direct way to develop theory is through the use of empirically tested hypotheses based in establishing cause-and-effect relationships. The most direct way to test cause-and-effect relationships is by a carefully devised experiment.[1] The close relationship of the experiment to the goals of science explains its wide acceptance and use in research.

By experimentation, the investigator attempts to find out what is related to what, and by control of the variables what cause is associated with an effect. Newly created facts about cause and effect are then put into contemporary theory that serves to explain and interrelate current knowledge. The strength of the experiment lies in the control pro-

---

1. In Carter V. Good, *Dictionary of Education* (New York: McGraw-Hill, 1973), experiment is defined as: the administration, under controlled conditions, of treatments to a group or groups that have been specifically constituted for the purpose, and the analysis of the effects produced or induced in the subjects or units as a result.

vided by the plan through manipulation of variables. Study of a natural situation provides little if any opportunity to control the contributions of variables to the setting being studied. The researcher has only limited opportunity to isolate variables for study in a natural setting. The experiment is valuable in educational research when the variables under study are amenable to manipulation either practically, ethically, or morally.

NATURE OF EXPERIMENTAL RESEARCH

The experimental approach is based in the idea of doing something with a situation rather than merely looking at it. In the strictest sense an experiment can take place only in a laboratory setting with the greatest possible control and study of the effects of manipulation. In the broadest sense any interjection of something different into a natural setting could be considered an experiment. In general the environment of the setting for the educational experiment does not allow the researcher complete control. With appropriate statistical procedures available to aid in data interpretation, the major task before the educational experimentalist is one of collecting valid data in sufficient quantities. To do this effectively he or she will be conducting research classed as quasi-experimental.[2] Although experimental in principle, most educational experiments lack the strict control provided only by a laboratory.

The study of the effects of "doing something with" involves a breakdown of observed differences into controlled and uncontrolled sources. The effects attributed to the uncontrolled sources are viewed as *random error* or differences that cannot be accounted for in the manipulation, while error associated with known sources is called *systematic error* or differences that can be accounted for. Obviously the experimenter loses systematic error as he/she loses control of the contributing variables. Some researchable questions allow the researcher more control than do others. In general researchers will use experiments where the nature of the question allows adequate control and where there are no ethical problems involved in introducing something different to that situation under study.

The study of rocks permits them to be chipped, pounded, ground to a powder, treated with acids and other compounds, and studied in regard to differences under carefully controlled conditions. Nature conducts innumerable experiments by introducing new conditions through natural sources. Of course changes by nature lack the control needed for rigorous study, but they are nevertheless experiments. Our culture and our researchers' inhibitions do not permit unlimited control through experiments on human beings and other animals, thus the use of the experiment is limited in the study of educational problems.

Depriving a subject of an educational benefit in order to study the effects is as unacceptable in educational research as is depriving a subject of a necessity for life or the introduction of a disease in order to seek a possible cure in medical research. This

---

2. "There are many natural social settings in which the research person can introduce something like experimental design into his scheduling of data collection procedures (e.g., the *when* and *to whom* of measurement), even though he lacks the full control over the scheduling of experimental stimuli (the *when* and *to whom* of exposure and the ability to randomize exposures) which makes a true experiment possible. Collectively, such situations can be regarded as quasi-experimental designs." See Donald T. Campbell and Julian C. Stanley, "Experimental and Quasi-experimental Designs for Research," *Handbook of Research on Teaching*, ed. N.L. Gage, (Chicago: Rand McNally, 1963), p. 204.

limiting factor is not a deficiency of experimental research, but the nature of manipulation in experimental research causes it to be less useful in the social sciences, behavioral sciences, and education than in the physical sciences. Biological sciences also suffer from the restriction placed on them by the nature of the subjects that they study.

In spite of these difficulties opportunities to use the experiment in educational research do exist, and its use is to be encouraged where the conditions are suitable for experimental manipulation. The empirical nature of the experimental approach and its capability to control through manipulation of variables make this research method a powerful generator of new knowledge. When strict experimental procedures are not feasible, the scientists turn to study of natural situations that are nearly comparable to desired actual experiments. The correlationalist using descriptive research studies nature's experiments, while the experimentalist studies the effects of variation that he or she has created. Carefully planned experimental strategies allow statements about causation by study of the effects of manipulation.

The Experiment in Education

The experiment should be used for educational research when laboratory-like conditions can be created for the research study. Many variables of educational concern can be studied by varying the conditions for separate groups and studying the effects that result from the different conditions. Different uses of classtime or different methods of presenting materials to students are examples of ways to provide the manipulation.

When the variable under study cannot be arbitrarily manipulated within subjects, such as the human characteristics of socioeconomic status, sex, aptitude, and so on, the researcher may find that much the same effect can be had by assigning to groups by differences on an attribute. A study may involve a question of the effects of being male or female in a particular situation. Rather than changing the sex of subjects under study, the control could come from studying the differences between a set of subjects who are all male and another set of subjects who are all female. Of course the plan of the study would have to give consideration to control of all other variables, but assuming that the control has been accomplished the manipulation would come through assignment rather than by direct manipulation.

The above discussion should reveal to the reader that near-laboratory conditions can be set up for many educationally based questions. The more detailed accounting of experimental designs given later in this chapter will point up more specifically how to gain the necessary control needed to establish the antecedent-consequence relationship of variables through the experimental approach to answering educational questions.

STEPS IN EXPERIMENTAL RESEARCH

The steps for experimental research fit the basic sequence used for the general scientific method. The overall plan will be focused on attacking questions that can best be answered by the research strategy of problem solving and will, in addition, be oriented to solution by development of an appropriate experiment.

Every experiment grows out of a doubt or indeterminate situation that provides a researchable problem. After the problem is put in question form, the next step is to seek the answer from colleagues, experts, and professional literature, especially reports of research studies. If a satisfactory answer is not found, the background knowledge is organized to develop a research hypothesis. The research hypothesis is a researcher's best guess as to the answer that he or she expects to find from the experimentally designed investigation of the problem. Each research hypothesis is developed and based on all the background knowledge that has been found to bear on the question. It will usually be tied to educational theory. Research hypotheses are developed to varying degrees of confidence. Some are much like a blind guess while others may rate very closely to a well established theory.

The research hypothesis is especially important to experimental research, since it is generally the alternate hypothesis to the statistically oriented null hypothesis used to interpret observed differences in the empirical data. The close relationship of the two hypotheses (research and null) is further revealed in the next section where they become a part of the researcher's experimental design.

The next step is to structure an experiment through a design to select subjects, gather empirical data, analyze them, and make an objective decision in regard to whether or not the data support the hypothesis. Since different types of designs yield different kinds of information, the methodology and structure of the experiment must be carefully constructed for the particular question under scrutiny. Basic statistical designs must be adapted to the special problem of the study, taking into consideration the effects of each decision on other components of the study. The structure of each study is so specialized that the developed design will be unique unto itself. Others may be similar to it but none will be exactly the same.

After the data have been gathered, organized, and analyzed, the conclusions are based on the experimenter's interpretation of the results. With a well designed experimental study having maximum control, the rejection of or the failure to reject the null hypothesis provides a ready-made decision about the support of the research hypothesis. In general the rejection of the null hypothesis will be cause to conclude that the research hypothesis had been supported. Failure to reject the null hypothesis generally indicates that the research hypothesis was not supported. Of course the investigator is free to expand the results with a narrative discussing the relationship to present educational theory and the implications of the study.

To review the steps of experimental research: the researcher first asks a question and, if he/she fails to find a suitable answer in the literature or from experts, proposes an answer stated as a research hypothesis. He or she then structures an experiment designed to gather data and analyze them and uses the results either to reject or not to reject the null hypothesis. Finally the researcher interprets that decision in terms of support or nonsupport of the research hypothesis. The major difference between historical research and descriptive research lies in the difference in structure of the experimental design, which is discussed in detail in the next section.

EXPERIMENTAL DESIGN

The process of planning and structuring experiments is commonly called *designing* experiments. The output of the process is an experimental design, and it includes all of the components of methodology needed to test hypotheses through a set of ground rules that uses empirical data as a basis for decisions of support or nonsupport of the research hypothesis. The design is used to allow objective interpretation of differences observed in the data.

Use of the Experiment in Inquiry

Experimental Treatment

Basic to the understanding of experimental design is the idea of different treatment for separate groups on a chosen variable (independent) and measurement of the same groups on another variable (dependent), to determine the effects of the different kinds (levels) of treatment.

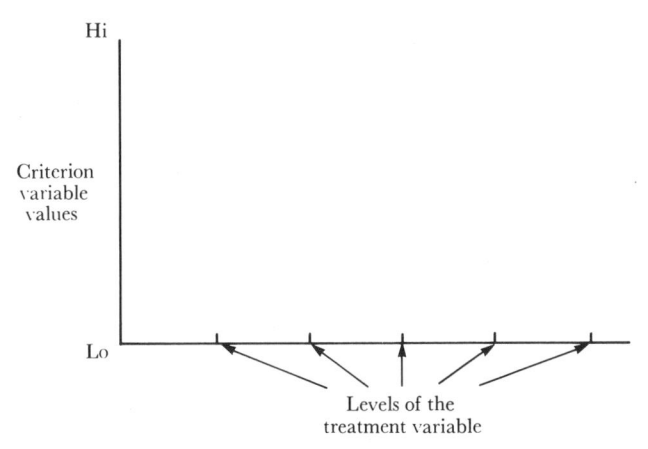

The study of experimental design here will be limited to designs in which there is one and only one criterion variable. The criterion variable, sometimes called a response or dependent variable, takes different values depending on the effects of different levels on treatment variables, also known as independent variables. Some experimental studies are designed to study the effects of different levels of treatment to one independent variable on one dependent (criterion) variable.

The effects of two or more treatment variables on a single criterion variable can be studied within a single experiment, but their effects are not necessarily independent. It seems reasonable to assume that combinations of effects are not predictable from separate effects. Studies of effects of more than one treatment variable must include as a part of the investigation a study of interaction among treatment variables.

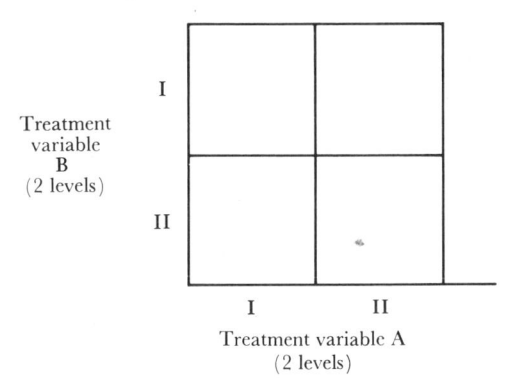

To determine a cause-and-effect relationship the treatment variable must be under the control of the experimenter. The control may be direct, as when the experimenter manipulates conditions by setting specific levels for the treatment variables. Different room temperatures for study can be set by the experimenter. The treatment variable would be temperature of rooms, the levels would be different temperatures, and the criterion variable would be some measure of how well the subjects were able to learn in the conditions of temperature differences.

The above example points up the two aspects of control, first, the control of the treatment variable and second, the control of other contributing variables. To view difference effects from one variable on the criterion variable, all contributions from extraneous variables must be held constant for the two groups.

The control for the treatment variable may be indirect, through the use of a priori classification of subjects to be studied. The effects of socioeconomic background on the school dropout rate cannot be studied by varying, at the experimenter's will, the level of the treatment variable for each subject in the study. However subjects from different levels of socioeconomic background can be assigned into like groups and studied for differences. The lack of a variable manipulated directly by the experimenter places this design as quasi-experimental. Since the experimenter is able to control conditions and assign levels on the independent variable, the design takes on the characteristics of an experiment except for the lack of direct manipulation.

The treatment variables that have had the levels set directly have been called *manipulated-type* variables, *active* variables, and *treatment* variables. The treatment variables which have had the levels set indirectly through traits or properties have been called *classification* variables, *assigned* variables, *attribute* variables, and *selection-type* variables. In general the statistical procedures will be the same for a design using either active or assigned independent variables.

Experimental treatment is composed of the differences provided by the researcher on the independent variable. This treatment must be clearly understood and explained in the design. Without a clear statement about treatment, the study lacks a vehicle to interpret differences that are observed on the criterion variable. The statistical test of significance is in terms of a "significant difference." The difference is in terms of the effects of treatment. If it is significant then the treatment levels (differences) are considered to be the source of the difference, if statistical significance is not found the treatment is viewed as having no effect.

The Null Hypothesis

The data gathered within an experimental design offer the opportunity of making a comparison of two or more sample means, or some other statistic, where the sample groups have received different treatments. For example, an experimenter may want to determine the effects of exercise on the performance of a cognitive task, such as reading comprehension. He or she may select at random (see chapter 5) two groups for study, assigning two levels of treatment on the independent variable (different treatment for each group) and measuring effects on the criterion variable. The two groups might be asked to read a passage and answer questions about the contents. The treatment levels for one group could be quiet restful activity for ten minutes before reading and questioning and, for the other group, ten minutes of vigorous activity before study. A mean score for each group could be obtained on the criterion variable, and the difference could be investigated statistically.

The experiment requires a decision about the observed differences between the two means of the criterion values. Both means and the difference between the means are subject to sampling error. If the two groups were to take the test questions under

Use of the Experiment in Inquiry

exactly the same conditions (no treatment) it is not likely that they would score, such that the means of both groups would be exactly the same value because of sampling error. A study of differences in experimental studies must take into account sampling error. May the difference observed between the two means be attributed to sampling error and viewed as a difference that appears by chance or is that difference so great that it would only rarely happen by chance? If the difference between the group means is considered as a rare occurrence with only sampling differences, then the observed difference will be presumed to be a result of the different treatment provided on the independent variable. In the preceding study the treatment provided is differences in amount of exercise. A design for this study could be shown as the model in figure 10.1.

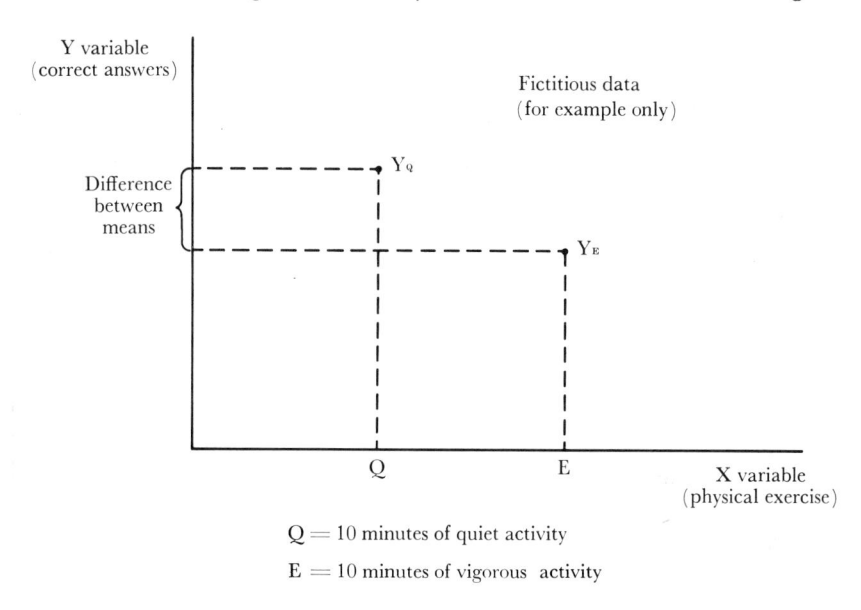

[Figure 10.1: A graph with Y variable (correct answers) on vertical axis and X variable (physical exercise) on horizontal axis. Points Y_Q at Q and Y_E at E are shown with dashed lines indicating the difference between means. Fictitious data (for example only).

Q = 10 minutes of quiet activity
E = 10 minutes of vigorous activity]

FIGURE 10.1 Effects of Exercise on Cognitive Functioning

A decision must be made as to the cause of the difference obtained on the dependent variable. Statistical procedures that lead to decisions about the source of the difference are called *tests of significance*. Significance is used to refer to a difference credited to experimental treatment. If the difference is sufficiently large to be considered a result of treatment, the difference is *significant*. Small differences are credited to sampling error. The test of significance will objectively make that decision about the source of differences based on the data of the samples and the structure of the design.

As mentioned earlier, the research hypothesis cannot be tested directly. A statistical statement, called the *null hypothesis*, provides the vehicle to be tested. The test of significance tests the tenability of the null hypothesis. Although *not* a true hypothesis in the sense of a rational guess, the null hypothesis gives a way to interpret the data and is closely related to the research hypothesis. The null hypothesis is a statement about differences on the criterion variable in regard to the source of those differences. It says in effect that any differences observed are there because of sampling error, not from treatment. A null hypothesis for the study about effects of exercise could be written as follows:

There is no significant difference between the group mean scores on the questions asked about the narrative read as a result of differences in amount of exercise provided the two groups.

This null hypothesis statement is a trial hypothesis that is testable statistically. One other hypothesis is implied when the null hypothesis is stated—that implied hypothesis is that there is a difference, and that the difference should be credited to treatment. Two, and only two, possible conditions exist—either the difference is there because of sampling error or because of treatment. The two conditions can be presented as follows:

$H_0 : \mu_Q - \mu_E = 0$ or $\mu_Q = \mu_E$
$H_1 : \mu_Q - \mu_E \neq 0$ or $\mu_Q \neq \mu_E$
   H_0 is the null hypothesis
   H_1 is the alternate hypothesis
   μ_Q and μ_E are the population means for the two groups
   0 includes any numerical value from the sample data that can be credited to sampling error
   $\neq$ means unequal

In general the alternate hypothesis is the experimenter's research hypothesis, and rejection of the null hypothesis as a tenable position is cause to support the research hypothesis. If the null hypothesis is rejected the experimenter believes that the possibility of the observed difference happening by chance is remote. Nevertheless the possibility that the difference did happen by chance exists in both theory and practice. Then how can an experiment prove that the difference came from treatment or if it came by chance? The experimenter can never be 100 percent positive that he has made a correct decision. In other words, he cannot *prove* anything from his study, but can only state that the research hypothesis was supported at certain levels of probability.

Decision Errors

The researcher hopes that his or her decision to support the research hypothesis or to fail to support it is a correct decision. Since the researcher cannot be sure of how his/her decision fits with the real world, he must make a study of the possible error associated with two different decisions. If he rejects the null hypothesis he may be rejecting a difference that occurred by chance. If he fails to reject he may be failing to reject a difference that did indeed come from experimental treatment. He could decide (by a statistical test) to reject the null hypothesis that he should not reject or he could be in error by not rejecting when he should reject. Each statement of a null hypothesis requires a significance level for the test of significance (usually .01 or .05). The significance level for a study is the probability of rejecting a null hypothesis when it should not be rejected. This is called an alpha error or type I error. An error associated with failure to reject the null hypothesis when it should be rejected is called a beta error or type II error.

Keep in mind that in reality either the null hypothesis is true or the alternate hypothesis is true. The decision about the null hypothesis is made without knowledge about the situation of real-world conditions. The relationship of the conditions is as follows: When H_0 is rejected and H_1 is true, the correct decision has been made. When the H_0

Use of the Experiment in Inquiry

Conditions / Decision	Real-world conditions	
	H_0 true	H_1 true
Reject H_0	Type I error Alpha (α)	OK Correct decision
Fail to reject H_0	OK Correct decision	Type II error Beta (β)

is not rejected and H_0 is true, the correct decision has been made. Rejection of H_0 when H_0 is true and failure to reject H_0 when H_1 is true are both errors.

Many decisions are nearly analogous to the above situation—the diagnosis of a patient as needing or not needing medication or surgery can be fit in the model. Each diagnosis by a physician is intended to be an OK decision, such that all patients needing medication or surgery receive it. Those patients who are diagnosed as needing medication when they do not, or are operated on when it is not needed, are victims of a type I error by the doctor. Those who do not receive medication when it is needed, or are not operated on when they should be, are victims of a type II error. Doctors and researchers hope to keep both types of errors to a minimum. Carrying or not carrying an umbrella and raining or not raining involve possible errors in judgment. See figure 10.2 for an analogy for experimental decisions using umbrella carrying.

Notice that the decision to carry or not to carry an umbrella determines what kind of error one can make. If carrying an umbrella, one cannot make a type II error. One makes a type I error if it does not rain when carrying it. A decision to not carry an umbrella cannot result in a type I error, but it will be the cause for a type II error if it rains. Of course to carry an umbrella when it rains and to not carry an umbrella when it does not rain results in no error at all.

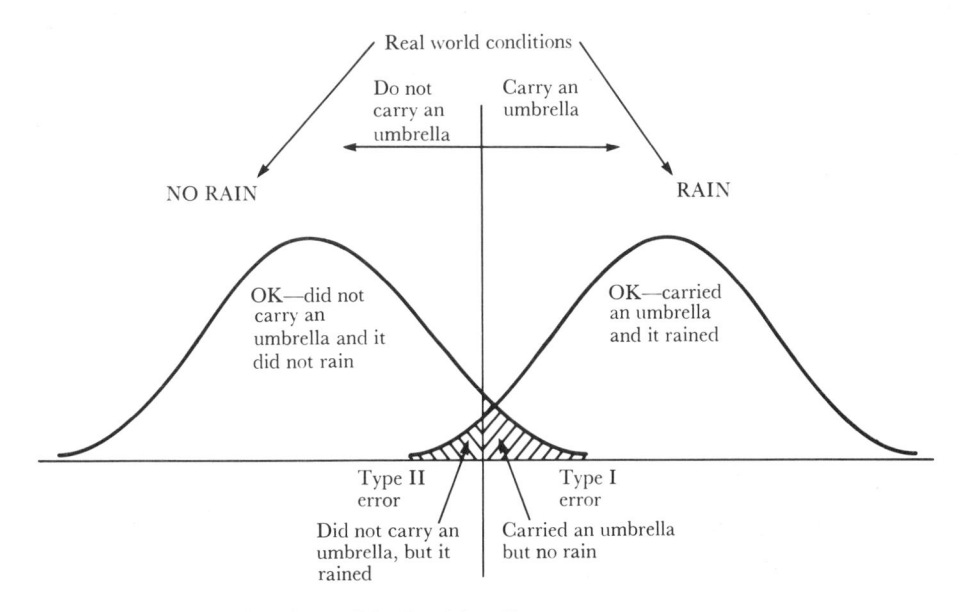

FIGURE 10.2 Study of Possible Decision Errors

Decisions about umbrella carrying are usually made without a careful structuring for each situation. Two types of people do not make individual decisions about carrying umbrellas—the person who never carries an umbrella and the person who always carries one. What possible error could each of these make? The one who never carries an umbrella will never make a type I error (α) but is subject to the type II (β). The one who carries an umbrella at all times is subject to the type I (α) but not the type II (β) error. The rest of the population fits at different places between these two extremes, with some more willing to carry umbrellas than others. Those who lean toward carrying an umbrella are protecting themselves from a type II error, while those who seldom carry one are more willing to risk a type II error to protect against a type I error. The relationship between the two errors is shown in figure 10.3. Part A shows the

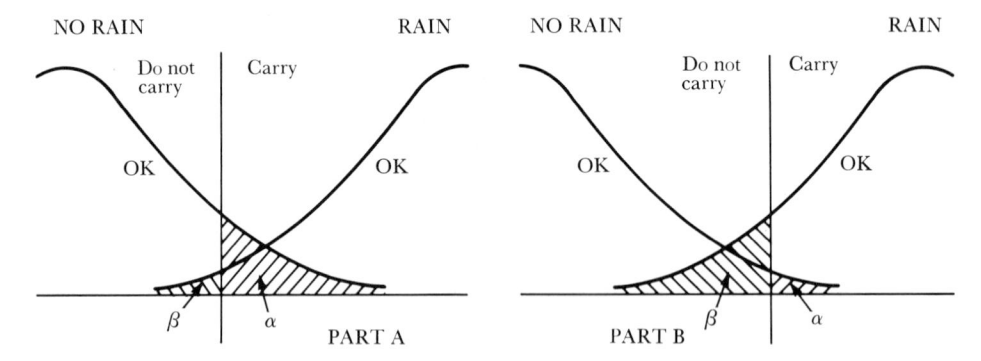

FIGURE 10.3   Relationship of Two Possible Errors

situation of the person who is protecting against the type II error, and part B shows the situation for protection against the type I error.

When testing a null hypothesis in a statistical design, a level for rejection of the null hypothesis is set using the probability of making an alpha error, the alpha error being one that results when the statistical test rejects a null hypothesis when it should not be rejected. An alpha of .05 as compared to an alpha of .01 is based on a study of the sampling error for the study. Figure 10.4 shows the relationship of the two types of errors. To reduce the probability of making an alpha error increases the probability of making a beta error. A study of the two probabilities permits a statement about the

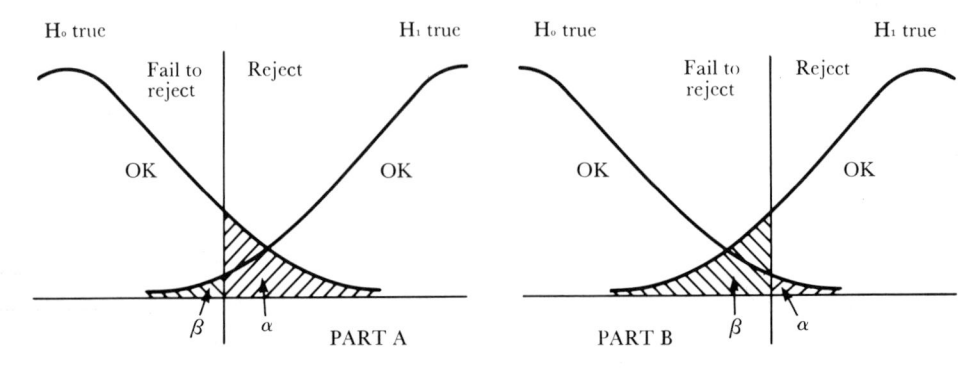

FIGURE 10.4   Relationship of Two Possible Errors

power of the test.[3] A relabeling of figure 10.3, as done in figure 10.4, shows the relationship of the two possible errors in the decision as to whether the null hypothesis is true or not true.

The null hypothesis is used in experimental design to fill the need for a clear rigorous procedure of decision making about what the data of an experiment indicate. It adds to the design a way of making an objective interpretation of whether the data confirm or contradict the research hypothesis being tested. The function of the experiment is to give a rigorous approach to inquiry, and the null hypothesis functions to give a rigorous method to making the interpretation of what data say rather than a subjectively determined decision on the part of the researcher.

If the significance level is set at .05 for a test of the observed difference between means, for example, the probability of saying that there is a difference when no such difference exists is .05 or less. If the null hypothesis is rejected the chances are five in 100, or less, that the difference could be a result of chance rather than a result of treatment applied. If the probability level is different, such as .01 or .001, a declared difference is said to be significant at that chosen level. The researcher hopes to choose a significant level that minimizes the combined probabilities of α and β, but that choice is difficult to make. Most studies in education use either the .05 or .01 level for tests of significance. The relationship of the seriousness of the two errors may help in the task of setting a significance level. If the seriousness of α is great compared to the seriousness of β, then the alpha should be set lower. Conversely α can be increased to protect the researcher from making a β error.

Can the researcher choose a significance level so that $\alpha = 0$? Yes, by saying that the decision rule for rejection is "H_o is always true." If such a decision is made β is at a maximum, and there is no reason to perform an experiment because the decision rule becomes independent of any data gathered for the study.

The null hypothesis is implied for any test of significance but should be stated in terms of variables under study in the experiment as a part of the methodology description. Tests of significance are used extensively with means of sample groups, but are also used with proportions, correlation coefficients, and other statistics. For each general type of test for significance there is often more than one specific procedure. Appropriate statistical procedures for the many tests of significance are to be found in books devoted to statistical procedures. Whatever procedure that is chosen for a study to test for significant differences is based on the principles discussed here. The experimental design of a study must include the most appropriate statistical procedure for the unique set of circumstances of the study.

Validity of Experiments

In an earlier section reference was made to the control of extraneous variables—those that are not a part of the treatment for the study but are contributing variables to the criterion variable measures. A criterion of experimental design that gives attention to weaknesses that relate to questions about control evaluates the *validity* of the experimental results in terms of how well the design provides the needed control. Validity is in turn evaluated in terms of two criteria based on the possible source of the weakness.

---

3. The power of a statistical test is the probability that the test rejects the null hypothesis when the null is false. Power is at a maximum when the probability of a type II error is least.

The two terms—internal validity and external validity—first appeared in an article in the late 1950s and the topic was further developed a few years later.[4]

Internal validity is concerned with the factors that contribute to making an experiment interpretable. It deals with the question, "Did the treatment make a difference in this study?"

External validity is concerned with the factors that contribute to making an experiment representative. It deals with the question, "To what populations and settings can this effect be generalized?"

Eight different classes of extraneous variables that have been presented as possibly producing confounding effects on the dependent variable are relevant to a study of internal validity. When the question of whether the treatment of the independent variable does indeed produce the effects observed on the criterion variable the following eight factors as competing influences should be attended to.[5]

1. *History.* To what extent could outside events that occur between start and finish of the study affect the criterion measurement?

2. *Maturation.* How did the passage of time per se function as an effect on the criterion measurement? Could differences be an effect of being older or growing more tired, less motivated, or such?

3. *Testing.* If the same test or an equivalent test is administered two times, how did the first test experience affect the criterion measurement?

4. *Instrumentation.* Did any calibration of measuring devices change from a pretest to a post-test? Did observers or scorers change any points of reference? Changes here could affect the criterion measurement.

5. *Statistical Regression.* When subjects have been selected for study on the basis of their extreme scores a terminal measurement on the same variable will cause the group mean scores to move toward the population mean. Could regression toward a population mean affect the criterion measure?

6. *Selection.* Did the manner of selecting subjects bias the characteristics of the groups and thus affect the criterion measure, by reflecting differences in the criterion measure as a result of the assignment rather than the treatment?

7. *Experimental Mortality.* Did the loss of some subjects chosen to be studied reflect a bias that could affect the criterion measures?

8. *Interaction.* Has interaction of any two of the above factors combined to create an effect not present in either individually that could affect the criterion measure?

When the question of representativeness is attended to, the following factors also become important:

9. *Reactive effect of pretesting.* Did any pretest increase or decrease the sensitivity of subjects to experimental treatment and thus make the conclusion invalid for anyone not taking the pretest?

10. *Interaction of selection biases and treatment.* Have the arrangements for the study per se been such that they create a change in subjects so that results would be invalid for generalizing to subjects who have not experienced the experiment?

---

4. Donald T. Campbell, "Factors Relevant to the Validity of Experiments in Social Settings," *Psychological Bulletin* 54 (July 1957): 297-312. For further development, see Donald T. Campbell and Julian Stanley, *Experimental and Quasi-Experimental Designs for Research* (Chicago: Rand McNally, 1963), which also appears as chapter 5 in N. L. Gage, ed., *Handbook of Research on Teaching* (Chicago: Rand McNally, 1963).

5. Discussion of these factors and those associated with external validity are based upon Campbell and Stanley, *Experimental and Quasi-Experimental Designs for Research.*

11. *Reactive effects of experimental arrangements.* Have the arrangements for the study per se been such that they create a change in subjects so that results would be invalid for generalizing to subjects who have not experienced the experiment?

12. *Multiple treatment interference.* Have effects of prior treatments that are not erasable limited the generalization to exclude those who have not had all treatments in sequence?

The preceding factors provide a set of guidelines for the researcher when he or she is checking a design for validity. Several standard designs are given specific attention in the Campbell and Stanley materials.[6] Three tables, on pages 178, 210, and 226 in the *Handbook*, structure the strength and weaknesses of sixteen different designs for experimental study. In addition, the twelve factors guide the investigator as he/she checks the specific design for confounding by extraneous variables.

What should be done if the experimenter finds that the question being studied does not allow a perfectly developed plan, and there are areas where the design is deficient? Most studies fall in the class of being less than perfect. Rarely, if ever, will conditions in educational settings permit a design with no weaknesses, even though laboratory-like conditions have been established for the study. If, after careful investigation of all possibilities, the study has one or more weaknesses, each should be listed as a limitation and pointed up to readers of the study's conclusions. To list a weakness as a limitation implies that the researcher has confronted the problem but was unable under the conditions to overcome it or that, if he were to overcome it, a greater weakness would be created elsewhere.

The researcher is placed in the position of selecting among alternatives. Many times the choice involves a sacrifice that creates a weakness because no single choice includes all of the desired characteristics. The art of researching involves the development of a study that minimizes the weaknesses. If either internal or external validity must be sacrificed, which should it be? "Internal validity is the prior and indispensable consideration."[7] If external validity were protected at the expense of internal validity, the researcher would be prepared to generalize questionable results. The study is affected negatively, and nothing is added to the body of knowledge about educational concerns.

Investigator and Experimenter Effects

A further study of research techniques in experimental research gives attention to effects contributed by those who are conducting an experiment. Chapter 11 in the *Second Handbook of Research on Teaching* gives excellent coverage to nine possible effects from the source of those conducting the experiment, as shown in figure 10.5.[8]

For discussion Barber isolates the roles of investigator and experimenter, although both roles could be played by one individual. The investigator originates the question, design, procedures, analysis, and interprets the results. The experimenter is responsible for the collection of the data. He/she conducts the study by administering the procedures, making the observations, and recording obtained data.

The investigator effects, listed in figure 10.5, are closely related to internal validity as the investigator selects the procedures to be used, and also to external validity in sample selection and so forth. Lowered validity can result from conclusions based on

---

6. Ibid., pp. 176-239.

7. Campbell, "Factors Relevant to the Validity of Experiments," p. 310.

8. Theodore Xenophon Barber, "Pitfalls in Research: Nine Investigator and Experimenter Effects," in R. M. U. Travers, ed., *Second Handbook of Research on Teaching* (Chicago: Rand McNally, 1973), pp. 382-404.

INVESTIGATOR AND EXPERIMENTER EFFECTS
Investigator Effects
I.   Investigator Paradigm Effect
II.   Investigator Loose Protocol Effect
III.   Investigator Analysis Effect
IV.   Investigator Fudging Effect
Experimenter Effects
V.   Experimenter Attributes Effect
VI.   Experimenter Failure to Follow the Protocol Effect
VII.   Experimenter Misrecording Effect
VIII.   Experimenter Fudging Effect
IX.   Experimenter Unintentional Expectancy Effect

FIGURE 10.5   Table from Chapter 11 of the *Second Handbook of Research on Teaching*

the investigator's design, experimental protocol, analysis of data, fudging of data, or any combination of these if deficiencies are involved. The experimenter effects are also associated with factors that might jeopardize internal and external validity. Misleading results can be produced by the experimenter's attributes, failure to follow protocol, errors made in recording data, fudging data, personal expectancies, or any combination of these. Deficiencies within the experimenter's tasks lower the validity of his or her conclusions.

Each of the nine effects is discussed at length in the chapter, and the reader should become familiar with these possible sources of invalidity. The ninth effect (Experimenter Unintentional Expectancy Effect) is presented in greater detail than the others, and the writer uses some studies of that effect to point up where researchers have been victims of pitfalls. Twelve summary statements give direction to ways that investigators and experimenters should function to avoid pitfalls that affect the validiy of experimental studies. Most statements are also applicable to descriptive studies, and some to historical studies.

SOURCES AND TYPES OF DATA

The source of data for most experimental studies in education will be human subjects who are observed on human attributes. Measurements will be made on characteristics, where the agreement is good, as to how a subject exhibits the degree of the characteristic that he has. Other characteristics will be measured where little agreement can be obtained about how a subject exhibits the degree of possession. A researcher would be able to obtain general agreement from educators about a student's ability to multiply by one place numbers by using a set of well prepared examples on a test. On the other hand, another researcher would expect to have much more disagreement from educators if he or she attempts to measure creativity with a paper and pencil test. Especially in the area of experimental research investigators are called upon to define human constructs that explain human behavior, and to gather quantitative data on a set of human subjects. The type of data which can be collected is dictated largely by the attribute being studied.

Sources of Data

Experimental research procedures provide excellent opportunities to study many attributes of a human population, but definitions of the variables in words may be inadequate. Operational definitions of how an attribute will be exhibited by a subject allow the experiment, with its potential control, an opportunity to study in areas that are difficult at best. The attributes that serve as criterion variables must be clearly defined if a study is to make a contribution to educational theory. Since the affective domain is becoming more and more a concern of the educator, measures of the attributes of aspiration, motivation, and the like are sources of data for experimental studies.

Sample groups of human subjects that have been systematically selected and provided treatment on an independent variable are measured on a dependent variable. The sources of data for experimental studies are the subjects in the groups. Measures on the criterion variable are studied for effects of treatment by analyzing the data with some statistical procedure. Sets of data from different sources or samples that have been subjected to different conditions make up the heart of an experimental study.

Types of Data

Data used within experimental designs are generated by measurement techniques that quantify the variable being studied. Both categorical and continuous variables provide data for experimental studies.

Categorical Variables. Those variables that only allow assignment to subclasses by the possession of a characteristic that defines a subclass are measured by the simplest rule of measurement. Either a subject has the characteristic of the subclass or he/she does not. The birthplace of a human subject could be assigned to one of the fifty United States, foreign, or unknown. In all, the categories would total fifty-two and each subject could be assigned to one and only one category. Subclasses could be by regions—New England, Midwest, and so on—or grouped in other ways. Where more than two subclasses are listed the variables are polytomous. With only two subclasses—male–female, above average–below average, and so forth—the variables are dichotomous.

Continuous Variables. Those variables that may take values from a continuous series are measured by a rule of measurement that allows at least an ordering where descriptors indicate more or less of the variable. With continuous variables each assigned value is interpreted to represent a range of possible values for each assignment. Just as a weight of 137 pounds is considered to represent a series of all possible values between 136.5 and 137.5 pounds, so are measurements of other human attributes, such as achievement, motivation, and creativity, used to represent a range of continuous values.

Categorical variables have been described before in the discussion of nominal measurement or measurement of nominal values. Continuous variables have been described before in the discussion of measurement of ordinal, interval, and ratio variables.

The identification of data as to type becomes important to the investigator as he or she looks for appropriate statistical methods. Statistical procedures exist for the analysis of data classed as nominal, ordinal, and interval or ratio. The last two have been combined because in practical statistical work in education any difference becomes unimportant, giving in essence three classes of measurement for statistical methods.

Experimental designs frequently apply methods, appropriate to a lower class of variables, to measurements of a higher class of variables. When doing that the investigator discards some information that he/she has in the data. If measurements of the variable of height were determined to the nearest one-half inch for a group of subjects, the groups could be studied on an interval scale or could be studied on a lower scale, such as ranks or classes. A set of six measurements for heights 76,75,66,64,60, and 58 in inches could be changed to ranks of 1,2,3,4,5, and 6 or to upper third, middle third, and lower third. Treating the heights as ranks utilizes the variable as ordinal, and division into thirds changes it to large categories although there is an order to the classes. Wide acceptance of the use of nonparametric statistics in the study of characteristics important to social sciences, behavioral science, and education makes the practice of discarding information understandable where questions arise about whether it is proper to use parametric procedures.

Experimental designs at times incorporate analyses of data by a statistical procedure that requires the investigator to assume that he or she has information which he actually does not have. Data that are ordinal may be treated by a procedure appropriate for interval and ratio data. Scores on mental ability tests are, in general, treated as if they were interval data, but the assignment of numerical descriptors does not include equal intervals. Differences between intervals in a scale for mental ability tests and many other scales of measurement used in education should not be compared as if they were assigned in equal units. A difference between scores of 95 and 100 is not necessarily the same difference as between 145 and 150, although each subtraction would be 5. The two fives are not the same distance on the scale. The units in the center of a scale for mental abilities are usually smaller than the units at the extremes. For the same reason a score of 150 is in no way twice a score of 75 when mental ability is being measured.

The practices of discarding information or assuming information should not be made without consideration of other statistical procedures for appropriate methods, but if the practical situation is best served by a particular procedure it should be used. The investigator must know the information that the data contain so that he/she is aware of assumptions underlying all procedures. "In other words, our understanding of precisely what we are doing is enriched by knowing the nature of the assumptions made at each stage in the application of any procedure.[9]

TOOLS OF EXPERIMENTAL RESEARCH

Experimental research uses two types of tools—one gathers the data while the other is used to analyze the data. Since the success of an experiment depends on comparison between or among sets of circumstances, tools to gather data for experimental studies must be objective in all respects. The statistical procedure chosen to analyze the data must be selected in regard to its ability to seek the messages contained in the data that relate to the answer for the study's question.

Tools to Gather Data

The first criterion for any tool to gather data for the experimental study is that it must be objective. Traits or characteristics which are readily observable can be measured with tools that produce highly objective data. Traits of major concern in education, behavioral sciences, and social sciences are, primarily, not readily observable. Because of the nature of the traits they become difficult to define and, in turn, difficult to measure with the desired objectivity.

A second criterion for a tool used to gather data for the experiment is that it must be valid for the study. The instrument being used for a study must possess acceptable

---

9. George A. Ferguson, *Statistical Analysis in Psychology and Education*, 3rd ed. (New York: McGraw-Hill, 1971), p. 16.

Use of the Experiment in Inquiry

validity for the purpose for which it is being used. Valid conclusions rest on valid data. The researcher must give attention to choosing an appropriate tool by considering the needs and the alternatives available. Proper selection of a tool provides valid data that are objective.

The tools discussed in the last two chapters may be used to gather data for experimental studies. Some are limited to gathering data for background and for aiding in developing a hypothesis. Others will be found appropriate for gathering data for analysis. A study based on an attitude change as a result of an intervening condition will probably use an attitudinal scale to measure attitudes of subjects under study. Other choices of measuring instruments should be equally appropriate.

The widespread use of testing instruments to measure the criterion variable for experimental studies in education should not cause one to consider tests as the only appropriate measuring devices for gathering data in an experiment. A test should be used only if it is capable of gathering the best data for analysis. If another type of device will generate better data it should be used. Do not become locked in on using a test for all situations. The nature of the criterion variable under study should be the major criterion for selection of the tool to gather data for analysis.

The process of gathering data is not a time consuming task in most experimental studies. Generally the gathering of data requires much less time for experiments than for historical or descriptive research. Careful planning of procedures to generate the data makes this aspect a rather insignificant part of the actual experiment. The plan should consider any possible effects on subjects produced by the procedures used to gather the data and recognize the importance of administration of tests and such on the validity of the data. When the planning incorporates special administration procedures to minimize each of the above difficulties, the procedures to secure the needed data become a series of routine tasks.

Tools to Analyze the Data

The experiment provides a unique opportunity for a researcher to obtain a decision arrived at objectively about what the data say in regard to his or her research question, and whether the data support or refute the research hypothesis. The tools used to analyze experimental data are designed to test the tenability of a null hypothesis. In general the research hypothesis will be an alternate hypothesis to the null hypothesis. Any rejection of the null hypothesis will be support for the research hypothesis, and failure to reject will represent failure to support the research hypothesis.

The analysis of a set of data from an experiment will generally be treated with a test of significance. A test of significance gives the researcher direction in interpreting the source of differences that are observed in statistics of different groups of subjects studied. Basically a study of sampling errors, any test for significant difference is designed to structure within the rules of the research design an objectively made decision about the effect of difference (levels) on independent variables as they are reflected in measurements of criterion variables.

A test of significance may involve one independent variable and one criterion variable, or it may involve more than one independent variable. The effects of the I.V.'s may be viewed singly and in combination with additional information about the effects of interaction between or among independent variables. The statistical reasoning associated with tests of significance provides a unique way of making rational conclusions about the effects of experimentally applied treatment.

The statistical analysis of a set of data depends heavily on the concepts of probability and making a comparison of what is actually observed with the probability of that occurrence by chance factors.

Statistical analysis is needed to study the variability (difference) that is imparted to those subjects studied in educational research. No two human beings are exactly alike. No one human being is the same at two different times because of intervening experiences. Statistical analysis allows an examination of the effects of treatment to permit statements in general, although there may be deviation from them in specific cases.

The statistical analysis results in a decision to reject the null hypothesis or to not reject it, thus completing the story begun earlier in the discussion about the null hypothesis. To review the total process, a test of significance consists of the following sequence of procedures. First, the researcher states a null hypothesis and assumes for statistical treatment that the applied treatment has had no effect. In most cases the research hypothesis appears as the alternate hypothesis that says the applied treatment has had an effect. Second, the researcher examines the data for differences between statistics for groups studied. Third, the question is asked about the probability of getting a difference as large or greater than the one obtained, owing to chance factors rather than treatment effects. Fourth, if the probability of getting a difference as large as the observed one by chance is small, the null hypothesis is rejected. Since a very unlikely event has occurred, the difference is viewed as significant. A significant difference means that the observed data have a difference that should not be attributed to chance but to the treatment applied. Failure to observe an unlikely event causes the researcher to view any differences as resulting from chance factors. This means that the null hypothesis will not be rejected.

The tools discussed in the rest of this section are presented as examples of a large class of statistical tests used to interpret sources of differences observed in sets of data. The number of tests available to the researcher seems endless. Newer statistical tests are being created to serve unique designs, and better tests are being developed to sophisticate techniques of analysis. The number of tools discussed here is limited to, but not intended to exhaust, the list of tests appropriate for the type of study that would be considered suitable for a first-time researcher. More advanced techniques are found in books devoted to developing understanding of a wide range of statistical procedures appropriate for educational research studies.

A full-blown study of statistics would reveal a series of theoretical frequency distributions which have been developed mathematically. These distributions are used in research statistical designs as models that assume that certain conditions exist. The best known of these models is the normal curve which is generated from an indefinitely large ($N = \infty$) population that has a mean equal to zero and a standard deviation equal to one (see figure 10.6). This model is chosen from a family of normal curves because of its usable characteristics.

The tendency for measurements of variables of most concern to educators to take the shape of a normal curve, when empirical frequency distributions are built for sets of obtained data, makes the *unit normal curve* in standard form a particularly valuable research tool. Because many physical traits are normally distributed and other traits have a tendency to generate empirical frequency distributions that approach normality, it seems reasonable to assume that many other traits are so distributed. Without information to show exceptions to this tendency, it seems rational to assume normal curve

Use of the Experiment in Inquiry

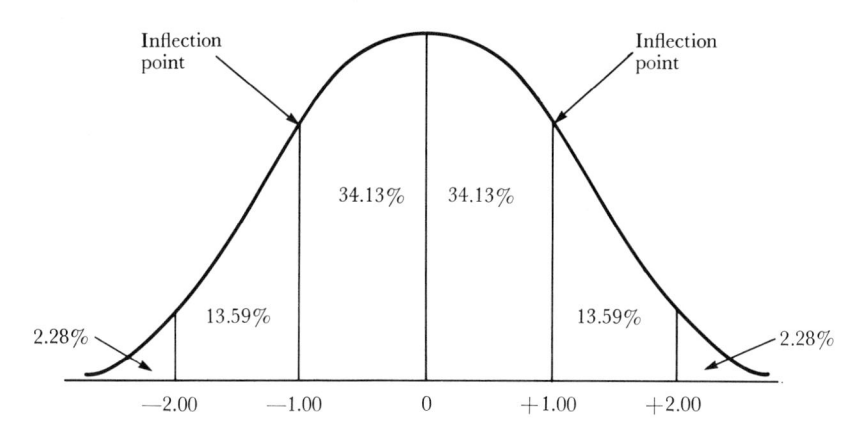

FIGURE 10.6 The Unit Normal Curve in Standard Form. Percentage of Area Associated with Basic Line Segments.

characteristics. Exceptions to this general rule are well known or should be discernible to the researcher. An inappropriate measuring device could artificially create a skewed empirical frequency distribution from an attribute that is normally distributed. A test which has been developed to measure mathematical understandings for middle-school students would not give a normally distributed set of scores for second-grade students. The distribution would be skewed positively because the difficulty level would be too high to measure second-grade pupil characteristics with high validity.

Theoretical frequency distributions such as the normal distributions are used to compare sets of gathered data with expected outcomes given certain conditions. The statistical test needs and uses a theoretical frequency distribution to indicate when a difference which is being interpreted should be considered as being so great that it should not be credited to chance happenings.

Other theoretical frequency distributions include the binomial distribution, the chi-square (χ^2) distribution, the t distribution, and the F distribution. Each has unique characteristics and the choice of a model is made in terms of the type of data used and the question being asked.

The *binomial distribution* is appropriate to use when data that fall into discontinuous categories are being compared to those outcomes which are expected to happen. For example, one might flip a coin 100 times and keep a record of the number of heads and the number of tails that appear. The binomial distribution is built on the equal probability of heads or tails coming up in one flip of the coin. The distribution indicates the probability of all combinations of events, e.g., 50 heads–50 tails, 51 heads–49 tails, 52 heads–48 tails, . . . , 100 heads–0 tails, or 49 heads–51 tails, 48 heads–52 tails, . . . , 0 heads–100 tails. By comparing the number of times that the coin comes up heads with what the binomial distribution says should appear, a decision can be made about whether the coin should be considered to be biased (bent or weighted in some way to cause it to be something other than fair). The fairness of a pair of dice can be checked in the same way to see if their behavior is so unusual as to cause them to be suspect. A record of the outcomes for many tosses of the dice (observed data) can be compared with what is expected (the binomial distribution) from a pair of unbiased dice.

Research data which fall in ordered categories can be analyzed statistically by comparing what is observed with the appropriate binomial distribution. An investigation of learning might study the effects of a condition in the environment on the rate of learning a new skill. A laboratory maze may have five choices, one of which—say number 2—has a pellet of food for a rat placed in the maze. A study of the learning rate can be made by counting the numbers of correct choices for food made by the rat. As the animal learns to choose the proper way through the maze the proportion will move away (be biased) from the binomial distribution for one correct choice out of five ($p = .20, q = .80$).

The t distribution is used primarily to test hypotheses about mean differences for two groups, and other comparisons of a statistic with a hypothesized parameter or zero. A different t distribution exists for each different sample number (N). Tabled values associated with degrees of freedom make the t distribution a relatively simple analysis tool but yet effective and useful for research studies. It has much the same properties as the normal curve except that it is leptokurtic. It is used in place of the normal curve when the sample size is small (less than 30 degrees of freedom).

F distributions are used to test hypotheses about differences among means much as the t distribution tests differences, but the F distribution permits a study of more than two means. The F ratio used with F distributions is a mean square estimate and for this reason has only nonnegative values and is skewed positively from the value of 0. A different F distribution exists for each pair of degrees of freedom that are contributed by the two variance estimates. Tables of significant criterion points for F tests of differences are available for comparing observed F values with tabled values. F distributions are also used to test hypotheses that involve two or more treatments as independent variables, and studies of interaction of effects of independent variables. The sources of differences are studied by partitioning total sums of squares into components, and the F ratios are checked against the tabled F distribution values.

The *chi-square distribution* is also a distribution that is skewed positively. Since it is a squared statistic it contains only nonnegative values and is skewed to the right of the value 0. Chi-square distributions can be used where not all assumptions for parametric tests can be met or for the type of data that is only categorical or ordered, i.e., nominal or ordinal. Many different types of problems can be solved using tests based on the chi-square distribution. Each test compares the numbers observed to fall into separate categories with numbers hypothesized to be expected to fall into the several categories.

The above mentioned theoretical frequency distributions provide well developed models to judge discrepancy between observation and hypothesis. Other theoretical distributions of frequency, bivariate distributions, and multivariate distributions are used in more sophisticated research designs and seem to be beyond the scope of this book. More information about all of these may be obtained in books devoted to statistical procedures.

A widely used theoretical distribution is the distribution that is generated by the differences obtained from many pairs of samples. It is important because many research studies are based in comparison of the performance of two groups that are considered to be equal in all ways except for different treatment for each group on one variable.

Given a population with a standard deviation of σ, two samples could be chosen at random. Another pair with the same number in each group could be chosen. Doing this

Use of the Experiment in Inquiry

an uncountable number of times gives an infinite number of pairs of samples with size N. Let us compute the mean for each sample in each pair, subtract the first mean from the second and keep a record of the differences. These differences can be arranged into a frequency distribution. That theoretical (because we cannot really accumulate an infinite number of differences) frequency distribution will have the following characteristics which are important to our study: (1) it will have a mean of zero; (2) it will be normally distributed; (3) its standard deviation can be determined; (4) proportions of areas under the curve can be determined from tables of the standard normal curve; and (5) differences can be located at points along the base line (figure 10.7) by z values $(z = (X - \overline{X})/s)$.

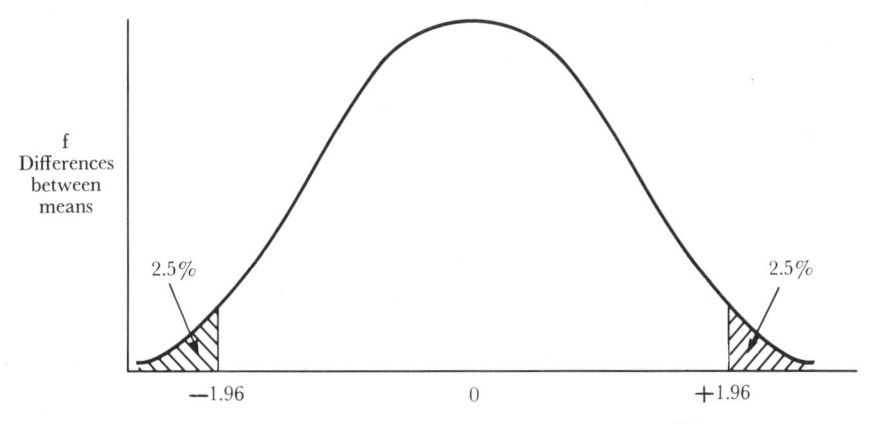

FIGURE 10.7 Differences between Pairs of Sample Means $(\overline{X})$

Since the distribution mean is zero the points on the base line are the differences between the pairs of samples. By putting the differences into units of the standard deviation, statements about probabilities of obtaining particular differences can be determined. Tables show that the interval between -1.96 and $+1.96$ includes 95 percent of the differences. Only 5 percent of the differences lie outside the two points ± 1.96. Beyond ± 2.58 lies only one percent of the differences. Using these points a method to test a null hypothesis at either the .05 level or the .01 level can be established.

Let us see how a theoretical frequency distribution of differences between two means could be used in a study of the comparison of two groups. A study of learning developed a methodology to answer the following question:

> What effect does practice in estimating the areas of rectangles have on the ability of students to estimate the area of circles?

A class of 32 fourth-grade students was given a series of lessons developing the concept of area, concluding with the development of the formula to determine the area of rectangles and a series of problems using the formula *length times width equals area* $(l \times w = A)$. For instruction on the final day the class was divided randomly and assigned to two groups of 16 each. For thirty minutes Group 2 worked individually and discussed together a set of problems involving measuring and determining the area of rectangles. Group 1 used the same set of problems, but before working each problem an estimate was made about the area and a comparison of the guessed value for the area was made with the obtained value for the area. At the end of thirty minutes each group was presented a set of circles that varied in size. Each student guessed the area of each circle, and a score value was determined for each student paper. The question now reduces to:

Is the mean accomplishment for one group superior to that of the other group?

A test of significance of the difference observed in our sample will test the null hypothesis:

There is no significant difference in mean scores on a test of estimation of areas of circles between a group that practiced estimating areas of rectangles and another group that did not (.05).

Included in the null hypothesis are all differences from 0 to the z-value criterion points of -1.96 and $+1.96$. Therefore any values between -1.96 and $+1.96$ will fail to reject the null hypothesis, as they will be considered small enough to have happened by chance. Differences less than -1.96, or larger than $+1.96$, will be considered as being great enough to be the effect of differences in time utilization.

An appropriate test of the significance of an obtained difference between two means is the *t-test* that utilizes a *t-ratio* to interpret the difference observed. By putting the difference between the two means in terms of a ratio based on the standard deviation of the theoretical frequency distribution, the difference can be tested for significant effects. The estimate of the standard deviation of the theoretical distribution can be obtained by the formula

$$s_{diff} = \sqrt{\frac{s^2}{N_1} + \frac{s^2}{N_2}}$$

s_{diff} = standard error of difference
s^2 = variance estimate
N_1 = number in sample 1
N_2 = number in sample 2

The *t-ratio* is derived by dividing the difference between the sample means by the standard error of difference (s_{diff}).

$$t = \frac{\overline{X}_1 - \overline{X}_2}{s_{diff}}$$

The variance estimate used in the formula for the standard error of difference uses the combined sum of squares of the two groups to get a pooled variance estimate:

$$s^2 = \frac{\Sigma x_1^2 + \Sigma x_2^2}{N_1 + N_2 - 2} \text{ or,}$$

$$s^2 = \frac{\Sigma X_1^2 - \frac{(\Sigma X_1)^2}{N_1} + \Sigma X_2^2 - \frac{(\Sigma X_2)^2}{N_2}}{N_1 + N_2 - 2}$$

Since the *t-ratio* for this study exceeds the critical ratio of $+1.96$, the null hypothesis is rejected (see figure 10.8). The observed difference is great enough to consider it as

Use of the Experiment in Inquiry

a very unlikely event with only a sampling difference. The difference is to be considered as an effect of the different treatment provided. For this study the conclusion is:

> The practice in estimating the area of rectangles was instrumental in increasing the mean criterion measurement significantly.

Using *fictitious data* for the two groups the procedure looks like this:

Scores for Group 1 (Practice)		Scores for Group 2 (No practice)	
19	14	9	10
11	17	14	14
20	9	11	13
13	15	12	14
14	16	12	13
14	15	11	10
13	16	18	17
16	12	8	11

$\Sigma X_1 = 234$ $\quad\quad\quad\quad\quad\quad\quad\quad\quad\quad$ $\Sigma X_2 = 197$
$\Sigma X_1^2 = 3540$ $\quad\quad\quad\quad\quad\quad\quad\quad\quad$ $\Sigma X_2^2 = 2535$
$\overline{X}_1 = 14.62$ $\quad\quad\quad\quad\quad\quad\quad\quad\quad$ $\overline{X}_2 = 12.31$

Variance estimate:

$$s^2 = \frac{3540 - \frac{(234)^2}{16} + 2535 - \frac{(197)^2}{16}}{16 + 16 - 2}$$

$$= \frac{3540 - 3422.25 + 2535 - 2425.56}{30}$$

$$= \frac{117.75 + 109.44}{30} = \frac{227.19}{30} = 7.573$$

Standard error of difference: $s_{\text{diff}} = \sqrt{\frac{7.573}{16} + \frac{7.573}{16}}$

$$= \sqrt{.4733 + .4733} = \sqrt{.9466} = .973$$

t-ratio: $t = \dfrac{14.62 - 12.31}{.973} = \dfrac{2.31}{.973} = 2.37$

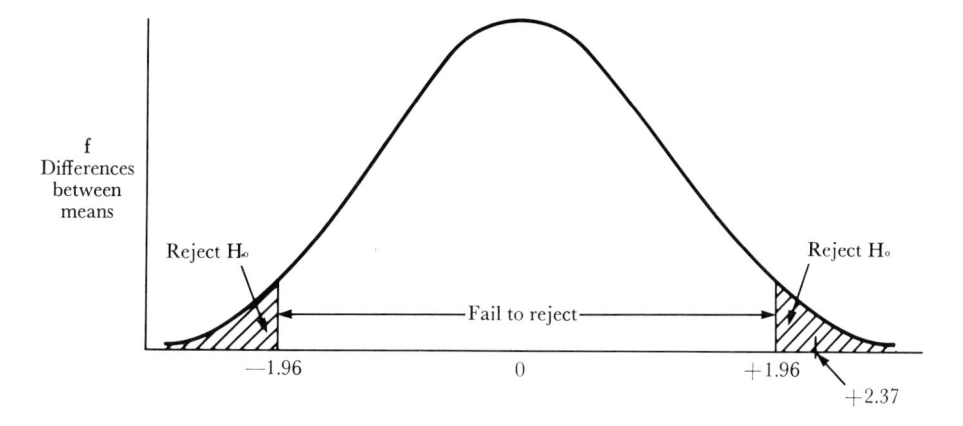

FIGURE 10.8 Comparing an Observed *t* Value with a Tabled *t* Value

The test that was administered to the above data used a *nondirectional* or two-tailed test. If the null hypothesis is changed to indicate a test of superiority for one of the groups over the other, a *directional* or one-tailed test can be used. If the test for the above data used a .05 level of significance and a directional test, the critical ratio changes from +1.96 to +1.64, and the hypothesis that the group that estimated areas of rectangles would exceed the other group would be rejected only if the critical ratio exceeded +1.64 (see figure 10.9). For a one-tailed test at the .01 level of significance,

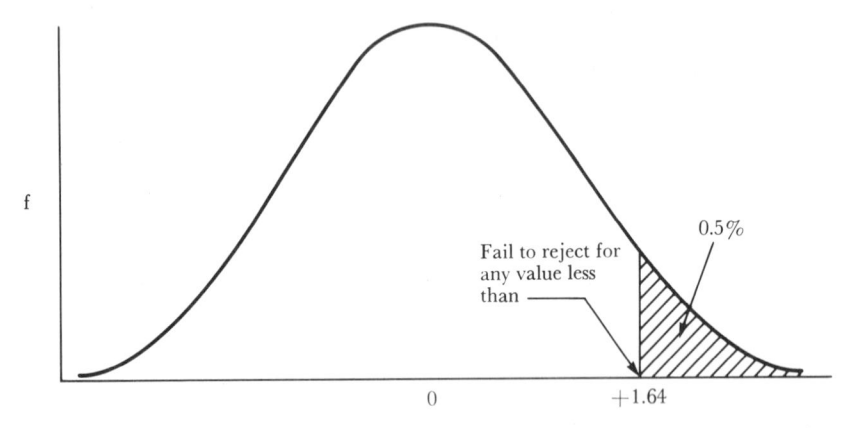

FIGURE 10.9 Rejection Area for a One-tailed Test

the critical ratio becomes +2.33. The data above would cause rejection of the null hypothesis at the .01 level of a one-tailed test, but not at the .01 level of significance of a two-tailed test.

If the denominator of the variance estimate for the *t* test procedure is less than 30, a correction must be made for the critical ratio points. The theoretical sampling distribution departs from normality as the N in the sample decreases. The distribution remains symmetrical, but it becomes leptokurtic (tall and thin rather than bell-shaped). A different *t* distribution exists for each different number of degrees of freedom associated with the variance estimate ($N_1 + N_2 - 2$). Tables have been constructed to give the *t-ratio* for one- and two-tailed tests and at varying levels of significance. If the degrees of freedom for the *t* test are less than 30, replace the standard normal distribution values (1.96, 1.64, 2.58, and 2.33) with the appropriate tabled value. An observed ratio from the data must exceed the tabled value to reject the null hypothesis.

Data from a study that involves more than two conditions on the independent variable *cannot* be analyzed with the *t* test. The *analysis of variance* allows the investigation of differences among three or more different groups. The basic principle underlying this procedure is a comparison of two variance estimates. The question is whether the means of the groups differ from one another (among group variance) to a greater degree than the scores in the groups differ from their own group means (within group variance). The *F* ratio is built from the two different sources of variance as follows:

$$F = \frac{\text{among groups variance}}{\text{within groups variance}}$$

The null hypothesis of no difference between these two estimates results in an expected *F* value of one (1.00) if treatment has no effect. As the groups depart from each other

Use of the Experiment in Inquiry

and the within variance is constant or decreases, the F value will increase. As with the t test, the F values that are small can result at a high probability because of sampling. Tabled F values indicate critical points for rejection of the null hypothesis. Observed F values that exceed tabled values cause rejection of the null hypothesis.

A further extension of tests of significance is the investigation of the effects of two independent variables simultaneously. Since an independent variable is called a factor, study of effects of two independent variables is called a two-factor study. If three independent variables are included the study becomes a three-factor study or three-way design. Tests for two or more factors are discussed in statistics books. The above parametric tests require that the data be treated using certain assumptions, namely:

1. That assignment to treatment groups is independent.[10] Selection of a subject for one group does not depend on or affect any other selection.
2. That population values are normally distributed.
3. That variances are equal.
4. That measurement assignment is in interval or ratio scale.

Nonparametric Techniques

When measurement is in nominal or ordinal scales, means and variances cannot be determined. Distributions of some populations are not known and cannot be obtained. When distribution characteristics are unknown or unavailable and/or means and variances cannot be obtained, *nonparametric* tests can be used to test differences between groups. Referred to as *distribution-free tests*, they are used with nominal and ordinal data and for data that have unknown population distributions. Discussion of techniques for treating data of descriptive studies included two procedures which are classed as nonparametric—the Spearman coefficient of rank correlation and the chi-square goodness-of-fit tests.

The chi-square tests are used when nominal variable classes are compared and when ordinal, interval, or ratio data have been categorized into distinct classes for data treatment. Chi-square tests are concerned with comparison of observed frequencies in discrete categories and expected frequencies in the same categories.

A one-sample test can be used to analyze the number of occurrences for several categories. An industrial firm might study employee absenteeism along the characteristic of the day of the week when the absences occurred. If there is no factor of selection then absences should occur about as often on any one day of the work week as on any other. To test whether absences are independent of the day of the week a chart could be built from gathered data as in table 10.1, and a chi-square value computed for differences between observed and expected frequencies.

TABLE 10.1 Absences for a Thirty-Day Period

Monday	Tuesday	Days of the week Wednesday	Thursday	Friday	Total absences = 985
212	187	172	183	231	Absent from work
197	197	197	197	197	Expected absences

10. Correlated techniques exist for studies that cannot meet this assumption. Examples: a special t test technique to test differences for correlated samples and repeated measures using the analysis of variance.

The expected value of 197 is derived by seeding one-fifth of the total absences (985) into each of the five categories determined by the days of the work week. The number of absences associated with each day is entered above the expected number and a chi-square value is obtained through use of the following formula:

$$x^2 = \Sigma \frac{(0 - E)^2}{E}$$

0 = number absent
E = number expected to be absent

If the actual absences had been distributed with 197 for each of the days, then x^2 would equal 0. As the observed values depart from expected values, the chi-square value will increase. Tabled values for chi square give the value needed for null hypothesis rejection. If the observed difference gives a chi-square value for the study that exceeds the tabled value, then the null hypothesis of no difference is rejected. The arithmetic for the above data is as follows:

$$x^2 = \frac{(212-197)^2}{197} + \frac{(187-197)^2}{197} + \frac{(172-197)^2}{197} + \frac{(183-197)^2}{197} + \frac{(231-197)^2}{197}$$

$$= \frac{15^2}{197} + \frac{-10^2}{197} + \frac{-25^2}{197} + \frac{-14^2}{197} + \frac{34^2}{197}$$

$$= 1.14 + .51 + 3.17 + 1.00 + 5.87$$

$$= 11.69$$

The chi-square value is compared to a table value for the appropriate degrees of freedom $(K - 1)$[11] at the significance level set for the test. The null hypothesis of no difference is rejected if the obtained value equals or exceeds the tabled value. For this study tested at the .05 level, the chi-square value must reach or exceed 9.49. The obtained value of the chi square 11.69 causes the rejection of the hypothesis of no difference. The results for this decision to reject the hypothesis of no difference indicate that absences should not be considered to be independent of the days of the week. Conclusions are then made from the inferences of the results.

Chi-square values are also used to test for (1) significant changes (before and after or pretest and post-test), (2) differences among independent samples, (3) the null hypothesis of no difference in breakdown of frequencies in contingency tables, and (4) special uses in other selected nonparametric techniques.

The *median test* is used to test the hypothesis that two groups come from populations that have the same median (or from one population). This test can be used only where the characteristic of order is associated with the measurement assignment. It cannot be used with nominal data. A study of the effects of two different environments on the activity rate of white rats could use the median test. By random assignment twenty animals can be assigned to two groups with one group (A) placed in an environment with certain characteristics and with the other group (B) placed in an environment where one of the characteristics is changed. After a specified period of time a measure of the activity of each animal in both groups could be measured. Since both groups originally came from the same population, the scores can be combined and an order of the twenty scores made and a median determined for the twenty animals. A

---

11. K = number of categories. In this case the number of work days (5).

Use of the Experiment in Inquiry

count can be made for the animals from group A that fall above the median and the number that fall below. The same count can be made for group B. If the environment has made no changes or caused no difference to arise in activity level, then 50 percent of each group should appear above the median and 50 percent below.

Group A	Group B
above 5	5 above
below 5	5 below

The ten animals above the median should be equally divided so that five animals from A and five animals from B are above the median, and five and five are below. The expected frequency value for each of the four cells is five. Applying the chi-square method, comparison can be made with the actual frequencies. Table 10.2 gives some

TABLE 10.2 Activity Scores for Twenty Animals

Group A		Group B	
27	19	20	23
25	23	28	28
29	23	30	33
22	20	25	29
32	30	32	30

possible values for activity measures for the twenty experimental animals. Table 10.3 shows the division of the two groups in regard to values that fell above and below the

TABLE 10.3 Division of Animals in Relation to the Median for Twenty Animals

Group A		Group B
32		33
30	Above	32
29	the	30
	Median	30
		29
		28
		28
27		25
25	Below	23
23	the	20
23	Median	
22		
20		
19		

median in each group. Combining the actual frequencies with the expected frequencies the data are as follows:

	Group A	Group B
Above the median	3	7
	(5)	(5)
Below the median	7	3
	(5)	(5)

Inquiry Methodologies

Applying the chi-square test at the .05 level with one degree of freedom (r − 1)(c − 1) the arithmetic and procedure is as follows:[12]

$$\chi^2 = \frac{(3-5)^2}{5} + \frac{(7-5)^2}{5} + \frac{(7-5)^2}{5} + \frac{(3-5)^2}{5}$$
$$= .8 + .8 + .8 + .8 = 3.20 \qquad \text{Tabled value} = 3.84$$

Since the obtained value for these data is less than the tabled value of 3.84, the null hypothesis is not rejected. The conclusion is that the difference in environment did not result in a significant difference in activity rate for the two groups.

A final example of the nonparametric techniques will be given, in which the normal distribution is used for the theoretical distribution. A pretest/post-test situation, or differences between matched pairs after different treatment, can be statistically analyzed with a nonparametric test.

The *sign test* merely studies the increases versus decreases of matched subjects or numbers in one group, which exceed matched subjects in other groups that have received different treatment. If there is no difference in treatment an increase or decrease will be a randomly determined event. Differences due to treatment are considered to have happened when the differences are beyond a critical point determined by the significance level. Use the values in table 10.4 for the following illustration.

TABLE 10.4 Results of Test on Fifty Addition Facts by Students in Two Treatment Groups after Matching on a Pretest

Group M	Group N	Sign M−N
43	41	+
47	40	+
19	24	−
33	33	0
38	42	−
46	42	+
32	30	+
22	23	−
47	45	+
29	27	+
39	39	0
49	46	+
44	46	−
40	38	+

Scores are arranged with matched subjects' scores side by side. If the increases (+) and decreases (−) for the two groups were randomly determined then the pluses should equal the minuses. Regarding the two zeroes as neither an increase nor a decrease, half of the signed numbers (12) would be the expected number of pluses and minuses. A z value is found by using a mean of .5N and a standard deviation of $.5\sqrt{N}$. Using the number of pluses (X), the z value is obtained by:

$$(1) \quad z = \frac{(X - .5) - .5N}{.5\sqrt{N}} \quad \text{or} \quad (2) \quad z = \frac{(X + .5) - .5N}{.5\sqrt{N}}$$

---

12. r = number of rows; c = number of columns.

If the number of pluses is more than .5N, then use X − .5. If the number of pluses is less than .5N, then use X + .5 in computation of z.

Using the data from table 10.4:

X = 8, N = 12, .5N = 6, so

$$z = \frac{(8 - .5) - 6}{.5\sqrt{12}} = \frac{7.5 - 6}{.5(3.46)} = \frac{1.5}{1.73} = +.87$$

Comparing the z value of +.87 with a table of areas under a normal curve, the null hypothesis of no difference is accepted. Rejection at the .05 level would occur for values beyond +1.96 or −1.96. For rejection at the .01 level values beyond +2.58 or −2.58 must be obtained. Directional tests would use criterion points of ±1.64 and ±2.33.

Small samples (Chase says less than eleven cases, and Siegel says less than twenty-six) should use the binomial distribution as a theoretical frequency distribution to compare observed results with expected results.[13]

The above examples serve to show how statistical procedures can be applied to research data. They represent a sampling of traditional techniques used to analyze data for messages contained therein. New procedures based on traditional thinking are being created as new and different situations arise in the field of inquiry. Each study should select the statistical design best able to handle that study's data.

A relatively new approach to old problems, and a technique that holds much promise for analyzing situations involving many independent variables, is the research design that utilizes the multiple regression approach. It is widely applicable to many different kinds of situations that arise in inquiry for the studies in psychology, sociology, and education. Although less well understood generally than analysis of variance procedures, it has been shown that "multiple regression analysis can do anything the analysis of variance does—sums of squares, mean square, F ratios—and more."[14] Although not an appropriate tool for those who are studying an introductory course in educational inquiry, it is a tool that the behavioral scientists will be going to more and more as they become accustomed to its use. Also see other material about regression analysis and other multivariate techniques in the bibliography at the end of part III.

SUMMARY

The experiment has been presented as a direct way to test hypotheses. This chapter has presented an overview of the use of the experiment in educational inquiry and its use of control of variables to establish cause-and-effect relationships among variables. The nature of the experiment lies in the idea of doing something with a situation (manipulation) and identifying changes that take place as a result of the manipulation.

The steps of the experimental method of inquiry follow the steps usually associated

---

13. Clinton J. Chase, *Elementary Statistical Procedures* (New York: McGraw-Hill, 1967), p. 187; and Sidney Siegel, *Non-parametric Statistics for the Behavioral Sciences* (New York: McGraw-Hill, 1956), p. 72.

14. Fred N. Kerlinger and Elazar J. Pedhazur, *Multiple Regression in Behavioral Research* (New York: Holt, Rinehart and Winston, 1973), p. 3.

with the scientific method approach. The research hypothesis plays an especially important role in experimental research since many experimental plans use a test of significance as a part of the analysis of data. Tests of significance use the null hypothesis to test for differences, and rejection of a null hypothesis is, in general, supporting evidence for a research hypothesis.

Experimental designs utilize experimental treatment where effects of different levels of an independent variable are studied in measures of the dependent variable. Through careful control within the research design, cause-and-effect relationships are identified.

Possible decision errors are associated with rejection of the null hypothesis or failure to reject it. The alpha error—rejection of the null hypothesis when it is true—is controlled by the researcher as he or she sets the significance level through an acceptable probability of making the error.

The validity of research results rests on the ability of the design to control variables not considered to be a part of the treatment. Internal sources of weakness, as well as external sources, have been discussed in twelve factors to provide guidelines for building validity into experimental results.

Tools used to gather data for experimental studies must be objective and must produce valid data for the study. The tools for analysis must be appropriate for the research design and type of data generated.

Theoretical frequency distributions serve as mathematical models that allow a comparison of observed values with values in the appropriate theoretical distribution. The *unit* normal curve values, the binomial distribution, the t distribution, F distribution and the chi-square distributions are used to judge discrepancy between observation and hypothesis.

The t test has been used as an example of a parametric test. Chi-square tests, the median test, and the sign test have been used as examples of nonparametric tests. Nonparametric tests are used when the data do not have the characteristics needed for tests of means and variances; however the basic principle of comparing obtained results with chance or theoretical frequency distributions remains the same. The technique of multiple regression has been proposed as a possible replacement for some presently used statistical techniques, as it becomes better understood by researchers.

The student should now have an understanding of the principles of experimentally designed research studies and ways to check the several parts of the process for their contribution to defensible results. The design must be completed before any of the experimentation begins, and it must be applied precisely as the plan states or the results of the study will be questioned by the readers of the research report.

11

Drawing Conclusions

> *Does my beginning begin and does my conclusion conclude? (A beginning should not go back to the flood, and a conclusion is not the same as a summing up.)*
> —Barzun & Graff,
> *The Modern Researcher*

The major contribution of a research study to the body of educational knowledge is based on the conclusions drawn from the results. Since these generalizations are presented as the researcher's interpretation of data, they must be based on *all pertinent* data. This assures that all valid inferences are made while, at the same time, interpretations that go beyond the data are avoided.

When developing the conclusions the researcher is involved in the most intellectually demanding aspect of the total research process. He or she must call on all of his/her ability to interpret data, generalize from it, and connect the study's findings to present knowledge. Any contribution of a research study to the body of knowledge about the educational process rests in the researcher's ability to interpret the results into valid conclusions. Valid conclusions are those which are in agreement with real-world conditions.

Conclusions of research studies are used to derive implications for educational practices in the school and other learning settings. Since conclusions for one research study must be viewed in light of other factors, a conclusion for one study will in itself most likely not be a direct implication for educational change. If a study of spelling achievement showed that students who drink a glass of "Mrs. Smith's Mineral Springs Water" learn more words while studying than students who use a traditional study method, it does not mean that *all* students who are studying a list of spelling words should drink from the same well. Other factors must be considered and practical application made in light of all known contributing factors. If the mineral springs water caused students' fingernails to turn a bright orange, one would have to consider both results and any other knowledge about how students learn to spell before making final decisions about how to structure activities for spelling classes.

Since most researchers work in an area of education that they know well, implications for practice may be suggested as a final part of many research reports. In essence, the research process is completed with the presentation of the conclusions drawn for the study. Curriculum development takes over after the conclusions of research are made public through the research report, journal articles, presentations before professional organizations, and personal contact with colleagues.

Conclusions are generally derived to give an answer to the researcher's question by reference to whether the research hypothesis was or was not supported by valid evidence obtained in the study. A carefully planned study will make for valid conclusions. The conclusions are justified and are valid to the degree that they are based on facts and hard data. The interpreter must look at the facts and base the conclusions precisely on what the facts imply.

When planning the study the researcher must consider the various outcomes that might result and the conclusions to be drawn in each case, so that procedures can be made to allow for any possible outcome. Since conclusions are made on available data they cannot be considered solely after the data are gathered but must be a part of planning procedures from the very start.

The major thrust is the interpretation of the results into meaningful statements about whether or not the research hypothesis was supported. If the study supports the research hypothesis, the conclusions should include a section that connects this contribution to related literature and research. A full-blown discussion of how the newly created knowledge will affect theory or cause other educators to alter their thinking is an important part of the section devoted to conclusions. If the study does not support the research hypothesis, an equally detailed discussion should be made of the results' relationship to theory.

The *interpretation of results* that were hypothesized is easy to make since there is agreement between the study's rationale and the results. The conclusions are for the most part ready-made, and a logical argument about connection with theory is already spelled out.

Limitations that were identified in the proposal and those which appeared during implementation must be given attention in regard to the extent of their influence on results. What appeared to be a major limitation might be less than expected or, on the other hand, an unanticipated limitation might become a major limitation by the end of data-gathering procedures. An anticipated high percentage of returned questionnaires may become a marginal percentage and emerge as a major limitation. On the other hand an anticipated limitation from a low percentage of returns might be overcome by an effective incentive to return the form, thus removing the limitation.

If statistical tests are used to assist in interpretation, the importance to overall conclusions must be made clear by the researcher. Statistical significance means that the results are unlikely to be found from chance happenings at a specified significance level with particular degrees of freedom. The meaningfulness and importance of the study must be further evaluated by the researcher. Small differences that are statistically significant may or may not be meaningful in practical terms. Significance for a correlation coefficient merely indicates that the derived coefficient is statistically different from zero. When a large number of cases has contributed to the measured relationship, very small coefficients can be tested as statistically significant when the relationship itself has little meaning to the study. The results of all other tests of significance need this same type of interpretation for meaningful conclusions. The investigator must go beyond the statistical test when drawing conclusions.

The *interpretation of negative results* is not as easily attended to as are supporting results. Too often the negative results are not used to create new knowledge. Results of nonsupport, as well as support, certainly can make a contribution to what is known about the educational process. Gilman observes how another field uses both positive and negative results for industrial research:

> It comes as quite a shock to most laymen to find that the results of more than 90 percent of the experimental research studies conducted by industry are inconclusive. Such costly research is maintained because of the small gains a company can make as a result of the few conclusive studies, and because of a research philosophy that even inconclusive tests are valuable in providing information that the corporation needs to know.[1]

A more open mind to negative results for educational studies could foster dissemination of information from these studies and give direction to future studies, and/or make a contribution to present knowledge.

Reports of studies that have results in opposition to the research hypothesis are usually written defensively with careful explanation about the shortcomings of the study and unexpected magnitude of the limitations. Any carefully planned study hypothesizes results based on a wide background of information about theory and results of other studies. If the prediction is made with perfect confidence about the outcome, then there is no need to conduct the study. The scientist is committed to establishing the true state of affairs, and a researcher must push into the unknown to add to our knowledge. Negative results provide an opportunity to reflect on theory and to reconsider it in light of the newly obtained information. The well formulated research study will create useful new knowledge with either positive or negative results.

BASES FOR RESEARCH CONCLUSIONS

Careful extrapolation of conclusions from the facts is a skill that a researcher must have to make a contribution to the educational scene. Since a researcher is free to conclude anything that he or she wants from the study, researcher self-discipline is needed to avoid the pitfalls of seeing only what one wants to see in the data. Self-imposed discipline also avoids making extravagant claims that are only suggested by the information and not truly warranted by fact. The bases for research conclusions must be validated data, and the extrapolation must go beyond the data with unsupported conclusions.

Historical Research

Since the purpose of historical research in education is utilitarian, any conclusions drawn must be based on data that have withstood the most rigorous criticism by the researcher. Historical research can lead to understanding only by avoidance of pitfalls that await the unwary. The greatest pitfall of all lies in drawing conclusions from limited amounts of data. Like the paleontologist who constructs a complete skeleton

---

1. David A. Gilman, "Why Don't You Publish It in the Journal of Nonsignificant Differences," *Contemporary Education* 43 (January 1971): 155-56.

from a few bones, the researcher using historical approaches to inquiry must recreate much of the past from a relatively small number of carefully documented clues. Objectivity and breadth of vision become the tools for providing valid conclusions to historically based studies.

After the choice of an integrating question, a hypothesis was developed, and evidence was gathered from relics and documents. The carefully prepared bibliography cards hold the needed information that has been subjected to formal criticism. The researcher is now ready to fit together a logically constructed pattern of truth as the answer to the original question. A general structure for the report of historical research uses a broad base of previous knowledge as a foundation, followed by the presentation of evidence central to the question in as direct and narrow a way as possible. This leads to the conclusion that broadens again to encompass, through generalizations, the findings of the study.

The conclusions must be written with the awareness that the reader will be directed only through the words and associated meaning. Although the writer knows what he/she wants the words to convey, the intended meaning may be lost by letting the actual written words express something different to the reader. The researcher must make sure that the meaning expressed is the meaning *intended*, by scrutinizing each word until he or she is assured that every word conveys exactly what it is meant to say.

Bad reasoning is a primary pitfall for historical studies. A study of logic might help in interpreting the data into conclusions. Logic could help to overcome some tendencies to beg the question, deny the antecedent, non sequitur, and such. Bad generalizations that are the result of use of words like "all," "every," and "never," when the data only cover a small area, could be improved by use of qualifiers, such as "nearly," "almost," and "perhaps." However too generous use of qualifiers results in an uninteresting and useless piece of material. Conclusions must be based on available data, but the writer does not want to avoid a commitment because data are incomplete.

Overgeneralization can result from failure to consider the negative instances. To form a conclusion that "it rains every time an outdoor cookout is planned since it happened on two occasions" without consideration of the several times that it did not rain, is an example of "failure to consider the negative instances." To avoid this danger consider all data and include in the plan procedures that assure that all possible outcomes are open to support.

A fallacy that awaits the unwary is condensing diversity into unity. This is the opposite of overgeneralizing and comes about by grouping a number of factors into one category. To say that the bombing of Pearl Harbor on December 7, 1941, was the reason that the United States entered World War II is an example of a complex system being reduced to one event. A senior approaching a teacher near the end of the semester with a statement saying that if he does not get at least a B in the course he will not be able to graduate, is reducing all of the college hours and their contributions to the present course. When teachers meet a newly devised curriculum they may be inclined to view it as nothing but the same old thing in a new dress—again the reduction fallacy has been put into play.

In sum, the drawing of conclusions requires both imaginative insight and scholarly objectivity to produce a logically conceived set of valid conclusion statements. Careful attention to detail and use of appropriate language remain as important contributors to making a historical study a contribution to educational knowledge.

Drawing Conclusions

Conclusions from historical research studies are generalizations that should be based in principles of probability similar to those used by more formally designed studies. By developing a hypothesis, gathering sufficient data, and verifying it for the study, the researcher can reach valid conclusions for historical studies. Implications about the validity of the conclusions in different times and places must be made much the same way that other conclusions are made or left to the reader for decision.

Descriptive Research

Many of the same difficulties in drawing conclusions from historical studies hold also for descriptive research studies because subjectivity is always involved. The major contributions for enhancing the validity of conclusions from descriptive studies over those from historical studies lies in the opportunity of descriptive studies to choose data from a complete setting rather than being forced to study only that information which remains from the past. At least in theory, all data about the present are available to the researcher, assuming that the tools are available to gather those that are needed for the study.

Methods of observation for descriptive studies, in general, provide more reliable data and results to be used as bases for conclusions. Although direct manipulation of variables is not possible, manipulation by selection of what to observe from present data gives the researcher and readers of the research increased confidence in his or her conclusions. In turn, users of the conclusions tend to have more confidence in implications that are drawn from validly based conclusions.

Since the *case study* is an intensive investigation centered on a particular subject, the researcher is limited in his/her ability to generalize. The researcher who uses the case study to probe deeply into a particular subject or unit is usually concerned more with that one particular case than with the development of far-reaching generalizations. A case study may provide the opportunity to uncover previously unsuspected relationships. The scientific approach does not allow a hypothesis developed from a set of data to be tested using the same data; therefore a hypothesis developed in a case study cannot be tested within itself.

A part of the conclusions from a case study should include any observed relationships as hypotheses. The empirical data used to develop the hypothesis should be presented and used to establish its rationale. Further investigation of its tenability lies in further testing using newly gathered data. The strength of the hypothesis and its acceptability is the function of the extent to which it has withstood the tests. For research, the case study's usefulness is as a producer of hypotheses rather than as a tool for testing hypothesis.

Researchers concerned with the study of effects may use a series of case studies where a change is introduced in a number of subjects and a study made of effects. Generally this use of the case study as a tool for gathering data for an experimental study is not a true case study where an in-depth investigation is made for bettering the subject being studied. It is used more as a data-collecting device than as a device to test a hypothesis.

A *survey* of present conditions is intended to culminate with statements about the present state of affairs and generalizations that interpet the data. In general the data for studies in a survey are collected using an observational technique—direct observation, questionnaire, opinionnaire, interview, or mechanical device. After organization of data by tabulation and graphing, statements about conditions can be made with direct reference to the tables and graphs. On the other hand, the generalizations are the researcher's conclusions, which are derived from the casual and meaningful aspects interpreted from the data.

To interpret the data the researcher must become familiar with it. A graph may reveal a characteristic that is hidden in a table. Meaningful patterns may be revealed by organizing data into ascending order, descending order, or alphabetical order. Try as many arrangements as possible for insight beyond interpretation by computational outcomes. Since the manner in which the data are prepared for further interpretation is critical, the researcher must be prepared to defend his or her procedure, keeping in mind the question that has been asked.

Any conclusions from a survey must be made in the context of a complex situation. The interaction of many factors makes hasty conclusions tenuous at best. The choice of what data to gather should contribute much help in drawing valid conclusions in a complex situation if consideration is given to possible conclusions during the planning stage. The plan of the study should assure that the data needed for valid conclusions are available in the results of the study. A good design is a prerequisite for valid conclusions.

The researcher using a survey has many tools and procedures to aid in collecting data, and he/she should not be guilty of relying on one tool, such as the questionnaire, for all surveys. A researcher falling into the pattern of using one tool would be guilty of committing a Type V error, defined as "the error committed by a researcher by rigidly adhering to one investigative design without a systematic approach."[2] By using the most appropriate tool or tools to collect the data and considering the total situation, the researcher can present generalizations as conclusions for research surveys that will score high in validity.

Developmental studies are important to education because of the need to know how human beings grow and develop and how they differ at various ages. Generally a specific trait or set of traits is studied for one selected group over a time period of several years. Terman used the longitudinal method to study over 1,500 subjects who were classed as gifted in 1921. A series of publications has reported results of the study. The reportings included conclusions based on data collected and related to present theory. In 1946, for example, twenty-five years after the study commenced, Terman concluded:

> Contrary to the theory of Lange-Eichbaum that great achievement is usually associated with emotional tensions which border on the abnormal, in our gifted group success is associated with stability rather than instability, with absence rather than presence of disturbing conflicts—in short, with well-balanced temperament and with freedom from excessive frustration.
>
> ... At any rate, we have seen that intellect and achievement are far from perfectly correlated. Why this is so, what circumstances affect the fruition of human talent, are questions of such transcendent importance that they should be investigated by every method that promises the slightest reduction of our present ignorance.[3]

---

2. For errors I-IV see Schuyler U. Huck et al., *Reading Statistics and Research* (New York: Harper and Row, 1974), pp. 375-76.

3. Lewis M. Terman and Melita H. Oden, *The Gifted Child Grows Up* (Stanford: Stanford University Press, 1947), p. 352.

Drawing Conclusions

Other conclusions that Terman felt had been established are given in the final chapter, on pages 377 to 379, of *The Gifted Child Grows Up*. The major thrust of the study in recent years has been to "increase our knowledge of the dynamics of human behavior, with special reference to the factors that determine degree and direction of creative achievement."

Longitudinal developmental studies require that someone or some group devote considerable amounts of time and money over the several years that the study continues. Problems also arise as the subjects under study move and/or become disinterested in the project. Study of a variable for change over a time span requires baseline data for conclusions about change. Important variables may be difficult to identify early in the project, therefore reducing the information needed to draw valid conclusions.

An alternative to studying change for one group over a time period makes use of what is called the *cross-sectional survey*. Changes due to development are studied by looking at various age levels at one point in time. Data are gathered on variables being studied and conclusions about development are made with regard to differences in the sample studied. The assumption is that if a time span were studied the data would look like that of the cross-sectional study. Conclusions drawn for cross-sectional studies are not affected by extraneous variables that change over time and affect data collected longitudinally. Part of observed changes over time is a result of change generally. A study of change per se with all contributing factors is best conducted by the longitudinal study. The researcher must draw his or her conclusions in the light of the total change. A study of typicalness might best be studied by a cross-sectional design.

A correlational study is designed to identify what the researcher hopes are meaningful and direct relationships between pairs of variables. Correlational techniques alone cannot ascertain which variable is the cause and which variable is affected. Conclusions for studies using correlational techniques will generally be hypotheses about relationships among variables. A correlational study may be conducted to establish a relationship (the conclusions) and generate a hypothesis about cause in an experimental study.

The correlational study may be conducted to establish the magnitude or strength after causal factors have been previously identified. Conclusions for studies using correlation in this way appear to be more like conclusions for experimental studies.

Experimental Research

The experimental design and the data generated by a design with high internal and external validity provide an opportunity for the researcher to draw highly valid conclusions. Without high internal validity, data cannot be interpreted into conclusions, and without high external validity, the results cannot be widely generalized.

Conclusions for experimental studies are, in general, intended to be tied directly to educational theory. The control of the experiment is intended to give the researcher a solid base for theory development. Levels of probability that are set for experiments allow statements that the outcome of the study did not happen by chance to be made with confidence.

Results of tests of significance have too often been used as conclusions for studies. Since the significance tests are an interpretative tool, researchers have been comfortable in letting the test of significance be the sole tool used for interpretation. What is needed is the interpretation by the researcher who views all of his or her information in total text. The importance of objectivity has overshadowed other important aspects for many investigators who use the experimental design as they draw the conclusions.

The present stage in the development of research in education, as in all behavioral sciences, does not allow the desired level of objectivity. As in all research of complex systems there seems to be a conflict between objectivity and import. What is hoped for in drawing conclusions for experimental research problems is a point at which both objectivity and import are maximal, which is the best that can be done until problems of inexactness are overcome.

Since the empirical distribution of the data determines the proper parametric or nonparametric comparative method to be used, appropriate methods must be chosen to interpret the data. Alternative forms of analysis can be proposed in the overall plan and a decision made concerning assumptions appropriate for parametric techniques. If the assumptions for a parametric test have not been met, then an appropriate nonparametric test can be employed. Recently there has been discussion about assumptions needed for use of parametric tests. An overview of current and historical thought is given in the *Review of Educational Research*.[4]

Following the statistical interpretation and with the results in hand, the researcher determines the inferences which can be made from the information. A well developed research hypothesis provides a firm base for conclusions in experimental studies, since rejection of the null hypothesis, in general, will be cause to support the alternate—the research hypothesis.

GENERALIZATION

The reader of a research report uses the researcher's conclusions to help him or her better understand educational concerns. Much of the generalizing done by the researcher must be put into the context of conditions that vary, given different settings. Complete descriptions of subjects, conditions, treatments, and all contributing factors allow the reader to generalize from a study to like situations. A study conducted on subjects in a rural midwestern community may have conclusions that are generalizable to similar subjects in other rural midwestern towns, but not to those in mountain communities of Appalachia or mid-city Miami, where the citizens are largely of Latin descent.

Some conclusions are widely generalizable while others are not. The less the studied trait is affected by environment, the greater the possibility of generalization. A study of a factor that is basic to the nature of humans, e.g., the effects of temperature on bodily functions, would be more widely generalizable than conclusions from a study of a factor based more in a culture, e.g., the effects of a counseling technique.

The section reporting the conclusions should also give attention to any limitations or weaknesses of the study. Since all research studies have inadequacies, limitations are associated with all stated conclusions. Any weakness that is relevant to the outcome of the study should be mentioned, and the magnitude of its contribution should be estimated.

Limitations that need to be listed are those that might have affected the results and, in turn, the conclusions. These usually come from less than ideal sampling techniques, limitations placed on methodology, and statistical design. Limitations are listed not

---

4. Paul Leslie Gardner, "Scales and Statistics," *Review of Educational Research* 45 (Winter 1975): 43-57.

Drawing Conclusions

only because of the responsibility that the researcher has to the reader, but also to instill confidence in the reader about the researcher's skill in researching. If obvious weaknesses are not listed, the astute reader will question whether the investigator was knowledgeable enough to recognize the limitation. A listing of a limitation usually indicates that the researcher was limited by condition. Limitations appear as the researcher makes choices among alternatives, where each alternative has desired characteristics but no one of them has all the desired traits. It is not likely that any one automobile has all of the desired features (especially price), but purchase of one says that, of all possible combinations, this is the one that is optimum. Selections for a research plan follow much the same logic, with weaknesses becoming limitations.

Limitations also come about through unpredictable events. Subjects may move or become ill, thus creating limitations outside the control of the researcher.

After the conclusions are presented and defended, the researcher may, at his/her choosing, speculate as to how the results might have been different given different conditions. He or she may also make interpretations that go beyond the data for the study. The one condition that is attached with any such addendum is that the researcher clearly states that he/she has gone beyond the data and that this particular section is only speculation.

IMPLICATIONS AND RECOMMENDATIONS

Conclusions from research studies carry some implications for practical application. A researcher may list any practical application that he or she feels is implied by his/her discovered principle. In general the curriculum specialists and other developmental people take over at this point and place the results in context with other factors for direct application.

An important section of the report for others interested in the research study is a section where the researcher makes recommendation for further study. He or she may have identified some closely related questions that need to be investigated or may have generated more questions through results of the study. His/her familiarity with the question under study allows and demands a good understanding of a wider scope about closely related questions. He or she is obligated to project into the future by giving personal ideas for recommended research.

The section on recommendations completes the task that commenced when the indeterminate situation was met and a study was developed to overcome the obstacle. However the structure for inquiry does not terminate the process here, since further study of the question is continued by replication of this study or by investigation of other closely related problem questions.

BIBLIOGRAPHY

Altman, Edward I. "Financial Ratios, Discriminant Analysis, and the Prediction of Corporate Bankruptcy." *Journal of Finance* 23 (September 1968): 589-609.

American Historical Association. *Guide to Historical Literature*. New York: Macmillan Co., 1961.

Anderson, Scarvia B. et al. *Encyclopedia of Educational Evaluation*. San Francisco. Jossey-Bass, 1975.

Andrews, Frank M., and Messenger, R.C. *Multivariate Nominal Scale Analysis*. Ann Arbor: University of Michigan — Survey Research Center, 1973.

Andriot, John L. *Guide to U.S. Government Guides & Periodicals*. McLean, Va.: Document Index (Box 195), 1969.

Babbie, E.R. *Survey Research Methods*. Belmont: Cal.: Wadsworth Publishing, 1973.

Barber, T.X. "Pitfalls in Research: Nine Investigator and Experimentor Effects." *Second Handbook of Research on Teaching*. Edited by R.M.W. Travers. Chicago: Rand McNally, 1973.

Barzun, Jacques, and Graff, Henry F. *The Modern Researcher*. New York: Harcourt, Brace, and World, 1970.

Beach, Mark. "History of Education." *Review of Educational Research* 39 (December 1969): 561-76.

Brickman, William W. *Research in Educational History*. Norwood, Pa.: Norwood Editions, 1973.

Brooks, Phillip C. *Research in Archives: The Use of Unpublished Primary Sources*. Chicago: University of Chicago Press, 1969.

Campbell, Donald T. "Factors Relevant to the Validity of Experiments in Social Settings." *Psychological Bulletin* 54 (July 1957): 297-312.

Campbell, Donald T., and Stanley, J. *Experimental and Quasi-experimental Design for Research*. Chicago: Rand McNally, 1963. Also appears as chapter 5 in N.L. Gage, ed., *Handbook of Research on Teaching*. Chicago: Rand McNally, 1963.

Chase, Clinton I. *Elementary Statistical Procedures*. New York: McGraw-Hill, 1967.

Conover, W.J. *Practical Nonparametric Statistics*. New York: John Wiley & Sons, 1971.

Edington, Eugene S. *Statistical Inference: The Distribution-free Approach*. New York: McGraw-Hill, 1969.

Eisenbeis, R.A., and Avery, R.B. *Discriminant Analysis and Classification Procedures*. Lexington, Mass: D.C. Heath & Co., 1972.

Ferguson, G.A. *Statistical Analysis in Psychology and Education*. 3rd ed. New York: McGraw-Hill, 1971.

Fisher, Sir Ronald A. *Statistical Methods for Research Workers*. 14th ed. Darien, Conn: Hafner Publishing, 1970.

Gardner, Paul Leslie. "Scales and Statistics." *Review of Educational Research* 45 (Winter 1975): 43-47.

Gilman, David A. "Why Don't You Publish It in the Journal of Non-significant Differences." *Contemporary Education* 43 (January 1971) : 155-56.

Good, Carter V. *Essentials of Educational Research*. New York: Appleton-Century-Crofts, 1966.

———. *Essentials of Educational Research*. New York: Appleton-Century-Crofts, 1972.

———. *Dictionary of Education*. New York: McGraw-Hill, 1973.

Good, Carter V., and Scates, Douglas E. *Methods of Research: Educational, Psychological, Sociological*. New York: Appleton-Century-Crofts, 1954.

Helmstadter, G.C. *Research Concepts in Human Behavior*. New York: Appleton-Century-Crofts, 1970.

Hempel, Carl. "The Test of a Hypothesis: Its Logic and Its Face." In *Philosophy of Educational Research*, edited by Harry S. Broudy et al. New York: John Wiley & Sons, 1973.

Hopkins, Charles D. *Describing Data Statistically*. Columbus, Ohio: Charles E. Merrill, 1974.

Horst, Paul. *Factor Analysis of Data Matrices*. New York: Holt, Rinehart and Winston, 1965.

Huck, Schuyler, U. et al. *Reading Statistics and Research*. New York: Harper & Row, 1974.

Johnson, H.H., and Solso, R.H. *An Introduction to Experimental Design in Psychology: A Case Approach*. New York: Harper & Row, 1971.

Katz, Michael B. *Class, Bureaucracy, and Schools*. New York: Praeger, 1971.

Kelly, Francis J. et al. *Research Design in the Behavioral Sciences MULTIPLE REGRESSION APPROACH*. Carbondale: Southern Illinois University Press, 1969.

Kendall, Maurice G. *Rank Correlation Methods*. 3rd ed. New York: Hafner Publishing, 1962.

Kerlinger, F.N. *Foundations of Behavioral Research*. 2nd ed. New York: Holt, Rinehart and Winston, 1973.

Kerlinger, F.N., and Pedhazur, E.J. *Multiple Regression in Behavioral Research*. New York: Holt, Rinehart and Winston, 1973.

Likert, R.A. "A Technique for the Measurement of Attitudes." *Archives of Psychology* 140 (1932): 1-55.

Lutz, Frank W., and Ramsey, Margaret A. "The Use of Anthropological Field Methods in Education." *Educational Researcher* 3 (November 1974): 5-8.

McReynolds, Paul, ed. *Advances in Psychological Assessment III*. San Francisco: Jossey-Bass, 1974.

Madge, J.H. *The Tools of Social Science*. New York: Doubleday & Co., 1965.

Masling, Joseph. "Role Related Behavior of the Subject and Psychologist and Its Effects Upon Psychological Data." Nebraska Symposium on Motivation. Lincoln: University of Nebraska Press, 1966.

Moehlman, Arthur H. et al. *A Guide to Computer-Assisted Historical Research in American Education*. Austin: University of Texas Press, 1969.

Mueller, J.H., and Schuessler, K.F. *Statistical Reasoning in Sociology*. Boston: Houghton-Mifflin, 1961.

Myers, Jerome. *Fundamentals of Experimental Design*. Boston: Allyn and Bacon, 1972.

Oppenheim, A.N. *Questionnaire Design and Attitude Measurement*. New York: Basic Books, 1966.

Pierce, Albert. *Fundamentals of Nonparametric Statistics*. Belmont, Cal.: Dickenson Publishing, 1970.

Poulton, Helen J. *The Historian's Handbook, A Descriptive Guide to Reference Works.* Norman: University of Oklahoma Press, 1972.

Schmeckebier, Laurence F., and Eastin, Roy B. *Government Publications and Their Use.* Washington: Brookings Institution, 1969.

Selye, Hans. *From Dream to Discovery.* New York: McGraw-Hill, 1964.

Siegel, Sidney. *Nonparametrics for the Behavioral Sciences.* New York: McGraw-Hill, 1956.

Sloan, Douglas. "Historiography and the History of Education." In *Review of Research in Education,* edited by Fred N. Kerlinger. Itasca, Ill.: F.E. Peacock, 1973.

Snidell, Peter S. "Anthropological Approaches to the Study of Education." *Review of Educational Research* 39 (December 1969): 593-605.

Sullins, Walter. *Matrix Algebra For Statistical Analysis.* Danville, Ill.: The Interstate, 1973.

Tatsuoka, Maurice M. *Multivariate Analysis, Techniques for Educational and Psychological Research.* New York: John Wiley & Sons, 1971.

Terman, Lewis M., and Oden, Melita H. *The Gifted Child Grows Up.* Stanford: Stanford University Press, 1947.

Tilly, Charles. "Computers in Historical Analysis." *Computers and the Humanities* 7 (September-November 1973): 323-35.

Van Dalen, Deobold B. *Understanding Educational Research.* 3rd ed. New York: McGraw-Hill, 1973.

Whallon, Robert, Jr. "The Computer in Archaeology: A Critical Survey." *Computers and the Humanities* 7 (September 1972): 29-45.

Woody, Thomas. "Of History and Its Method." *Journal of Experimental Education* 15 (March 1947): 175-201.

PART IV

Aids to Inquiry

From time to time the researcher turns to an auxiliary for the special assistance which it can give to the process of inquiry. Three of these that can contribute substantially to effective inquiry are the library, the research proposal, and the research report. Each of the final three chapters gives attention to one of these research aids.

The library is used to provide ready-made answers to questions. More importantly, its contribution is to give the researcher background knowledge about problems that are being investigated through empirical procedures. The chapter on the library is intended to aid the student who is searching for knowledge related to a specific topic of concern.

The research proposal is used to structure a complete plan of procedure for isolating a problem for research and developing a way to arrive at an answer to the implied question. It is widely used today not only for its contribution to the researcher but also to those sponsoring or funding research projects.

The research report serves the purpose of communicating to others what research has been performed and the conclusions drawn from it. In addition to the detailed report, which gives complete documentation, the condensed report that is appropriate for a professional journal is used to disseminate information gained from research studies.

12

The Library

The college or university library serves many purposes. It is a convenient place to step into when one is caught in the rain, a quiet place to study when the dormitory is noisy, a source of information for assignments of readings, and a valuable source of information. The search for information will be the major concern in this chapter, and, though the search may be time consuming, it is a necessary part of educational inquiry. Skill in the use of the library is necessary to avoid spending excessively large amounts of time trying to locate information about a specific problem.

The next step after clear formulation of a problem is to learn whether the question has been answered by someone else and to gather information about closely related problem areas. Most of what is known can be found in libraries. Every year thousands of books, monographs, journals, documents, and other materials are added to libraries. This body of knowledge is useful to the person who seeks answers to questions that arise, and can be used to provide a sound basis for further search for answers through research studies.

Skillful use of the library gives direction to the specific materials needed for an exhaustive search for all possible information related to a study. An attempt to find needed materials without library skills results in much wasted effort. An evening wasted in the library can be one of the most frustrating experiences for a student. An evening in which the time is used efficiently can be rewarding both in the material located and in achieving a personal sense of accomplishment. This chapter is designed to help students make trips to the library personally rewarding and productive.

In general all libraries have the same facilities and offer the same services for students, but each library is organized uniquely and the regulations vary from one library to another. Most campus libraries have printed guides about layout, regulations, services, and special facilities. Some libraries conduct tours to explain exactly how they can be used. If a conducted tour is not available, a personal orientation tour will familiarize the student with how and where information can be obtained. Essential to the use of the library for inquiry are:

1. Location of the card catalog and its organization.
2. Location of the stacks. Find if they are open to students, or if special permission can be arranged to use closed stacks; it should be obtained.
3. Determination as to whether periodicals are distributed through the stacks. If they are centrally located in a periodicals room, find it.
4. Location of the reference section and its organization.
5. Location of special collections, such as indexes, curriculum materials, rare books, reserve books, and microfilms.
6. Location of study and listening carrels.
7. Information about borrowing books by interlibrary loan.
8. Procedures for checking out a book and tracing a book that is listed but not on the shelf.

This early orientation to the total workings of the library will do much to allow efficient work. For special problems that arise the professional staff members of the library are anxious to provide their expert skill and knowledge to help in any way that they can. The reference section is an especially important part of the library since most of the search in the library for research purposes is for material that is unknown to the person looking. The sources are discovered through the use of indexes, abstracts, and other reference materials. Much of this chapter is devoted to use of the tools necessary in obtaining the information needed for the study.

INDEXING THE LIBRARY

Most of us learned at an early age to use the index to a book when looking for a particular topic or to determine whether the book covers a topic of interest. The index is used rather than resorting to a page-by-page search. The library should be approached in the same way, by using the appropriate indexes. Generally the main card catalogue indexes all material in a library, but other special lists in other card catalogues throughout the library give a second listing in special areas and/or augment and supplement the main card catalogue index.

Most large libraries use the Library of Congress classification system. Letters of the alphabet serve as principal headings (see figure 12.1), with numerals standing for subcategories. For extensive holdings and libraries with individual collections this seems superior to the Dewey Decimal system still used extensively as a classification system in public libraries and some college and university libraries.

All books will be coded and placed on the shelves serially by the code prescribed by the classification system being used. A library guide gives directions within the library's specific organizational layout.

Typically the entries for the catalogue will be on a 3 by 5 card and will include all or part of the information given in the Library of Congress listing. One card for each piece of material will be alphabetized by the first letter of the last name, and if the

The Library

		Classifications in the Library of Congress System
A		General Works—Polygraphy
B		Philosophy, Religion, Psychology
C		History—Auxiliary Sciences
D		History and Topography
EF		American History
G		Geography, Anthropology
H		Social Sciences
I		vacant
J		Political Science
K		Law
L		Education, General Works
	LA	History of Education
	LB	Theory of Education
	LC	Special forms and applications
	LD	US Universities and Colleges
	LE	American Education (Outside US)
	LF	European Education
	LG	Asia, Africa, Oceania
	LH	School Periodicals
	LI	vacant
	LJ	Fraternities, Societies
	LT	Textbooks
M		Music
N		Fine Arts
O		vacant
P		Language, Literature
Q		Science
R		Medicine
S		Agriculture
T		Technology
U		Military Science
V		Naval Science
W		vacant
X		vacant
Y		vacant
Z		Library Science—Bibliography

FIGURE 12.1 Major Headings for Library of Congress Classification

material is authored by more than one person a card will be entered for each author (see figure 12.2). When no author credit is given the card will be entered alphabetically by name of editor, organization name or such.

```
LB1028.B755
    Broudy, Harry S., comp.
Philosophy of educational research [by]
Harry S. Broudy, Robert H. Ennis [and]
Leonard I. Krimerman. New York, Wiley [1973]
    xvi, 942 p. 23 cm. (Readings in
educational research)
    Bibliography: p. 893-921.
    1. Educational research. I. Ennis, Robert
Hugh, 1927- joint comp. II. Krimerman,
Leonard I., joint comp. III. Title.


ISBN 0-47110625-9      27J173
370/.72     72      72-002332
```

FIGURE 12.2 Example of an Author Card

```
LB1028.B755
    Philosophy of educational research.
Broudy, Harry S., comp.
    Philosophy of educational research [by]
Harry S. Broudy, Robert H. Ennis [and]
Leonard I. Krimerman. New York, Wiley [1973]
    xvi, 942 p. 23 cm. (Readings in
educational research)
    Bibliography: p. 893-921.
    1. Educational research. I. Ennis, Robert
Hugh, 1927- joint comp. II. Krimerman,
Leonard I., joint comp. III. Title.


ISBN 0-47110625-9      27J173
370/.72      72      72-002332
```

FIGURE 12.3 Example of a Title Card

Expect to also find a card listed alphabetically by title, disregarding *a, an,* and *the* (see figure 12.3), and by subject (figure 12.4), either in the main index or in a separate index contiguous to the main index. The subject card helps to identify material when neither a title nor an author is known and when a survey is being made of an area. In searching subject indexes and indexes for periodical literature, the key to success is the determination of proper topic headings to use in the index. A list of topics or descriptors is given for each index and can be used to select possible information related to the question under study. An item is generally listed only once, so a complete search requires consultation with a number of issues of indexes for periodical literature. Begin with the most recent issue and work back through older issues. Bibliographies found with published articles give additional sources. Remember when using bibliographies

```
LB1028.B755
    Educational research
Broudy, Harry S., comp.
    Philosophy of educational research [by]
Harry S. Broudy, Robert H. Ennis [and]
Leonard I. Krimerman, New York, Wiley [1973]
    xvi, 942 p. 23 cm. (Readings in
educational research)
    Bibliography: p. 893-921.
    1. Educational research. I. Ennis, Robert
Hugh, 1927- joint comp. II. Krimerman,
Leonard I., joint comp. III. Title.


ISBN 0-47110625-9      27J173
370/.72      72      72-002332
```

FIGURE 12.4 Example of a Subject Card

for sources that bibliographies cite only sources prior to the publication of the bibliography, and can never bring the search to the present.

If bound periodicals are distributed by classification through the library an index for these will, in general, be located with the main index.[1] The periodical index *may be* found in the same location with the collection of current issues. If current issues and bound issues are together in a special collection, expect to find the periodical index with it. The entries for the periodical index indicate the names of periodicals and issues that the library has in its collection.

To find entries within the journals, special indexes need to be consulted. One general index to popular magazines and two for professional educational literature are widely used in educational research:

> *Readers' Guide to Periodic Literature.* New York: H. W. Wilson Co. 1900 to date. From 1900 to 1929 the *Guide* covered all periodic literature including educational journals. Since 1929 the *Guide* lists only popular magazines, and is helpful in obtaining information outside professional education.
>
> *Education Index.* New York: H. W. Wilson Co. 1929 to date. A cumulative author-and-subject index to the contents of over 200 educational periodicals, plus proceedings and yearbooks on education and most publications of the US government that deal with education. This index replaced entries about education in *Readers' Guide.* For entries about education pre-1929 see the *Guide.* From September 1961 to September 1969, the author index was dropped in the *Education Index.*
>
> *Current Index to Journals in Education.* New York: CCM Information Service. 1969 to date. A monthly companion to *Resources in Education,* this publication indexes articles in over 300 education journals and *articles about* educational concerns in *other* professional journals. In total, nearly 750 periodicals are indexed for educationally directed articles. A main entry section is arranged alphabetically by clearinghouse name, and numerically by clearinghouse accession number. An EJ accession number is also listed. Other information and an annotation are given in the entry (See figure 12.5).

Instructions for the use of each periodical index, the journals listed, and a key to abbreviations accompany each issue. A few minutes spent in learning how to use a new index will save much time in searching. The primary use of an index for periodicals would be for a search within a subject area. Major subjects are broken down into subcategories, e.g., "RESEARCH, Education," with subtopics of "Aims and Objectives" and "Methodology." (Figure 12.6) Subcategories will change from issue to issue, depending on what is being listed. A search for reports about a specific person's research can be made by author or by title, if a title is known but the author's name is not known. The many ways to use indexes become apparent as they are used in searches for information.

Other indexes that educators find helpful include *Social Sciences and Humanities Index, New York Times Index, State Education Journal Index, An Annotated Index*

---

1. A periodical is a publication, popular or professional, that is issued at regular times and intended to continue indefinitely. For example, *Time* and *Educational and Psychological Measurement.*

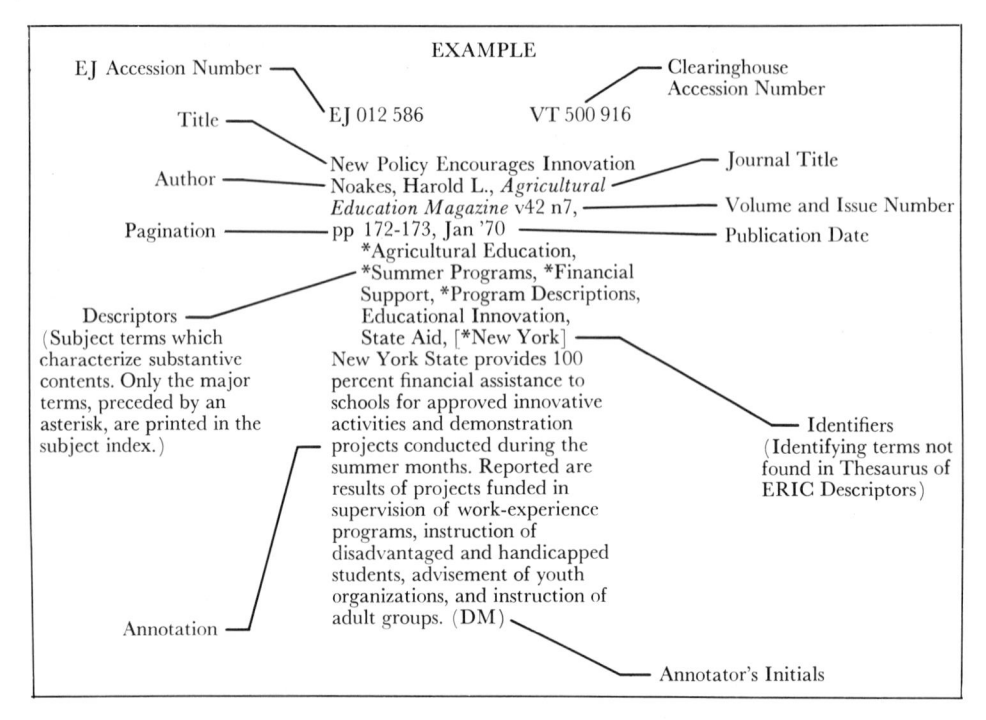

```
                                    EXAMPLE
       EJ Accession Number ─────────╮              ╭───── Clearinghouse
                                     ╲            ╱        Accession Number
              Title ─────╮    EJ 012 586      VT 500 916
                          ╲  New Policy Encourages Innovation ──── Journal Title
             Author ───────  Noakes, Harold L., Agricultural
                             Education Magazine v42 n7, ───────── Volume and Issue Number
         Pagination ──────── pp 172-173, Jan '70 ───────────────── Publication Date
                             *Agricultural Education,
                           ╭ *Summer Programs, *Financial
                           │ Support, *Program Descriptions,
        Descriptors ───────  Educational Innovation,
    (Subject terms which     State Aid, [*New York] ─╮
    characterize substantive New York State provides 100
    contents. Only the major percent financial assistance to
    terms, preceded by an    schools for approved innovative
    asterisk, are printed in the activities and demonstration ──── Identifiers
    subject index.)          ╭ projects conducted during the       (Identifying terms not
                             │ summer months. Reported are         found in Thesaurus of
                             │ results of projects funded in       ERIC Descriptors)
                            ╱  supervision of work-experience
                           ╱   programs, instruction of
                          ╱    disadvantaged and handicapped
                         ╱     students, advisement of youth
                        ╱      organizations, and instruction of
         Annotation ───╯       adult groups. (DM)╲
                                                  ╲──── Annotator's Initials
```

FIGURE 12.5 Entry from *Current Index to Journals in Education*

of *State Education Journals, Index to American Doctoral Dissertations, Art Index, Music Index, AIM-ARM Index,* and *Cumulative Book Index.*

ABSTRACTS

Publications that briefly summarize research studies enable the scholar to keep up with work being performed in the field without going to original reports. Enough is reported about each study to give a clear picture of the problem and the scope of the study. In general an abstract will be complete enough to allow one to decide whether a reading of the original article would be profitable. Some sources for abstracts follow.

Resources in Education (RIE),[2] first published in 1966, is a monthly publication of the Educational Resources Information Center (ERIC), a federally funded project that has the charge of identifying and listing each month publications of interest to educators. Résumés of project reports, speeches, and other materials that are difficult to find through other sources are given. Cost for microfiche (MF) and hard copy (HC) are given with an ED number (Example: ED 085 666) for access to the ERIC materials. Many large libraries keep complete files of ERIC listings on easy-to-read microfiche cards. ERIC has a goal of having a copy of each important document of educational research and research-related materials on file plus other educationally oriented data.

---

2. Originally *Research in Education* (1966–74), the title change to *Resources in Education* reflects the broader scope of the documents to be found in ERIC.

RENNER, John Wilson, and Lawson, A. E.
Piagetian theory and instruction in physics. bibliog pors Phys Teach 11:165-9 Mr '73
Promoting intellectual development through science teaching. pors Phys Teach 11:273-6 My '73
—and others
Evaluation of the Science curriculum improvement study. bibliog Sch Sci & Math 73:291-318 Ap '73

RENTAL services
Twelve reasons for renting electronic test equipment. R. E. Herzog. il Ind Educ 62:66-7 Mr '73

RENTSCH, George J.
Need for alternative schools within the public school system. por Sch Mgt 17:8-9+ Ap '73

RENZULLI, Joseph S.
Talent potential in minority group students. bibliog Excep Child 39:437-44 Mr '73

REPARATION
Making the victim whole. D. E. J. MacNamara and J. J. Sullivan. bibliog Urban R 6 no3:21-5 '73

REPAIRING
See also subhead Maintenance and repair under subjects, e.g. Audio-visual equipment—Maintenance and repair; School buildings—Maintenance and repair

REPEATED measurements designs. *See* Experimental design

REPERTORY grid technique. *See* Research, Educational—Methodology

REPETITION
Repeating questions in prose learning. W. M. Boyd. bibliog J Educ Psychol 64:31-8 F '73
See also
Reviews

REPORT cards
When a computer fills out students' report cards. J. H. Mulski and M. Levy. il Ind Educ 61:57-9 O '72

REPORTERS and reporting
Needed improvements in education news coverage as perceived by media and education gatekeepers. H. K. Jacobson. bibliog J Educ Res 66:274-8 F '73

REPORTS and records
Computer aids
GRADER: an automated gradebook system. N. J. Castellan, jr. il Educ Tech 13:56-60 Ap '73
Improving the education of migrant children. P. F. Hogan. il Am Educ 9:20-4 Ap '73
When a computer fills out students' report cards. J. H. Mulski and M. Levy. il Ind Educ 61:57-9 O '72

Forms
Evaluation of educational media. W. E. Hug. il Improv Col & Univ Teach 21:33-4 Wint '73

REPORTS to parents
Good news notes: painless plan for polishing PR. Nations Sch 91:40 Mr '73
School and home communications. A. L. Casey. Sch & Com 59:35 Ap '73

REPOUSSÉ work
Metal mask. R. Reinke. il Arts & Activities 73:36-7 Mr '73

REPRESSION (psychology)
Research findings on the kibbutz adolescent: a response to Bettelheim. J. Jay and R. C. Birney. Am J Orthopsych 43:347-54 Ap '73

RESEARCH
See also
Religious research

Methodology
Adolescence of political socialization. R. M. Merelman. bibliog Sociol of Educ 45:134-66 Spr '72
Problems in the analysis of patterns of abilities; with reply by G. S. Lesser. D. Feldman. bibliog Child Develop 44:12-20 Mr '73

Colleges and universities
Fictitious conflict between research and education. J. E. Lannutti. Educ Rec 54:83-4 Wint '73
In-service education: the university's role. P. W. Kirby. Educ Lead 30:431-3 F '73
Plea for research subjectivity. E. Scriven and A. Harrison. Improv Col & Univ Teach 21:38-9 Wint '73
Research and publication in the small college; a comparative study of faculty members' perceptions and attitudes. S. A. Clark. bibliog J Educ Res 66:328-33 Mr '73
Teaching-research controversy. J. H. Wilson and R. S. Wilson. Educ Rec 53:321-6 Fall '72; Same cond. Educ Digest 38:56-9 F '73

Graduate schools
Publication by the graduate student: some negative considerations. J. W. Cortada and J. H. Stone Educ Forum 37:179-81 Ja '73

RESEARCH, Educational
Capsulized R&D; Council of educational development and research. C. Reynolds. Am Educ 9:back cover Mr '73

Administration
Surveys for local education agencies: theoretical and practical considerations. F. J. Brieve and A. P. Johnston. Calif J Educ Res 24:79-92 Mr '73
Who does what—when, where and why? Cooperative institutional research program. il Col Mgt 8:40-1 Ap '73

Aims and objectives
In-service education: the university's role. P. W. Kirby. Educ Lead 30:431-3 F '73
Plea for research subjectivity. E. Scriven and A. Harrison. Improv Col & Univ Teach 21:38-9 Wint '73

Bibliography
California educational research association; research papers of the fifty-first conference. Calif J Educ Res 24:93-8 Mr '73

Criticism
How we all failed at performance contracting. E. B. Page. bibliog Phi Delta Kappan 54:115-17 O '72; Reply. J. K. Miller. bibliog 54:394-6 F '73

Evaluation
Good news: research on the nongraded elementary school. B. N. Pavan. bibliog El Sch J 73:333-42 Mr '73
Retrospect and prospect in educational research. W. Taylor. Educ Res 15:3-9 N '72

Implementation
Relationship of educational research to educational technology. A. M. Gallegos and H. F. Rahmlow. bibliog il Educ Tech 13:44-7 Ap '73
Research results for the classroom. E. J. Schneider and M. K. Burton. il Todays Educ 62:44-5 Mr '73

Methodology
Application of repertory grid techniques to the study of choice of university. W. A. Reid and B. J. Holley. bibliog Brit J Educ Psychol 42:52-9 F '72
Classroom behavior of teachers; ed. by N. Flanders and G. Nuthall; symposium. bibliog il Int R Educ 18 no4:427-568 '72
Dependent variable: measurement issues in reading research. R. Farr and J. J. Tuinman. Read Res Q 7:413-23 Spr '72
Eta-squared and partial eta-squared in fixed factor ANOVA designs. J. Cohen. Educ & Psychol M 33:107-12 Spr '73
Learner analysis; some process and content concerns. T. M. Schwen. bibliog il AV Comm R 21:44-72 Spr '73
Research-service model for support of handicapped children. M. J. Guralnick. bibliog Excep Child 39:277-82 Ja '73
Technique for minimizing subject-observer looking interactions in field settings. J. A. Grimm and others. bibliog J Exp Child Psychol 14:500-5 D '72
What you see is not necessarily what you get. H. G. Petrie J Educ Res 66:inside cover F '73
Wheel and the table: the relative merits of two alternative instruments for collecting semantic-type data. C. Orpen. Brit J Educ Psychol 42:86-7 F '72
Within-subject variation, measurement error, and selection of a criterion score; with reply by F. M. Henry. R. Hetherington. Res Q (AAHPER) 44:113-18 Mr '73

State and federal aid
Trailblazer in an age of R&D. D. A. Erickson. bibliog Sch R 81:155-74 F '73

Student participation
Involving undergraduates in research. A. Rothstein. JOHPER 44:71-2 Mr '73

Teacher participation
Action research: a valuable professional activity for the teacher. B. G. Rainey. Clearing H 47:371-5 F '73
Undergraduate-graduate research collaboration program. F. V. Scalzi and P. Kovacic. J. Chem Educ 50:205-7 Mr '73

Teaching
Research: the preservice missing link. M. B. Marks. J Teach Educ 23:453-6 Wint '72

California
See also
California educational research association

Great Britain
Retrospect and prospect in educational research. W. Taylor. Educ Res 15:3-9 N '72

FIGURE 12.6 A Page from *Education Index*

Included in each issue of *Resources in Education* are document résumés, subject index, author index, institution index, new thesaurus terms, lists of other ERIC products, how to order ERIC publications, and how to order ERIC document reproductions. A companion publication, *Thesaurus of ERIC Descriptors,* lists descriptors for searching ERIC materials, descriptor groups, and a rotated descriptor display to aid in choosing likely descriptors.

An integral part of the ERIC operation is a series of clearinghouses scattered around the country, each devoted to a special interest area, for example—urban education. The clearinghouses acquire, review, abstract, and index documents for *Resources in Education.* In addition they prepare bibliographies and interpretive summaries of ERIC-listed materials on special topics. Current addresses of all clearinghouses are listed in each issue of *Resources in Education.*

Computer searches can be made of all material listed in ERIC at one of several places that have the listings computerized. *ERIC tapes* and *ERIC tools* are also available for special uses. Special announcements about changes within ERIC are given in each issue of *RIE,* and current mailing addresses for computer searches and other services are also listed.

Psychological Abstracts gives summaries of studies, books, and articles on all fields of psychology and many educational articles. Published by the American Psychological Association, each issue is indexed by subject and author. This is a good source for experimental research.

Dissertation Abstracts International: Abstracts of Dissertations Available on Microfilm or as Xerographic Reproductions gives a monthly compilation of doctoral dissertations submitted by United States, Canadian, and European universities. Each issue is arranged by broad topic with subject and author indexes. Complete copies or individual pages may be purchased. This publication continues *Microfilm Abstracts* (vol. 1–11, 1938–51) and *Dissertation Abstracts* (vol. 12–29, 1952 through June 1969).

Other abstracts of interest to educators include *Exceptional Child Education Abstracts, Sociological Abstracts, Child Development Abstracts and Bibliography,* and *Mental Retardation Abstracts.*

REVIEWS OF LITERATURE

The following books give reviews, usually organized chronologically, of educational research. Articles listed by subject topics organize and integrate research performed. This is usually the best place to get an early grasp of what has been reported, up to the date of publication of the review.

Encyclopedia of Educational Research is a publication of the American Educational Research Association, printed in about ten-year intervals (1940, 1950, 1960, and 1969). Long critical essays by specialists which summarize and interpret research within very specific areas of education (e.g., Physiology and Psychology of Reading) make up the encyclopedia. Needed research is indicated and excellent comprehensive bibliographies accompany each article. An excellent overview of research in special areas of education makes this a good starting point for a search of the literature.

Review of Educational Research supplements the *Encyclopedia of Educational Research* by reviewing major research findings for more active fields between issues of the *Encyclopedia.* Before June 1970, each issue was devoted to a series of specific articles about a broader field, for example, Educational Evaluation. Since that date, reviews have been made about specific fields, but there is no general theme running through all the articles of one issue.

ENCYCLOPEDIAS

An encyclopedia is a work which contains a collection of articles giving general information about subjects or topics. An encyclopedia should be used as a first source to investigate a subject about which little is known, or as an overview.

The Encyclopedia of Education is comprehensive, covering the history, theory, research, and philosophy as well as the structure and fabric of education. *Education Yearbook, 1972 to date* updates the *Encyclopedia of Education*. An encyclopedia of a general nature may be of use to the educational researcher. *Encyclopaedia Britannica, Encyclopedia Americana*, or, of more special nature, *Encyclopedia of the Social Sciences, International Encyclopedia of Social Sciences, Encyclopedia of Sports*, and *Encyclopedia of Mental Health* may be of value to a researcher's review of literature. To locate encyclopedias about other very specialized areas, the library main card catalogue can be consulted under the heading, "Encyclopedia."

GUIDES

Helpful to the location of materials are books classed as "guides"—they help a person obtain needed information, but many times they include basic information themselves.

Documentation in Education, by A. J. Burke and M. A. Burke, is a discussion of how to do research in education with long and useful bibliographic essays on the materials helpful in conducting research.

Sources in Educational Research: A Selected and Annotated Bibliography, by Theodore Manheim, cites and annotates basic titles useful in general educational research and covers subject-oriented research, for example, comparative education.

Mental Measurements Yearbook, by Oscar K. Buros, gives information regarding forms, manuals, grade levels, publishers, and prices of educational, psychological, and vocational tests, plus reviews of the tests by testing experts. Published roughly at six-year intervals, these yearbooks represent the most thorough coverage of standardized tests available and include complete listings of books about testing, along with annotations.

Handbook of Research on Teaching, edited by Nathaniel L. Gage, is composed of articles about research on teaching. Special chapters on topics give overviews of research in special subject matter areas. Chapter five, "Experimental and Quasi-experimental Designs for Research on Teaching," by Donald T. Campbell and Julian C. Stanley, has been printed separately and is a classic in the history of research design. Chapter 10, "Analysis and Investigation of Teaching Methods," by Norman E. Wallen and Robert M. W. Travers, is a must for all studies of the methodology of teaching.

Second Handbook of Research on Teaching, edited by Robert M. W. Travers, was prepared to update the first handbook but when completed became much more comprehensive; however topics tend to be narrower in scope. Part II, "Methods and Techniques of Research and Development," is composed of chapters devoted to deep coverage of very specific topics of concern to a researcher, for example, "The Use of Direct Observation to Study Teaching," and "The Assessment of Teacher Competence."

Guide to U.S. Government Serials & Periodicals, by John L. Androit, includes an extensive listing of Government publications about education.

Government Publications and Their Use, by Laurence F. Schmekebier and Roy B. Eastin, aids in identifying, locating, and using government publications.

REFERENCES TO REFERENCES

There are works that discuss information sources and how to use them in reference work, and others that give comprehensive reviewing service for reference books.

American Reference Books Annual, published each year by Libraries Unlimited, Inc., aims to review all reference books published or distributed in the United States. The section on Education is subcategorized for easy use by anyone searching literature. Included in some reviews are book reviews that have appeared in periodicals, giving an overview of reviews for the one book. A cumulative index to the first five editions is being compiled by Joseph Sprug and should be available by the time this book is published. It is titled *Cumulative Index to ARBA: An Author-Title-Subject Index to 8,796 Titles in American Reference Books Annual, Volumes 1–5, 1970–1974.*

A Guide to Reference Books, 8th edition, edited by Constance M. Winchell, lists by author, subject area, and type of reference important books in English and other languages. Supplements by Eugene P. Sheehy have augmented the listing of the eighth edition.

A Guide to Reference Material, by A. J. Walford, published in three volumes by the Library Association is international in scope and includes United States publications.

Reference Books: How to Select and Use Them, by Saul Galis and Peter Spielberg, lists about 200 basic reference books that are frequently used in the humanities and social sciences, and gives a concise summary of the contents of each book.

Introduction to Reference Work, by William A. Katz, in two volumes gives detailed descriptions of reference works and how they are used. Part II, chapter 4, "Search Strategy," analyzes how a reference librarian finds answers. The accompanying flow charts give direction to organized library searches, and are considered valuable aids in developing skill in the use of the library.

DICTIONARIES

Dictionary of Education, edited by Carter V. Good, and prepared under the auspices of Phi Delta Kappa, gives entries for educational terms and terms from closely related disciplines.

Roget's International Thesaurus of Words and Phrases (or the abridged title) lists closely associated words as families. A writer can use a thesaurus to choose the word most closely related to an idea that he or she needs to express in his/her writing.

Webster's New International Dictionary of the English Language is a general dictionary for use in writing.

A glance at the reference section of a university library will reveal many books not mentioned in the foregoing sections. The very brief coverage given here is intended to provide the reader with a way into a set of materials that will, in turn, lead to sources of information—areas not covered here but useful for special problems include almanacs, biographical references, directories, atlases, gazetteers, reports of statistics, bibliographies, newspapers, and so on.

The Library

A thorough understanding of how to use sources in locating information must be attained to build background for research problems and to find answers to questions. This working knowledge must be updated by checking for new reference materials, such as *American Reference Books Annual*. Current publications of older references should be checked for coverage since they may expand their coverage or drop some coverages included in the past.

In addition to keeping current on the preceding references, the student needs to remain informed about bibliographical and information-retrieval systems currently available. Since this approach to locating sources is expanding so rapidly a detailed accounting here would be less than useful in a short time, the burden will be on the student to find up-to-date information about systems similar to ERIC and its retrieval systems. The art of choosing descriptors for computer searches is needed for use with these facilities, which are expanding explosively at present, in order to lessen the drudgery of the systematic search through mounds of knowledge. An up-to-date listing of the materials listed in retrieval systems is available from the Washington office of Educational Resources Information Center.

ORGANIZING THE INFORMATION

If successful, a search of the literature for information about a subject results in a need to record it, organize it, and report it. While in the library, much can be done to facilitate the above tasks by structuring the recording of the information when it is first written down. What is recorded is dictated by the purpose or need for the information. Since our discussion is directed toward research, this section will discuss gathering background information for research studies—other purposes will, in most cases, follow similar procedures but different information will be recorded.

Use of Cards

The first need for data recording is something to record on. Information should *always* be recorded on bibliographical cards. Do *not* try to beat the system by using the back of envelopes, sheets of wrapping paper, or even newly acquired notebooks and/or paper from the bookstore—USE CARDS. The cards allow much more flexibility in arranging the material into interpretable form and for developing a narrative report.

The size of the card is not crucial, but 4 by 6 is usually considered minimum, and 5 by 8 is more widely used. If one tends to write quite a lot about each source, the larger cards will avoid use of more than one card for an entry.

Information for the Card

The card should first have a complete bibliographic entry for the item as it would appear in a bibliography. The student should decide (with the help of any regulations that apply to selection) what form the final bibliography will be in (APA, Campbell, Turabian, Dugdale, or such) and learn that form. The example in figure 12.7 is in Campbell's form.[3] Other styles will vary somewhat but, in general, they include the same information. For a book: (1) author or publishing agent; (2) complete title; (3) place of publication; (4) publisher; and (5) date of publication. Other informa-

---

3. William G. Campbell and Stephen Vaughan Ballou, *Form and Style Theses, Reports, Term Papers* (Boston: Houghton-Mifflin, 1974).

> Anderson, Harry E., Jr., and W. L. Bashaw. "An Experimental Study of First Grade Theme Writing," American Educational Research Journal, 5:239-247, March, 1968.
>
> B. The purpose of the present study is to examine differences in mode of discourse for first grade themes. The general hypothesis is that stimulation in a given mode of discourse will improve the quality of compositions in that mode but decreases the quality of themes in another mode.
>
> C. Experimental
>
> D. Ratings of themes by readers
>
> E. Analysis of variance
>
> F. Results of the present study would seem to support Piaget's conjecture in some respects. The D themes required some logical organization of thought but a minimum of abstraction as compared to the writing of A themes. The discussion
>
> (over)

FIGURE 12.7   Side One of a Bibliographical Subject Note Card

tion will be included for special cases—see the style manual. An entry for a periodical is different and usually includes (1) author, (2) complete title, (3) name of magazine or journal, (4) volume number, (5) pages, and (6) date. Entries for other types of materials take special formats, and the manual should be consulted for information needed and the form to be used.

In addition to the entry, list the library call numbers somewhere on the card. With computer preparation of cards, call numbers are now being written across the top of cards rather than down the left side. Example: LB1028.S39. This may be included on the card above the bibliographic entry.

The final bibliography is easily assembled by alphabetizing the cards by author and typing directly from the cards. Make sure that all of the information for the entry is on the card before leaving the book or article.

Additional information can be recorded on the card as needed. The information to be recorded is chosen for its significance to the investigation. Generally it will be (1) a quotation, (2) a paraphrase, or (3) a summary. If a direct quotation is recorded indicate by quotation marks. *Record the page number* since it is needed in the footnote for a direct quotation, a paraphrase, and a summary. Direct quotations are discouraged in final writing, but a direct quotation on a card can be used as such if the meaning is lost in a paraphrase.

Recording information for a *research study* should include as a minimum the following *additional* information (see figure 12.7):

1. Purpose of the study. Include question asked and hypothesis.
2. Research method used (historical, descriptive, or experimental).
3. Kind of data used (test scores, judges' ratings, and so on).
4. Statistic used (chi square, median test, and so on).
5. Results and researcher's conclusions.
6. Personal reaction.
7. Any other information that the researcher deems important.

Selection of important and significant material from an article based on the writer's opinion or other general writings requires skill that is developed by trial and error.

The Library

The best guide is to record only what will bear directly on the subject, plus a summary of additional information found in the article. Those engaged in historical research in the library will be engaged in this type of note taking almost exclusively. Carefully selected notes that are complete and understandable provide the basis for answering the question by giving the background information and/or data to be used in drawing conclusions. Carelessly collected and recorded notes provide little if any support to answering the research question, and can cause great inconvenience and frustration.

Some Notes on Note Taking

1. Use cards. One note to a card. 4 x 6 cards are easy to handle. 5 x 8 cards allow for more narrative.
2. Write the bibliographical entry and library call numbers at the top of the note card.
3. Classify cards by subject heading and/or color coded edges on cards to help in final organization. The classification may be organized around an outline for final writing.
4. Be sure that each note is written clearly and completely in a way that it will be understood when needed. Do not plan to recopy since this introduces a chance for error. Use a typewriter if possible.
5. Develop skill in paraphrasing so that the original meaning remains, but is in your own words. Mark clearly all direct quotations and record the page number.
6. Organize a filing system for all notes. Find a secure permanent place and file the notes as soon as they are made. If they must be carried about, an accordion folder with your name and address on it is a convenient way to transport them.

Selected List of Educational Journals

There are many publications that report educational research, and a thorough search of their contents can be made through appropriate indexes; however some journals are more research-oriented than others. At the risk of limiting your search (do not let this replace a more thorough search), the journals in the following list are presented as being research-oriented publications:

> *American Educational Research Journal*
> *Educational and Psychological Measurement*
> *Educational Researcher*
> *Harvard Educational Review*
> *Journal of Educational Measurement*
> *Journal of Educational Research*
> *Journal of Educational Sociology*
> *Journal of Experimental Education*
> *Journal of Special Education*
> *Measurement and Evaluation in Guidance*
> Most psychological journals including:
> > *Journal of Educational Psychology*
> > *Journal of Experimental Psychology*
> > *Journal of Psychology*
> > *Journal of School Psychology*
> > *Psychological Review*
> > *Psychological Bulletin*

Reading Research Quarterly
Research Quarterly
Review of Educational Research
Sociology of Education

SUMMARY

The researcher spends time locating answers to important questions. Closely related to answering questions is the storage of the answers. Most information is to be found in libraries, making them an integral part of the research process. Researchers use libraries primarily to gather information about the field being studied, knowing that valid research is based on their knowing as much as they can about closely related topics. Skillful use of the library requires (1) an overall understanding of its organization, (2) knowledge of reference materials—indexes, guides, and such—to ferret out the needed information, and (3) skills in recording the information.

Indexes for the library have been presented to familiarize the reader with a way of quickly locating possible needed information. In addition to the card catalogue that lists most materials except periodical articles, the *Readers' Guide to Periodical Literature, Education Index,* and *Current Index to Journals in Education* are all used to give complete coverage to educational information. For other areas more specific indexes are available. Other aids to library search are abstracts, reviews, encyclopedias, guides, handbooks, yearbooks, dictionaries, and reference to references.

Bibliographical and information-retrieval systems should be consulted to complete the coverage of the literature. The Washington, D.C. office of the Educational Resources Information Center lists currently available retrieval systems and their contents.

Information should be recorded on 4 by 6 or 5 by 8 cards, and should include a complete bibliography entry, plus pertinent information. For reporting about research the information should include the purpose of the study, type of research, kind of data, statistics used, results, conclusions, and a reaction statement.

Some suggestions about note taking have been given, to aid students in developing skills in recording information about research questions. A selected list of journals that are research-oriented has also been provided as an aid to the search for studies about educational concerns.

BIBLIOGRAPHY

Allen, George. *Graduate Student's Guide to Theses and Dissertation: A Practical Manual for Writing and Research.* San Francisco: Jossey-Bass, 1973.

Barzun, Jacques, and Graff, Henry F. *The Modern Researcher.* New York: Harcourt, Brace, and World, 1970.

Best, John W. *Research in Education.* New York: Prentice-Hall, 1970.

Boyd, Jessie Edna et al. *Books, Libraries, and You.* New York: Scribner's Sons, 1955.

Brogan, Gerald E., and Buck, Jeanne T. *Using Libraries Effectively.* Belmont, Cal.: Dickensen, 1969.

Campbell, William Giles, and Ballou, Stephen Vaughan. *Form and Style: Theses, Reports, Term Papers.* Boston: Houghton-Mifflin, 1974.

Computers and the Humanities. (Periodical—all issues). Flushing, N.Y.: Queens College of the City University of New York.

Hillway, Tyrus. *Handbook of Educational Research,* pp. 97-113. Boston: Houghton-Mifflin, 1969.

Todd, Alden. *Finding Facts Fast.* New York: William Morrow, 1972.

13

The Research Proposal

From time to time funding agencies, both public and private, release calls for proposals for educational research projects. These announcements say in essence, "We have some money to spend on worthwhile research and if you want to utilize some of it in your quest for knowledge write a report in the form of a proposal telling us (1) what you are seeking, (2) how you intend to go about finding it, (3) how it is significant to educational theory, (4) how you are qualified, and (5) how much money you will need to see the task to completion." Each call for proposals gives some idea about how the above information is to be submitted and what types of studies the funding agency sees as important. In most cases guidelines to be used for proposals are available to interested persons. The guidelines are structured so that detailed information will be provided about the points listed above.

Proposals serve to open communication between funding agencies and researchers. When finally accepted, the proposal is a contract that serves as a two-way insurance policy. The funding agency says, "We are willing to back you financially if you do what you have included in your proposition." The researcher says, "If you will finance me I will carry out the research as proposed." The proposal is the vehicle used to encourage search for knowledge about educational concerns. This chapter is designed to prepare you to organize a framework for proposed research in proposal form.

Proposals are not unique to the field of education. Research and development contracts with funding agencies are common also to the business world. Although proposals for research in education and research in business may be prepared for different purposes they have much in common. The following is excerpted from a publication prepared from a lecture given before the Technical Writers' Institute and is directed to business proposals:

A PROPOSAL IS AN OFFER TO SELL
— Something
— To someone
— At sometime
— For some price

Figure 9

A. Defining a Proposal

Let us first consider what a proposal really is. As shown in Figure 9, it is an offer to sell a specified something to a specified someone at some specified time for some specified price. In most cases, the something must be specified in extensive detail, even though none of the items to be delivered may exist at the time the proposal is submitted.

The someone may be complicated, too. Frequently, the party who buys the thing, the potential customer, may not be the party to whom the seller must deliver the thing. To the potential customer, the proposal must be credible; he must be persuaded that the seller (or bidder) can and will deliver as specified, and must further be persuaded this particular seller offers the best combination of such factors as low cost, high quality, and cost and performance reliability. *Furthermore, the proposal must be sufficiently clear and free from ambiguity that the party who is to accept delivery understands exactly what he is to get and how it will perform.*[1] (Italics added)

Most of the following discussion about educational research proposals is analogous to the above quotation. Especially important to our discussion is the last italicized sentence, and the application of those criteria should be made for proposals of all kinds.

To obtain financial support for a research project, a proposal is required. Candidates for advanced degrees and students in research classes and seminars are also asked to submit proposals for intended research. In general the proposals called for from students are the same as proposals from funding agencies, with one exception. Most proposals from students will omit the section on budget unless a class instructor includes it as a simulation of a proposal for funds. The discussion of the educational research proposal in this chapter does not include the development of a budget. The guidelines for funding proposals are very specific about how the budget is to be presented, and can easily fit as an addendum to our discussion here. The cost of conducting the research is not less important for students since an unlimited income for a student is a rare occurrence. This remains a consideration for the student who is planning to conduct a research study for a class or degree assignment and who lacks large amounts of money, but is not included in proposals of this type.

The components developed within our framework will, in general, be used in all educational proposals, but the arrangement will vary from one set of guidelines to another. The procedures about proposal building presented here are built around a set of instructions that this author has used with students of educational research for several years. Student reactions to various forms have helped develop the product to its present level of sophistication, and it seems to have withstood the test of time. The guidelines are reproduced in figure 13.1, for reference to the elements that make up a proposal. The four broad topics: Background of the Problem; Presentation of the Problem; Methodology; and Bibliography are discussed separately. The proposal pro-

---

1. Louis L. Ullman, *Preparing Effective Proposals*, 2nd ed. (Troy, N.Y.: Technical Writers' Institute, 1971), p. 5.

vides a structure for the research plan, and allows the integration of the several parts into a logically conceived strategy.

THE PROPOSAL TITLE

Each proposal should have a title. If possible the title of the final report can be developed and serve as a title for the proposal. It should include:
1. the variables being studied;
2. the relationship between the variables; and
3. the population being studied.

An appropriate title for a study can be easily adapted from a well developed research question. The following title meets the three criteria:

> Effects of Replacing Arithmetic Drill Time with Informal Investigation on Arithmetical Computation and Understanding of Fifth-Grade Students.

The above title comes from the research question given in chapter 4:

> What are the effects on arithmetical computation and arithmetical understandings when classtime used for drill is replaced by informal investigations of problems involving large mathematical concepts?

BACKGROUND OF THE PROBLEM

This section should be developed as a context for placement of the research question. It begins the "chain of reasoning" development for the proposed research, and leads the reader into the specific question being investigated. A brief historical development should guide the reader to a discussion of present status, and project the possible outcomes into the future. (Occasionally a full-blown review of literature is requested but this aspect is usually left for the final report.) Knowledge of the field should be reflected in citations and summaries of significant publications and journal articles through reference to the problem area.

A part of the background section should be devoted to pointing up the importance of the study for education, and if needed a case should be built for conducting the study. Whether a study is significant to the field of education depends on the contribution of possible conclusions to the existing body of knowledge about the process of education.

The development of the theoretical framework of the study may be sufficient to show the importance, but the educational significance may lie in reference to one or more of the following points.

1. *Practicality.* A close relationship of the study and a practical problem lends support to proposed research.
2. *Generalizability.* A study that is generalizable over many varied populations of students would be more acceptable than one that is limited in scope.
3. *Opportuneness.* Research that relates to currently considered social problems is well received.
4. *Theorization.* The ability of the study to analyze sets of facts and create new understanding of theory can be readily justified.
5. *Scholarship.* A study may be justified by its contribution of new approaches to research procedures for educational problem solving.

Elements of a Research Proposal

I. BACKGROUND OF THE PROBLEM:

All research is a chain of reasoning. In this section, describe the facts, theories, personal concerns, or actual conditions in practice that have led you to regard this to be research worthy of study. Theory, historical development, and present status deserve consideration, and a projection of the research into the future with considerations of possible outcomes should be presented. The significance and relevancy must be demonstrated in this section, and you should indicate the nature of the problem.

Justification for your selection of the problem should be based on one or more of the following:

1. Gaps in needed knowledge of the area.
2. Need for clarification of conflicting educational practices.
3. Need for a better understanding or knowledge to evaluate alternative practices, policies, or research procedures for scholarly work in the field.

The competence to work in this field should be reflected by ability to cite references of significant publications and current journal articles related to the problem. Summarize points of view, significance, and relevancy by reference to the chosen problem.

II. PRESENTATION OF THE PROBLEM:

This section should propose a clearly defined problem presented as:

1. A question you propose to answer.
2. A hypothesis (sub-hypotheses) to test.

Delimit your problem by fencing in and isolating your problem from all other problems of the field. Be cognizant of the fact that not all of the world's ills will (or can) be solved by this study.

Include in this section:

1. Definition of terms.
2. Assumptions.
3. Delimitation—the isolation of your problem from all others.
4. Limitations—any restriction to generalizability of results or other limiting aspects of the study.

The Research Proposal

III. METHODOLOGY:

The methodology should be presented in detail and each step explained specifically, so that another researcher will be able to repeat the study exactly as you intend to carry it out. Discuss in operational terms the statement of procedure in regard to:

1. Sample — selection of subjects, materials to be examined, or where searches are to be made.
   a. The description gives a good clue to generalizability.
   b. The characteristics of the sample provide an operational statement of groups to whom you hope to generalize.
2. Design — indicate how you will structure your procedures so that you can gather data which will be indicative of whatever effect you want to measure. The design should:
   a. Utilize the technique that best fits the problem.
   b. Yield the most reliable and valid data.
   c. Be manageable, feasible, and economical in both cost and time.

The methods by which you propose to process and treat the data should be described in such a fashion that their appropriateness to the problem is clear. Your method of tabulating and organizing the data should be shown and methods of data analysis described. Describe all statistical procedures to be applied to the data.

IV. BIBLIOGRAPHY:

Include in this bibliography:
1. The references which led you to select the problem.
2. References which are pertinent to the basic problem of the study.
3. Any material that is closely related to the problem under study.

V. CHECK YOUR PROPOSAL AS *A CHAIN OF REASONING*:

It should:
1. Give background for the problem.
2. Present the problem.
3. Tell how you intend to attack the problem by finding the answer to a question implied by the problem.
4. Present a selected bibliography to guide an interested person into the literature.

FIGURE 13.1 Guidelines for Developing a Research Proposal

Reasons for selecting the topic and its significance should be built into the background narrative, and the relationship of the study to theory should be exhibited. Justification for selection can be based in the three reasons listed in figure 13.1. For a funding agency the case of importance should be made by showing how the study fits with the criteria of the guidelines, and by indication of its importance in the long-range funding policy of the agency. The significance of a student's proposal for a class or degree requirement is judged by the instructor and/or committee members. Close working relationships should be kept between the person developing a proposal for a thesis and the thesis chairman, to make sure that the proposed study is considered to be significant to the field of study.

PRESENTATION OF THE PROBLEM

This section focuses the reader's attention to the specific area of concern for the study and develops the rationale for the study as a basis for the next section on methodology. The major focus will be on the problem question and the hypothesis developed for the study.

After a short introductory paragraph, the carefully prepared research question (see chapter 4) should be presented. A lead-in sentence, such as, *The study will be based in the question* or *The purpose of the research study will be to answer the following question*, will immediately bring the reader to the problem area. An additional discussion may be needed to delimit the problem area so that there is no ambiguity about what is being covered. As this study is "fenced in," other closely related areas, but not a part of this study, are "fenced out."

A logical next step is to present a carefully prepared statement that hypothesizes the answer that is expected for the proposed question. This is the research hypothesis (see chapter 4) that has been developed from past personal experience and reading.

The variables under study must be defined. A definition of any other word not using common meaning, a word used in a special way, or any word that has been created for the study needs to be presented.

Basic assumptions need to be given attention in this section. Assumptions are beliefs that the researcher holds to be basic to the proposed study. Examples: (1) multiple-choice test items can be developed to measure creativity or (2) the physical sciences are best studied as an integrated program in the secondary school.

Any anticipated restrictions on generalizability of the results should be pointed up now as *limitations* of the study. All studies are limited in some way since the perfectly reliable and valid study is yet to be developed. By listing limitations the researcher points up particular places that may limit the ability to generalize. Limitations develop where methodology is less than ideal, and may be the result of the nature of the question asked, the population being studied, or inadequate procedures which cannot be made adequate.

In the field research report the two sections of the proposal—"Background" and "Presentation of the Problem"—will, with minor changes such as order and arrangement, make up the first chapter of the research report. The following section (methodology) will, in general, be exactly the same in the proposal and final report except for the tense change from future to past, and usually is presented as chapter 3 in the final report.

METHODOLOGY

The section on methodology explains the procedures that will be used to answer the question and/or test the research hypothesis. This component of the proposal should be presented in such detail that another researcher would be able to take this section and repeat the study in exactly the way that the present researcher intends to carry it out. The detail in methodology is required if the study is to be replicated on another set of subjects. As much as possible, all conditions must remain the same in all replication. If conditions differ, then no comparison of results can be made.

Carefully detailed methodology also serves to eliminate any difficulty created by ambiguously stated procedures. It serves as a written record of what was agreed on by the researcher and the funding agency or committee for an advanced degree, and it can be an insurance policy for both the researcher and the agency or committee. This "two-way insurance policy" serves much the same purpose for research as the written contract does for the field of business.

For the historical study a general plan for gathering data should be augmented, with specific plans as to where searches will be made, what information will be sought, and how conclusions are to be drawn. Some freedom is given the historical researcher to extend beyond materials cited in the proposal. Since he or she may discover more sources after the plan has been implemented, it would fail to serve the idea of inquiry to handcuff the investigation with that limitation. Descriptive and experimental research studies are not given this freedom and must be conducted just as the proposal presents it.

If a study is to be generalizable, then special care must be taken in the selection of subjects for providing the data. Random procedures should be used to select names of subjects to receive questionnaires, or to supply data for descriptive studies. For experimental studies and descriptive studies involving tests of significance between groups, selection and assignment of subjects is crucial. If conditons preclude random assignment, a description of the sample may allow generalization to populations with like characteristics. In additon to describing the procedures, a statement should be included about any possible effects of sampling on generalizability of the results.

The design element of methodology describes how arrangements are to be made to supply the most desirable data with minimum contamination from irrelevant variables, and to assure valid data for basing results and subsequent conclusions. The method of recording, tabulating, and organizing the data should be shown and any statistical procedures to be applied should be defended as those most appropriate to the study.

Treatment of the independent variable for experimental studies must be clearly defined. If the investigation involves a study of teaching methods, each method must be explained at length. The difference between or among methods is the treatment for experimental studies of educational methods. Chapter 10 of the *Handbook*, "Analysis and Investigation of Teaching Methods," by Norman E. Wallen and Robert M.W. Travers, is a classic source for aid in studies of teaching methods; the bibliography lists many methodological studies conducted before 1963.[2] Part IV of the *Second Handbook* treats methods in topics of subject matter rather than in a separate section.[3]

---

2. N. L. Gage, ed., *Handbook of Research on Teaching* (Chicago: Rand McNally, 1963), pp. 448-505.

3. Robert M. W. Travers, ed., *Second Handbook of Research on Teaching* (Chicago: Rand McNally, 1973), pp. 1072-1322.

The design section must include a time schedule for data collection and procedures for recording. Effects of data-gathering procedures on the results should be discussed—how is the setting changed by introducing a test session, tape recorder, human observer, or such? Data analysis in the form of name and description of statistical techniques must be presented in this section.

Since the null hypothesis is what the test of statistical significance tests, it must be included as a part of the methodology section of the proposal for studies which use a test of significance. If the writer wants to show the relationship of the research hypothesis to the null hypothesis for his or her study, the research hypothesis can be repeated here, but such repetition does not replace its presentation in the section, "Presentation of the Problem."

The completeness of this section should be checked by answering the question:

> Could someone else trained in research methods take this section of the proposal, follow the listed procedures, and complete the research in the same way that I would?

When the question can be answered in the affirmative, all of the points needed for a complete plan of methodology have been attended to.

BIBLIOGRAPHY

A necessary element for all proposals is a selected bibliography. The bibliography may be extensive if a review of literature is requested, but in most cases it will be something less than that. It should include references which led the researcher to select the problem, those which are necessary to understand the basic problem, and other closely related material that relates to the problem under study.

PREPARING MATERIALS

Any materials, e.g., questionnaires or tests that will be developed especially for the study, must be included—usually in an appendix—in the proposal. Since the study is still in the proposal stage, a final form is not required, but rough outlines with types of questions to be asked and general coverage should be included for questionnaires. If a test is to be developed, a table of specifications with sample items would be required by most proposal guidelines.

Standardized test instruments that are being used in part or adapted especially for a study should be included with special attention given to how they are to be used in the study. Standardized tests that are readily available need only a reference but less used or relatively unknown tests should be included in a proposal as a part of an appendix.

SUMMARY

The research proposal has been presented as a chain of reasoning that expands the research study from a vague idea in the head of a researcher to a set of meticulously planned procedures, designed especially to answer the research question. It is the formally stated plan designed to overcome some specific obstacle in the educational process.

The Research Proposal

The elements of the proposal are:
1. Background to the problem;
2. Presentation of the problem;
3. Methodology; and
4. Bibliography.

These have been discussed individually, and a section has dealt with materials that are to be specially prepared for the study.

A set of guidelines for developing the proposal through the above elements has also been provided as an example of what to include in proposals. Other sets of guidelines will, in general, include much the same information, but the organization may take other forms. Proposals may or may not include a complete review of related literature, depending on the set of guidelines.

The proposal serves as a communication between a researcher and a sponsor that indicates:
1. What is being sought;
2. How the researcher intends to find it;
3. The significance of the study;
4. The researcher's qualifications to study the problem; and
5. How much funding will be needed to see it to completion (only for proposals requesting a budget for funding).

BIBLIOGRAPHY

Ary, Donald et. al. *Introduction to Research in Education.* New York: Holt, Rinehart and Winston, 1972.

Gage, N.L., ed. *Handbook of Research on Teaching.* Chicago: Rand McNally, 1963.

Guba, Egon G. "Guides for the Writing of Proposals." In *Educational Research: New Perspectives,* edited by J.A. Culbertson and S.P. Hencley. Danville, Ill.: The Interstate, 1963.

Krathwohl, D.R. *How to Prepare a Research Proposal.* Syracuse, N.Y.: Syracuse Bookstore, 1965.

May, Charles. "The Nature of, and a Proposal for, Conducting Educational Research Studies." In *Methods and Techniques of Educational Research,* edited by Ralph H. Jones. Danville, Ill.: The Interstate, 1973.

Resta, Paul E., and Baker, Robert L. *Components of the Educational Research Proposal.* New York: American Book Co., 1972.

Smith, G.R. "How to Write a Project Proposal," *Nation's Schools* 76 (August 1965): 33-35, 57.

Travers, R.M.W., ed. *Second Handbook of Research on Teaching.* Chicago: Rand McNally, 1973.

Ullman, Louis L. *Preparing Effective Proposals,* 2nd ed. Troy, N.Y.: Technical Writers' Institute, 1971.

Wiersma, William. *Research Methods in Education—An Introduction,* 2nd ed. Itasca, Ill.: F.E. Peacock, 1975.

14

Writing the Research Report

A necessary part of any research study is the writing of the report to convey the results and conclusions to interested persons. The two major levels of research—*conducting* and *writing*—require different talents from the researcher. A researcher must be able to function well at both levels and be able to bridge the gap between them.

Most persons find that they work better at one of the levels and most researchers find conducting to be the stronger area. This may explain why research teams usually include one person who is charged with the major part of the writing. Since monetary funds are so important to research studies, specialists in writing proposals have emerged on the educational scene. Other writers seem to be stronger through interest and/or skill in writing the final report. In general, what holds for the proposal writer is equally applicable to the report writer. Since what is known of the study will be relayed in proposals and final reports, the importance of what is written and how it is written determines the readers' impressions, their confidence in the conclusions, and, in turn, the contribution of the study to the body of knowledge about educational concerns.

Research reports take different forms and have different emphases depending primarily on the audience. A detailed report that gives a complete description of what has been done is written as a documentation and as a record for reference. The student thesis or dissertation is an example of a complete research report. The components of the dissertation provide a model for other detailed reports.

Many times a research report is in the form of a very limited (100–200 words) coverage of the study. It is usually in the form of an abstract that focuses on the conclusions, with only a skeleton of methodology. The purpose of this report is to give the reader enough information to let him or her judge whether the study is of personal interest professionally.

The researcher may prepare a condensed report of the study for publication in a professional journal.[1] The purpose of this type of report is to provide enough information about the problem, methodology, results, and conclusions to allow the reader to evaluate the study. In general each journal has a form for all studies reported in it. Without the guidelines of a specific journal the style manual of the APA serves well for most reports of this type.[2]

FORM AND STYLE

The form and style referred to in the scholarly writing of research involves basically two parts, (1) the substance of the report or the information conveyed and its logical arrangement, and (2) the technical format and aspects of the mechanics of writing or the way in which something is written down.[3]

The *mechanics* of style gives consideration to format and arrangement for headings, tables, figures, footnotes, bibliography and the like. It also includes spelling, punctuation, capitalization, italics, quotations, and abbreviations. Most departments of universities, schools within universities, or universities as a whole have adopted what they call an acceptable mechanics style for papers, essays, theses, and dissertations for the unit. The style that has been adopted for use, either by the school or the funding agency, should be adhered to precisely. Without direction to a particular style the writer should choose one for his/her writing and follow it exactly. Several styles are listed in the reference section for this chapter.

The most important characteristic of writing style is *consistency*. The best way to prepare a paper is to be consistent within a style; second best is to be in error within the style but consistent throughout the report.

A maxim for the research writer is—*use a style manual*. Most of the technical decisions are arbitrary in isolation, but the plan fits all of the decisions into a scholarly form for reporting scholarly work. For example, Campbell's style book says to indent each paragraph eight typewriter spaces, while other styles indent other numbers of spaces. One may arbitrarily choose nine. What is the right number of spaces to indent for paragraphs? To this author's knowledge that question has not been answered, as each style develops its own unique format. The important question is not, "What is the correct number of spaces?" The important question is, "What does my style manual say is correct?" At best many decisions are arbitrary on the part of the author of the style manual, but his or her format results in a report that is in a form that is an aesthetically pleasing and orderly presentation.

Since a style manual can be used for the mechanics of the report, the rest of this chapter will be devoted to the aspect of substance and its arrangement in the research report. Style manuals give varying amounts of treatment to this topic but each will include some important suggestions about what to include and how to arrange it.

---

1. Since a copy of a detailed research report would be inappropriate for this book, examples of the condensed report as published in professional journals are included in the appendix.
2. American Psychological Association, Council of Editors, *Publication Manual of the American Psychological Association*, 2nd ed. (Washington, D.C.: The Association, 1974).
3. Jane Angell, "Technical Aspects of Form and Style," in Ralph H. Jones, ed., *Methods and Techniques of Educational Research* (Danville, Ill.: The Interstate, 1973).

Writing the Research Report

Most research reports are organized around five or six components[4] presented within the framework of the three major areas of *planning, investigation,* and *generalization.*

In general the first three chapters of a report are devoted to the planning activities, the fourth chapter reports the results, and the fifth (sometimes a sixth) reports conclusions and generalizations drawn from the study. Not all reports are divided into chapters, but the basic divisions are the same components as found in the several chapters. Ballou's *Model* is in the form of a six-chapter report, but is not a report of a research study. The unique feature of the book is the discussion of each section as it appears in the report. The substance of the *Model* provides helpful suggestions concerning content and style and is a valuable aid to anyone writing a research report. It is presented in a way that permits the flexibility needed when writing about a study based in a specific type of educational research. It also includes some rationale for the choices made about acceptable format and prepares the researcher to write about historical, descriptive, or experimental research.

PLANNING

The first two components of the research report are usually devoted to explaining the groundwork for the development of the problem into researchable form and for reporting a review of related knowledge about the study. Chapter 1 deals basically with the material used in the first two sections of the proposal, "Background of the Problem" and "Presentation of the Problem." It includes a brief background to the problem, the problem question, delimitations, hypotheses, definitions, assumptions, limitations, and any other information which is considered important to readers of the study.

Chapter 2 should include a reporting of all related literature including research that deals directly with the study. In general this will be new writing. If the proposal included an extensive review of literature this section is much the same as the proposal's section on related literature.

This chapter serves two purposes. First, it shows the reader that the researcher is knowledgeable about the field. Second, it brings the reader up to date about the subject under study. Although there are differences of opinion about how to report the readings, an organization by topics of variables under study seems to be the most common. For example, if the study is about the relationship of intentional and incidental learning for retarded children, a logical division of the review might be "Teaching the Retarded Child," "Incidental Learning," and "Intentional Learning." Within each topic a time sequence, commencing with the earliest writing and finishing at the present, makes a logical and meaningful format. The special nature of historical research may cause this section to be omitted or treated briefly in its reports.[5]

A good practice to use in introducing chapter two is to repeat the problem question in an introductory paragraph. The repetition of parts of the report may seem contrary to good writing style, but writing the research report is different from other types of

---

4. Stephen V. Ballou, *A Model for Theses and Research Papers* (Boston: Houghton, Mifflin, 1970).

5. The rest of this chapter on writing of the research report primarily applies to the quantitative methods of descriptive and experimental research. The reader is directed to chapter 8, "Historical Research," for writing about historically based studies.

writing. Persons read the report for different reasons and, in general, do not read it from cover to cover. Some may be interested only in results and conclusions, others in methodology, and others may only have an interest in a review of the literature. The person reading only chapter 2 will be saved the time it takes to look through the first chapter to find the question if it is included as an introduction to the review of literature.

The researcher must decide what material is related before writing the review of related knowledge. For example, a study of the effectiveness of phonics instruction as an aid to spelling achievement is based in language arts. Does this mean that every study in language arts should be reported, since all language arts studies are related? Of course not. At the same time, to limit the report to studies conducted on only the same question may leave the chapter blank or, at best, quite limited. The decision is best made in light of what the writer sees as relevant. All relevant literature should be included in the review.

The substance of the chapter comes from the carefully prepared note cards that have already been written in the library. Some of the selection of material will have already been made and some screening made earlier, but now comes the need to make the final selection and order of the report of the review of related information. Ballou says: "As a general guide, sufficient sources should be cited to establish the theoretical framework within which the immediate study finds its setting."[6]

After deciding what citations to use, the writer must decide how to arrange the material and the manner in which it will appear. Most writers find the review a difficult writing task. Since this is a report of someone else's work the writer is restricted in providing his or her input. The report, being objective, precludes subjective additions, but, at the same time, the narrative must have a continuity and be written so that it is interesting—not an easy task.

A series of paragraphs of direct quotations or a series of paragraphs each reporting a study will be of little use to the report. Direct quotations are to be avoided except for rare cases where the meaning would be lost in a paraphrase or the original writer has expressed it so well that it is best to keep it in that form for emphasis. In any case a footnote or citation of a reference, whether a paraphrase or quotation, must be made for each idea included in the chapter.

Good (also poor) examples of organization of the review of literature can be found in copies of theses and dissertations in university libraries. The student should read some of the reviews, pick out examples of good techniques, and note poor practices in order to direct his/her writing to proper organization. Further sources for ideas about organization are selections within the *Encyclopedia of Educational Research* where the writers are reviewing literature about research in particular areas.[7] To avoid repeating each one separately, the use of grouping for studies that have much the same outcome is illustrated well in the *Encyclopedia*. Other examples of writing in this difficult area can be found in the *Review of Educational Research*[8] and *Second Handbook on Research*[9] where writers give reviews of research on specialized topics.

---

6. Ballou, *A Model for Theses*, p. 23.

7. Robert L. Ebel, *Encyclopedia of Educational Research* (Washington, D.C.: American Educational Research Association, 1969), (also 1940, 1950, 1960).

8. *Review of Educational Research* (Washington: American Educational Research Association, all issues).

9. Robert M. W. Travers, ed., *Second Handbook of Research on Teaching* (Chicago: Rand McNally 1973), parts III and IV, pp. 530-1322.

Writing the Research Report

A complete review of literature will include results of research studies and articles of opinion by experts knowledgeable about the topics of concern. The concluding section of the chapter should tie together the relationships that were separated by the topical division of the chapter. The summary should serve two major functions. First, it should strengthen the presentation of the review as a background for the study. Second, it should provide the researcher with a starting point for comparing his or her results with other opinions and connecting his/her conclusions with theory. It should not present any conclusions or include any reactions of the writer.

INVESTIGATION

The investigation part of the study is reported in the chapters dealing with design and results. The design is usually reported in chapter 3 and the results in chapter 4.

Since the proposal spells out specifically what procedures and materials will be used, the writing of chapter 3 involves only the change of tense from future (proposal) to past (final paper). Of course any changes that were made should be reported in the final report, with the reasons why the original plan had to be abandoned. The reader is referred to the chapter on the research proposal (chapter 12) for the basic components for this section of the research report.

A part of the final report (usually chapter 4) is devoted to a reporting of the results of the study. This reporting should be an objective presentation of results, including tables that organize the data collected, statistical analysis, and/or descriptive analysis. A well organized report of results should be sequenced and presented in such a way that it will be clear to the reader whether the data support or fail to support the research hypothesis.

All of the presented data should be relevant and essential to the question and/or the conclusions. Sets of original scores and other data that may be important to a few readers can be placed in the appendix of the report. Original scoresheets, questionnaires, and other gathered facts should be kept on file but, in general, are not a part of the research report. If it is necessary that some be included they should be placed in the appendix.

The research report writer must keep in mind that his or her writing of results is expository writing, rather than interpretive. Preparation of the section of results must include guidelines that insure inclusion of any data that fail to support the research hypothesis, as well as data that support it.

Finally the results need to be synthesized and reported by identifying relationships among findings that reinforce each other or that are contradictory to each other. The summary of this section of results and the summary of the chapter of related literature provide the input for the final section of generalization. A careful fitting of the results into present theory can be made from this base.

GENERALIZATION

The last major part of the research report synthesizes an answer to the research question and discusses the implications of the study. This is the section where the investigator draws his or her conclusions in light of the results (see chapter 11), and projects the study of the problem into future research studies.

The substance of the generalizations is usually presented in two chapters and carries the results through to the solution of the problem, connecting the study's results to present theory. A section on implications indicates suggested changes in practice, and recommendations project subsequent research on this topic into possible future studies.

The chapter that interprets the results by drawing the conclusions (usually chapter 5) may include the sections on implication and recommendations. If they are a part of chapter 5, then the last chapter presents a summary of the complete study. If the fifth chapter is reserved for drawing conclusions and connecting them to theory, then the sixth chapter may include implications, recommendations, and summary. If the report requires a very long summary it should be placed in a separate and concluding chapter.

The limitations of the study should be included in the discussion of the research conclusions, since they are limitations placed on the generalizations. The investigator should point up for the reader any aspect of the design that might reduce the validity of the conclusions and, in turn, the generalizations derived from them. A listing of the limitations is made to inform the reader that the investigator is aware of certain weaknesses that resulted because of the nature of the problem and the restriction of not being able to develop an ideal set of procedures. The fact that the researcher is aware of the limitations should strengthen the confidence of the reader toward the researcher. For example, failure to list the fact that all tests are unreliable to a degree might cause the reader to question whether the researcher knew of this when he or she drew conclusions. Limitations of lack of control of certain variables might exist, not because of poor researching precedures, but from something beyond the control of the management of the investigation.

The summary of the study should present the problem being studied, a statement about the procedures, findings, implication to theory and practice, and recommendations. The summary should give the reader a good overview of the study and should transmit the real message of the study to education.

REFERENCE MATERIALS

Each report is expected to include a bibliography and may include one or more appendixes. Together they form an addendum to the report narrative that gives the reader an opportunity to go beyond the bare essentials that were included in the study.

The appendix, or appendixes, consists of the supplementary material that may be of interest to some or all of the readers, but its inclusion in the basic narrative would be awkward and/or cause the continuity to be broken. Material for the appendix could consist of:

1. Presentation of original data
2. Tables that contain data not directly related to the major question
3. Lengthy quotations
4. Copies of standardized tests not readily available to all readers
5. Instruments constructed for the study (questionnaires, tests, opinionnaires, and the like)
6. Documents, letters, and any supportive evidence for significance

Either preceding or following the appendix is a bibliography consisting of an entry for every piece of material cited in footnotes, plus other entries which the writer considers to be important to his/her study and its theoretical framework.

The bibliography serves to give the reader the advantage of the writer's knowledge about relevant materials and also as a step into the vast amount of knowledge about

Writing the Research Report

educational concerns closely related to this study. The decision about what to include must be made by the writer, keeping in mind that including materials which are not relevant does little to help the reader. If a very long bibliography is necessary it may be divided into parts according to the form of the publication being listed. Books may be catalogued together in one group, periodicals in another, and such. For historical studies the division may be made by listing primary sources and secondary sources separately.

Some bibliographies include an annotation of a sentence or short paragraph about each item as a convenience to the reader. The *annotated bibliography* entry should describe the content of the material cited and its relationship to the study.

ABSTRACT

The investigator may need to write an abstract of his or her study in the form of a condensed report of about 100 to 200 words, focusing on the methods, results, and conclusions of the study. The abstract is intended to give just enough information for the reader to decide whether the study will be of personal interest.

The abstract should include the research question, a description of the subjects, a brief accounting of methodology, the results, and derived conclusions. The conclusions, being the most important part of the study, receive major emphasis in an abstract.

Careful use of words for this very condensed version is necessary to convey the real meaning of the study to the reader. Make every word count and check carefully the logic of the abstract so that the continuity from conception to completion is not lost in the reduction.

WRITING JOURNAL ARTICLES

Articles within a journal should be as much alike as possible to avoid distracting the reader with various formats. To achieve needed consistency throughout the journal, manuscripts need to be much alike in form to allow consistency in the printed page. Accomplishment of the goal of consistency is best reached by a set of rules and/or guidelines in the form of a manual prescribing the style to be used for manuscripts. Before writing for a particular journal the report writer should find out the proper form to use. When writing a report without specific directions the writer should use the guidelines of the APA *Publication Manual*.

A journal article consists of five components: *Introduction*; *Methodology*; *Results*; *Discussion*; and *References*. A title page that gives the title, author's name and institutional affiliation, an abstract (100–200 words), and if needed an *appendix* support the main body of the article.

The *title* of the article should inform the reader of the variables under study and summarize the principal idea of the report. The title of the proposal, if well written, can serve as a title for the research report (see chapter 13, "The Proposal Title"). To assure proper indexing for retrieval systems, avoid misleading words and words that serve no purpose. For example, shorten titles by omitting any reference to methods, results, and beginning phases, such as "An Experiment of" or "A Study Designed to." A title should not exceed fifteen words.

The *abstract* of the study usually appears under the by-line and allows the reader to quickly review the study. The abstract for a journal article is much the same as the abstract discussed in the previous section.

The *introduction* of the article provides the background and presents the problem studied, much as the proposal did. It includes the problem question, definitions of the variables, and the research hypothesis, as well as an adequate background section.

The *methodology* section should describe procedures in detail to allow the reader to evaluate research methods and establish the degree of validity of the results and conclusions. Attention should be given to characteristics of subjects, how they were selected and assigned, and any other information that will help the reader understand the study. A detailed accounting of all procedures and treatment, including statistical analysis, allows the reader to judge the validity of results. Measuring instruments and special apparatus should be described.

Down to this point the article is very much like the research proposal except the tense has changed from future to past. The intent to inform causes these two elements to cover approximately the same topics to the same degree. The remaining sections—results and discussion—are new to the final article.

The *results* section organizes, tabulates, and summarizes the collected data and reports the results of the statistical treatment. Included are results that support the hypothesis and any results that fail to support it, but conclusions are not drawn.

The *discussion* section reports conclusions and interpretation of the results in regard to implications and recommendations. The reader should be made aware of whether or not the research hypothesis is supported, and how this result fits with theory. Any speculation on the part of the writer should be clearly presented as what it is—speculation. Implications to practice in education can be presented here and mention of recommendations for further research may be included.

The *references* section includes an entry for each citation in the article. A bibliography is not included for a journal article except when it serves a special purpose or when one is requested by the journal staff. In general an appendix is not included, but may be included if needed to present necessary material that would break the continuity of the article if included in its body.

WRITING STYLE

Each writer will develop a unique style of writing about research and will use guidelines to the advantage of his or her style. Keep in mind that the process being written about is *inquiry*, and you are reporting objectively about a question and its answer.

The writing should be concise and straightforward, to inform, rather than impress, the reader. For a report to be accurate the language must be precise. To make the report meaningful the important points must be emphasized. A combination of accuracy and emphasis of important points, along with careful attention to detail in giving a logically organized presentation, will result in a report which is capable of disseminating the information from the study to the field of education.

While thinking about the research, think about the reporting of the research. Preplanning a report through an outline begun early in the process will contribute much to a meaningful final report of the study by presenting the material in a logically organized arrangement. With preplanning, the actual writing will fall into about six steps.

1. Writing the first draft. The first draft is best written without too much concern about choice of words or grammar, but more attention to thoughts, ideas, and facts that need to be included in the report.

Writing the Research Report

2. Revision of the first draft. Attention is given to rewriting unclear sentences and paragraphs, filling gaps, correcting sentence structure, spelling, grammar, and punctuation while choosing exact words to convey the meaning. (Check the style manual.)
3. Additions of footnotes, tables, figures, and appendices. A table of contents can now be made. (Check the style manual.)
4. A final editing. It should give attention to consistency of statements throughout the paper and readability of the material with smooth transitions between ideas. This step should result in the paper being a logical presentation of the chain of reasoning set as a goal for the research.
5. Read the paper thoroughly. Read it word for word, comma for comma, checking for every detail of format to see that style guidelines are followed. After this step the only remaining corrections are typing errors.
6. Final typing and correction of typing errors.

If the research writer has used clear and concise language, presented his or her case in a logically organized manner, and given the needed attention to detail by rereading and proofreading, the efforts expended in research will be rewarded by the scholarly reporting needed as an integral part of the research process.

Without reporting one's research to colleagues and to other interested professional persons, the time spent in research is largely wasted except for the aesthetic rewards earned by the researcher. The difference between a major contribution and a lesser contribution for the same study lies in being able to write a scholarly report of the research. *This author hopes that the reports of your research efforts are at the same high level as your research efforts.* Good luck.

BIBLIOGRAPHY

American Psychological Association, Council of Editors. *Publication Manual of the American Psychological Association,* 2nd ed. Washington, D.C.: The Association, 1974.

Angell, Jane. "Technical Aspects of Writing Form and Style." In *Methods and Techniques of Educational Research,* edited by Ralph H. Jones. Danville, Ill.: The Interstate, 1973.

Ballou, Stephen V. *A Model for Theses and Research Papers.* Boston: Houghton-Mifflin, 1970.

Barzun, Jacques, and Graff, Henry F. *The Modern Researcher.* New York: Harcourt, Brace and World, 1970.

Campbell, William Giles, and Ballou, Stephen Vaughan. *Form and Style: Theses, Reports, Term Papers.* Boston: Houghton-Mifflin, 1974.

Cook, David R., and LaFleur, N. Kenneth. *A Guide to Educational Research,* 2nd ed. Boston: Allyn and Bacon, 1975.

Dugdale, Kathleen. *A Manual of Form for Theses and Term Reports,* 4th rev. Bloomington: Indiana University Press, 1972.

Ebel, Robert L. *Encyclopedia of Educational Research.* Washington, D.C.: American Educational Research Association, 1969.

Perrin, Porter G. *Writer's Guide and Index to English,* 4th ed. Chicago: Scott, Foresman, 1968.

Review of Educational Research. Washington, D.C.: American Educational Research Association, 1931 to date.

Travers, Robert M. W., ed. *Second Handbook of Research on Teaching.* Chicago: Rand McNally, 1973.

Turabian, Kate U. *A Manual for Writers of Term Papers, Theses and Dissertations,* 4th ed. Chicago: University of Chicago Press, 1973.

APPENDIX

Examples of Research Reports from Professional Journals

THE EFFECT OF KEYED RESPONSE SEQUENCING OF MULTIPLE CHOICE ITEMS ON PERFORMANCE AND RELIABILITY*

JOHN C. JESSELL and WALTER L. SULLINS
Indiana State University

Most test constructors agree that proper sequencing of multiple choice test items, with respect to keyed response position, is a desirable test characteristic. Nearly every basic educational measurement textbook devotes some discussion to item sequencing, usually recommending that the correct answer appear in each position about an equal number of times and that the items be arranged randomly. The theoretical rationale underlying such procedures is that if one were to choose the same option for each item of a test, he could not obtain a score beyond that of a chance score. Other reasons are to avoid providing test-takers with systematic devices which would enable them to "beat" the test and to establish a safeguard against an unconscious bias by the test constructor to allow the correct response to occur appreciably more often in one option position than in another.

Although detailed methods for arranging items in proper sequence have been given (Anderson, 1952; Mosier and Price, 1945), there is little empirical evidence that keyed response arrangement is related to test performance. The purpose of this study was to investigate the effects on test reliability and student performance of response sequencing that would be extremely unlikely under a random model.

PROCEDURE

Test Forms

The items of the test were based on two units of study in an introductory life science course and were representative of content covering the topic areas of genetics and parasitology. The

---

From the *Journal of Educational Measurement*, Volume 12, No. 1, Spring 1975, pp. 45-48. Copyright 1975, National Council on Measurement in Education, Inc., East Lansing, Michigan. Reprinted by special permission.

*The authors wish to thank Dr. Charles Gehring, Associate Professor of Life Sciences, for his cooperation in providing subjects and the test used in the study. Appreciation is also extended to Thomas Cahill, doctoral fellow, for his assistance in data collection.

test was the fourth in a series of five examinations administered over the semester. The items which were constructed by the instructor had been used in previous testings, conformed to item-construction principles, and met the criteria of acceptable difficuly and discrimination.

The original form (Form 1) of the test, which consisted of 60 multiple-choice items with four options for each item, was arranged in an ideal format with each option as the keyed response for one-fourth of the items and with the keyed response position appearing no more than twice in sequence.

Form 2 of the test was arranged so that the initial seven items of the test were keyed according to the second option (letter B) with the format of the remainder of the test identical to that of Form 1.

For Form 3, seven items in the middle portion of the test (items 27 thru 33) were keyed with the second option as the keyed response. All other items were keyed in accordance with Form 1.

Form 4 was arranged so that the final seven items were keyed with the second option as the keyed response and all other items keyed as in Form 1.

Items of Forms 5, 6, and 7 were arranged similarly to those of Forms 3, 4, and 5 except that 14 sequential items were identically keyed. The initial 14 items, the middle 14 items, and the final 14 items were keyed with the second option as the keyed response for Forms 5, 6, and 7 respectively. All other items of these forms were keyed in accordance with Form 1.

The choice of the second response position (option B) as the keyed response for each of the arranged, sequential patterns was an arbitrary one. It was decided to use the same response position as the keyed response for each arranged pattern for each form, since varying the response position might introduce an uncontrolled variable.

Sample

The test forms were administered to 454 Indiana State University freshmen enrolled in an introductory life science course during the Fall semester, 1973-74. A single televised lecture session with six laboratory and discussion sections was the instructional format. The test was administered to the six sections over a two-day period. The seven forms were uniformly distributed among the six sections and were distributed within sections in a random fashion.

The fact that the test was administered over a two-day period to six different sections at six different time periods, raises the possibility that information was exchanged among the students of the various sections. Since there were seven different forms of the test, the likelihood of such a development occurring so as to affect the results of the study is small.

RESULTS

The results for the seven test forms are presented in Table 1. The numeral codes identifying the forms are the same as those used in the previous section. Although the Kuder-Richardson Formula #20 reliability estimate for Form 1 was higher than for other forms, inspection revealed no practical differences in reliability estimates; thus no tests of statistical significance were performed. Similarly, the standard errors of measurement were nearly identical.

Mean performance on the forms ranged from 35.33 to 39.00, with Form 1 yielding the highest performance. Results of a test of significance among the means of the forms are presented in Table 2. The computed value of F (1.16) indicated no statistically significant differences among the means. Since the standard deviations were similar (8.55 to 9.70), no test for homogeneity of dispersion was performed.

DISCUSSION

The results of this study do not support the intuitively appealing notion that multiple choice test items should be keyed with the correct answer appearing in each position about the same number of times, and randomly sequenced with respect to the keyed response position. The sequential patterning of keyed responses employed for purposes of this study were of such a nature that their probability of occurring (under a random arrangement model) would be near zero, nevertheless neither test reliability nor student performance appeared to be affected.

Table 1

Summary Statistics for the Seven Forms

FORM	KR20	SEM	Mean	St. Dev.	N
1.	.89	3.25	39.00	9.70	67
2.	.85	3.40	35.33	8.73	66
3.	.86	3.32	38.23	8.82	64
4.	.86	3.36	37.21	9.11	63
5.	.88	3.33	37.43	9.43	67
6.	.84	3.39	37.59	8.55	64
7.	.84	3.42	36.37	8.56	63

These findings demonstrate that it is unnecessary to follow elaborate schemes to achieve a balanced distribution of keyed responses. With the exception of the occasional "pattern sleuth" or "pattern marker," it would appear that examinees pay less heed to response patterning than might be supposed. It would be presumptuous, however, to conclude that no care should be

Table 2

Analysis of Variance Among the Seven Forms

Source	SS	df	MS	F
Forms	566.47	6	94.41	1.16
Error	36226.50	447	81.04	
Total	36792.97			

taken to avoid extreme and/or lopsided keying distributions. For a single testing and for a sequence of achievement tests in a course over a term, some attention toward achieving a nominal spread of correct response options is warranted.

The results of this study may or may not be applicable to students below or above the level of university freshmen, but this would need to be determined through further investigation.

REFERENCES

ANDERSON, S. B. Sequence in multiple-choice item options. *Journal of Educational Psychology*, 1952, **43**, 364-368.

MOSIER, C. I. & PRICE, H. G. The arrangement of choice in multiple-choice questions and a scheme for randomizing choices. *Educational and Psychological Measurement*, 1945, **5**, 379-382.

AUTHORS

JESSELL, JOHN C. *Address:* Dept. of Graduate Studies in Education, Indiana State University, Terre Haute, Indiana 47809. *Title:* Professor of Education. *Degrees:* B. S. Southern Connecticut State College, M.Ed. Ohio University, Ph.D. University of Wisconsin. *Specialization:* Guidance and Counseling; Educational Measurement.

SULLINS, WALTER L. *Address:* Center for Educational Research, Indiana State University. Terre Haute, Indiana 47809. *Title:* Associate Professor of Education. *Degrees:* B.S., M.S. Kansas State College, Ph.D. University of Maryland. *Specialization:* Statistics and Educational Measurement.

A LONGITUDINAL STUDY OF WHO SEEKS COUNSELING WHEN[1]

W. HARRY SHARP
University of Houston

BARBARA A. KIRK[2]
University of California, Berkeley

This study undertook to determine when, over a four-year period, those members of the entire 1966 entering freshman class at the University of California, Berkeley, who sought counseling initiated their contacts. Generally speaking, the rate of initiation declined steeply over time, both by years and quarters within years. An occasional reversal occurred for females. Also studied were characteristics of the students as related to time of initiating counseling, utilizing scores on the School and College Ability Test (Form UA), Omnibus Personality Inventory (Form F), and Strong Vocational Interest Blank (Forms M and F) administered in freshman orientation. Neither male nor female clients differed significantly by test results when time of counseling initiation was considered by the four academic quarters. By year, quarter by quarter, and by parts of quarters, the Omnibus Personality Inventory yielded significant results on some scales.

Educators are concerned increasingly with the form, magnitude, and focal point of stresses affecting college students. Murray (1938) provided a productive "need-press" model for the research of Stern, Stein, and Bloom (1956). The latter conceptualized the behavior of students as an ongoing field process, "the resultant of the transaction between the individual and other structural units in the behavioral field [p. 35]." The work of Dubos (1968) has led to the conceptualization of the campus as an eco-system(s). Regardless of the conceptual framework, few would differ with the conceptualization of a transactional relationship in which different kinds of students respond to internal and external stresses differentially.

When a student comes to a college counseling center, one may assume that the student is reacting to specific stimuli. In many cases, the stimuli may be distressful. Either internal or external stimuli, or both, may influence the student's decision to seek professional counseling. Three questions related to the transactional relationship between the student and his campus can be studied in college counseling centers: (a) When do students initiate counseling? (b) Is there a relationship between whom the client is (his characteristics) and when he initiates counseling? (c) Is there a relationship between when the student initiates counseling and his expressed problem(s)? Another manner of stating the three questions is: When do students come for counseling? Who are they? Why do they come when they come? The present article, one of a series (Kirk, 1973), attempts to answer the first two questions.

Academic calendars on any campus are highly regimented. Students register at prescribed times; classes begin on a specified date; faculty give tests during the middle of the term and require completion of major papers toward the end; final examination schedules are fixed by the administration. Faculty have considerable latitude in terms of what they require of students, but they have relatively little latitude in terms of when it is required, since they are responsible for completion of grading by deadlines. Thus, the initiation of counseling may

---

From *Journal of Counseling Psychology*, 1974, Volume 21, No. 1, pp. 43-50. Copyright 1974 by the American Psychological Association. Reprinted by permission.

[1] The authors wish to thank Austin Frank for his critical reading of the manuscript and for his suggestions.

[2] Requests for reprints should be sent to Barbara Kirk, Counseling Center, Building T-5, University of California, Berkeley, California 94720.

speak rather directly to the source of external stress imposed upon the student by the academic community. Snyder and Kahne (1969) concluded, "we have forceful evidence that the nature, intensity, and location of educational and other stresses strongly affect patterns of the use of psychiatrists by students [p. 28]."

However, little work has been done to discover when students initiated counseling. Baker (1963) studied the pattern of incidence of appeals for services over six academic years by semesters at the Clark University Psychological Clinic. Students initiated the services at a greater rate during the first than they did during the second semester. The highest initiation rate occurred during the first half of the first semester. He suggested and later confirmed (Baker & Nidorf, 1964) that the high rate of initiation during the first half of the first semester reflected freshmen difficulties of initial adjustment to college. The similarity of initiation rate patterns for first semesters and second semesters suggested the operation of common precipitating factors. Baker reasoned that one such factor was the regularly occurring examination periods, and he speculated that students may react to examination stress by anticipating the stress and initiating assistance prior to examinations. Other students delay their reactions to stress and seek assistance following the examination period. From his results Baker hypothesized "that the effect of examination-stressers is in part a function of personality differences among students [p. 363]," but this important point has yet to be explored.

Snyder and Kahne (1969) compared the term-by-term use of the psychiatric service by the class of 1965 at Massachusetts Institute of Technology, Cambridge. The class was divided into groups by academic discipline. The data were consistent with the hypothesis that departments presented their students with significantly different stresses at different times. Students enrolled in one science program made their greatest use of the psychiatric service during the first term as majors in the program. Students in another science program made the greatest use of the psychiatric service during the first term of their senior year.

Since students who use a counseling service are different from those who use a psychiatric service (Kirk, 1973) and since the matter of when students initiate counseling is related to the transactional relationship between the characteristics of the students and the campus, both students and administrators can be assisted by understanding the interaction. The present study follows an entering class over four years and addresses itself to the questions: When do students come for counseling, and who comes when?

METHOD

New freshmen who enrolled in the fall quarter of 1966 at the University of California, Berkeley, were followed through June 1970. The later date was the time graduation might have been expected to occur. Scrupulous records of the exact date of first initiation of counseling were maintained by the Counseling Center and were analyzed for this freshman class. Enrollment data, which would reflect attrition within this class alone for each of the 15 academic quarters, were not available at the time of this study. Thus in the results reported below, the percentages of students initiating contact at any one time were based on the class entering enrollment data (1,761 men and 1,292 women) and after the first quarter were spuriously low in terms of those remaining on campus. Nevertheless, the data do reflect the pattern of use of the Counseling Center by members of the class who began college in September of 1966.

The academic calendar over the four-year period was used as the baseline for the analyses. Clients were grouped in four different time periods: by year (first, second, third, and fourth), by calendar quarters combined (all fall, winter, spring, and summer quarters), by individual academic quarter (fall of 1966 to spring of 1970, 1-16), and by combined parts of quarters (registration week, first week of instructions, . . . , final examination week equal to five parts in all).

The time periods were defined in the following manner. The first year included those students initiating counseling prior to their enrollment in September of 1966 through the end of the spring quarter of 1967. The second and subsequent years included students initiating counseling from the end of the previous spring quarter through the end of the appropriate spring quarter. Thus, students initiating counseling either prior to school or during the summer quarter were categorized in the following school year.

The academic quarters were defined in the following manner, fall quarters, for example, extended from the end of summer quarters through the end of the fall quarters, including the short gap prior to the quarter with the succeeding quarter. The remaining quarters were defined in the same fashion. Students who sought counseling prior to their enrollment in September of 1966, were included in the fall quarter of 1966 category.

The quarter was divided into the following categories: registration week, the first week of instruction, the five weeks of instruction subsequent to the first week of instruction, the last four weeks of instruction, and final examination week. The five-week period of instruction included presumably the time when instructors would have given mid-term examinations.

During the week preceding registration in the fall of 1966, all incoming freshmen were asked to complete the School and College Ability Test, Form UA (SCAT), the Omnibus Personality Inventory, Form F (OPI), and the Strong Vocational Interest Blank, Forms M and F (SVIB), for each sex respectively. Of the 401 male and 319 female clients who were then seen one or more times for counseling during four years, test data were available as follows: 90.5% of the men and 95.2% of the women had taken the SCAT; 81.8% of the men and 93.6% of the women had taken the OPI; and 87.5% of the men and 92.4% of the women had taken the SVIB. The tested clients were assumed to be reasonably representative

TABLE 1

Number and Percentage of Original Class Initiating Counseling (by Academic Quarter) and Omnibus Personality Inventory (OPI) Scales, Which Show Significant Differences between Quarters

Quarter	Men (N = 1,761) n	%	n	Theoretical Orientation M	SD	Social Extroversion M	SD
Prior to enrollment	29	1.6					
1. Fall 1966	86	4.9	76	20.7	5.4	19.0	8.3
2. Winter 1967	66	3.7	56	22.2	5.0	19.9	7.1
3. Spring 1967	55	3.1	42	22.4	4.9	21.3[c]	7.1
First-year total	236	13.4					
4. Summer 1967	7	.4	6	22.0	3.0	13.5	5.1
5. Fall 1967	38	2.2	28	21.8	5.5	20.7	7.1
6. Winter 1968	29	1.6	26	22.3	6.0	20.4	6.4
7. Spring 1968	12	.7	10	15.9[a]	5.0	26.3[d]	6.3
Second-year total	86	4.9					
8. Summer 1968	1	.1	—	—	—	—	—
9. Fall 1968	20	1.1	17	22.4	5.3	17.7	8.0
10. Winter 1969	17	1.0	14	18.4[b]	4.5	20.3	4.5
11. Spring 1969	12	.7	9	23.7	4.9	15.6	6.8
Third-year total	50	2.8					
12. Summer 1969	8	.5	5	21.4	3.1	21.6	6.9
13. Fall 1969	13	.7	11	23.9	5.2	18.5	7.5
14. Winter 1970	6	.3	5	22.0	6.0	15.6	4.2
15. Spring 1970	2	.1	2	19.5	2.1	24.0	9.9
Fourth-year total	29	1.6					
All fall quarters	186	10.6					
All winter quarters	118	6.7					
All spring quarters	81	4.6					
All summer quarters	16	.9					
Four-year total	401	22.8					

[a] The mean of Quarter 7 was significantly less than the means of Quarters 1, 2, 3, 5, 6, 9, 11, and 13 ($p < .01$).
[b] The mean of Quarter 10 was significantly less than the means of Quarters 2, 3, 11, and 13 ($p < .05$).
[c] The mean of Quarter 3 was significantly greater than the mean of Quarter 4 ($p < .05$).
[d] The mean of Quarter 7 was significantly greater than the means of Quarters 1, 2, 4, 9, 11, 13, and 14 ($p < .05$).

of the total client population being studied. The only SVIB scales used in the present study were the Masculinity-Feminity for both sexes and the Occupational Level for males.

Analysis of variance was the major statistic used to test differences between groups. Kramer's (1956) extension of the Duncan multiple-range test to group means with unequal numbers was used to determine where significant differences were located. Males and females were treated separately.

RESULTS

When Students Came for Counseling

Analysis by sequential quarters. Tables 1 and 2 present the number of students beginning college in September of 1966 who initiated counseling during the first through fourth years by quarter. An analysis of variance of 14 quarters in Table 1 showed—Theoretical Orientation: $MS_{between} = 53.7$, $MS_{within} = 26.9$, $F = 1.99$, $p < .05$; Social Extroversion: $MS_{between} = 94.8$, $MS_{within} = 52.7$, $F = 1.80$, $p < .05$. An analysis of variance of 15 quarters in Table 2 showed—Thinking Introversion: $MS_{between} = 114.5$, $MS_{within} = 53.9$, $F = 2.13$, $p < .05$; Altruism: $MS_{between} = 528.$, $MS_{within} = 27.7$, $F = 1.91$, $p < .05$; Practical Orientation: $MS_{between} = 51.8$, $MS_{within} = 25.6$, $F = 2.02$, $p < .05$.

TABLE 2

NUMBER AND PERCENTAGE OF ORIGINAL CLASS INITIATING COUNSELING (BY ACADEMIC QUARTERS) AND OMNIBUS PERSONALITY INVENTORY (OPI) SCALES, WHICH SHOW SIGNIFICANT DIFFERENCES BETWEEN QUARTERS

Quarter	Counseling initiation Women (N = 1,292) n	%	Thinking Introversion n	M	SD	Altruism M	SD	Practical Orientation M	SD
Prior to enrollment	19	1.5							
1. Fall 1966	67	5.2	65	26.9	6.5	21.9	5.5	11.2	4.6
2. Winter 1967	46	3.6	40	27.0	8.2	22.8	5.6	11.3	5.1
3. Spring 1967	31	2.4	28	27.0	7.3	23.7e	5.2	10.4	6.2
First-year total	163	12.6							
4. Summer 1967	5	.4	5	28.4	7.9	21.8	6.7	12.2	6.7
5. Fall 1967	44	3.4	38	28.6	7.1	22.0	3.9	10.3	5.1
6. Winter 1968	22	1.7	19	25.6	7.1	20.0	5.4	11.8	4.5
7. Spring 1968	17	1.3	14	27.4	7.9	22.3	6.7	11.6	4.6
Second-year total	88	6.8							
8. Summer 1968	4	.3	2	26.0	5.7	15.5	10.6	16.0	—j
9. Fall 1968	12	.9	8	29.6a	7.1	22.1	3.4	9.3	5.7
10. Winter 1969	7	.5	3	17.0b	2.7	16.3	0.6	18.7g	5.9
11. Spring 1969	3	.2	2	10.0c	8.5	11.0f	2.8	21.0h	2.8
Third-year total	26	2.0							
12. Summer 1969	5	.4	5	34.2d	4.9	18.6	5.4	6.6i	1.5
13. Fall 1969	25	1.9	23	25.0	8.0	20.1	5.2	12.3	4.7
14. Winter 1970	8	.6	6	22.7	11.4	22.3	4.5	14.2	6.9
15. Spring 1970	4	.3	3	31.3	2.5	19.7	5.5	7.7	4.0
Fourth-year total	42	3.3							
All fall quarters	167	12.9							
All winter quarters	83	6.4							
All spring quarters	55	4.3							
All summer quarters	14	1.1							
Four-year total	319	24.7							

aThe mean of Quarter 9 was significantly less than the mean of Quarter 15 at $p < .05$.
bThe mean of Quarter 10 was significantly less than the means of Quarters 1, 2, 5, 9, and 12 ($p < .05$).
cThe mean of Quarter 11 was significantly less than the means of Quarters 1 through 7 and 12 through 15 ($p < .05$).
dThe mean of Quarter 12 was significantly greater than the means of Quarters 13 and 14 ($p < .05$).
eThe mean of Quarter 3 was significantly greater than the means of Quarters 6, 11, and 13 ($p < .05$).
fThe mean of Quarter 11 was significantly less than the means of Quarters 1, 2, 4 through 7, 9, 13, and 14 ($p < .05$).
gThe mean of Quarter 10 was significantly greater than the means of Quarters 1, 2, 3, 5, 6, 9, 12, and 15 ($p < .05$).
hThe mean of Quarter 11 was significantly greater than the means of Quarters 1, 2, 3, 5, 6, 7, 9, 12, 13, and 15 ($p < .05$).
iThe mean of Quarter 12 was significantly less than the mean of Quarter 14 ($p < .05$).
jData not included in analysis because of lack of variance.

Students initiated counseling at a diminishing rate over the four-year period. Senior women, however, showed an increased rate during the fourth year when compared with the third year. A pattern of counseling initiation was found over each year with fall quarters representing the highest rate and subsequent quarters decreasing.

Analysis by combined parts of quarters. Table 3 presents data by parts of quarters. Only those students initiating counseling during the specifically defined period of time were included in the data presented in Table 2. An analysis of variance for male OPI scores in Table 3 showed—Impulse Expression: $MS_{between} = 267.1$, $MS_{within} = 98.1$, $F = 2.72$, $p < .05$; Personal Integration: $MS_{between} = 407.5$, $MS_{within} = 98.4$, $F = 4.1$, $p < .005$; Anxiety Level: $MS_{between} = 112.4$, $MS_{within} = 20.2$, $F = 5.55$, $p < .001$; Response Bias: $MS_{between} = 60.8$, $MS_{within} = 17.8$, $F = 3.4$, $p < .01$.

TABLE 3

COUNSELING INITIATION BY PARTS OF QUARTERS, FOUR YEARS COMBINED, AND DIFFERENTIATING OMNIBUS PERSONALITY INVENTORY (OPI) SCORES FOR MEN

Part of the quarter	Men (N = 1,761) n	%	Women (N = 1,292) n	%	n	Impulse Expression M	SD	Personal Integration M	SD	Level Anxiety M	SD	Response Bias M	SD
1. Registration weeks	89	5.1	62	4.8	75	29.4	11.2	32.4	10.1	13.2	4.5	14.2	4.2
2. First weeks of instruction	46	2.6	30	2.3	38	31.7	9.3	30.4	9.9	12.5	4.8	13.9	4.2
3. Next five weeks	103	5.8	116	9.0	89	33.6[a]	9.6	28.1[b]	9.6	10.5[d]	4.5	12.3[f]	4.0
4. Next four weeks	103	5.8	66	5.1	84	30.3	9.6	31.0	10.4	12.4	4.4	13.6	4.5
5. Final examination weeks	14	.8	5	.4	9	36.6	5.6	20.7[c]	6.4	8.2[e]	5.1	10.2[g]	3.2
Total	355	20.2	279	21.5	295								

[a] The mean of Part 3 was significantly greater than the means of Parts 1 and 4 ($p < .05$).
[b] The mean of Part 3 was significantly less than the mean of Part 1 ($p < .01$).
[c] The mean of Part 5 was significantly less than the means of Parts 1, 2, 3, and 4 ($p < .05$).
[d] The mean of Part 3 was significantly less than the means of Parts 1, 2, and 4 ($p < .05$).
[e] The mean of Part 5 was significantly less than the means of Parts 1, 2, and 4 ($p < .05$).
[f] The mean of Part 3 was significantly less than the means of Parts 1 and 4 ($p < .05$).
[g] The mean of Part 5 was significantly less than the means of Parts 1, 2, and 4 ($p < .05$).

The patterns of initiating counseling during an academic quarter differed somewhat on the basis of sex. Men initiated counseling with approximately equal frequency during registration week and the periods that presumably included and followed the administration of midterm examinations. Women initiated counseling at a considerably higher rate during the period following the first week of instruction and including midterm examinations than during the period following midterm examinations, not only relative to themselves but also to the men. The third highest rate for both sexes occurred during registration week. The lowest rate for both sexes took place during final examination week.

Student Characteristics in Relation to Time of Initiating Counseling

Analysis by combined quarters. Neither male nor female clients differed significantly by test results when time of counseling initiation was considered by the four academic quarters, that is, all fall quarters versus all winter quarters, etc.[3] Thus, based upon entering tests, clients

---

[3] Where no significant differences are found among test scores for contrasted groups, the scores are not reported. Fairly complete data on the counseled group as a whole are available in Kirk (1973).

who initiated counseling during the fall quarters did not differ from those initiating counseling during any of the other quarters. The same finding was true for those initiating counseling during the winter, spring, and summer quarters.

Analysis by academic years. When clients were grouped by the year in which they initiated counseling, the SCAT and SVIB scales did not yield significant differences, but some OPI scales did. These are presented in Table 4. An analysis of variance of the scales in Table 4 showed—Impulse Expression: $MS_{between} = 279.4$, $MS_{within} = 93.7$, $F = 2.98$, $p < .05$; Personal Integration: $MS_{between} = 380.8$, $MS_{within} = 146.1$, $F = 2.61$, $p < .05$; Altruism: $MS_{between} = 276.9$, $MS_{within} = 56.2$, $F = 4.93$, $p < .005$; Intellectual Disposition Category: $MS_{between} = 9.6$, $MS_{within} = 3.5$, $F = 2.77$, $p < .05$.

TABLE 4

OMNIBUS PERSONALITY INVENTORY (OPI) SCALES, WHICH SHOW SIGNIFICANT DIFFERENCES BY YEAR OF INITIATING COUNSELING

	Men			Women						
Years	Impulse Expression				Personal Integration		Altruism		Intellectual Disposition Category	
	n	M	SD	n	M	SD	M	SD	M	SD
First	194	32.8a	9.6	156	28.4	12.2	21.1	7.7	4.6	1.8
Second	70	29.0	10.2	81	27.1	11.9	20.2	7.1	4.3	1.8
Third	41	30.9	9.6	23	21.2b	14.2	14.7c	9.3	3.6d	2.5
Fourth	23	29.9	8.8	35	25.6	10.4	19.7	6.0	4.9	1.8
Total	328			295						

aThe mean of the first year was significantly greater than the mean of the second year ($p < .05$).
bThe mean of the third year was significantly less than the means of the first and second years ($p < .05$).
cThe mean of the third year was significantly less than the means of the first, second, and fourth years ($p < .05$).
dThe mean of the third year was significantly less than the means of the first and fourth years ($p < .05$).

Male clients who initiated counseling during the first year had Impulse Expression scores significantly greater than those male clients who initiated counseling during the second year.

Female clients who initiated counseling during the third year had significantly lower Personal Integration, Altruism, and Intellectual Disposition Category scores than those initiating counseling during the first year. A significant difference in the same direction was found between females initiating counseling during the third year and the second year on the Personal Integration and Altruism scales. A similar difference was found between women initiating counseling during the third year and the fourth year on the Altruism and Intellectual Disposition Category scales.

Analysis by sequential quarters. When the temporal period was considered on a quarter-by-quarter basis, neither the SCAT nor SVIB scales differentiated male or female clients. Male clients were differentiated on the basis of the Theoretical Orientation and Social Extroversion scales of the OPI. These data are presented in Table 1.

Men who initiated counseling during the spring quarter of 1968 had significantly lower Theoretical Orientation scales than did men initiating counseling during eight other quarters. Similar differences were found for men who initiated counseling during the winter quarter of 1969 and those initiating counseling during four other quarters. The Social Extroversion scores of men initiating counseling during the spring quarter of 1967 were significantly higher than the scores of those initiating counseling during the summer quarter of 1967. Men who initiated counseling during the spring quarter of 1968 had higher Social Extroversion scores than did men initiating counseling during seven other quarters. Overall, it is interesting to note that for three of the four academic years, the spring quarter Social Extroversion scores were the highest.

Female clients were differentiated on the basis of the Thinking Introversion, Altruism, and Practical Outlook scales of the OPI. These data are presented in Table 2.

Women who initiated counseling during the fall quarter of 1968, the winter quarter of 1969, the spring quarter of 1969, and the summer quarter of 1969 (i.e., academic year 1968-69), differed significantly on the Thinking Introversion scale from women who initiated counseling during a number of other quarters. Female clients who initiated counseling during the fall quarter of 1968 and the summer quarter of 1969 had relatively high Thinking Introversion scores in comparison to other clients. Those who initiated counseling during the winter and spring quarters of 1969 had relatively low Thinking Introversion scores. Female clients initiating counseling during the spring quarter of 1967 had significantly higher Altruism scores than did those initiating counseling during the winter quarter of 1968, the spring quarter of 1969, and the fall quarter of 1969. Clients who initiated counseling in the spring quarter of 1969 had lower Altruism scores than did clients initiating counseling during nine other quarters. Only two female clients, however, initiated counseling during the spring quarter of 1969.

Females who initiated counseling during the winter, spring, and summer quarters of 1969 had Practical Outlook scores that were significantly different from those of females who initiated counseling during a number of other quarters. Again, caution must be exercised due to the small numbers in each of these three cells.

Analysis by combined parts of quarters. Females who initiated counseling during various parts of the quarter did not differ on the basis of SCAT, OPI, or SVIB data. Male clients did differ on four OPI scales. These data are presented in Table 3.

The mean scores for these four scales rise and fall in perfect lock-step fashion across the five segments of the quarter, the Impulse Expression scale moving in the opposite direction from the other three scales. The scores for the few men initiating counseling during final examination weeks were most deviant, followed by the scores for those in the middle five weeks when midterm examinations were being given. The scores for those initiating counseling at the other times were essentially similar.

DISCUSSION

Since a detailed study of the pattern of initiation of counseling by an entering class over four years has not been reported previously, one can only compare the present results with earlier inferential findings. As this study confirms, counseling starts are greatest just after the class arrives on campus and decline rather steeply over time. Every year fall quarters are heaviest and from the standpoint of overall counseling center management, provision must be made for high fall intake.

A previous study showed that women are more prone to use counseling resources than are men (Kirk, 1973). In the current study, in contrast to men, women tended to initiate contacts earlier in the quarter, which perhaps suggests greater dependence and/or concern for getting on the right path quickly. Also in contrast to men, women increased their initiation of counseling in the fourth year over that of the third year, perhaps showing greater concern over plans after graduation.

The data relating the psychological characteristics of clients to the academic calendar are impressive, particularly for men, when the corresponding parts of quarters are combined over all four years. As shown in Table 3, the differentiating scales come not from the SCAT or the two SVIB scales but from the OPI, and three of these four scales, Impulse Expression, Personal Integration, and Anxiety Level, are from the social-emotional adjustment cluster of the instrument (Heist & Yonge, 1968). The student groups are not distinguished one from the other by the clusters of OPI scales assessing intellectual orientation or authoritarianism. That the Response Bias scale is differentiating too is not surprising, since high scores on it are related to making a good impression and low scores may indicate "a low state of well-being or feeling of depression [Heist & Yonge, 1968, p. 5]."

As mentioned earlier, the mean scores for these four scales move together, with the Impulse Expression scale going in the opposite direction from the other three. Clinically, as well as psychometrically within the OPI, when personal integration is low and anxiety is high (high anxiety is associated with *low* Anxiety Level scores), there tends to be less control of impulsiveness, and the picture in Table 3 is consistent; in the busy, stressful times surrounding midterms and finals, the students who initiate counseling are those who, at entrance, test as being most psychologically vulnerable. The relatively few men who started counseling at finals time were a standard deviation above the general mean on Impulse Expression and a standard deviation below the mean on Personal Integration, Anxiety Level, and Response Bias. They were also more homogeneous as a group than any other, as the standard deviations show.

Why similar results were not obtained for women is not clear. However, in year-by-year comparisons, women who came in the third year differed from women initiating counseling at other times. They appeared to be less intellectually oriented, personally integrated, and altruistically inclined. It can be hypothesized that in their junior year they may have been having particular problems of identity in reference to the institution they were attending. For men, those initiating counseling in their freshman year had relatively higher Impulse Expression scores, which suggests recognition of difficulty in academic or general adjustment.

Remember that the contact rates are based on entering totals and do not take normal attendance attrition into account. The rates also do not take account of return contacts or amount of usage of counseling but only the frequency with which students first request service. Patterns of return usage may be quite different. The small numbers in many cells also require caution in interpreting some of the results. However, the appearance of significant differences in characteristics tested at entrance in relation to time of first seeking counseling indicates the potential for research on the transaction between specific campus environmental stress and psychological characteristics at the time of enrollment.

REFERENCES

BAKER, R. W. Pattern of initial contacts with a university psychological clinic and its relation to academic stressors. *Journal of Clinical Psychology,* 1963, **19,** 361-363.

BAKER, R. W., & NIDORF, L. J. Pattern of occurrence of psychological disturbance in college students as a function of year level. *Journal of Clinical Psychology,* 1964, **20,** 530-531.

DUBOS, R. *So human an animal.* New York: Scribners, 1968.

HEIST, P., & YONGE, G. *Omnibus Personality Inventory Manual.* New York: Psychological Corporation, 1968.

KIRK, B. A. Characteristics of users of counseling centers and psychiatric services on a college campus. *Journal of Counseling Psychology,* 1973, **20,** 463-470.

KRAMER, C. Y. Extension of multiple range tests to group means with unequal numbers of replications. *Biometrics,* 1965, **12,** 307-310.

MURRAY, H. A. *Explorations in personality.* New York: Oxford University Press, 1938.

SNYDER, B. R., & KAHNE, M. J. Stress in higher education and student use of university psychiatrists. *American Journal of Orthopsychiatry,* 1969, **39,** 23-35.

STERN, G. G., STERN, M. I., & BLOOM, B. S. *Methods in personality assessment.* Glencoe, Ill.: The Free Press, 1956.

(Received October 30, 1972)

AN EXPERIMENTAL STUDY OF FIRST GRADE THEME WRITING*

HARRY E. ANDERSON, JR. and W. L. BASHAW
University of Georgia

Mode of discourse is one of several variables of obvious importance in research on composition writing. Braddock, Lloyd-Jones, and Schoer (1963, pp. 8-9) list, in addition to writer variables, the important composition variables of topic, mode of discourse, time afforded for writing, and the examination situation. They specify that mode of discourse includes narration, description, exposition, argument, and criticism. They also point out that mode of discourse has been largely ignored by composition researchers, in spite of the fact that it has more effect than variations in topic on the quality of writing. Kincaid (1953), for instance, found mode of discourse, argumentative or expository, to be a significant factor in college freshman themes, particularly for the relatively inferior student. Also, Seegers (1933) had earlier shown an effect of mode of discourse on sentence structure. Seeger's study involved argument, exposition, narration, and description.

Descriptive and argumentative modes of discourse appear to be most common, but these modes have not been studied at the first grade level. According to Piaget's (1932 and 1951) theory of child development, first grade children should do much better in the descriptive mode than in the argumentative mode. In any case, specific instruction in descriptive discourse should be more effective than instruction in the argumentative topics because, Piaget's theory states, children at this age level are *only initially* learning logical, abstract organization. But specific instruction in one mode, is apt to effect the quality of writing in another mode, especially for young children.

The purpose of the present study is to examine differences in mode of discourse for first grade themes. The general hypothesis is that stimulation in a given mode of discourse will improve the quality of compositions in that mode but decrease the quality of themes in another mode.

METHOD

Subjects. The sample consisted of all first graders in a suburban elementary school. The results of the study are based on compositions by 92 students including 50 males and 42 females. Themes of students not present for the complete experiment were eliminated from analyses of final results.

Themes and treatment. Each student wrote two descriptive (D) themes and two argumentative (A) themes. For the D themes the students were told to write to a friend, giving a physical description of the school. The A themes also involved writing to a friend, but telling him why he would like to go to this school.

The treatment consisted of 10-minute discussion periods. One discussion session (T_D) focused on the physical description of the school. Another session (T_A) centered on studies,

---

Reprinted from *American Educational Research Journal*, vol. 5, no. 2 (March 1968): 239-47. Copyright 1968, American Educational Research Association, Washington, D.C., and reprinted with their permission.

*The research and development reported herein was performed pursuant to a contract with the United States Department of Health, Education, and Welfare, Office of Education, under the provisions of the Cooperative Research Program. The researchers are grateful for the assistance and cooperation of the following persons: Mr. Jasper Griffin, Superintendent of Cobb County, Georgia, Public Schools; Mrs. Gaynell Walker, co-ordinator of Elementary Education, Cobb County Public Schools; and Mr. William Leverett, Principal of Milford Elementary School, Marietta, Georgia.

games, and activities that would make the school attractive for a friend. A third discussion session was neutral (T_N). It was designed to avoid argumentative and descriptive discussion; the title of the T_N session was, "If I Were No Bigger Than a Peanut."

Experimental procedure. For the writing and discussion sessions, the students were taken out of their regular classrooms and randomly assigned to one of six groups depending on theme writing order (viz., *AD* or *DA*) and type of treatment (viz., T_D, T_A or T_N) received in the experiment. The first two themes were written on two successive days, the treatment and third theme were handled on the third day, and the fourth theme was written on the fourth day. Groups (1) and (2) attended the same discussion session as did, respectively, groups (3) and (4), and groups (5) and (6). It may be helpful, also, to note that the themes were written in May, at the end of first grade.

Local teachers were trained in the conduct of the writing sessions. The teachers also collaborated with experimenters in writing materials for the discussion sessions. Three of the teachers were then trained and rehearsed for conducting the T_D, and T_A, and T_N sessions.

Rating scales and reliability. A seven-point *D* and a seven-point *A* rating scale was established for the rating of themes. Themes written by students absent one or more days in the experiment were used for the scale anchor points and for practice sessions. A presentation of the anchor themes will be helpful not only in understanding the rating scales but also in gaining insight into the vocabulary, grammar, and spelling extant in first grade themes. From low to high at scale points two, four and six, the argumentative anchor themes were as follows:

Rank 2—Low Argumentative

I Like Miffe Scool.
I Like The RooMs.
I Lik The techer
We have picher
We bareball.
I Like picher
I Like Techer

Rank 4—Medium Argumentative

Why do my friend likes Milford
school by kows they like school
I like Milford school
I like to go to school
I like school by kowo it is fun
I like Milford school to
I play in school to
I play in school

Rank 6—High Argumentative

my friend will like Milford skool
be kus it is insiting and
he will like Milford be kus
it's Fun and he will like
the wokr and he will like
the nis techr's and he will
like the prisubl and he will like
The Cafutieu

Likewise, the descriptive anchor themes were:

Rank 2—Low Descriptive

Milford Has Big windows
the CaFoteReo is Hooked
onto the ottorem

Rank 4—Medium Descriptive

the playground is a big
plase. the Lunch Room
has big Window.
 ther are 5 1st Grade.

Rank 6—High Descriptive

there is 810 and 26
teacher. a store is down
the road. there is a
fire stashe. by the school
Is a mike Jug. and
across is two stashe.

For helpful "interpretation" of the descriptive themes, we should note that Milford Elementary School had 810 students, 26 teachers, five first grade classes, a "store down the road", a fire station nearby, two filling stations across the road, a Milk Jug business stand next door, a large playground, and a large window in the cafeteria which is adjacent to the auditorium. As may be noted from the anchor themes at all three points in both scales, presence of argument or description was emphasized as the criterion variable to the exclusion of other factors such as spelling, grammar, sentence structure, vocabulary and mere length.

Ratings were made by five first grade teachers who attended training and practice sessions where the criterion (i.e., presence of argument or description) was emphasized in the use of the above anchor themes. The themes were randomly assigned to the raters within the limits of two restrictions: (1) the student was not in the rater's first grade class, and (2) the student was not in experimental sessions with the rater. A number code replaced student names which were removed from the themes so that the rater would not known the writer's identity, nor whether the theme was a D or an A type, nor even if the theme was a pre- or post-treatment theme. Each theme was rated on the D scale and on the A scale.

We will hereafter, for ease of presentation, use a capital letter to designate the theme type; a 1 or 2, respectively, for pre- and post-treatment themes; and a small letter to represent the appropriate rating scale. For example, $D1a$ designates a pre-treatment descriptive theme rated on the argumentative scale.

The initial ratings were made on small slips of paper attached to the themes and were used for experimental analyses. After the initial ratings, however, small samples (N's from 12 to 14) of $D1$, $A1$, $D2$, and $A2$ themes were randomly chosen for re-ratings, but no theme was re-rated by the same rater. Each theme was re-rated on both scales, but one set of the ratings, $A1d$, was eliminated for lack of variation. For the seven remaining sets of ratings, the correlations between first and second ratings ranged between .75 and .96 with a mean of .86, so it seems reasonable to assume a fair amount of reliability in the ratings of the themes.

Experimental hypotheses and analyses. The experimental hypotheses for the study were as follows:
(1) The effects of T_D will be to raise the d quality of both D and A themes but to reduce the a quality of these themes.
(2) The effect of T_A will be to raise the a quality of both D and A themes but to reduce the d quality of both themes.

Several alternative analyses were possible in the study. The writers chose a set of analyses that they judged would most directly test this hypotheses. It was decided to focus on pre- and post-treatment differences using analysis of variance.

The T_N groups were used as a control in the experiment and the T_D and T_A groups were compared to the T_N groups by Dunnett's (1955) procedure. A suggested modification for unequal samples was used where necessary (Steel and Torrie, 1960, p. 114). All tests were one-tailed and were made at the .05 level of significance. When treatment differences were not in the hypothesized direction, tests were not made.

RESULTS

For the conservation of space, complete rating means will not be presented. The pre-treatment rating means for the males ranged from 1.00 to 4.20 with an overall mean of 1.76; for the females from 1.00 to 5.20 and a grand mean of 2.29. The male post-treatment rating means again ranged from 1.00 to 4.20 and the overall mean was 1.88; for the females, from 1.00 to 5.60 and a grand mean of 2.23.

The pre-treatment ratings were analyzed within treatment for sex and order effect with the following significant results (i.e., $p < .05$). For those in the description treatment, order effects were significant in the $D1d$ ratings ($F = 9.15$, $df = 1$ and 29) and in the $A1a$ ratings ($F = 5.05$, $df = 1$ and 29). Sex-by-order interaction effects were significant ($F = 6.58$, $df = 1$ and 24) for the $A1a$ ratings in groups assigned to the argumentative treatment. Finally, for the groups in the neutral treatment, the sex effects were significant in the $D1d$ ratings ($F = 9.42$, $df = 1$ and 27) and in the $A1d$ ratings ($F = 5.13$, $df = 1$ and 27).

Rating differences were obtained as follows: *D2d-D1d, D2a-D1a, A2d-A1d,* and *A2a-A1a*. These four sets of data were analyzed separately for tests of hypotheses and, because of the significance of some sex and order effects in the pre-treatment analyses, sex and order as well as treatment were specified as major sources of variation in the analyses. The sample sizes are $T_D, N = 33$; $T_A, N = 28$; and $T_N, N = 31$.

For the $D2d-D1d$ ratings, the overall treatment means were as follows: $T_D = -.12$, $T_A = -.25$, and $T_N = -.10$. No significant effects were found either in the analysis of variance or using Dunnett's *t*-test.

The treatment means for the $D2a-D1a$ ratings were $T_D = -1.00$, $T_A = .07$, and $T_N = .39$. In the analysis of variance, both treatment ($F = 5.75$ with 2 and 80 df) and treatment-by-order interaction ($F = 4.26$ with 2 and 80 df) are significant ($p < .05$). The mean difference between T_A and T_N is not even in the expected direction, but the mean difference of $T_D - T_N = -1.39$ is larger than required by Dunnett's method ($D' = .957$; $p <.05$) so we conclude that the a quality of the D themes was reduced under T_D and the first hypothesis is supported by the results.

The treatment means for the $A2d-A1d$ ratings were $T_D = 1.76$, $T_A = .11$, and $T_N = -.19$. In the analysis of variance, the following effects are significant (at least $p < .05$): treatment ($F = 15.43$ with 2 and 80 df), order ($F = 5.10$ with 1 and 80 df) sex-by-order ($F = 4.17$ with 1 and 80 df), treatment-by-order ($F = 6.30$ with 2 and 80 df), and sex-by-treatment-by-order ($F = 4.06$ with 2 and 80 df). The significant interactions indicate that several one-way analyses might be more appropriate, but we are primarily interested in the treatment means. The mean difference $T_A - T_N$ is not in the expected direction, but $T_D - T_N = 1.95$ which is larger than the difference required by Dunnett's method ($D' = .900; p < .05$) so we conclude that T_D had the effect of raising the d quality of the A themes.

DISCUSSION

There is some possibility of rater-theme interaction with respect to A themes rated for d quality and D themes rated for a quality. The possibility of a type of halo effect in which a quality affects d ratings and vice versa certainly could have a confounding effect in the $A2d$-$A1d$ and $D2a$-$D1a$ comparisons. Further study and analysis would be required to determine the likelihood and possible impact of such a rating problem. If such a phenomenon existed, it should have had no effect on the $A2a$-$A1a$ and $D2b$-$D1d$ comparisons.

The descriptive discussion period did not raise the d quality of the D themes but other effects of T_D on the D themes are significant and in the expected directions. The effect of T_D raised the d quality of the A themes and lowered the a quality of both the D and A themes. Indeed, the descriptive discussion had the largest effect of all three treatments and the first hypothesis regarding the effects of T_D received major support by the study.

The argumentative discussion appears to have had little effect on the quality of the themes with the exception of the a quality of the A theme which was raised almost significantly after the discussion. A larger sample would have provided for significant evaluation of the $A2a$-$A1a$ difference, but the second hypothesis is not substantiated by this set of data.

Piaget (1951; particularly pp. 23-24) purports that in the 7-8 year old child, there is a diminution of ego-centrism and an increase in logical forms. Elsewhere (1932, p. 73 and pp. 125-126), he explicitly states abstract, logical thought in verbal communication for the child begins somewhere between seven and eight years of age. The data reported herein were collected at the end of the first grade, so the children are, on the average, slightly more than seven years of age and fall into the 7-8 year bracket designated by Piaget.

The results of the present study would seem to support Piaget's conjecture above in some respects. The D themes required some logical organization of thought but a minimum of abstraction as compared to the writing of A themes. The discussion of physical description of the school had the expected effects in three of the four sets of ratings. The effects of the argumentative discussion, however, are not as clear. The children, according to Piaget's theory, may not be advanced enough, from a developmental standpoint, to profit from the argumentative discussion.

Longer treatment sessions might have produced more significant effects. Experienced first grade teachers, however, opined that a longer treatment period might well dampen the treatment effects because of the children's attention. Nevertheless, the question of longer treatment periods must remain open for further study.

Finally, note must be taken of the words used in the themes. The children were encouraged to disregard spelling altogether and, as can be inferred from the scale anchor themes, the children used a great many words that they did not know how to spell. Indeed, spelling appeared to be no factor whatever in terms of the use of words in the themes.

REFERENCES

BRADDOCK, RICHARD, LLOYD-JONES, RICHARD, and SCHOER, LOWELL. *Research In Written Composition*. Champaign, Illinois: National Council of Teachers of English, 1963, 142 pp.

DUNNETT, CHARLES W. A. Multiple Comparisons Procedure for Comparing Several Treatments with a Control. *Journal of the American Statistical Association,* 50: 1096-1121; December, 1955.

HAHN, ELISE. "An Analysis of the Content and Form of the Speech of First Grade Children." *The Quarterly Journal of Speech,* 34: 361-366; October, 1948.

KINCAID, GERALD LLOYD. *Some Factors Affecting Variations in the Quality of Students' Writing.* Unpublished Ed.D. thesis, Michigan State University, 1953, 124 pp.

MCCARTHY, DOROTHEA AGNES. "Language Development of the Preschool Child." *Institute of Child Welfare Monograph Series* (University of Minnesota), 1930, No. 4, 174 pp.

PIAGET, JEAN. *The Language and Thought of the Child.* New York: Harcourt, Brace and Company, 1932, 246 pp.

PIAGET, JEAN. *Judgment and Reasoning in the Child.* London: Routledge and Kegan Paul Ltd., 1951, 260 pp.

SEEGERS, J. C. Form of Discourse and Sentence Structure. *Elementary English Review,* 10: 51-54; March 1933.

STEEL, ROBERT GEORGE DOUGLAS and TORRIE, JAMES H. *Principles and Procedures of Statistics.* New York: McGraw-Hill, 1960, 481 pp.

TEMPLIN, MILDRED. *Certain Language Skills in Children.* Minneapolis: The University of Minnesota Press, 1957, 183 pp.

(Received February, 1967)
(Revised July, 1967)

AUTHORS

ANDERSON, HARRY E., JR. *Address:* University of Georgia, Athens, Georgia 30601 *Title:* Professor and Associate Director, R&D Center in Educational Stimulation *Age:* 38 *Degrees:* B.A., Michigan State Univ.; M.A., Memphis State Univ.; Ph.D., Univ. of Texas *Specialization:* Statistics; research design.

BASHAW, W. LOUIS *Address:* University of Georgia, Athens, Georgia 30601 *Title:* Associate Professor of Ed. Psychology *Age:* 31 *Degrees:* B.S., M.S., Ph.D., Florida State University *Specialization:* Educational measurement; statistics.

Glossary

ABSTRACT. A brief summary of a study's formal report. Also a formal summary of a journal article used by APA to replace a concluding summary.

ACTION RESEARCH. A tool of curriculum development used for the study of local problems to guide, correct, and evaluate educational decisions and actions. It may include research procedures as defined for our study.

ANTHROPOLOGICAL APPROACH. Ethnographic fieldwork that attempts to see how each discrete fact relates to the total of facts collected on the sociocultural situation. Uses direct observation and participation of the researcher in the flow of living. Can be applied to the educational scene.

A POSTERIORI. Related to reasoning from observed facts (inductive).

A PRIORI. Related to reasoning from experience or propositions (deductive).

ASSUMPTION. An aspect of a research study that is presumed to be true with or without general agreement in the discipline base, taken as self-evident to start a train of reasoning for the study.

ATTITUDINAL SCALE. A data-collecting device intended to measure personal attitude toward a specific thing or concept. It usually records reactions on a rating scale.

BIAS. Not neutral. An inclination to some form of prejudice. Examples: sampling — statistical—.

CANONICAL CORRELATION. A multiple correlation technique that adds more than one dependent variable to the regular multiple regression model.

CASE STUDY. An encompassing study of some entity using all available evidence. The object of study may be a person, defined group of persons, event, institution, or community.

CENTRAL LOCATION. A value used to represent a set of scores in a frequency distribution. Examples: arithmetical average (mean), median, mode.

CHANCE ERROR. A difference between two values that appears without bias, such that the sum of such errors approaches zero as a limit.

CHECKLIST. An aid to direct observation which lists items to be given attention. Check marks indicate presence, absence, or frequency of occurrence for each item.

CLOSE-ENDED. A structure that does not allow for contingency beyond the frame of reference. Example: a close-end question which allows for only specified responses.

CONCLUSION. The end product of a process of reasoning. The researcher's interpretation of the study's results stated as a generalization.

CRITERION VARIABLE. The dependent variable. The measured variable in an experimental study which is used to judge the effects of experimental manipulation.

DATA. Information. Factual information used as a basis for reasoning or calculation, especially for testing a research hypothesis.

DECISION ERRORS. Mistakes made in tests of statistical significance when a null hypothesis is rejected and it should not be (Type I error) or a null hypothesis is not rejected when it should have been (Type II error). The probability of making a Type I error is the significance level for the test of significance.

DELIMITATION. A fixation of the limit for some aspect of the research study. A series of delimitations explains the scope of the study. Used to clarify the area of concern for the study.

DEMOGRAPHIC DATA. Vital information about subjects under study. Usually not a part of the data used to reason about the study's hypothesis but, rather, to explain characteristics of studied subjects.

DEPENDENT VARIABLE. Criterion or measured variable. *See also* CRITERION VARIABLE.

DEVELOPMENTAL STUDY. A research endeavor that studies change, e.g., growth, function, or organization of something, or some concept over a long time span.

DIRECT OBSERVATION. Taking note of phenomena under circumstances that allow no intervention between the one observing and that which is being observed.

DISCRIMINATION ANALYSIS. A technique for discriminating to which group an individual belongs. It is based on a prediction using a dependent variable that represents membership in a group.

ECOLOGICAL FALLACY. A danger that arises when a researcher correlates variables when using aggregated data. Determination of a direct relationship between the variables becomes difficult.

EDUCATIONAL RESEARCH. Structured scientific inquiry of educational questions that provide answers which contribute to the generalizable knowledge about educational concerns.

EXPERIMENTAL RESEARCH. A study made under laboratory-like conditions to allow for control of variables and manipulation to study cause-effect relationships. Most studies in education are considered experimental if the conditions approach those in a laboratory setting.

EXPERIMENTAL TREATMENT. The manipulation of a variable(s). Effects of the manipulation are viewed through measurement of a criterion variable.

EXTERNAL VALIDITY. Degree to which results of the study are generalizable. Deals with the question: To what populations can the studied effects be generalized?

FACT. Any bit of information that has validity for use as data for a research study. Facts are used to test the tenability of research hypotheses. *See also* OBSERVATION.

FACTOR ANALYSIS. A method to analyze relationships among a set of values in a matrix. Used to determine what is unique to one variable or common to several variables.

FREQUENCY DISTRIBUTION. An arrangement of data according to the frequency of occurrence for each possible value in the range of score values. It may be presented in tabular or graphic form. *Theoretical* frequency distribution is a frequency distribution built on a mathematical structure for all possible values. Usually a sampling distribution obtained by direct reference to probability considerations.

GENERALIZATION. A conclusion drawn from relevant data. Also the process of inferring beyond the sample studied to a greater population using sample information.

GOODNESS OF FIT. The extent to which a set of obtained frequencies agrees with frequencies based on a set of theoretically or empirically generated expected values.

Glossary

HYPOTHESIS, NULL. A statement that there is no difference in measures of the criterion variable except what would be expected for sampling. Requires that a significance level be stated (.05, .01, . . .). The statistical hypothesis is what the test of significance tests.

HYPOTHESIS, RESEARCH. The statement of what the researcher deems to be the most probable answer to the study's problem question. A tentative statement which is subject to verification through subsequent investigation.

IMPLICATION. A close connection of a study's conclusions to suggested changes in the educational scene. Suggested change in the educational setting as a result of drawn conclusions.

INDEPENDENT VARIABLE. A variable to which values can be assigned at will. The variable that the researcher manipulates in an experimental study.

INFERENCE. The act of generalizing from sample data to values of population parameters. Also the making of general statements from the study of particular cases.

INQUIRY. A systematic investigation of some question, stated or implied. A search for knowledge based on a problem-solving procedure, which is based on looking for an answer to a clearly presented question.

INTERNAL VALIDITY. The degree to which the effect of the experimental stimulus is *not* confounded by extraneous variables. Deals with interpretation of the question: Did treatment make a difference?

KURTOSIS. The relative degree of flatness or peakedness of a frequency distribution.

LABORATORY CONDITIONS. An environment which has the same state of affairs as a laboratory where strict control of all variables is possible. Constitutes ideal conditions for experimental studies of educational concerns.

LEVEL. One of the treatments on the independent variable. If two groups are studied, where different temperatures are provided for each group, the factor of temperature has two different levels—one for each group.

LIMITATION (RESEARCH). Any restriction that the study has in regard to inferring or generalizing beyond the subjects studied. Limitations should be kept at a minimum—the art of researching lies in being able to deal with each study and its limitations.

MANIPULATION. The differences on the independent variable(s) supplied by the experimenter. The effects of this manipulation will be observed in the criterion variable.

MEAN SQUARE. The variance (σ^2). The average (mean) value of all of the squared deviations of each score from the mean. (See page 158.)

MEASUREMENT. A process of assigning by rule a numerical description to observation of some attribute of an object, person, or event.

MECHANICS OF STYLE. The functional details of format for written scholarly works. See a style manual.

MEDIAN. That point in a distribution of scores which divides the set of scores into two equal parts. Fifty percent of the scores fall above the median and fifty percent below.

MICROFICHE (MF). A four-by-six film on which material may be reduced by twenty-four times (1/24 of the original). Used to reproduce written material for convenient and inexpensive storage. One sheet can hold over seventy-five pages of material. ERIC uses microfiche for storage.

MULTIPLE REGRESSION. A prediction method that uses more than one predictor (independent) variable to predict values on a predicted (dependent) variable.

MULTIVARIATE. More than one variable on either the independent or dependent dimension, or both. Any technique that is a simultaneous analysis of k independent variables and m

dependent variables (either or both k and m greater than one) is considered to be multivariate.

NOMOGRAPH. A procedure for testing the significance of difference between two percentages. Only a rough estimate—for cases that border on significance, a chi-square technique should be used.

NONPARAMETRIC STATISTICS. Methods for tests of significance which may be applied to analyze data without any assumption as to the shape of the distributions involved. Used for nominal and ordinal data and for special cases of interval and ratio data where assumptions cannot be met.

NON SEQUITOR. Something that does not logically follow from premises or previous statements.

NORMAL CURVE. A graphical representation of the normal distribution.

OBSERVATION. The act of gathering data on which to base research conclusions. Also any fact that is the result of the process of observing is called an observation. Thus observation generates the basic elements of science, facts which are called observations.

OPEN-ENDED. A structure that allows for contingencies beyond the frame of reference. Example: an open-ended question which allows the respondee to create any response.

OPERATIONAL DEFINITION. A statement that describes something in terms of observable properties or behaviors. This description by operations avoids lengthy ambiguous word definitions for constructs.

OPINIONNAIRE. A self-reporting device intended to obtain a subject's opinions on some specific subject.

PARAMETRIC TEST. A test of significance which uses values computed on samples in order to make conclusions about characteristics of populations. Sample statistics are used as estimates of population parameters.

PERIODICAL. A publication issued at intervals as part of a continuing series with no predetermined date for termination.

PILOT STUDY. A miniature study conducted on a group which is not to be used as a part of the major study. Used to try out the mechanics of procedures and/or instruments.

POPULATION. Any defined aggregate of persons, objects, or events. A population may be described by a statement such as "all students enrolled in Education 393 for the fall semester 19___," or, if practical, the elements of the population may be listed.

PREDICTION. In general, a forecast. Statistically, prediction is made by use of regression equations that utilize knowledge about relationships and values on one or more variables to predict on a criterion variable.

PRESENTISM. To invoke the present on the past. The one who studies the past must *not* interpret the past with a frame of reference based in the present.

PRIMARY SOURCE. Firsthand evidence that has no intervention between the researcher and the object or account. The source must be original or firsthand to be classed as primary.

PROBLEM QUESTION. The indeterminate situation being studied presented as a question. The answer to the problem question is the object and output of the research study.

PROBLEM SOLVING. A process of inquiry which combines inductive methods and deductive methods with the use of a research hypothesis. In general, any process used to overcome a felt difficulty.

PROPOSAL. A document that pulls together all of the aspects of an intended study. A logical chain of reasoning translates an indeterminate situation into a step-by-step plan for creating new knowledge.

Glossary

Q METHODOLOGY. Procedure used to gather and interpret data to research individuals on psychological traits. It usually studies the way an individual sorts a deck of cards that have been prepared for the study. Correlations among responses from different individuals allow study between persons.

QUALITATIVE DATA. Information in the form of statements or narrative as opposed to quantitative data that have been expressed numerically.

QUANTIFICATION. The assignment of meaningful numbers to observations for the purpose of mathematical interpretation.

QUANTITATIVE DATA. Information that has been expressed in terms of mathematically manipulative numbers. (Assignment of numbers merely for identification is not a procedure of quantification.)

QUESTIONNAIRE. A list of questions about a specific topic organized so that it can be reacted to by subjects under study. Includes directions for the respondee so that it can be self-administered.

RANDOM ASSIGNMENT. Assignment procedures made such that selection into groups for study has the qualities of equiprobability and independence. The two groups are equated for study by statistical tests of significance.

RANDOM ERROR. An error ascribable to chance. There is no bias or system to chance errors. When errors involve system or bias they are referred to as constant errors in that they do not cancel out over many instances as do random errors. *See also* CHANCE ERROR.

RANDOM SELECTION. Procedures to study material, sources, or subjects such that each element chosen for study is selected with equal probability and independence. Random selection may include stratification and proportional stratification to control for important contributing variables. Samples chosen at random allow generalization back to the parent population.

RANGE. The difference between the lowest and highest score in a distribution. $[(X_h - X_l)$ or sometimes $(X_h - X_l) + 1]$.

RATING SCALE. A device used to score some particular attribute. Usually a chart for an observer to use, but may also be used by a human subject to rate himself. *See also* SCALE.

RECOMMENDATION. A statement made at the end of a research report to indicate what additional studies should be made or how other techniques could be employed for study of the same question.

REFERENCE BOOK. A published work designed to direct the reader or consulter to other sources of information. In general, not a source of data for research studies, but widely used by researchers who are searching the literature for their studies.

REGRESSION. Prediction of values of one variable when given values on another and a measure of the relationship between the two variables. *See also* MULTIPLE REGRESSION.

RELIC. A physical object which has been preserved, either by plan or by happenstance, but was not created deliberately to transmit a record for future consultation.

REPLICATION. A reproduction of a research study using the same design on a new set of subjects. No deviation of procedures is allowed in a replication study.

REPRESENTATIVE SAMPLE. A sample of subjects which takes the same characteristics as the parent population.

RESEARCH. Structured inquiry that (1) utilizes acceptable scientific methodology to solve problems, and (2) creates new generally applicable knowledge.

RESEARCH REPORT. A writing that covers all aspects of a research study—planning, investigation, and generalization—all receive equal emphasis. An extensive review of literature is, in general, included except for a journal manuscript.

RESULTS. The presentation of the data for the study. It includes the outcomes of statistical tests and graphs or tables to organize the data for interpretation.

SAMPLING ERROR. The difference between a particular sample value and its corresponding population value. A test of significance is a study of sampling error estimated to be a part of the study.

SCALE. A measuring instrument constructed such that individuals may be assigned by rule to one of a limited number of points ordered hierarchically. Fine discriminations are not intended, but equal interval between points is assumed.

SCATTER DIAGRAM (SCATTERGRAM). A visual representation of the relationship between sets of values on two variables. Constructed by plotting a point for each pair of values obtained from a common subject.

SCIENTIFIC APPROACH. The common strand that is a part of any systematized attack of inquiry that uses accepted procedures to answer questions.

SELF-REPORTING DEVICE. Any data collecting device which allows the studied subject to report his/her inner thoughts about something.

SIGNIFICANCE LEVEL. The probability of making an alpha (Type I) error. Usually set at .05 or .01 for most studies in education.

SIGNIFICANT DIFFERENCE. An observed difference in a study that is so great that the statistical test rejects the hypothesis that the difference appeared by sampling alone. A difference becomes statistically significant when the observed difference exceeds the criterion point for rejection of the null hypothesis.

SKEWNESS. A distortion or unbalancing effect within a set of data, caused by deviate or atypical scores.

SOCIOGRAM. A device used to get preferences within a group to determine the social structure of that group. Usually a map showing by names and lines the choices of the individuals.

STANDARD DEVIATION. A measure of the variation of a set of scores obtained by taking the square root of the variance. *See also* VARIANCE.

STANDARD ERROR. The standard deviation of some sampling distribution. It is a measure of the variability of a statistic over repeated sampling. A standard error of difference between means is the standard deviation of a sampling distribution built from differences between means of pairs of samples.

STATISTICAL INFERENCE. *See* INFERENCE.

STATUS STUDY. Gathering of information about school conditions for making administrative decisions. Largely, demographic data is used to make decisions other than instructional.

STRATIFICATION. A modification applied to random sampling, whereby subjects for study are selected randomly from subgroups of the population. A sample of university students could be selected from the four strata of class rank.

STRUCTURE. A framework of a subject topic such that its understanding permits many other things to be related to it. The interrelatedness of many things is explained and/or revealed by a structure.

STYLE MANUAL. A set of rules concerning format for scholarly writing. Covers all aspects of the mechanics of preparing a document for submission and/or publication. Example: *Publication Manual of the American Psychological Association.*

Glossary

Survey. A field study that deals in cross section with a large number of cases at a particular time. The purpose is to determine characteristics of a definite population or to generalize from subjects of a sample to a parent population.

Systematic error. Observations which consistently overestimate or underestimate a true value.

Table of specifications. A two-way table that organizes specific objectives according to behaviors and subject-matter topics. It serves as a blueprint for a test to build relevance and balance into the test instrument.

Taxonomy. A classification system according to general principles or relationships. Used to organize problem-solving strategies (chapter 1), and educational objectives (chapter 7).

Test instrument. A measuring device built as a series of tasks to which a person is to respond. When scored, the test gives a quantification of the characteristic that the test is designed to measure. It serves the same purpose for educational and psychological measurement that rulers, liter jars, and such do for physical measurement.

Tests of significance. A set of statistical procedures designed to make decisions about the tenability of the null hypothesis.

Unhypothesis. A nickname for the null hypothesis. Since the null hypothesis does not involve conjecture it does not have that property usually associated with hypothesis development.

Usability. As a test characteristic usability refers to the ease with which the test can be administered, scored, and interpreted.

Validity. Is the degree to which an observation describes consistently what is being observed. Test validity is concerned with how well the test measures what it is used to measure. It is the most important single characteristic associated with test instruments.

Variability. Differences associated with phenomena. Variation within nature and within measurement is a concern for the researcher as well as the statistician.

Variable. A property whereby elements of a group differ one from another. Used interchangeably with "trait," "characteristic," or "attribute," it refers to ways of identifying differences between elements under study.

Variance. (σ^2). The mean (average) square of the squared deviation scores. A measure of variation in two dimensions. (See page 158.)

Index

Abstract, 222; of research, 243
Abstraction, hypothesis, 80
Action research, 19, 106
Affective domain, 141
Allen, George, 231
Alpha error, 182
Alternate hypothesis, 180
Altman, Edward I., 167
American Educational Research Journal, 229, 264
American Historical Association, 130
American Reference Books Annual, 226, 227
Analysis, 25, 27; correlational, 27; documentary, 72; inferential, 27; information, 27
Analysis of variance, 196; repeated measures, 197
Anderson, Harry E., 264
Anderson, Scarvia, 31
Andrews, Frank M., 212
Androit, John L., 131, 226
Angell, Jane, 244
Answers, common sense, 4; and questions, 4; yes or no, 42
Antecedent-consequence. *See* Cause-effect
Anthropological approach, for descriptive studies, 153-54
Anthropological research, 153
A posteriori, investigation, 64

Appendix, proposal, 240
A priori, 168
Arrett, Glenn W., 85
Ary, Donald, 31
Assignment: from absolute zero, 97; by categories, 95; by coin flip, 66; by intervals, 96; at random, 66; by rank, 96; of treatment, 66
Assignment rules, limitations, 95
Assumptions, 26; research, 237
Attention, 78
Attitudinal scale, 148
Attributes, 74
Author card, example, 219

Babbie, Earl R., 147, 153, 155
Bailyn, Bernard, 120
Ballou, Stephen V., 245
Barber, Theodore Xenophon, 185
Barzun, Jacques, 129
Baslaw, W. L., 264
Beach, Mark, 126
Becker, Carl L., 3
Best, John, 10
Beta error, 182
Bias, 147; external, 66; internal, 67; in sample selection, 64, 65; sources of, 67, 81
Bibliographic entry, example, 228
Bibliographical cards, 227

Index

Bibliography: annotated, 249; assembling, 228; divided, 249; Part I, 31-32; Part II, 113; Part III, 212-14; Library, 231; Proposal, 241; Research Report, 252
Binomial distribution, 191
Biserial, 164
Bivariate analysis, tables, 156
Bloom, Benjamin S., 19, 106
Blueprint, for a test, 105
Boas, George, 4, 6
Borich, Gary D., 19
Boyd, Jessie Edna, 231
Brickman, William B., 118
Brogan, Gerald E., 231
Brooks, Phillip C., 131
Brownell, William A., 49
Bruner, Jerome S., 23, 39
Buros, Oscar K., 103, 225

Campbell, Donald T., 174, 184, 185
Campbell, William Giles, 231
Canonical correlation, 167
Carroll, Lewis, 25
Case study, 207; tool for data-gathering, 207
Categorical variables, 187
Cause and effect, 4, 13, 127, 173, 177
Central location, measures, 159
Chance error, sources, 101
Characteristics, human, 81
Chase, Clinton J., 201
Checklist, 55, 82;
    contributions, 82, 83
    example, 83
    use, 83
Chi square
    computation, 168
    distribution, 168, 191, 192
Clarification, of practice, 25
Cliff, Norman, 84
Close-ended,
    questions, 145
Cognitive domain, 106
Common sense, 4, 8
Comparative studies, 73, 178
Computer: bibliographology, 132; checklists, 132; library cataloging, 132; searches, 224
Computer contribution: calculation of, 70; storage, 132
Computers and the Humanities, 132
Computer Studies in the Humanities and Verbal Behavior, 132

Conception, 80, 89
Conclusions, 9, 55, 138, 203-11; basis for, 28, 205; descriptive study, 140; discuss limitations, 248; historical study, 128; as hypotheses, 127; as interpretation, 73; to knowledge, 28; and limitations, 210; validity, 90; writing, 206
Conjecture, 127. *See also* Guesses
Conover, W. J., 170
Contingency coefficient, 164
Continuous variables, 187
Control, experimental, 177
Cook, David R., 252
Cordell Collection of Dictionaries, 131
Correction factor, in scientific approach, 21
Correlation, appropriate coefficient, 164
Correlationalist, as a historian, 120
Correlational study, 138, 209
Correlational techniques, 163-64
Correlator, 138, 171
Credibility, of data, 125
Criterion variable, 177, 187
Criticism: external, 124; guiding principles, 125; internal, 124
Cronbach, Lee J., 100
Current Index to Journals in Education, 221; example of entry, 222
Curriculum development, and research process, 204

Data: descriptive study, 140; directing organization, 71; historical study, 127; ordering, 27; organization, 69; qualitative, 27; tables, 156; tabulation, 27; tentative, 127; validation, 124
Data collection, points in planning for, 70
Data coordination, gathering and treatment, 71
Data recording, information for cards, 227, 228
Data sources: primary, 123; secondary, 123
Data treatment, 71, 72; what kind of data, 110-11
Decision errors, 180, 202
Deduction, 5
Defining, traits, 98
Definition, of terms, 44. *See also* Operational definition
Definitions, 25
Delimitation, in proposal, 236, 237; study's scope of, 44

Index

Demographic data, 146; to describe sample, 64
Dependent variable, experimental design, 177
Depositories, source of facts, 131
Description, numerical, 94
Descriptive research, 68, 115-16; interpretive tools, 155; nature, 137; steps, 139
Descriptive study, 135; conclusions for, 69, 207; data organization, 155; types, 207
Descriptors, for an index, 220
Design: abstracted, fit to reality, 62; choices within, 63; experimental, 53, 176; statistical, 53; two meanings, 53
Development, 10
Developmental procedures, 19
Developmental study, 208
Dewey decimal, 218
Dewey, John, 6, 8, 77
Dichotomy: forced, 164; natural, 164
Dictionary of Education, 25, 226
Difference, between means, 179, 193
Difficulty index, formula, 109
Directional test, 196
Direct observation, proceduress, 82, 144
Discriminant analysis, 167
Discrimination: test item, 110; valid measurement, 110
Disprove, 46
Dissemination, negative results, 205
Dissertation Abstracts, 224
Dissertation, format, 30
Distribution-free tests, 197
Distribution of scores, questioned normality, 73
Diversity into unity, 206
Documentation in Education, 225
Documents, 122; examples of, 122; source of information, 69
Dugdale, Kathleen, 252

Easiness index, formula, 109
Eastin, Roy B., 131
Ebel, Robert L., 102, 105, 246
Ecological fallacy, in data analysis, 153
ED number, 222
Edington, Eugene S., 170
Education: art of, 17; science of, 16, 17
Education in the Forming of American Society, 120
Education Index, 221; sample page, 223

Educational and Psychological Measurement, 104, 229
Educational Information Networks (EDUCOM), 133
Educational journals, research oriented, 229
Educational Measurement, 104, 111
Educational measurement, problems, 93
Educational objectives: affective, 107; cognitive, 106
Educational research, defined, 15
Educational Researcher, 229
Effects, treatment, 179
Eisenbeis, R. A., 212
Elkind, David, 57
Empirical, 17
Encyclopedia of Education, 225
Encyclopedia of Educational Research, 224, 246
Englehart, Max D., 31
Environment, changes, 88
Equal intervals, 188
Equal probability, 58, 63, 66
ERIC, 132, 222; clearinghouses, 224; Washington address, 132
Error: random, 174; systematic, 174; as variability, 100
Errors: decision, 180; relationship, 181; in problem question, 43; reduction, 81
Ertl, J. P., 78
Ethics of research, 24, 174
Evaluation, 10; educational, 19
Evaluative procedures, 18
Event sampling, examples, 89
Evidence: classification, 124; negative, 46; positive, 46; validation, 123
Existing data, analysis, 153
Experiment, the, 69; art of, 57; definition, 173; in education, 175; strength, 173; validity, 183
Experimental mortality, 184
Experimental research, 68, 115-16; comparison, 188; nature, 174; steps, 175-76
Experimental treatment, 177
Experimentalist, as a historian, 120
Experimentation, 9, 73; as an art, 73
Experimenter effects, 185
Explanation, 3, 4
External validity, 184

Fact, 126; interpretation, 126; into results, 126; public, 7
Factor analysis, 167

Falsification, of records, 122
F distribution, 191
Ferguson, George A., 27, 57, 188
Fisher, Sir Ronald A., 166, 212
Forced choice, 151
Format: dissertation, 30; journal manuscript, 30; thesis, 30
Frame of reference, gathering data, 81
Framework, theoretical, 29
F ratio, 196
Frequency distribution, 159, 202; theoretical, 190
Funding agencies, proposals, 233

Gage, N. L., 174, 184, 225
Galis, Saul, 226
Gardner, Paul Leslie, 95, 110
Generalizability, restrictions, 238
Generalization, 5, 28, 63, 210, 247; beyond the sample, 63; insufficient data, 4
Generalization stage, 21, 28
Gephart, William J., 10, 12, 18
Gilman, David, 205
Good, Carter V., 25, 118, 120, 122, 129, 135, 173, 226
Goodness of fit, 155, 168
Government Publications and their Use, 226
Graff, Henry F., 129
Graphs, 157; principles in building, 157-58
Guba, Egan G., 241
Guesses: educated, 46; hierarchy of, 48
Guide to Reference Books, 8th ed. 226
Guides to Research in Educational History, 118
Guide to U.S. Government Serials and Periodicals, 225
Guion, Robert M., 104

Handbook of Research and Teaching, 225
Harvard Educational Review, 229
Hastings, J. Thomas, 19
Hays, William L., 93
Helmstadter, G. C., 10, 11, 141
Hempel, Carl, 118
Hillway, Tyrus, 31
Historical inquiry, scientific approach, 117
Historical novel, 128
Historical research, 68, 115-16; broadened scope, 119; conclusions for, 205; contribution of computers, 131; goal, 118; limitations, 117; major tools, 134; methodology in a proposal, 238; outline

Historical research (*continued*)
evolution, 72; problem identification, 120; problem isolation, 120; scientific method, 119; sources for data, 121, 122; special tools, 134; in steps, 119
Historical writing, 128
History, 184
Hoaxes, examples, 122, 123
Hodges, J. L., 58
Hollerith, Herman, 131
Hopkins, Charles D., 27, 49, 87
Horst, Paul, 167
Huck, Schuyler V., 213
Human behavior, methods of observing, 89
Human nature, 21
Humpty Dumpty, 25
Hypothesis, 6-7, 44-46; alternate, 180; a priori, 168; cause-effect, 138; conceptual scheme, 80; descriptive study, 140; direct test, 7; evolution of, 50; examples of, 45; in historical research, 121; null, 47; purposes of, 45; research, 5, 170; use of, 13

If-then statements, as hypotheses, 80, 127. *See also* Cause-effect
Illusions, optical. *See* Optical illusions
Illusions, psychological, 79
Implication, 28; from conclusions, 211
Import and objectivity, 210
Independent variable, 189; in experimental research, 177
Index, definition, 162
Indianapolis Star, 123
Indirect measurement, 98
Induction, 5
Induction-deduction relationship, 5, 13
Inference, in descriptive research, 170; from samples, 56-58
Information: definition of, 53; nonnumeric, 69; selecting sources of, 54
Ingle, Robert B., 10
Inquiry, educational, 45; structure of, 21, 29; writing about, 250
Instrumentation, 184; to gather data, 79; mechanical, 87; purposes, 88
Interaction, 184
Internal validity, 184
Interpretation, 72, 87; test responses, 101
Interval scale, 96, 111
Interval scaling, results, 96
Interview, personal, 149

Index

Introduction to Reference Books, 226
Investigation stage, 21, 27
Investigator effects, 185
Item, difficulty, 109

Jessell, John C., 253
Johnson, H. H., 212
Jones, Lyle V., 93
Jones, Ralph H., 31
Journal of Counseling Psychology, 256
Journal of Educational Measurement, 104, 229, 253
Journal of Educational Psychology, 229
Journal of Educational Research, 229
Journal of Educational Sociology, 229
Journal of Experimental Education, 229
Journal of Experimental Psychology, 229
Journal of Psychology, 229
Journal of School Psychology, 229
Journal of Special Education, 229
Journals, research-oriented, 229
Judgments, value, 17

Kagan, Jerome, 39
Katz, Michael B., 117
Katz, William A., 226
Kelly, Francis J., 213
Kendall, Maurice G., 163
Kendall's concordance, 164
Kendall, Tau, 164
Kerlinger, Fred N., 11, 24, 35, 42, 48, 94, 95, 110, 142, 153, 166, 201
Keypunch card, 155
Kirk, Barbara A., 256
Knowledge, 17; storage, 24
Knowledge, present, source of, 6
Kohlberg, L., 121
Krathwohl, D. R., 107
Kuder Preference Record Form, 151
Kurtosis, 160; leptokurtic, 160; mesokurtic, 161; plalykurtic, 160

Laboratory conditions, 73; educational inquiry, 175
Law, natural, 17, 49
Learning, human, 39
Lehmann, E. L., 58
Lehmann, Irvin J., 31
Leptokurtic, 160
Level: significance of, 180-83; of treatments, 177

Library, 215, 217-31; classification system, 218; components, 218; flow chart, 226; indexing, 218; purpose, 217; as a research tool, 130; skills, 24, 130, 226
Library of Congress, 218; classification headings, 219
Library search, 226
Light, Richard L., 74
Likert, Rensis A., 148
Likert scaling, 72, 149
Limitations: on historical data, 117; in proposal, 238; relationship to conclusions, 204; sources, 211
Line, formula, 163
Line of best fit, 165
Linguistic analysis, 133
Literary analysis, 133
Logic, conclusions for historical studies, 206
Lutz, Frank W., 154

McGrath, J. H., 10
McReynolds, Paul, 154
Madaus, George F., 19
Madge, J. H., 213
Manhelm, Theodore, 31
Manipulation: by assignment, 175; of conditions, 55; experimental, 177; of variables, 73
Masling, Joseph, 149
Material, for appendix, 248
Maturation, 184
May, Charles, 241
Mean, 160
Meaningful numbers, 54
Mean square, 160
Measure, meaning, 93
Measurement, 93-112; definition, 94; indirect, 98; interval rules, 96; levels, 94-98; nominal rules, 95; as observation, 88; ordinal rules, 96; purpose, 93; ratio rules, 97; rules, 94, 98, 144, 188; subjects, 93
Measurement and Evaluation in Guidance, 229
Mechanical devices, limitation, 88, 151
Mechanics of style, writing research, 244
Median, test, 198
Mental Measurement Yearbook, 103, 104; included information, 103, 225
Metaphysical, 20; statements, 17; questions, 17
Methodology, 27

Microfiche (MF), 222
Modern Researcher, The, 129
Moehlman, Arthur H., 131, 133
Mouley, George J., 31
Mueller, J. H., 213
Multiple regression, 142, 166, 201
Multivariate, problems, 80
Myers, Jerome, 213

Natural law, 49
Natural phenomena, 3
Need: to choose, 10, 12, 18; to do, 10, 12, 19; to know, 10, 12, 13
Negative instances, in historical research, 206
Neilson, N. P., 85
Neilson- Arnell scorecard, 85
Nomical scale, 95, 96, 111
Nominal scaling, results, 95
Nominal variable, 142; examples of, 95
Nomograph, 161
Nonlinear coefficient, 164
Nonparametric statistics, 73, 99, 197
Nonsupport, of hypotheses, 47
Normal curve, 190; standard form, 191
Note taking, organizing, 227-29
Null hypothesis, 47, 178, 180-83; example of, 47; interpretation of rejection, 189; in proposal, 239; statement, 180, 194
Nunnally, Jum C., Jr., 110

Objectivity and import, 210
Observation, 9, 77; aids, 87; attention, 78; conception, 78, 80; controlled, 89; as data, 78; direct, 82; hypothesis, 202; objectivity, 81; obstructions, 81; perception, 78, 79; preparing for, 82; sensation, 78, 79; structure, 82; use, 88-89
Observational techniques, 70
Observed t, compared to table, 195
Observer: agreement, 7; between-observer differences, 82; training, 82
One-tailed test, 196
Open-ended, questions, 145
Operational definition, 26, 98, 187; experimental, 26; measured, 26
Opinionnaire, 148
Oppenheim, A. N., 147, 161
Optical illusions, 79
Ordinal scale, 96, 111, 143
Ordinal scaling, results, 96

Page, Ellis B., 21
Parametric, 99
Parametric test, meeting assumptions, 210
Pearson correlation coefficient, 162
Pearson r, 164
Pedhazur, Elazar J., 166, 201
Perception, 79, 89
Periodical, definition, 221; index for library, 221
Periodical index, instruction to use, 221
Perrin, Porter G., 252
Phenomena, natural, 3
Phi, 164
Phi Delta Kappa, 12
Piaget, Jean, 57
Pierce, Albert, 213
Pilot study, 140
Plan, structure for, 28
Planning stage, 21, 23
Platykurtic, 160
Point biserial, 164
Points for rejection, 193
Population: definition of, 56; parent, 56
Poulton, Helen J., 130
Power test, 109
Power, test of, 183
Prediction, 101, 163, 165
Premise: major, 5; minor, 5
Presentism, 117, 128
Pretesting, reactive effect, 184
Primary source, 123
Principal component analysis, 133
Probability in sample selection, 58, 60
Problem, 20-21, 35; background of, 29; clarification, 43; identification, 8; narrowing, 120; presentation, 24, 29; question, 43; research, 24; selection of 40 ,41; sources of, 37; of a study, 43; widening, 120
Problem dimensions, 120
Problem question, 20, 22, 23, 54, 139; criteria for, 42; in proposal, 236
Problem solving, 5-7, 10, 48
Problems: from practice, 37, 38; sources of educational, 35; from theory, 38, 39
Procedures, effects on results, 239
Professional journal, manuscript format, 30
Proof, 46, 180
Proposal 28, 215; budget in, 29, 234; as a chain of reasoning, 237; components of, 234; guidelines for preparation, 236-37; for student research, 234; title, 235. *See also* Research proposal

Index

Propositions, as assumptions, 26
Prove (Proof), 46
Psychological Abstracts, 224
Psychological Bulletin, 229
Psychological Review, 229
Purpose of a study, 43

Q methodology, 152
Q sort, 152
Qualitative data, 27, 142; organization of, 71; retrieval methods, 68
Qualitative study, 54
Quantification, 81, 87
Quantitative data, organization of, 71, 171
Quantitative study, 54
Questioning subjects, 89
Questionnaire, 145; bias in respondees, 68; entry examples, 146; format, 145-49; percentage of returns, 147
Questions, 3, 41-43; close-ended, 145; open-ended, 145
Questions and answers, 4

Ramsey, Margaret, 154
Rand corporation, 58
Random assignment, 66
Random disk files, 69
Random error, 174
Random numbers, 58; table of, 59; using a table of, 58
Random sample, 57; proportional, 61, 62; stratified, 60
Random selection; in sampling, 57
Range, 160
Rank biserial, 164
Rank, correlation, 162
Ranking, 85, 86; example, 87
Rating scale, 55, 83; development of, 84; divisions, 84; naming point, 84; numbering points, 84; objectives, 85
Ratio scale, 97, 111
Readers' Guide to Periodic Literature, 221
Reading Research Quarterly, 229
Recommendation, further research, 28, 211
Reference Books: How to Select and Use Them, 226
Reflective thinking, 5
Regression, making predictions, 163
Rejection points, 193
Relationship: cause and effect, 4, 69; measures of, 161
Reliability, 100, 101; relation to validity, 101

Relics, 122; examples, 122; information from, 69
Replication, 9
Report, research. *See* Research report
Representativeness, of historical data, 127
Representative sample, 61, 63, 65; questionnaire, 147
Research: acceptance of results, 64; accepted procedures, 63; action, 19; applied, 35; art of, 77; basic, 35; characteristics, 12, 13; contribution of, 21; correlational, 137; definition, 11; descriptive, 14; educational, 15; experimental, 14; historical, 9, 14; as inquiry, 1; is not, 9; levels, 243; personal reward, 21, 22; plan for, 29; scientific, 10, 74; self-discipline, 36; writing, 243
Research hypothesis, 44, 45, 47, 176, 179, 189; examples of, 44; in historical research, 119, 129; in proposal, 237; relationship to conclusions, 204
Research in Education (RIE). *See Resources in Education*
Research plan, procedural points, 74, 75
Research proposal, 215, 233-241; as an insurance policy, 233, 238
Research Quarterly, 229
Research questions, list of, 41-42
Research report, 215; format, 30; material arrangement, 245; steps in writing, 150-51
Research study, educational significance, 235; planning for, 51
Resources in Education (RIE), 222
Resta, Paul E., 241
Results, 27: fit to theory, 247; from facts, 126; interpretation, 204; nonsupport of hypothesis, 204; summary of, 27; synthesis, 28
Retrieval systems, 227
Review of Educational Research, 210, 224, 229, 246
Review of literature: organization, 246; in proposals, 235; purposes, 245; summary, 247
Rewriting, 250, 251; research report, 128
Rice, J. M., 15, 16, 17
Roget's International Thesaurus of Words and Phrases, 226
Rules, of measurement, 94

Sample: definition of, 56; representative, 56, 89

Index

Sampling: event, 89; qualitative data, 68; systematic, 58, 63, 65; techniques of, 57; time, 89; without randomness, 62
Sampling error, 56, 178, 189
Saretsky, Gary, 10
Sax, Gilbert, 32
Scale: appropriate statistics, 97; defining relations, 97; development guides, 84, 85, 148; Likert type, 72; measuring, 97; rating, 83; units, 84
Scates, Douglas E., 135
Scatter diagram (scattergram), 158, 165
Schmeckebeir, L. F., 131, 226
Schwab, Joseph J., 114
Science: nature of, 21; philosophy of, 11; role of, 69; ultimate goals, 49
Scientific approach, 6, 16, 35
Scientific method, 6, 7-9; application to educational questions, 17; steps in, 8
Scientific research, 10
Scientific thought, 15
Scorecard, 85; example of, 86; use of, 85
Secondary sources, 123
Second Handbook of Research on Teaching, 185, 225, 246
Selecting samples, 56, 64
Selection bias, 64, 65
Self-reporting device, 150
Sensation, 79
Seventh Mental Measurements Yearbook, 103
Seyle, Hans, 173
Sharp, Harry W., 256
Siegel, Sidney, 73, 170, 201
Significance, test of, 179
Significance level, 180
Significant difference, 179
Sign test, 200
Skewness, 191; in a frequency distribution, 160
Sloan, Douglas, 118, 120
Smith, G. R., 241
Snidell, Peter S., 214
Sociogram, 151; example, 152
Sociology of Education, 229
Sociometry, 151
Source of data, 54, 55
Sources materials, accumulation, 121
Sources in Educational Research, 225
Spearman correlation coefficient, 162
Spearman rho, 164
Sprug, Joseph, 226

Standard deviation, 160
Standard error, of difference, 194
Standardized test, evaluation, 104
Standards for Educational and Psychological Tests, 104
Stanley, Julian C., 101, 174, 184
Statistical inference, 56
Statistical regression, 184
Statistical significance, 178 and conclusions, 204
Statistical test, difference between means, 195; nonparametric, 142
Statistics, nonparametric, 73, 188
Status study, 135-37
Stratification: how many variables?, 61; on two variables, 61; proportionally, 62; of samples, 60-62
Stratified random sampling, 60
Strong's Vocational Interest Blank, 151
Structure, 23; of inquiry, 13, 21, 22; for observation, 91
Study, adequacy of, 54
Stufflebeam, D. L., 32
Style, Mechanics, 244
Style manual: APA, 227; Campbell, 227; Dugdale, 227; Turabian, 227
Subject card, example, 220
Subjects, selection of, 56, 238
Sullins, Walter L., 253
Summarizing, 27
Summary tables, 28
Support, of hypotheses, 47
Survey, 207; cross-sectional, 209; data interpretation, 208
Syllogism, 5
Synthesis of historical data, 128
Systematic error, 174

t distribution, 191-92
t ratio, 194
t test, 194; calculation of, 194; correlated sample, 197
Table, of random numbers, 59
Table preparation, guidelines, 156
Table of specifications, 105, 106; behaviors, 107; components, 106; example, 108; topics, 107
Tally sheet, as checklist, 82
Tatsuoka, Maurice M., 214
Taxonomy, of problem-solving strategies, 10, 12, 18, 144

Index

Taxonomy of Educational Objectives:
  affective domain, 107; *cognitive domain,* 106, 107
Terman, Lewis M., 208
Terms: invented, 25; technical, 25
Ternstrom, Stephen, 117
Test: balance, 107; characteristics, 102; construction, 105; development, 104; as measuring device, 105; preparing form, 110; purpose, 105; reliability, 99; standardized, 103; steps in construction, 105; validity, 99
Testable, directly, 7
Test administration, importance, 102
Test evaluation, guidelines, 104
Testing devices, 88
Test instrument, 88, 150; as a measuring device, 105, 189; standardized, 103
Test items, steps in writing, 108-10
Test of significance, 48, 179, 183, 189; distribution free, 73; interpreting outcomes, 209; procedure sequence, 190; ranking tests, 73
Tetrachoric, 164
Theoretical, frequency distribution, 190
Theory, 48; definition of, 48; development of, 48; uses of, 49
Thesaurus of ERIC Descriptors, 224
Thompson, Stith, 4
Thorndike, Edward L., 49
Thorndike, Robert L., 110
Tilden, Freeman, 42
Tilly, Charles, 132, 133
Time sampling, examples, 89
Title card, example, 220
Titles, indexing for retrieval systems, 249
Todd, Alden, 231
Tools, for historical research, 129
Travers, Robert M. W., 32, 53, 225
Treatment: assignment, 66; experimental, 177; independent variable, 239; levels, 178
Tukey, J. W., 74

Turabian, Kate U., 252
Turner, Frederick J., 131
Twain, Mark, 81
Type I error, 180-82
Type II error, 180-82
Type V error, 208

Ullman, Louis L., 234
Unhypothesis, 47
Usability, 100; of measuring devices, 102

Validity, 99, 100; condition for, 101; external, 184, 209; historical data, 125-26; importance, 101; internal, 184, 209; measuring device, 99; physical measurement, 99; relation with reliability, 101
Value judgments, 17
Van Dalen, Debold B., 32, 78, 125, 128
Variability, 190; of measurement, 100
Variable: active, 178; assigned, 143, 178; attribute, 178; classification, 178; continuous, 100; definition of, 13; descrete, 100; major, 25; manipulated-type, 178; selection-type, 178; treatment, 178
Variance, 160, 165
Variation, effects on reliability, 101
Verification, of fact, 126
Vernadsky, Vladimir, 15
Volunteer subjects, 67

Webster's New International Dictionary of the English Language, 226
Weighing evidence, 127
Whallon, Robert Jr., 132
Wiersma, William, 241
Winchell, Constance, M., 226
Woody, Thomas, 125
Words, special meaning, 25
Working outline, 72
Worthen, B. R., 32
Writing, journal articles, 249, 250